THE GREAT CHURCH IN CAPTIVITY

A STUDY OF THE PATRIARCHATE OF CONSTANTINOPLE FROM THE EVE OF THE TURKISH CONQUEST TO THE GREEK WAR OF INDEPENDENCE

THE GREAT CHURCH IN CAPTIVITY

A STUDY OF THE PATRIARCHATE OF CONSTANTINOPLE FROM THE EVE OF THE TURKISH CONQUEST TO THE GREEK WAR OF INDEPENDENCE

BY

STEVEN RUNCIMAN

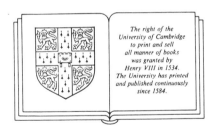

The right of the University of Cambridge to print and sell all manner of books was granted by Henry VIII in 1534. The University has printed and published continuously since 1584.

CAMBRIDGE UNIVERSITY PRESS

CAMBRIDGE

LONDON   NEW YORK   NEW ROCHELLE

MELBOURNE   SYDNEY

Published by the Press Syndicate of the University of Cambridge
The Pitt Building, Trumpington Street, Cambridge CB2 1RP
32 East 57th Street, New York, NY 10022, USA
10 Stamford Road, Oakleigh, Melbourne 3166, Australia

First published 1968
First paperback edition 1985

Printed in Great Britain by the University Press, Cambridge

Library of Congress catalogue card number 68–93302

ISBN 0 521 31310 4

CONTENTS

Contents

PREFACE

In 1960 and 1961 I had the privilege of giving the Gifford Lectures at the University of Saint Andrews, where my subject was the Church of Constantinople from 1261 to 1821. In 1966 I had the privilege of giving the Birkbeck Lectures at Trinity College, Cambridge, where my subject was the Church of Constantinople and its relations with the Protestant Churches in the sixteenth and seventeenth centuries. This book is based on both those series. In it I have strayed from the original design of my Gifford Lectures, in which I had given equal space to the Church before 1453 and after 1453. The Church of the later Byzantine Empire has been the subject of a number of learned studies; and I doubt if I have anything much to add that cannot be found in other works. The story of the Greek Church under the Ottoman Sultans is, however, comparatively little known. But in order to understand what happened to the Great Church, as its adherents loyally called it, during the dark centuries of its captivity, it is necessary to have a picture of what it had been and how it had operated before the captivity began. I have therefore reduced my 1960 Gifford Lectures to become a preliminary section which aims at a description of the Church as it was in the last years of the Byzantine Empire, and have amplified my 1961 Gifford Lectures, in the belief that they are of greater value and with the aim of including the full substance of the Birkbeck Lectures without upsetting the proportions of the book. If, even so, I have given a little more detail to the Greek Church's relations with other Churches than to its other aspects, I hope that it will be forgiven me in view of the importance nowadays of the Oecumenical Movement.

Even so, I have had to be somewhat selective. A detailed account of everything that is known about the later Greek church would fill many volumes and would be at the same time curiously uneven in its detail. The indigenous sources on which such an account must be based are scanty, fewer, indeed, than those that are available for the last period of Byzantine history. The records of the Patriarchal administration have suffered from fires at the Patriarchate and in the monasteries and from political mishaps. The Turkish governmental records about the minorities are perfunctory. The Greek chronicles are few, and, though fairly reliable as far as they go, do not go very far. Though there were many cultured Greeks during these centuries, only one great lay historian emerged, the brilliant but somewhat erratic Demetrius Cantemir, and one great ecclesiastical historian, his contemporary, Dositheus, Patriarch of Jerusalem. Were it not for the reports and accounts of foreign diplomats, churchmen and travellers, there are whole periods about which we should be very ignorant. Even for the career of the most remarkable and most controversial of all the Constantinopolitan Patriarchs of the period, Cyril Lucaris, we are principally dependent on a collection of documents made by an English chaplain.

The story has often been obscured by bitterness, prejudice and ignorance. It is not always edifying. Not even the most devoted Philhellene can claim that all the Greeks behaved well. There were indeed during these centuries a number of noble and wise and courageous Greeks, who are all the more to be admired because of the circumstances in which they lived their lives. But servitude does not usually bring out the best in men. If absolute power corrupts absolutely, so too does absolute impotence. If the Greeks were guilty of intrigue and corruption, it must be remembered that they were dealing with masters who themselves were all too often corrupt intriguers. But it would be equally wrong to assume that all the Turkish rulers were brutal and arbitrary tyrants. Many Turkish officials did indeed have a brutal contempt for the Christian minorities; but if they maltreated the Greeks it was chiefly because they knew that they could not count on Greek loyalty to their rule. Hellenism survived, nurtured by the Church, because the Greeks unceasingly hoped and planned for the day when they would recover their freedom. The Turks cannot wholly be blamed if such aspirations provoked them into acts of cruel oppression. But there were Turks such as the Sultan Suleiman the Magnificent, whom his own people surnamed the Lawgiver, or the great viziers of the Köprülü family, who were consistently just and friendly towards the Greeks; and even the Conquering Sultan Mehmet himself, once his savage lust for conquest was sated (and he was no more savage than many of his contemporaries in Renaissance Europe), was proud to call himself Emperor of the Greeks as well as of the Turks. On a humbler level relations between the two races were often genuinely friendly. If we denounce the Greeks as deceitful or the Turks as savage we shall get nowhere. Nor, similarly, should we let our feelings for or against the great Church of Rome affect our objectivity. A historian has his personal tastes and sympathies; but erudition will not produce understanding unless it is tempered with tolerance and freed from prejudice.

The Greeks themselves have tended to neglect the history of their forefathers under Turkish domination. They do wrong; for, though it contains much that is melancholy for a Greek to recall, it also bears witness to the brave and unquenchable vitality of Hellenism and to the spiritual strength of the Holy Orthodox Church. The story also has an international interest; for it shows what can happen to men and women who are forced to become second-class citizens. In these days, when there are still countries in which large sections of the population are second-class citizens, it is, perhaps, not without relevance.

It would take too long to list all the scholars, past and present, to whom I am indebted in this work. I have tried to pay tribute to them in my reference notes. Many of them have given me personal help and advice. Amongst friends who have encouraged me, I should first like to pay my respectful thanks to His All-Holiness Athenagoras, Oecumenical Patriarch, whose wisdom and kindness have meant much to me. I am deeply grateful to the officials of the Patriarchate, and to many other Orthodox divines in all parts of the world. I have received nothing but kindness from the

Turkish authorities when I have asked them for help. In this country my principal debt is to the staffs of the British Museum Reading Room, the London Library and the Library at Lambeth Palace. I am, as ever, grateful to the Syndics and staff of the Cambridge University Press for their patience and assistance. I owe a particular debt of gratitude to Mr S. J. Papastavrou. Finally I wish to express my gratitude to the University of Saint Andrews for having provided me with the stimulus out of which this book was begun and to my own academic parent, Trinity College, Cambridge, for having encouraged me to delve deeper.

Note. I have not attempted to be consistent in the transliteration of proper names, but in each case have used the form that seems most familiar.

S. R.

Elshieshields,
Dumfriesshire
October 1967

BOOK I

THE CHURCH ON THE EVE OF
THE TURKISH CONQUEST

CHAPTER I

THE BACKGROUND

Of all the roads that a historian may tread none passes through more difficult country than that of religious history. To a believer religious truths are eternal. The doctrine that he preaches and accepts gives expression to their everlasting validity. To him the historian who seeks to discover and explain why the doctrine should have appeared at a particular moment of time seems guilty of unwarranted determinism. But Revealed Religion cannot escape from the bounds of time; for the Revelation must have occurred at a particular moment. The Christian religion, above all others, is concerned with the relations of time and eternity. Its central doctrine, the Incarnation, is not only an eternal truth but an event in history; it is a bridge between the temporal and the eternal. The institutions of Christianity, however divine their inspiration, have been ordered and governed by men and are affected by the temporal processes to which man is subject. The articles of faith, whatever their transcendental validity, have been spread around the world by the agency of man, and their transmission has been affected by changes in worldly circumstances and outlook. It may be that man is continually refreshed by messages from on high. It may be that there is a divine ordering of history. But the historian himself is mortal, restricted by the limitations of temporality; and he must have the modesty to know his limitations. His business is to tell the story and to make it, as best he can, intelligible to humanity.

Nevertheless, if the story is to be intelligible, more is needed than a presentation of mundane facts. Many great and wise men have told us that history is a science and no more. It is true that in the collection of historical evidence accuracy and objectivity are required, especially when the subject concerns religion, a sphere in which judgment is too often influenced by personal conviction and prejudice. But the historian's methods cannot be entirely empirical. Human behaviour defies scientific laws; human nature has not yet been tidily analysed; human beliefs disregard logic and reason. The historian must attempt to add to his objective study the qualities of intuitive sympathy and imaginative perception without which he cannot hope to comprehend the fears and aspirations and convictions that have moved past generations. These qualities are, maybe, gifts of the spirit, gifts which can be experienced and felt but not explained in human terms.

For the study of the Orthodox Faith of Eastern Christendom some such intuitive gift is needed. It is a Faith which has always been suspicious of attempts to reduce religion to a near-philosophical system and which has always preferred to cling to esoteric and unwritten tradition. Its genius is apophatic, dwelling on the ignorance of man face to face with the Divine; all that we can know about God is that we know nothing; for His attributes must from their nature be outside the realm of worldly knowledge. Its theology and its practices are characterized by antinomies that are not easily resolved by a logical observer. It may well be that no one who has not been nurtured in the atmosphere of the Orthodox Church is in a position to understand it fully, still less to describe it. The objective student before he begins his study must charge himself with sympathy and must forget the taste for dialectical precision that is apt to characterize Western theology.

The effort is the greater because most Western students have been reared on stories of the passionate debates that raged amongst the Eastern Fathers of the Early Church over minutiae of doctrine. The Eastern Church is not tolerant of demonstrable error, that is to say, any doctrine that seems to impair the essential message of Christianity. Truths revealed by the Holy Scriptures and explained and defined by the action of the Holy Spirit at the Oecumenical Councils of the Church, exegesis by Fathers of the Church whose divine inspiration cannot be called into question, and tradition handed down from the apostolic age are all sacred and to be

4

accepted; and it may be that the Holy Spirit may still deign to give us further enlightenment. But beyond that point the Church has been shy of dogmatic definitions, preferring to rely on traditions that were not written down until a need arose. The pronouncements of the Oecumenical Councils were made to counter doctrines that seemed to damage the true meaning of the Trinity or of the Incarnation. Nearly all the works of the Greek Fathers were written to answer specific questions from an anxious inquirer or from a challenging controversialist. The ancient taste of the Greeks for speculative philosophy was not extinguished. It was, rather, encouraged so long as it kept itself apart from dogma. None of the philosophers ventured to work out a complete compendium of theology. The Greek Church did not and could not produce a Thomas Aquinas. It still has no *Summa Fidei*.[1]

This apophatic attitude had its strength and its weakness. It permitted a certain tolerance and elasticity. There is a word which we meet continually in Greek Church history, the word οἰκονομία, 'economy'. The word means literally the administration of the house. Greek theologians use it sometimes to denote the method of operation; the 'economy of the Holy Spirit' is the method in which the Holy Spirit operates on the Church. Economy is, however, more frequently used to mean a wise handling of the *oecumene*, the inhabited world; and in this sense it became roughly equivalent to the 'dispensation' of Western theologians. In the interests of harmony and good will the Church—that is to say, the Orthodox Church—can overlook or condone minor errors in belief or liturgical practice and minor breaches in canonical

---

[1] For a general account of the Orthodox Churches and their attitude to theology see S. Bulgakov, *The Orthodox Church*; N. Zernov, *Eastern Christendom*; P. Evdokimov, *L'Orthodoxie*; and two excellent short summaries, J. Meyendorff, *L'Eglise Orthodoxe*, and T. Ware, *The Orthodox Church*. The only *summa theologiae* fully accepted by all the Orthodox is John of Damascus's Πηγὴ Γνώσεως (often known as *De Fide Orthodoxa*), which leaves many theological issues untouched. For statements of doctrine which are considered as being perfectly Orthodox but need not be accepted in all details see below, p. 347, n. 2.

correctitude; they can be covered by the grace of the Holy Spirit for the greater good of Christendom. Unlike dispensation in the West, the term is deliberately imprecise and ungoverned by fixed rules. Western theologians, approaching the question with the legalism that is their inheritance from Scholasticism, have sought in vain for an exact definition. Even Orthodox theologians have described it in varying and often contradictory terms. Sometimes it seems to critics to be over-elastic: as when Basil declares that, while it was morally wrong for Jacob to deceive his blind father and steal the inheritance from his brother Esau, we must show economy towards his sin because it was for the ultimate benefit of mankind. But in general economy was admirable, and all the more so because it was not hedged by rules and restrictions.[1]

The difference between the Eastern and the Western attitudes was due largely to historical developments. When the Roman Empire collapsed in the West, the Roman Church was left as the repository not only of Roman traditions and Roman law, as opposed to the customs introduced by the new barbarian rulers, but also of learning and education. In the chaos of the invasions, with the former lay governors fleeing or dispossessed, ecclesiastical officers were often called upon to take over the administration of cities and whole districts. Moreover, when orderly government was restored, there were for many centuries few literate men outside of ecclesiastical ranks. Churchmen provided the lawyers and clerks on whom the lay rulers depended. This all tended to give the Roman Church a legal outlook. The Papal chancery was obliged to fill itself with trained lawyers, whose tastes began to dominate theology. Roman theologians liked clear-cut definitions. The apophatic tradition, of which Augustine had been so eminent an advocate, tended to give way to Scholastic tastes, to the desire to turn theology into a systematized philosophy.

In the East Roman Empire lay life was never interrupted until the Turkish conquest. It survived in exile even during the half-

---

[1] The best concise interpretation of economy is given in R. L. Langford-James, *A Dictionary of the Eastern Orthodox Church*, pp. 47–9.

century of the Latin occupation of Constantinople. In Constantinople the lawyers remained laymen; and there was always a highly educated laity which provided most of the philosophers and many even of the theologians. The scope of canon law was small; the Church never acquired a legalistic outlook. Nor did the ecclesiastical establishment acquire an overriding authority. In the West 'the Church' came in ordinary parlance to mean the hierarchy and the priesthood. In the East the Church always meant the whole body of Christians, past, present and future, including the angels in heaven. The priesthood was not a class apart. Communion in both kinds continued to be administered to the laity.[1]

There was thus never any serious conflict in the East between the lay and ecclesiastical authorities. The Patriarch was a great personage; he was, so to speak, the keeper of the Empire's conscience. But the Emperor was the unquestioned head of the Oecumene, God's living viceroy on earth. The whole Eastern Church viewed with disapproval the desire felt by the Western Church in the middle ages to subordinate all lay powers to the authority of the supreme Pontiff. But the accusation of Caesaropapism often levelled against the Byzantine Church is not just, however applicable it might become to the Church in Tsarist Russia. The Orthodox believed in making the distinction between the things which are Caesar's and the things which are God's, though they might dispute about the exact place where the line should be drawn.

This attitude had its weakness. The reluctance to make of theology a complete philosophical system led to a reluctance to make of religion a complete guide for the conduct of life. It was for the ministers of the Church to uphold morality and to denounce sin; but the daily ordering of existence should be left to the lay authorities. As a result the hierarchy in the East could never exercise the same moral influence as the hierarchy in the West; and the attitude goes far to explain the curious dichotomy in the

---

[1] See Bulgakov, *op. cit.* pp. 9–17.

2-2

Byzantine character, with its intense and genuine piety and conviction that life in this world was but the prelude to the true life to come, and its practical, self-seeking, cynical and often unscrupulous handling of mundane affairs.

The weakness was enhanced by the structure of the Eastern hierarchy. In the Western Empire Rome had always been the one great metropolis. Only the African cities could rival her; and the African bishoprics never fully recovered from the Donatist schism. The impact of the barbarian invasions made it all the more necessary for the Roman bishopric to insist on her pre-eminence. She was left as the heir of the Roman Empire, sitting crowned on the ruins thereof, not a ghost, as Hobbes imagined, but a living vigorous force, the guardian not only of the Faith but of the traditions of Roman civilization. Amid the political disruption of the West it was inevitable that men should long for unity and should see in the Roman Pontiff the one power that was in a position to maintain unity. In the East there had been many great cities. Each had its church, none of which was ready to submit to the dominance of a rival. The historian Dion Cassius truly remarked that there is no equivalent in Greek to the Latin word *auctoritas*;[1] and this dislike of authority characterized the churches in the Greek world. It is possible that, but for the destruction of the city in A.D. 70, the Church of Jerusalem under the vigorous leadership of James, the son of Joseph, and his successors, might have established a hegemony, though the Gentile Churches would doubtless have soon rebelled against its Judaistic tendencies.[2] As it was, each Church in the East was held to be of equal rank. The Holy Spirit had descended equally to all the Apostles at Pentecost; and their successors, the bishops, thus enjoyed charismatic equality. None could dictate to any other on matters of faith or doctrine. If such decisions were needed, then all bishops, representing all the churches, should come together, and the Holy Spirit would descend again as at Pentecost. But in time administra-

---

[1] Dion Cassius, *Historia Romana* (ed. U. P. Boissevain), II, p. 452.
[2] See S. Brandon, *The Fall of Jerusalem, passim.*

tive needs led to the creation of an ordered hierarchy. Bishops were grouped together under metropolitans; and the bishops of the two greatest cities of the East, Alexandria and Antioch, each acquired certain disciplinary rights over a vast province; and each eventually was given the title of Patriarch. But there was a lack of uniformity. Certain Churches, such as that of Cyprus, the Church of St Barnabas, were recognized as being disciplinarily autonomous, just as certain archbishops were free of metropolitan control. In the West it was difficult to maintain in practice that all bishops were equal when the Roman Pontiff so obviously overtopped them all. Even the Easterners admitted him, as bishop of the Imperial City, to be the senior hierarch in Christendom, whose views and rulings were entitled to special respect. The position was complicated by the foundation of a new Imperial capital at Constantinople, whose bishop had, reasonably, to be raised to Patriarchal rank and given disciplinary authority over a great province. But the Patriarch of Constantinople, with his power restricted on the one side by the presence and the overriding majesty of the Emperor and on the other by the democracy of the Church and the egalitarian claims of the bishops, could never attain the status enjoyed by the Pope in the West. These restrictions, combined with the looser attitude of the Orthodox towards theology and their definite dislike of a monolithic structure, weakened the administrative cohesion and efficacy of the Church organization.

The strength and the weakness of the Byzantine Orthodox ecclesiastical organization and religious outlook were to be revealed when the Church had to undergo the cruellest fate that can befall a community: sudden subjection to an alien and infidel domination. It is the aim of this study to examine the effects of the Ottoman conquest upon Greek ecclesiastical history and religious life. But it is necessary first to give a picture of the Byzantine Church as it was during the last centuries of its independence, in order to assess the consequences of the conquest and of the long years of servitude.

The Background

The history of the Church of Constantinople can be roughly divided into four epochs up to the Turkish conquest. The first lasts from the foundation of the new capital to the Arab invasions of Syria and Egypt. Christendom was still undivided and nominally conterminous with the old Roman Empire, whose official religion it had recently become. But already divergences were appearing. Many centres, in particular the three great religious metropoles of Rome, Alexandria and Antioch, were developing their own characteristic theological outlook; and the differences were enhanced and complicated by great Christological controversies. Arianism had spread through Christendom without a definite core and therefore died out, except amongst the barbarians settled in the West, where the challenge of Arianism guided theological developments. Nestorianism, the product of the Antiochene school, failed within the Empire. The Nestorians went off to build up their remarkable missionary church under alien domination. Monophysitism, the product of the Alexandrian school, was more successful. Helped by political dissatisfaction, it resulted in the establishment of heretic churches in Syria and Egypt which drew off most of the congregations there. But its successes were local; neither it nor Nestorianism found adherents in the Western world, which was little touched by the problems that they raised. In the official Church the Roman view in general prevailed— largely, so cynical orientals thought, because the crudity of the Latin language prevented Roman theologians from appreciating the nicer points at issue and enabled them thus to provide comprehensive formulae. During these controversies the Church of Constantinople played a not very impressive part. It was something of a parvenu church, and it was seated at the seat of the secular government. Its hierarchs were too often required to express the views of the Emperor of the moment; and there was as yet no strong local tradition to counter Imperial influence. The great Cappadocian Fathers of the fourth century and John Chrysostom a generation later were beginning to build up a characteristic school of thought. But it was not till we come to

Maximus the Confessor at the end of the period that we begin to see a definite Constantinopolitan theology.[1]

The second period lasts from the Arab invasions of the seventh century to the Turkish invasions of the eleventh. Alexandria and Antioch have now passed under infidel rule and will never again play a leading part in Church history. Rome has her own troubles and is only fitfully concerned with the East. Constantinople is now the unquestioned capital of Christian civilization. The bounds of its Patriarchate are roughly those of the Empire, making of it a national church, the church of the Empire, the *oecumene*, as the Byzantines now, with philological inaccuracy, called the dominions subject to the Emperor. The proximity of the Imperial government was still an occasional cause of embarrassment to the Church authorities. The long and bitter quarrels over Iconoclasm, when a succession of Emperors tried to force a controversial doctrine on a mainly unwilling people, had to be resolved before Church and State could settle down together in a relationship that remained undefined but, apart from minor disturbances, was generally accepted and understood.[2] With the close of the controversy Byzantine theology can be said to have taken on its lasting characteristics. The Liturgy and the practices of the Church were established in forms that have scarcely been altered since that day. There were no fundamental theological disputes for some centuries. The Church shared in the prosperity of the Empire and worked together with the State on great missionary enterprises. Among the most splendid achievements of the period were the conversion of the Balkan Slavs to Orthodox Christianity in the ninth century and the conversion of the Russians at the end of the tenth.

The period that followed was one of decadence and transition.

[1] For the Christological controversies and the quarrels between the Patriarchates see the chapters by A. Bardy in A. Fliche and V. Martin, *Histoire de l'Eglise*, IV, pp. 163 ff., and by A. Gardner in *Cambridge Medieval History*, I, pp. 487 ff.; also Zernov, *op. cit.* pp. 39–80.

[2] See below, pp. 134, 152. For the vast literature on Iconoclasm see the bibliography in *Cambridge Medieval History*, IV, 1 (new edition), pp. 840–8.

The Background

The Turkish invasions, though they were stemmed, resulted in the loss to the Empire of most of Anatolia, its chief granary and source of manpower. The Church suffered along with the State. The Christian life of Anatolia came almost to a halt. Many Christians fled to the coastlands or to greater safety beyond the sea. Others allowed themselves to be converted to the conquering faith of Islam. The rest remained as Christian enclaves *in partibus infidelium*, impoverished and half-isolated. At the same time the Empire had to face Norman invasions from the West and the loss of Byzantine Italy, and the claims of the reformed Hildebrandine Papacy. All these factors led to the movement which we call the Crusades; from which at first Byzantium gained certain material advantages, but which led to worsening relations between Eastern and Western Christendom. Early in the period there had been a bitter quarrel between the Churches of Constantinople and Rome; and before the period was over political misunderstandings combined with religious rivalry to produce enmity and open schism, till the climax was reached of the Fourth Crusade.[1]

The Latin conquest, temporary though it proved to be, ushered in the final period of Byzantine political and ecclesiastical history. The religious life of Byzantium and its whole moral and intellectual atmosphere during the last two centuries before the fall of Constantinople were fundamentally affected by the disruption and shock of the Latin conquest, by the courageous revival of the Greeks and by the disintegration and decay that followed ironically soon after their recovery of Constantinople. It is necessary to remember this political background. The Crusaders failed in their attempt to annex the whole Empire. They, jointly with the Venetians, held Constantinople for half a century. Frankish lordships in Greece itself and in the islands lasted for some two centuries; and the Venetians acquired some islands and ports of strategic and commercial value. But Byzantium lasted on in exile, based round the ancient city of Nicaea. The Nicaean Empire provides one of the most admirable episodes in Byzantine history.

---

[1] For a full bibliography of the schism, *ibid.* pp. 942–52.

It was ably ruled, first by Theodore Lascaris, son-in-law of one of the last Emperors, and then by his son-in-law John Vatatzes, an even more remarkable man. Though there had been other Greek succession states, the Despotate of the Angeli in Epirus and the Empire of the Grand Comnenus at Trebizond, the Nicaean Empire was soon recognized by most Greeks as the legitimate Empire. The Despotate of Epirus faded out about the end of the thirteenth century; and, though the Empire of Trebizond was to outlive the Empire of Constantinople and remained a commercial and intellectual centre of some importance, it played only a minor part in international history. It was with the efficient Empire of the Nicaeans that the future seemed to lie. John Vatatzes's son, Theodore II, was a man of high intellectual tastes but no politician. On his death in 1258 the throne was seized by an ambitious noble, Michael Palaeologus, founder of the last Byzantine dynasty. He not only began the reconquest of the Greek peninsula, but in 1261 his troops entered Constantinople, and extinguished the Latin Empire.[1]

For Byzantium, religiously as well as politically, the recovery of the capital was a moral triumph and a triumph of prestige. But it created new difficulties. To rehabilitate Constantinople was costly. An alliance had been made with the Genoese, in order to counter the Venetians; and the Genoese had to be paid with concessions that virtually gave them control of the Empire's commerce. The West burned for revenge; and Michael could only protect himself by an expensive foreign policy and by promises of union with Rome which offended most of his ecclesiastics, who were already hostile to him owing to the unscrupulous circumstances of his usurpation. The treasure accumulated by the thrifty Nicaean Emperors was spent. Unwise economies were made over the defence of the eastern frontier. There seemed to be no immediate danger there; whereas in the Balkans the Bulgarian Empire of the Asen dynasty had been a potential threat, and now

[1] See D. M. Nicol, 'The Fourth Crusade and the Greek and Latin Empires', *ibid.* pp. 279–330.

13

the Serbian Empire of the Uroš dynasty was growing ominously powerful.

Michael's European policy was effective. There was no apparent challenge from the West during the reign of his son, Andronicus II, who was therefore able to make peace with his Church by jettisoning his father's ecclesiastical schemes. But Serbian power was increasing; and the weakened eastern frontier was threatened by a vigorous Turkish emir called Osman, whose people, known from his name as the Osmanlis or Ottomans, began to encroach into the Empire. The Emperor was short of soldiers and rashly hired a mercenary band of Catalans. The Catalan company turned against its employer, blockaded Constantinople for two years, ravaged all the provinces and introduced the Turks into Europe, before retiring to establish itself at Athens. Andronicus II's reign ended in revolt; he was dethroned by his grandson, Andronicus III, in 1328.

Decay continued under the new Emperor. The Serbs were at their zenith under the great king Stephen Dusan, and seemed for a time likely to absorb the whole of Byzantium. The Ottoman advance continued. Brusa had fallen in 1326. Nicaea fell in 1329 and Nicomedia in 1337; and soon almost the whole of Byzantine Asia was lost. When Andronicus III died in 1341 his son, John V, was a child. He was to reign for fifty years, during which he was driven from power first by his father-in-law, John VI Cantacuzenus, from 1347 to 1355, then, from 1376 to 1379, by his son Andronicus IV, and lastly, for a while in 1390, by his grandson John VII. The civil war with John Cantacuzenus was particularly bitter and harmful. Religious as well as political issues were involved. In the midst of it there was a disastrous visitation of the Black Death, in which about a third of the Empire's population seems to have perished. Both sides called in Ottoman aid, with the result that the Ottoman Sultan was able to establish himself irremovably in Europe. By the time of John V's death in 1391 the Ottoman Empire had annexed Bulgaria and most of Serbia and stretched to the Danube, with its capital at Adrianople, in Thrace.

The Emperor's dominions were restricted to the cities and environs of Constantinople and Thessalonica (though that was temporarily in Turkish hands), to a few coastal cities in Thrace, and to most of the Peloponnese, where a cadet of the Imperial house was Despot.

John V's ultimate successor, his younger son Manuel II, was unable to stem the decay. It seemed clear that the Empire was doomed to fall into the hands of the Turks unless help came; and only the powers of Western Europe were in a position to provide help. But their price was religious union, a price which most Byzantines were not prepared to pay. John V had gone to Italy to seek for allies and had personally submitted to the Pope at Rome. But he could not carry his people with him, and he ended his Italian tour detained for debt at Venice. Manuel II travelled as far as Paris and London in his search for aid, but avoided committing himself to Church union. One Western army came to fight the Turks but was crushed by them at Nicopolis in 1396. There was a respite next year when the Turks, who had just begun to lay siege to Constantinople, were forced to withdraw to face the armies of Timur the Tartar. Their defeat by Timur led to civil wars, in which Manuel managed to recover a little territory. But they soon recovered. In 1422 they were again before Constantinople, only retiring because of plots within the Ottoman dynasty. In 1423 the governor of Thessalonica, despairing of the future, sold his city to the Venetians; but the Ottoman Sultan took it from them seven years later.[1]

Manuel II died in 1425. His eldest son, John VIII, less prudent and more desperate than his father, journeyed to Italy and pledged his Empire to union with Rome at the Council of Florence in 1439. The union was bitterly opposed at Constantinople. Had it resulted in effective aid, the opposition might have been silenced; but the one ensuing Western expedition was annihilated by the Turks at Varna in 1444. John died at the end of 1448, in an atmosphere of bitterness and gloom. His successor, his brother Con-

[1] See G. Ostrogorsky, 'The Palaeologi', *ibid.* pp. 331–88.

stantine XI, was a brave and capable man; but there was nothing that he could do. In 1451 the Ottoman throne passed to a young man of high brilliance and ruthless ambition, Mehmet II, who was to be surnamed the Conqueror. Early in April, 1453, he laid siege to Constantinople. After a heroic defence lasting for six weeks it fell to him on 29 May 1453. In 1460 his troops overran the Peloponnese. In 1461 they extinguished the Empire of Trebizond. Greek independence was ended.[1]

It was in this atmosphere of gathering gloom that the Byzantines lived during the last two centuries of their Empire. The disillusion was all the more bitter because the period of the Nicaean Emperors had been one of regeneration and hope, and the recovery of Constantinople had seemed to open a new era of glory. There was always an element of pessimism in Byzantium. Even in its most splendid days men had whispered of prophecies foretelling that the Empire would perish. On stones in the city and in the books of such great seers and magicians as Apollonius of Tyana and the Emperor Leo the Wise the lists of all the Emperors had been given, and the names were drawing to an end. It was natural that in the deepening darkness many of the Byzantines should seek refuge in mysticism and should emphasize the other-worldly side of their faith. Yet, paradoxically, the cultural life of Byzantium was never so brilliant as in the two centuries before its fall. The art of the period was perhaps the most beautiful and certainly the most human that Byzantium ever produced; and it was produced so long as there was money to pay for it. The intellectual brilliance lasted on to the end, led by scholars whose vigour and originality were as fine as any of their forefathers' and whose renown spread to foreign lands. Many of these scholars hoped that regeneration might still be achieved, even though it might involve integration with the West and an abandonment of ancient traditions. But others believed that there could be no escape from the coming political doom and that the only task to be performed was to see that the Faith and all that it meant did not

[1] See S. Runciman, *The Fall of Constantinople, passim.*

perish in the holocaust. This conflict, complicated by cross-currents, gave a bitter intensity to the religious life of the dying Empire, adding to the problems that faced the harassed Church.[1]

These problems can be roughly grouped under five headings. First, there was the problem of the organization of the Church; how could the machine be kept adaptable enough to meet the needs of the changing political world? Secondly, there was the problem of the relations between Church and State, which needed adjustment, now that the Emperor ruled effectively over a small and dwindling proportion of the Orthodox congregations. Thirdly, what was the relationship of the Byzantine Church to be with other Churches, in particular the great Church of the West, now that Western Europe was, materially and culturally, taking the lead in Christendom? Fourthly, what were the duties of the Church towards education, especially now that the secular State was collapsing? Fifthly, new controversies over theology had arisen, touching especially on the deep and delicate question of mysticism; and their repercussions had not been stilled.

All these problems were intertwined; and they had not been resolved when the infidel conquerors came, bringing in their train problems for which it would be even harder to find a solution.

[1] See J. Gill, *The Council of Florence, passim*; D. Geanakoplos, *Byzantine East and Latin West*, pp. 84–111.

CHAPTER 2

THE STRUCTURE OF THE CHURCH

THE HIERARCHY

To the Byzantines, as to the Orthodox Christians of today, the distinction between the Church and the Churches was clear and emphatic. The Church is the Body of Christ, joined to Him in a unity that yet preserves the reality of their difference. As the Body of Christ it is the domain in which the Holy Spirit works; it is the life of the Holy Spirit in humanity. But it is not limited to humanity alone. The whole company of angels is part of it. It unites the living and the dead, the heavenly host and all creation. It began before the beginning of the created world and is the eternal end of creation. As such it is invisible. But it also belongs visibly to history. It reached the fullness of its existence with the Incarnation, and it was realized with the descent of the Holy Spirit at Pentecost. In this earthly sense it has its limits in time and space. On earth it must operate as a society, and as a society it must have its earthly structure.

There must therefore be some organization of the Church on earth; there must be the Churches, and there must be persons qualified to act as their officials and their ministers. As Paul wrote to the Corinthians, 'And God hath set some in the Church, first apostles, secondarily prophets, thirdly teachers, after that miracles, then gifts of healings, helps, governments, diversities of tongues'. That is to say, there must be some sort of a hierarchy. This should not impair the fundamental equality before God of all members of the Church. Earlier in the same passage Paul says: 'Now there are diversities of gifts, but the same Spirit. And there are differences of administrations, but the same Lord. And there are diversities of operations, but it is the same God which worketh all in all.'[1] According to Orthodox belief, Christ Himself laid the founda-

---

[1] I Corinthians xii. 4–6, 28.

tions of the hierarchy by calling the twelve Apostles by name. They were the witnesses of the Word. To them was entrusted the power to confer the gifts of the Holy Spirit upon the newly baptized and to ordain others to perform priestly functions. They were, to use a favourite word of Greek theologians, Χαρισματικοί, men of Grace, who both administered the Sacraments and prophesied and taught. A little below them were the seventy disciples mentioned in the Gospels and the apostles mentioned in the Acts and the Epistles, with Paul at their head, and all those that saw the risen Lord. But even Paul does not quite rank with the twelve whom the Incarnate God Himself had chosen. It was the twelve who at the beginning bestowed on believers the grace of the Spirit by the laying-on of hands; but it was soon decided that this power could be handed down by the hierarchy which was thus instituted and which derived and still derives its authority down the ages from a direct and uninterrupted succession from the Apostles. The Apostolic Succession is thus of essential importance to the Orthodox.[1]

It is uncertain when the three hierarchical orders of bishop, priest and deacon were evolved. By the third century the pattern was in general use. Though every priest is charismatic by ordination, the bishop alone is fully charismatic. He was now the charismatic unit. In theory all bishops were equal. Each represented his local church; each was elected into his seat by the will of the clergy and congregations of the bishopric and was empowered to exercise his functions when he had received the grace conferred by consecration at the hands of an already consecrated bishop, in the Apostolic Succession. But already, with the growing number of Christian churches and congregations, a closer organization was required. It was inevitable that the bishops of the greater cities should take the lead and even acquire some sort of authority over their poorer brothers. There was justification in the Gospels for this. Though the twelve Apostles had been equal in authority yet

[1] For the Apostolic Succession of the priesthood see P. Evdokimov, *L'Orthodoxie*, pp. 161–4.

Our Lord had from time to time picked out certain of them, notably Peter, James and John, for special distinction. There was thus a precedent for later allotting to certain of the bishops special honours and duties. This allotment was often combined with the theory that the holders of sees whose founder had been an Apostle were entitled to particular reverence and even particular authority. In the West this second theory came to overshadow the belief in the equality of bishops. The Bishop of Rome, as the heir of Peter, was considered to have an overriding authority, though in practice one may wonder whether this authority was not based originally on the fact that Rome was the Imperial capital. In the East the theory that an apostolic origin conferred special rights upon a see was never fully or logically developed, though it was not without its influence. The Easterners were always ready to give the see of Rome a primacy of honour, but more because of the greatness of the city than because of any prerogative inherent in the heirs of Peter. The Bishop of Alexandria, which was the greatest city in the East, was held almost from the outset to rank above his brother of Antioch, a city that was not quite so great; and yet the see of Antioch had been founded by Peter and that of Alexandria by Mark, who was not one of the Apostles. The see of Ephesus, founded by John the Divine, ranked some way below them. It is true that the bishops of Constantinople found it useful at a later date to claim that their see had been founded by Andrew; but that somewhat unhistorical claim was never pushed very far as an argument for giving the see authority. In fact, the emergence of certain sees into a position of practical authority was an administrative necessity; and of necessity it was to the bishops of the greater cities that authority was entrusted.[1]

The ecclesiastical organization was imperfectly formed until the fourth century. But when the Empire had become Christian the Emperors wished for a Church whose organization would be roughly parallel to that of the lay government. The bishops were

---

[1] The whole question of the apostolicity of the great sees has been treated at length by F. Dvornik, *The Idea of Apostolicity in Byzantium.*

grouped together under the bishop of the metropolis of the province; and these metropolitans were grouped together again according to the great lay dioceses that Diocletian had instituted, under the presidency of the bishop of the capital of the diocese. When a new Imperial capital was founded at Byzantium, administrative convenience demanded that its bishop, hitherto under the Metropolitan of Heraclea in Thrace, should be raised to the first rank of bishops. He was given authority over the diocese hitherto dominated by Ephesus, together with some of the Bishop of Antioch's diocese; and he was soon raised, against Roman protests, to rank next under the Bishop of Rome, because the new capital was officially New Rome. About the same time, though more for reasons of sentiment than of administration, the Bishop of Jerusalem, who had hitherto been under the Metropolitan of Caesarea, was raised to be head of a diocese comprising all Palestine and the lands across the Jordan, districts that had formed part of the diocese of Antioch. The Bishops of Constantinople and Jerusalem, together with those of Alexandria and Antioch, were each given the additional title of Patriarch; and they were arranged in honorary rank, first Constantinople, then Alexandria, then Antioch and finally Jerusalem, with the Bishop of Old Rome ranking above them all. The elevation of Constantinople to the second place among the five had not been achieved without protests from both Rome and Alexandria.[1]

The rivalries of the Patriarchates during the great Christological controversies of the fourth, fifth and sixth centuries do not concern us here. But it is important to remember that the Orthodox world never lost its belief in the charismatic equality of bishops. Each bishop was a guardian of the Faith; each had an equal right to pronounce on a doctrinal issue. But he was not infallible. If a point of doctrine had to be defined, then all the bishops in Christen-

---

[1] For the emergence of the Patriarchates and their order and their disputes see A. Bardy in A. Fliche and V. Martin, *Histoire de l'Eglise, passim*; Dvornik, *op. cit. passim*; N. H. Baynes, 'Alexandria and Constantinople: a study in Ecclesiastical Diplomacy', *Byzantine Studies*, pp. 97–115.

dom, as heirs of the Apostles, should meet together in a Council that the Holy Spirit would inspire. Each bishop was free to air his views, even though they might be opposed to those of the Patriarch. In practice this put the Eastern bishops at a disadvantage when arguing with Western bishops, who were more strictly disciplined and tended more and more only to express views laid down by their superior, the Pope.

A bishop attended such an Oecumenical Council not only in his charismatic quality but also as representative of his congregation. Every baptized Christian had the right to attend; for a Council should express the opinion of the whole Church on earth. In fact it was seldom that members of the laity were present; it was usually left to the bishop to speak for the people, and only he had the right to vote on an issue. When the Empire became Christian, it was for the Emperor, as chief magistrate under God, to summon the Council, on behalf of the Christian commonwealth. It was generally held that his presence, or that of his personal representatives, sufficiently expressed the participation of the laity.

The decisions of the Council were officially unanimous. In fact, unanimity was invariably reached by the drastic device of anathematizing bishops who voted with the minority, depriving them thus of episcopal rank and the right to vote. The pronouncements of the Council were issued by the senior hierarch. In the case of an Oecumenical Council this was, until the schism with the West, the Bishop of Rome. They were then promulgated throughout the Oecumene, the Christian world, by the Emperor and thus received the force of law.[1]

Only the decisions of an Oecumenical Council were binding on the whole of Christendom. The Orthodox Eastern Churches recognized the traditional seven, from the First Council of Nicaea in 325 to the Second Council of Nicaea in 787. Their findings ranked next to the Holy Scriptures as being essential articles of

[1] F. Dvornik, 'Emperors, Popes and General Councils', *Dumbarton Oaks Papers*, VI (1951), pp. 1–23; S. Bulgakov, *The Orthodox Church*, pp. 90–2. Evdokimov, *op. cit.* pp. 159–61.

faith. There were also local Councils, held within one Patriarchal area, to deal with local heresies or schisms. The findings of some of these Councils were accepted by other churches and attained a dogmatic value next to those of the Oecumenical Councils. The decrees of the Council of Carthage, held in 426, are considered to apply universally. The Councils of Constantinople, held in the fourteenth century to consider Palamite doctrines, were rated by the other Eastern Patriarchates to have oecumenical value, and their decrees became articles of faith among the Orthodox. Councils of this type that concerned the whole Patriarchate of Constantinople were summoned by the Emperor. There were also purely local Councils, known as ἐνδημοῦσαι, summoned by the Patriarch and attended by neighbouring metropolitans and bishops, to deal with matters of ecclesiastical legislation.[1]

According to Byzantine theory the Church was administered, both as regards its daily needs and its larger political issues, by a vast organization at whose head was the pentarchy of Patriarchs. Just as the Roman Empire in its later days had often recognized at the same time more than one Emperor, each supreme in his sphere, and yet the Empire remained one and undivided, so the Church remained one, though it was governed by five independent Patriarchs, whose position and rank had been authorized by the Oecumenical Councils. The theory of the pentarchy was not fully promulgated till about the eighth century; but it had been the basis for Church government in the East since the end of the fourth century. The schism with the Roman Church did not in theory reduce the pentarchy to a tetrarchy. The place of Rome thenceforward was and still is vacant, until such time as her Bishop abandons the errors of his predecessors. Then she will return to her position as the senior of the five Patriarchates, *prima inter pares*. In the meantime the Patriarch of Constantinople enjoys the acting primacy.[2]

From the time of the Arab conquests in the seventh century and

---

[1] See Evdokimov, *op. cit.* pp. 159–61.
[2] N. Zernov, *Eastern Christendom*, pp. 75–7.

the somewhat arbitrary redistribution of ecclesiastical provinces by the Iconoclastic Emperors in the eighth, the territory effectively governed by the Emperors lay within the sphere of the Constantinopolitan Patriarchate. Only such lands as the Empire possessed west of the Adriatic and such lands as it reconquered temporarily in Syria lay outside. These extraneous territories had finally been lost during the eleventh century. But the Patriarch's authority extended over a number of autonomous Churches. Of those that still acknowledged it in the later Byzantine period the oldest was the Caucasian Church, at whose head was the Archbishop of Iberia (or Georgia). He seems to have been appointed locally, nominally by his Church and actually by the King of Georgia, and to have been always a native Georgian, as were his bishops. He was autonomous; but his appointment was confirmed by the Patriarch, unless it was impossible to communicate with Constantinople. In general the Caucasian Orthodox, though they used their own language and liturgy, were as loyal to Constantinople as circumstances permitted.[1]

The Balkan Churches were in a different position. Soon after the conversion of the Slavs they had been allowed to use their own language together with the liturgy that Cyril and Methodius had composed in Slavonic. Under the First Bulgarian Empire the Bulgar Tsar had insisted on appointing his own local Patriarch; but after the Byzantine reconquest the Balkan Churches, while retaining their native liturgy and priesthood, were placed under a Greek archbishop, the Archbishop of Bulgaria, who was stationed at Ochrid. In the thirteenth century the rulers of the revived Bulgarian and Serbian Empires proclaimed the autonomy of their Churches, and appointed their own Patriarchs. But the title was not considered fully canonical and was only accorded fitfully and grudgingly by Constantinople. Both Patriarchates faded out with

[1] See P. Peeters, 'Les débuts du Christianisme en Géorgie', *Analecta Bollandiana*, 50 (1932), pp. 6–58, and 'Histoires monastiques géorgiennes', *ibid.* 36–7 (1917–18), pp. 116 ff. The Georgian Church was officially under the Patriarchate of Antioch until the eleventh century. See also R. Janin, 'Géorgie', in *Dictionnaire de théologie catholique*, VI, coll. 1251–60.

the Turkish conquest of the Balkans in the fourteenth century; but each Church remained autocephalous, under the nominal suzerainty of Constantinople. The later Churches of Wallachia and Moldavia, though for some centuries to come they used the Slavonic liturgy, were more directly under Constantinople.[1]

The Russian Church showed even greater differences. It employed the Slavonic liturgy; and most of its clergy had at first come from Bulgaria. But from the early eleventh century to the early fourteenth the head of the Church, the Metropolitan of Kiev and All Russia, was a Greek, appointed by the Patriarch of Constantinople. From the fourteenth century onwards a Russian was often appointed, usually alternately with a Greek. The latter would still be nominated by the Patriarch, the former by the chief Russian prince of the time and confirmed by Constantinople. The Church was autocephalous but was thus kept in close contact with Constantinople; and the connection was made closer by the many Russian pilgrims who visited the city and the many Russian monks who settled on Mount Athos.[2]

The Orthodox Church of Cyprus, under its archbishop, enjoyed a historic claim to autonomy and independence from any Patriarchate. But in the thirteenth and fourteenth centuries the attempts by the Lusignan government of the island to subordinate it to the Latin Church induced the Orthodox in the island to tighten their links with the Patriarch of Constantinople, who thus obtained a vague and unofficial authority over it. The Metropolitan of Trebizond, appointed by his Emperor, the Grand Comnenus, so long as that Empire lasted, was in fact autonomous, though his appointment was supposed to be confirmed by the Patriarch of Constantinople, whom by the terms of a concordat, dated 1260, he recognized as his superior.[3]

---

[1] D. Obolensky, 'The Empire and its Northern Neighbours', *Cambridge Medieval History*, IV, I (new edition), pp. 473–518; M. Dinić, 'The Balkans, 1018–1499', *ibid.* pp. 519–66, both with bibliographies. See below, pp. 379–80.
[2] D. Obolensky, 'Byzantium, Kiev and Moscow', *Dumbarton Oaks Papers*, XI (1957), pp. 21–78; W. K. Medlin, *Moscow and East Rome*, pp. 38–45, 62–6.
[3] See below, p. 65.

These international rights and privileges added to the prestige of the Patriarch, who was at the pinnacle of the Byzantine Church organization. But basically, at least in principle, the Church was democratic. The parish priest was appointed by the local bishop, officially on the request of the congregation; and the priests of the bishopric officially elected the bishop. By an old tradition legalized by Justinian I, when a vacancy in a bishopric occurred, the priests, aided on special invitation by the leading laymen of the bishopric, met and submitted three names to the bishop whose duty it was to perform the consecration, that is to say, the metropolitan of the province, and he made his choice from among them. Occasionally, however, the Patriarch himself intervened directly to choose the candidate and perform the consecration. In the case of a metropolitan the same procedure was ordained, as he was elected as a simple bishop, though, as he was regularly consecrated by the Patriarch, the Patriarch chose between the candidates. In fact by the ninth century the metropolitan was chosen from three names submitted to the Patriarch by the synod of the province, that is to say, its suffragan bishops, the lower clergy no longer playing any direct part in the election. In all cases the election was ratified by the Patriarch, who bestowed the ὠμοφόριον, or pallium, and by the civil power, the Emperor or his local representative. The Patriarch, as Bishop of Constantinople, should have been elected by the same process as any other bishop. But by the eighth century it was the metropolitans of the Patriarchate, together with the high officials of the Patriarchal Court, sitting together as the Synod of the Great Church, who selected the three candidates; and it was the Emperor who made the final choice, even substituting a candidate of his own if none of the three pleased him. All metropolitans were expected to attend the meetings at which the candidates were chosen unless they were specially excused from coming to Constantinople.[1] By the concordat of 1260 the Metropolitan of

---

[1] L. Bréhier, *Le Monde Byzantin*, II, *Institutions de l'Empire Byzantin*, pp. 507–13; Constantine Porphyrogenitus, *De Ceremoniis* (C.S.H.B. edition), I, pp. 564–6: Pseudo-Codinus, *De Officiis*, M.P.G., CLVI, coll. 176–7.

Trebizond was permanently excused, officially because his journey might be long and dangerous but actually in recognition of his semi-autonomy.

According to the official formula the Patriarch was elected by the decree of the Holy Synod and the promotion of the Emperor. His investiture took place in the Imperial Palace in the presence of the high dignitaries of Church and State. Until 1204 the scene was the Palace of Magnaura, where the Emperior in person announced the election with the formula: 'The Divine grace, and Our Majesty which derives from it, raises the most pious [*name*] to be Patriarch of Constantinople.' After 1261 the investiture was held in the triclinium of the Palace of Blachernae; and about the same time the formula was changed. The Emperor now said: 'The Holy Trinity, through the power that It has given Us, raises you to be Bishop of Constantinople, New Rome, and Oecumenical Patriarch.' By the beginning of the fifteenth century the formula and the setting had changed once more. The investiture now took place in a church in the presence of the Emperor; but it was a high lay official who pronounced the words: 'Our great and holy Sovereign and the Sacred Synod call Your Holiness to the supreme throne of Patriarch of Constantinople.' The theologian Symeon of Thessalonica, writing in about 1425, regretted the change of words as there was no mention of God, though he liked the recognition given to the Holy Synod. When the election had thus been proclaimed the Emperor gave to the Patriarch the cross, the purple soutane and the pectoral reliquary cross which symbolized his office. After this investiture the new Patriarch rode in procession through the streets of Constantinople to the church of Saint Sophia, where he was consecrated by the Metropolitan of Heraclea, in memory of the days when Byzantium had been a suffragan see under Heraclea.

As the latest formula showed, the electoral rights of the Holy Synod were recognized throughout the history of the Empire. It was for the Synod, too, to depose the Patriarch should that be thought necessary. The Emperor could legally do no more than convoke the Synod to discuss the question of deposition. Very occasionally the Synod deposed a Patriarch without consulting the Emperor, as in the case of Athanasius I, who was ejected in 1293 because he was too strict; but he was so strongly supported by the lower clergy and the people that the Emperor was able to enforce his re-election eleven years later. Strictly speaking the only ground for deposition was that the original election had been somehow uncanonical; but this could be interpreted very loosely.

A candidate for the Patriarchate, like a candidate for any bishopric, had to be over thirty-five years of age—a rule that Emperors had sometimes neglected when forcing a pet candidate upon the Synod. He must not be a civil servant or a tax-collector, unless there were a special dispensation for him. He might be a married man or a widower, so long as he had only been married once and his wife had not been previously married. If she were living she would have to consent to retire into a convent. He might be a layman; and monks who had not taken priestly orders counted as laymen. If a layman, he would be hurried through the ecclesiastical orders; but three months should elapse before he could be invested. If this interval were omitted, as in the case of the great Patriarch Photius, there were grounds for questioning the legality of the appointment. By the canons of the fourth-century Councils no bishop might be transferred from one see to another; and this rule remained officially in force till the eve of the fifteenth century. As time went on bishops were drawn more and more from the monasteries. During the last 250 years of the Empire, with very few exceptions, the Patriarchs were former monks, most of whom had already taken priestly vows. Only one complete layman was appointed, a professor called George of Cyprus, elected in 1283.[1]

The Patriarch enjoyed high prestige; but, quite apart from limitations imposed upon him by the Emperor, his power was also

[1] Bréhier, *op. cit.* II, pp. 477–86. Constantine Porphyrogenitus, *De Ceremoniis* (C.S.H.B. edition), I, *loc. cit.*; Symeon of Thessalonica, *De Sacris Ordinationibus*, M.P.G., CLV, col. 440.

limited by the Holy Synod. He was held responsible for the proper celebration of services and for religious discipline throughout the Empire, but he could only legislate on such matters through the Synod. Major religious legislation was initiated by the Emperor, as being the source of law. He did so in the form of a communication to the Patriarch, whose business it was then to inform the Church and to see that the new laws were obeyed. In the event of a scandal within the Church the Patriarch could take direct action. He could suspend a metropolitan who misbehaved; and, if a metropolitan permitted abuses within his province, he could intervene to suspend the guilty clergy. But no bishop could be deposed without the authorization of the Holy Synod.[1]

In the great days of the Empire the Patriarch enjoyed an enormous revenue. This came partly from an annual grant from the Imperial exchequer, partly from landed property in all parts of the Empire, including valuable estates in Constantinople itself, and partly from rents paid by monasteries that had been founded by a Patriarch. Each source of revenue was earmarked for a special object. Foreign invasions and the Latin conquest had disorganized the whole system; but the Nicaean Emperors seem to have re-endowed the Patriarchate with country estates, and after the reconquest of Constantinople a third of the city's revenues were set aside for it. In addition, a proportion of the fees paid for licences by professional fishermen and huntsmen living in or near the capital was handed to the Patriarch to defray the cost of the candles and oil needed to light the great cathedral of Saint Sophia. The Turkish advance lost to the Patriarch more and more of his country property; but he continued to receive rents from such Patriarchal monasteries as survived in the Turkish dominions. By the end of the fourteenth century his income had fallen so greatly that he could no longer fully maintain the Patriarchal palace.[2]

This palace adjoined Saint Sophia, to which it was connected by covered passages. It included administrative offices and reception halls, among the latter the Great Secretum and the Small

---

[1] Bréhier, *op. cit.* II, pp. 442–6, 489–90. [2] *Ibid.* pp. 518–23.

Secretum, in which Synods met, according to their size, as well as several oratories and a magnificent library, which seems to have survived almost intact till 1453. During the Latin occupation the Venetians had controlled it and kept it undamaged. The Patriarch's own living-quarters were suitably modest; but he owned suburban villas to which he could retire; and he often preferred to reside in some nearby monastery.

In the old days, his chief official had been the Syncellus, who had been his political adviser and acted as liaison between the Imperial and Patriarchal courts. But this office seems to have faded out during the thirteenth century, perhaps because the intimate arrangements of the small court at Nicaea made it super-fluous. The Archdeacon, who had been the Patriarch's deputy in all liturgical matters, disappeared about the same time. But five great offices remained throughout the Byzantine period. They were headed by the Grand Economus, who was in charge of all properties and sources of revenue and who administered the Patriarchate during an interregnum; by the Grand Sacellarius, who, in spite of his title, had nothing to do with the Purse but was in charge of all the Patriarchal monasteries, assisted by his own court and a deputy known as the Archon of the Monasteries; by the Grand Skevophylax, in charge of all liturgical matters, as well as of the holy treasures and relics belonging to the Patriarchate; by the Grand Chartophylax, originally the keeper of the library but, after the disappearance of the Syncellus and the Archdeacon, the Patriarch's Secretary of State and director of personnel; and finally by the Prefect of the Sacellion, keeper of the Patriarchal prison and in charge of the punishment of ecclesiastical offenders. These five officials were members of the Holy Synod and ranked above all metropolitans. Till 1057 they were appointed by the Emperor; but the great Patriarch Michael Cerullarius had won the right to make his own appointments, though later Emperors tried to withdraw this right from the Patriarchs. Lower in rank, below the metropolitans and not members of the Synod, were such officials as the Referendarius, who carried the Patriarch's messages to the Emperor; the Mandaton, who arranged the daily liturgies; a Logothete, or chief accountant; a Protonotary, who received and presented petitions; a Hieromnemon, who organized meetings of the Synod and counted the votes at them; a Hypomimnescon, who was the chief private secretary, as well as assistant secretaries and the professors attached to the Patriarchal School. There was also a Master of Ceremonies, and a number of priests appointed to assist the Patriarch in his liturgical duties. The many clergy serving in Saint Sophia counted as forming part of the Patriarchal establishment.[1]

The metropolitans maintained similar organizations, on a smaller scale. Each had his Economus, his Skevophylax, his Sacellarius and his Chartophylax, performing equivalent functions within the metropolitan see. The bishops maintained simpler but still similar courts, though there were small local divergences. Bishops' revenues came from estates in the diocese and from rents paid by monasteries that were neither Imperial nor Patriarchal foundations. The bishop also received the κανονικόν, a tax levied on priests at the moment of their ordination. This was a tax that the civil authorities disliked and always tried to discourage the priests from paying. In 1295 the Emperor Andronicus II decreed its abolition; but in practice it was still paid, as it was difficult to punish bishops who refused to ordain priests unless they received the money. The bishop could also charge a fee for registering a betrothal. The bridegroom paid one gold piece and the bride provided twelve ells of cloth.[2]

Every bishop held a court of justice at which suits involving clerics were heard and from which appeals could be made to the Patriarchal court. The canons of the early Councils forbade clergy to appear before secular courts; and the ban was on the whole respected. The bishop was supposed to work in with the civil authorities; and if he had a strong personality he would dominate the local governor. He was, however, forbidden to touch anything that concerned military affairs. When Andronicus III

---

[1] Bréhier, *op. cit.* II, pp. 496–506.   [2] *Ibid.* pp. 517–18.

reformed the system of civil justice by introducing itinerant judges to tour the provinces, the bishop was put in charge of the local tribunal which the judge from time to time visited. This was convenient as enemy invasions often now made it impossible for a civil officer to visit the frontier districts, whereas the bishop was supposed to remain at his post, even under an enemy occupation. The conquering Turks made few difficulties about this. But many bishops in fact deserted their sees. During the last decades of the Empire the Patriarch had continually to order bishops to return to their posts. In towns annexed by the Turks the bishop came to be recognized by the new masters as the magistrate in charge of the Christian population.[1]

To supervise the rural parts of his diocese the bishop had in earlier days appointed a *chorepiscopus*, a 'country bishop', to assist him. Later he employed an exarch, or visitor. We know little about the organization of the parishes. The parish priest was a local man, recommended by the headman of the village and appointed by the bishop. He might be a married man, so long as the marriage had taken place before he reached the rank of sub-deacon, and so long as neither he nor his wife had been previously married. By the late Byzantine period he was almost invariably a married man, bachelors being considered to be less respectable; though occasionally a local monk who had taken priestly orders might be put in as a stop-gap. He lived and maintained his church off the tithes paid by the parishioners and off the patrimony of the church, usually a small glebe which he farmed himself. He was usually a man of humble birth and simple education; but his ordination by the bishop gave him sufficient grace to perform the mysteries. The parish was closely supervised by the bishop's exarch.[2]

On the whole the Byzantine ecclesiastical organization ran smoothly. During the later Byzantine period there were comparatively few major Church scandals. The Emperors no longer, as in earlier years, tried to make cynical and worldly appoint-

---

[1] See below, pp. 79–80.   [2] Bréhier, *op. cit.* II, pp. 466–7, 475–6.

ments. Patriarchal letters continued to fulminate against absentee bishops and bishops who sold justice; but steps were always taken to end the abuses. There was always some nepotism. Bishops were permitted to provide for needy relatives out of their revenues; and they interpreted this permission rather too widely. The main problem was caused by the shrinking of the Empire and the increasing number of bishoprics passing under alien and often infidel control.

In the list of bishoprics suffragan to Constantinople attributed to Epiphanius and actually dating from the early seventh century, that is to say, before the province of Illyricum was annexed to the Patriarchate, 524 are mentioned, of which 371 were seated in Asia. In the list known as the *Taxis*, published by the Patriarchate about the year 901, the total number is 505, of which 405 are Asiatic. The bulk of the Balkan peninsula was at that time in the hands of Slavs and Bulgars, only newly converted to Christianity; and their few Churches were not yet organized. Of the 505 bishops, 54 were metropolitans, each with a group of bishops under his jurisdiction; but there were 50 autocephalous arch-bishops, who depended directly on the Patriarch and had no suffragans. These autocephalous bishoprics gradually faded out. The metropolitanates were arranged in an order of precedence. The senior was the see of Caesarea-Mazacha. Next came Ephesus, then Heraclea in Thrace, then Ancyra. Thessalonica only appears as sixteenth in the *Taxis* list; and the other European sees were lower still.[1]

The invasions of the Turks and their gradual conquest of Asia Minor altered the picture. Constantinople would not admit at first that the loss of so many Asiatic bishoprics was final. But by the end of the twelfth century it was clear that the Turks had come to stay. Many of the bishops from the occupied territories fled to Constantinople, intending to return when circumstances allowed. Some of the cities were destroyed during the wars; and there could be no returning to them. But several bishops were

---

[1] H. Gelzer, *Texte der Notitiae Episcopatum*, pp. 3–10.

able to go back, even though the sees were not liberated; while a few others stayed at their posts and managed to carry out their duties. But, under a régime that was not given to urban life, a number of cities declined fairly rapidly, while others were deserted by their Christian population. Of the Christians who did not migrate many within two or three generations had passed over to the religion of their new masters. But a number of Christians remained in Turkish territory, mostly in the larger towns but a few in isolated mountain villages. In general they were allowed to practise their religion without hindrance, and their bishops were permitted to stay with them and, except in times of war, to keep in touch with Constantinople. But the former ecclesiastical divisions were becoming meaningless. The Byzantines could not bear to abandon the historic titles of their sees. It was not always necessary. Cities such as Caesarea and Ankyra retained their importance and much of their Christian population. But the Patriarchal lists show a steady diminution in the number both of metropolitan and of suffragan sees. Varying forms of readjustment were used. If the metropolitan city had dwindled away the see might be allotted to a suffragan bishop. For example, the title of Metropolitan of Sardis, a see that had ranked sixth in precedence in the old lists, was given in the thirteenth century, when Sardis was no more than a village, to its former chief suffragan, the Bishop of Philadelphia, whose city remained free and important until the end of the fourteenth century. Similarly, the Bishop of Heraclea in Pontus acquired the title of Metropolitan of Claudiopolis. Sometimes a metropolitan see that had lost its flock or was too poor now to maintain its own organization was given, as it were, on loan to some still active neighbouring metropolitan. The phrase used was κατὰ λόγου ἐπιδόσεως, 'temporary in principle'; and the temporary incumbent was called the Proedrus of the see. Sometimes, when the see had clearly been lost for ever, the title was preserved by giving it as an additional honour to a bishop who might live far away from the original see. Hyacinthus Critobulus, Metropolitan of Ouggro-Valachia, north of the

34

Danube, in the late fourteenth century, held also the title of Metropolitan of Melitene, a city situated near the banks of the Euphrates. Eventually metropolitan titles *in partibus infidelium* were given to high clergy at the Patriarchal court, to raise them to episcopal rank and authority, a device that was to be followed later at Rome.

The Latin occupation of various European provinces did not have quite the same effect, as the Greek congregations there remained virtually undiminished. Sometimes the Greek bishop had been removed and replaced by a Latin. He would then retire to the Byzantine court, waiting till he could be reinstated. If he died there, a titular bishop would be appointed to succeed him. Sometimes the Greek bishop remained, side by side with a Latin bishop; and sometimes, more rarely, he was left undisturbed. In both those cases he was under pressure to acknowledge Roman authority and to defer to the upper Latin hierarchy. But he could often keep in touch with Constantinople, and there was no real interruption of tenure. Many of the sees were recovered by the Byzantines; and the bishops reverted easily and gladly to the old allegiance; or, if the bishop had been ejected, he or his successor returned from exile.

The return of the Empire to Constantinople in 1261 had been followed almost at once by the loss of most of its Asiatic provinces. In consequence the sees situated in Europe rose in importance. The historic sees of Asia kept their precedence. Caesarea and Ephesus, though the cities were in alien hands, continued to rank first and second in order. But Thessalonica rose from sixteenth to twelfth place early in the fourteenth century, and, a few years later, to fourth, just behind Heraclea in Thrace. Lists made in the latter years of the Empire show diminishing numbers as well as the changed order. The *Ecthesis* of Andronicus II, drawn up in 1299, gives 112 metropolitans, which was twice as many as had existed a century before; but, except in Europe, hardly any of them had more than one or at most two suffragans, while those of them that had passed wholly into alien hands, with the exception of a few in the first rank, were listed in an appendix and credited with no suffragans. A *taxis* published in the early years of the fifteenth century gives seventy-eight metropolitan sees, calling them *Eparchies*, of which forty have titles which suggest that they were still active. The final position is shown in a memorandum issued in 1437 for the benefit of the Council of Basle. It gives sixty-seven metropolitans, many of whom have no suffragans. Eight were in the territory around Constantinople and seven in Greece. Thirty-six were in Turkish territory and sixteen in independent Christian lands, Wallachia, Moldavia, Russia, the Caucasus and Trebizond.[1]

With the decline in numbers came an increase in titles. The metropolitans of the leading sees became exarchs, with the epithet of ὑπέρτιμος, 'most honourable'. About the end of the fourteenth century the Metropolitan of Caesarea became Exarch of the East, the Metropolitan of Ephesus Exarch of Asia, the Metropolitan of Heraclea Exarch of Thrace and Macedonia, the Metropolitan of Philippopolis Exarch of Europe. Soon afterwards exarchates were allotted to nearly all the surviving metropolitans, the Metropolitan of Thessalonica, for example, becoming Exarch of Thessaly and the Metropolitan of Nicomedia Exarch of Bithynia. This was not, as some historians have thought, an attempt to compensate for lost grandeur by a pathetic use of empty titles. The exarchate represented something definite. In the civil world the exarch had been the governor of a province so far removed from the capital that he had to be given special viceregal powers. Bishops had had their exarchs to represent them in country districts which they had no time personally to supervise. The bestowal of the office on metropolitans in the fourteenth and fifteenth centuries was a recognition by the Patriarch that he could no longer administer areas under foreign control. As exarch the local metropolitan was empowered to act as his deputy.[2]

---

[1] *Taxeis* of the early fourteenth and early fifteenth century are given in *M.P.G.* cvii, coll. 386–94, 397–404. For the list of 1437, 'Terre Hodierne Graecorum' (ed. S. Lambros), *Neos Hellenomnemon*, vii (1910), pp. 360 ff. For the sees under Turkish domination see A. Waechter, *Der Verfall des Griechentums in Kleinasien im XIVten Jahrhundert*, pp. 61–5.   [2] Bréhier, *op. cit.* ii, pp. 472–3.

A further complication was caused by the growing disparity in size between the Patriarchal territory and that of the dying Empire. The Emperor was still the Sacred Emperor, the head of the Christian commonwealth, whose duty it was to give the Church the backing of the State. He could no longer give such support. As the list of 1437 showed, more than three-quarters of the metropolitans had their sees in territories ruled by foreign potentates, some of whom were Christians, but not necessarily on cordial terms with Constantinople, but by far the most important of whom was an infidel Sultan. The Patriarch was thus involved in foreign politics, and his interests there were by no means identical with the Emperor's. In Turkish lands his bishops had increasingly to be prepared to take charge of the secular as well as the religious administration of their flocks. The Church was faced by new preoccupations and new problems of which its Fathers had never dreamed. By 1453 its position was so awkward and anomalous that some reorganization was long overdue. The Turkish conquest may not have provided the happiest solution; but at least it provided a solution.

THE MONASTERIES

It was typical of the attitude of the Byzantines towards religion that, highly as they respected the Patriarch and the hierarchy, they were personally far more deeply influenced by individual monks and holy men. They resented any attack on the hierarchy by the lay authorities, unless the particular hierarch had made himself unpopular. But, if there were a conflict between the hierarchy and the monasteries, it was the monks who could count on the stronger popular support.

Byzantine monasticism differed greatly from that of the West. There was no fixed Rule; there were no monastic Orders. Each monastery had its own constitution, usually laid down when it was founded. These constitutions fell into two main types. One was derived straight from the early monasticism of Egypt, from the traditions of the Fathers of the Desert, those ascetes who had retired from the world into the wilderness to lead lives of holy and humble contemplation, in solitude at first, but as time went on gathering together into small groups, so as to give each other a little mutual protection and to perform mutual services and acts of charity. The group formed what came to be called a Lavra. The second type is derived from the reforms that Basil the Great introduced, in an attempt to make monastic life more orderly and more complete. He believed that the monks, the μοναχοί, or 'solitary men', should always be combined into communities, in which they should live lives of perfect communism under the rule of an elected head who should command perfect obedience, and that they should work as well as pray. It was from his recommendations that Benedict derived his Rule and the whole of Western monasticism grew up.[1]

Under Justinian I laws were passed to make every monastic establishment follow the Basilian pattern. All monks were to lead a communal life and every monastery must have a communal refectory and dormitory. No separate cells were to be permitted, except for penal confinement, inside or outside of the monastic building. The monk was to have no personal property. Before taking his final vows he could dispose of his worldly goods as he wished, though, if he were married, his wife and children were entitled to the proportion of his estate that they would have received on his death. His wife must consent to his retirement; and it was usual that she should enter monastic life at the same time. He could inherit property after entering the monastery, but only if he had already made arrangements for the disposal of any such inheritance. Though early Councils had forbidden it, a monk was allowed to become the guardian of a minor and a trustee for his property. Any man or woman could take monastic vows whenever he or she pleased, with the exception of runaway slaves and of government officials whose term of office had not expired.

[1] For monastic origins see S. Schiwietz, *Das Morgenländische Mönchtum*, I, *passim*, esp. pp. 48–90, 148–225.

The noviciate lasted for three years; and during those years the novice could, if he wished or if he were considered unsuited for the life, return into the world. When his noviciate was completed he made his profession before the abbot and took the vows of chastity, poverty and obedience. The abbot then tonsured him and gave him his robe, the 'angelic habit', and the kiss of peace.

According to Justinian's legislation the monastery was under the absolute control of the abbot, called either the *higumene*, the 'leader', or the *archimandrite*, the 'head of the flock'. He was elected by a majority vote of the monks, but he could not take office until he was blessed by the bishop of the diocese, who gave him his pastoral staff. The bishop also controlled the foundation of monasteries. At this time nearly all were founded by laymen; but building could not begin until the bishop had inspected and blessed the site, planting a cross there, and had approved the foundation deeds. Till Justinian's time there had been a number of institutions where both sexes lived in common. This was now strictly forbidden. Women's monasteries were organized along the same lines as the men's, the abbess being elected and having the same absolute power as an abbot. Under the abbot was the *economus*, in charge of the worldly possessions of the monastery, the *chartophylax*, or registrar, and the *bibliophylax*, or librarian. A monk was not necessarily a priest, though a priest could become a monk; but there were always a few ordained monks in each establishment, in order that the church services could be performed; and if the elected abbot were not a priest it was customary for him to be ordained. For female establishments the bishop provided chaplains.

Imperial legislation did not interfere in the internal running of the monastery. Its constitution was laid down in two foundation-deeds, the *brevion*, which listed the endowments and gave the founder's wishes with regard to liturgical duties, and the *typicon*, which regulated the rights and duties of the monks. Subject to these requirements the abbot had complete control over discipline. Monks who disobeyed the rules or otherwise misbehaved were punished by enforced fasts and other austerities and in more serious cases by being excluded from the liturgy and from receiving blessings, and, at the worst, by solitary confinement. Later Patriarchs issued codes for the punishment of monks; but the abbot could always use his discretion. He also decided upon the number and duration of church services, along the lines laid down in the *brevion*. The services usually consisted of psalmody throughout the Seven Canonical Hours, an hour or more of prayer before dawn, followed by the sunrise mass, the ὄρθρος, with all night services on the eve of the greater saints' days and of the major feasts of the Church and such other days as the founder might have ordained.[1]

Justinian's legislation was repeated and confirmed in 692 by the Quinisextine Council, the Council *In Trullo*, which added laws forbidding the disaffection of monasteries and the secularization of monastic property. It also fixed the minimum age for novices at ten and it added a year to the noviciate, at least for voluntary candidates. It was already customary for offenders against the State to be relegated to monasteries and to be tonsured at once. An enforced entry into monastic life remained throughout the Byzantine period the usual fate for fallen politicians and officials, from Emperors downwards.[2]

In spite of Justinian and the Quinisextine Council it proved impossible to abolish the *lavras*, with their loose pre-Basilian organization. Where such communities existed and seemed to be competently run, they were left alone. They had been particularly numerous in Syria and Palestine; and when those countries were overrun by the Arabs some of them moved to Asia Minor and re-established themselves there.

The Iconoclastic Emperors of the eighth century found the monks to be their fiercest opponents and tried to curtail if not to

---

[1] Justinian, *Novellae* (ed. K. E. Zachariae von Lingenthal), I, pp. 133, 535, 538, 539, 554; A. Knecht, *System des Justinianischen Kirchenvermögensrechtes*, pp. 57–60.

[2] C. J. Hefele, *Histoire des Conciles*, revised and translated by H. Leclercq (Hefele–Leclercq), III, 1, pp. 560 ff., esp. pp. 568–9.

abolish the monasteries. But their laws were repealed before the end of the century and the records destroyed. The effect of their rule had been to loosen episcopal control; and many abuses had reappeared, including monasteries of mixed sexes. The Second Council of Nicaea in 787 reaffirmed earlier legislation, though mixed monasteries were permitted so long as the sexes occupied completely separate buildings. A law issued a few years later forbade monks to act as guardians of minors, though they might still be trustees of property. More effective reforms were instituted at this time by Theodore the Studite, who reintroduced the strict Basilian rule for a group of monasteries which he dominated. He seems to have envisaged a sort of informal Order, not unlike that later founded in the West by the Cluniacs. But only a few establishments followed him.[1]

The period that followed, up to the Latin conquest of Constantinople, was the great age of Byzantine monastic prosperity. There was very little uniformity. New monasteries were continually being founded, some by holy men who gathered disciples around them, some by rich laymen and laywomen, some by bishops, some by Patriarchs and some by Emperors. Patriarchal foundations, wherever they might be, were controlled from the Patriarchal court, by the Sacellarius. Imperial foundations were directed by the Emperor's officials, without any ecclesiastical intermediary. A few great monasteries were proclaimed by special Imperial decree to be *autodespotae*, withdrawn from all jurisdiction, civil or ecclesiastical. The local bishop retained certain rights over the foundation of a new establishment. He still had to approve and bless the site, and he opened the building when completed, with a procession and a reading of the foundation-deeds. It was ordered now that the founder must arrange for at least three monks to occupy the site as soon as the bishop had planted a cross on it, and that the building must be ready within three years.[2]

The foundation of so many new monasteries, each endowed

---

[1] See A. Gardner, *Theodore of Studium*, esp. pp. 66 ff.

[2] L. Bréhier, *Le Monde Byzantin*, II, *Institutions de l'Empire Byzantin*, pp. 545–6.

with properties that were sometimes huge, together with endowments given by the pious to already existing establishments, began to create problems. The Imperial authorities were alarmed to see vast tracts of land passing inalienably into monastic hands. But tenth-century legislation aimed at limiting the endowments proved ineffectual and had to be abandoned. Difficulties arose for the monks also; for many of their properties were now far apart. Stewards, known as ἐπίτροποι, had to be appointed; and it was not easy for the Economus to supervise them. Sometimes the Imperial or ecclesiastical authorities would put a foundation under a lay protector who administered its property, allowing the monastery an income adequate for its needs and keeping for himself any additional profits that he could make. Such a monastery was called a *charisticum*, and its protector the *charisticarius*. The authorities liked the system as it meant that the estates were efficiently managed; but it was liable to be abused. Many founders stipulated that their foundation should never become a *charisticum*.[1]

Nearly all the monasteries were now Basilian and coenobitic, that is to say, following a communal life. In rural monasteries the monks mainly laboured in the fields, though each had a library, some of which were well kept up and might contain monks who copied manuscripts. The monks were also supposed to tend the local poor and sick. In urban monasteries, though the monks usually had gardens and orchards to maintain, there was more intellectual activity, and the social activities were wider. The monasteries provided confessors for neighbouring families and tutors for their children. They ran hostels for pilgrims, sick-wards and dispensaries, many of the establishments having social duties assigned to them by the *typica* given them by their founders. Nuns as well as monks did useful social work, caring for destitute children and nursing the sick, some of them having a good medical training. The influence enjoyed by the monks and nuns was principally due to their social activities. They moved amongst the people and understood their needs. The monasteries were further

---

[1] Bréhier, *op. cit.* II, pp. 550–9.

useful in providing places of refuge for the aged. In them you would find elderly folk who would otherwise have been a burden on their families, together with large numbers of quite well-to-do retired officials or widowed housewives, who wished to end their days in an atmosphere of sanctity. They contained manumitted slaves and penitent sinners and even a certain number of criminals hiding from justice. There was no class-consciousness in them; the retired nobleman would work and pray side by side with the retired peasant, and, in theory if not always in practice, no one might enjoy special privileges. For an ambitious boy of humble birth a monastic career provided the easiest ladder to climb, as the hierarchy recruited its staff more and more from the abler and better-trained monks. Not all the monasteries were estimable. Some were little more than comfortable residential clubs; others were filled by lazy men and women who lived by begging and who thought nothing of smuggling out and selling books and other treasures from the libraries; others, again, were animated by a narrow anti-intellectualism or by political passions and prejudices.[1]

There were monasteries all over the Empire. Their number is impossible to estimate. The twelfth-century traveller Benjamin of Tudela said that there were as many monasteries in Constantinople alone as there were days in the year. In fact, at that time there were probably in the city and suburbs as many as 175 establishments, some, like the great monastery of Studium, containing several hundred monks, others not more than ten.[2] A large provincial city such as Thessalonica probably housed at least twenty establishments.[3] In addition there were monasteries for either sex all over the countryside, many of them being in groups. In the middle Byzantine period the most famous group was situated on Bithynian Olympus. It was there that Theodore the Studite started his career and planned his reforms.[4] There was another group settled,

---

[1] *Ibid.* pp. 564–5.
[2] Benjamin of Tudela, *Itinerary* (trans. M. N. Adler), pp. 11–14.
[3] O. Tafrali, *Thessalonique au XIVe siècle*, pp. 99–107.
[4] See above, p. 41.

mainly in caves, in the Cappadocian hills, given more to contemplation and less to learning and social works than the Olympian group. When the Turks overran Cappadocia many of these monks fled and established themselves on Mount Latmos, on the Aegean coast, south of Smyrna. The communities there were famed in the twelfth century for their austerities.[1] The most famous of all groups was settled on the peninsula of Mount Athos. The Holy Mountain had been settled by hermits from early in the middle ages, and a few small lavras were soon established there. They had already organized themselves into a community under a *protos*, or headman, when in 963 a monk from Trebizond called Athanasius, who enjoyed the friendship of the Emperor Nicephorus Phocas, founded a great monastery there known as the Grand Lavra. In spite of its name it was not a lavra but followed the Studite coenobitic rule. By the end of the century five more monasteries had been founded on the Mountain, and the group had been given a constitution by the Emperor. A monastery reserved for Georgians was founded in about 979, a monastery for Russians in 1169 and one for Serbians in 1197. In the eleventh century the Amalfitans had an establishment there which followed the Latin rite; and a Seldjuk prince converted to Christianity founded a monastery early in the twelfth century. The constitution of the Mountain ordained that there should be a council or synod consisting of the heads of all the establishments, which should elect the *protos* and act as his advisory body. He, with its advice, judged disputes between the monasteries and confirmed the election of abbots. The constitution was revised in 1052, when many of the smaller and older lavras had disappeared. By then the Grand Lavra contained 700 monks, and the whole population of the peninsula approached 10,000. There were no establishments for women. Indeed, no female creature was officially allowed on the mountain, though the ban could not be extended to birds of the air and in time hens were grudgingly admitted, and, later still, female cats,

[1] F. Miklosich and J. Müller, *Acta et Diplomata Graeca Medii Aevi*, IV, pp. 298-301; T. Wiegand, *Der Latmos, passim*.

as mice and snakes would not obey the rules and were breeding too plentifully. The ban in theory was not made to ensure chastity but to show respect to the Patroness of the Mountain, the Holy Virgin, who should have no rivals. Great austerity was demanded of the monks; but already by the end of the eleventh century they had begun to import lay brothers to help them with their flocks and gardens, and boys to wait on their persons; and some scandals ensued, especially when the shepherds tried to smuggle in their womenfolk. Each monastery kept boats for fishing, for obtaining supplies for the mainland and for marketing its timber; and most of them acquired estates on the mainland, with which they had to keep in touch. Stewards had to be appointed for those distant properties; and the Grand Lavra kept a steward at Constantinople, to act as a diplomatic and financial agent there. By the end of the twelfth century the monasteries on Olympus were in decay; they had never fully recovered from the Turkish invasions of the previous century; and Mount Latmos was dangerously close to the frontier. Athos emerged as by far the most important monastic settlement. The history of later Greek monasticism is largely a history of Mount Athos.[1]

By that time the lavra type of monastery had virtually disappeared. But the disadvantage of coenobitic life of the Basilian or Studite type was that the absence of solitude made holy contemplation difficult; it was not easy to be a mystic in such an establishment. In earlier days a would-be contemplative would set himself up as a hermit in some remote cave or on top of a pillar, where he would mortify his flesh. If his retreat were sufficiently remote he might be left in peace. But, if it were accessible, the fame of his holiness would spread, and a stream of pilgrims of all sorts would come to him for advice, political as well as spiritual. A saint such as Symeon Stylites was a real power in the State. But in the course of the middle Byzantine period these individualistic holy men grew rarer. The last recorded Stylite, called Luke, lived

[1] For Mount Athos see P. Meyer, *Die Haupturkunden für die Geschichte der Athos-Kloster, passim.*

in the tenth century.[1] His slightly younger contemporary, also called Luke, was one of the last solitary hermits to wield a political influence. Provincial governors in Greece would come to his hermitage in Styris to consult him; and his fame reached the Imperial court owing to his successful prophecy about the Byzantine reconquest of Crete from the Saracens. When he died, his dwelling-place was turned by Imperial decree into a monastery.[2] But by the end of the tenth century a hermit would usually retire to some spot like Mount Athos where he would be out of reach of the world but yet have spiritual comforts at hand. This was due to an ever-increasing devotion to the Liturgy among the Byzantines. Even a holy man could not bear to deprive himself of taking part in the Mysteries.

To accommodate solitaries and mystics who yet wished to be part of a monastic group there were regulations permitting a monk to obtain his abbot's permission to leave his monastery for an establishment that allowed greater solitude, or even for a hermit's cell. But it was more usual for such a monk to be given a separate cell within the monastery or close by and a dispensation from certain labours. As a rule a monastery was allowed to have only five of these solitaries, or *kelliots*. The Church authorities inclined to believe that mystics should keep to the coenobitic life until they were sure of their vocation. Symeon the New Theologian, the eleventh-century founder of later Byzantine mysticism, spent most of his career in an active coenobitic monastery in Constantinople and only retired to the country when he was exiled as the result of a monastic intrigue; and even in the country he directed a small monastic community.[3]

The Latin conquest interrupted Byzantine monastic life. In the territories conquered by the Latins many monasteries were pillaged and ruined, particularly during the sack of Constanti-

---

[1] E. Delehaye, *Les Saints Stylites, passim*.
[2] *Vita S. Lucae Junioris*, M.P.G., cxi, coll. 441–80, *passim*.
[3] See Nicetas Stethatus, *Vie de Syméon le Nouveau Théologien*, ed. I. Haussher and G. Horn, with introduction, in *Orientalia Christiana*, xii.

nople in 1204. Others were occupied by Latin Orders, such as Daphne, near Athens, which for two centuries housed Cistercian monks. Those that were left to the Greeks were deprived of endowments. The Athonite establishments lost most of their mainland estates, though they soon recovered them when the Nicaean Emperors acquired control of Macedonia. The Nicaean court was too thrifty to found monasteries. The only important foundation of the period was one at Ephesus, Saint Gregory the Thaumaturge, the creation of the scholar Nicephorus Blemmydas, who attached an excellent school to it. A few monasteries were founded by the Despots of Epirus; and in the Empire of Trebizond monastic life was uninterrupted. The great monastery of Sumela, founded in the fifth century and continually re-endowed by the Grand Comnenus, was in the later middle ages the richest monastic establishment in the East.[1]

When Michael VIII recaptured Constantinople he found its monasteries impoverished and decaying. Some had disappeared; others had lost their endowments. With the approval of the Church authorities he ordered the amalgamation of smaller and poorer houses into workable units. Neither he nor his successors made new foundations, preferring to repair and re-endow older foundations. Michael himself rebuilt and renamed the Monastery of Saint Demetrius. His daughter Maria, widow of the Mongol Ilkhan Abaga, repaired the monastery later known as Mary of the Mongols. The noble Theodore Metochites restored the Monastery of the Chora and was responsible for commissioning its mosaics and frescoes, which are today perhaps the loveliest surviving works of Byzantine art.[2] It was only in the provinces that there were new

[1] For Nicaean foundations, see Nicephorus Blemmydas, *Curriculum Vitae, et Carmina* (ed. A. Heisenberg), p. 39. For Trebizond, Mgr Chrysanthos, 'Η Ἐκκλησία τοῦ Τραπεζοῦντος, pp. 471–8; Miklosich and Müller, *op. cit.* v, pp. 276–81.
[2] R. Janin, *La Géographie ecclésiastique de l'Empire Byzantin*, pt. i, iii, *Les Eglises et les monastères*, pp. 95, 222–3. For the Church of the Chora, P. A. Underwood, *The Kariye Djami*, i, pp. 316. Michael VIII's one foundation was on the small isle of Oxya.

foundations, at Mistra, the capital of the Despotate of the Morea, at Megaspileon in the Peloponnese or in towns farther north such as Castoria.[1] The strange rocks of Meteora in Thessaly, long a resort of hermits, acquired a number of monasteries early in the fourteenth century, chiefly owing to the pious generosity of Serbian kings. They formed a monastic republic, on the lines of that of Mount Athos.[2]

During the last period of Byzantine history the monasteries were, thus, fewer and poorer than before, though, with the general decline in population and wealth, the proportion of monks to laity and their proportionate wealth was probably much the same. To some extent their tribulations had been salutary. Since the Iconoclastic period the monasteries had not played a great part in intellectual or even in spiritual life. With rare exceptions, such as Theodore Studites and Symeon the New Theologian, the important religious thinkers had belonged to the hierarchy or even to the laity. From 1261 onwards the monasteries took a livelier part in religious thought. Mount Athos in particular became a centre for theological discussion. But there were certain disadvantages in having the main centre of monastic thought on an isolated mountain, away from the intellectual circles of Constantinople. The monks were not necessarily anti-intellectual, though many of them came from poor homes and never received more than a rudimentary education. In the greater Athonite houses the libraries were full, well tended and well used, with copyists busying themselves over secular as well as religious manuscripts. But there was an inevitable tendency towards suspicion of secular learning.

The Mountain was not without its scandals. In 1292 the Emperor Andronicus II placed its houses, which had been under a loose Imperial control, directly under the Patriarch Athanasius I, a stern disciplinarian, so as to ensure stricter discipline. Twenty years later he issued a Bull further tightening the constitution of

---

[1] Miklosich and Müller, *op. cit.* v, pp. 191–3.
[2] See D. M. Nicol, *Meteora, the Rock Monasteries of Thessaly*, pp. 70 ff.

the Mountain.[1] In 1402 Manuel II was shocked to find how lax the monasteries had become again and legislated to enforce the old rules.[2] Part of the trouble was that a new type of monastery had grown up on the Mountain. This was the idiorrhythmic, in which each monk had his own private cell and kept some of his private property, coming together with his fellows only for church services and for dinners on the greater feast-days. Otherwise he could keep to himself or in a small group. These groups, or 'families', would elect a superior who was responsible for discipline; but there was no abbot. A superior, whose term of office was limited, would act as president and represent the monastery on the Holy Synod of the Mountain. The idiorrhythmic monk did not disdain work of all sorts; but there was no one who could oblige him to work. Discipline inevitably slackened; and, though the system might be useful for contemplatives who wished to be left alone, it was far too convenient for men who wished to combine holiness with indolence. Manuel II would have liked to abolish the idiorrhythmic rule; but it was too late.[3]

The period also saw the monks playing a larger part in Church politics. They had always formed a potential political force, which had come to the fore in Iconoclastic days as the chief opponent of Imperial policy; but it had not been greatly felt in the following centuries. But from the thirteenth century onwards there was a party in the Church, supported in general by the monasteries, which was in fairly constant opposition to the Imperial court and the upper hierarchy. The dividing line between the parties was never clear cut and the issues varied. On the whole the monastic party was both conservative and democratic. It supported tradition in religious affairs, therefore bitterly opposing any concessions to be made to achieve union with the West; and it was suspicious of philosophers who sought to pry into theology in defiance of its apophatic inheritance. At the same time it

[1] Meyer, *op. cit.* pp. 54, 190–4.
[2] *Ibid.* pp. 203–10.
[3] *Ibid.* pp. 57 ff.

49

opposed the autocracy of the Emperor and disapproved of the luxury of the Court and the upper hierarchy, though it was willing to ally itself with the landed nobility, whose economic interests were often similar to those of the greater monastic establishments. As we shall see, this party warfare played an important role in all the questions that troubled the later Byzantine Church.

The whole lay population of Byzantium was involved in these ecclesiastical struggles. In Eastern Christendom the laity was far more important than in the West. In early Christian times the laity played an important role in the Church organization; and that tradition was never lost in the East, where laymen never ceased to receive communion in both kinds. The clergy, despite the respect given to them for the charismatic succession that enabled them to perform the Mysteries, could not in Eastern theory complete the sacrament alone without a congregation. To that extent the laity took part in the ministry. The laity were not devoid of *charisma*; baptism made them 'a people of God, a royal priesthood'. If need be, any baptized man or woman could perform the rite of baptism. Nor was theology the monopoly of the priesthood. Any layman might be equally inspired by the Holy Spirit.[1]

This was reasonable in view of the high standard of lay education in Byzantium. In the West the barbarian invasions had left the Church in sole charge of education. In the East lay education had never been interrupted. It is true that monks were usually employed to tutor young children, and many of the monasteries ran schools, while the Patriarchal Academy, which is the oldest school to survive to this day, provided an excellent education. But education was essentially a secular affair. The University, though its life was often interrupted, was a department of the State, not of the Church.[2] Even clerics who entered the Church early in life had usually passed through some lay schooling; and many of the

[1] For the position of the laity see D. J. Geanakoplos, *Byzantine East and Latin West*, pp. 79–80.
[2] For education see below, pp. 112 ff.

50

leading theologians only entered the Church late in life or remained laymen till their deaths. At the Council of Florence in 1439 the Emperor complained that his lay advisers were much more learned than his bishops.[1] This long tradition of lay learning made it difficult for the Church to dominate religious and philosophical thought.

In Byzantine ecclesiastical party conflicts there was a natural tendency for the lay intellectuals to be allied with the court and the upper hierarchy, much of it lay-educated, against the monks and the members of the hierarchy educated at Church schools. But a controversy such as the Palamite, where a fundamental but intricate point of theology was concerned, cut across the usual dividing line. Moreover, the lay intellectuals, with their own views about theology, did not always follow the recommendations of the hierarchy or of the court. Therein the monks were stronger; for the general populace was under their influence. Not only did their charitable social work keep them in touch with the people and win them its affection; but the fact that they provided tutors and, still more, confessors and spiritual advisers, widened their moral control. It was rare for a member of the hierarchy to act as a spiritual adviser, though we have a case of a Metropolitan of Chalcedon who in about 1400 acted as spiritual adviser and confessor to a noble lady called Eudocia, and whose letters to her have survived and are admirable for their calm common sense. In general even the richest families employed monks, and could not fail to be affected to some extent by their views.[2]

The influence of the Church was enormous but uneven. The Byzantine had deep religious feelings, particularly in two respects. He had a profound admiration for what he conceived as holiness; and he was passionately attached to his liturgy. The act of worship was the basic expression of his faith. When he attended a service

[1] J. Gill, *The Council of Florence*, pp. 228–9.
[2] For spiritual advisers in the late Byzantine period see S. Salaville, 'Une lettre et un discours inédit de Théolepte de Philadelphie', *Revue des études byzantines*, v (1947), pp. 101–15, and V. Laurent, 'La direction spirituelle des grandes dames de Byzance', *ibid.* viii (1950), pp. 64–84.

in his church building he knew himself to be part of the Church of Christ; he was in touch with the Divine. The worst of punishments was to be deprived of this privilege. But services required priests; and a priest could withhold communion. Excommunication was a very rare sentence, but all the more formidable because it was seldom imposed. Moreover, without an ordained priest there could not be a celebration of the Mysteries. Even in the most backward village, where the priest was a peasant like his flock and shared most of its daily life, he was nevertheless the priest, the magician, so to speak, whose operations were necessary for the well-being of the community. He tried, as best he could, to carry out the instructions of his superiors. But they were distant, and the bishop's exarch might not be able to pay him regular visits; and in that case he would take his troubles to the abbot of the nearest monastery. Sometimes, as in Greece under the Franks, the hierarchs might be Latins or Latinizers. In that case he sought to carry on undefiled the traditions of his forefathers; he became the little local champion of Greek Orthodoxy, a role which grew during the centuries of Turkish domination.

In the cities the faithful could go to some great cathedral whose ceremonies, conducted by bishops, were more splendid and more magical. To the last the services in Saint Sophia kept a special prestige. But in the later Byzantine period there was a tendency for smaller and smaller churches to be built; they were liked because of the more intimate atmosphere that they provided. The Byzantine revered the great tradition that was represented by the Emperor and the Patriarch. The glorious ritual of the Imperial Palace and the Great Church were part of his heritage that he would support passionately against external attack. But holiness impressed him still more deeply; and he saw holiness in terms of visible other-worldliness, in poverty and simplicity and self-denial. In older days he would listen to the stylite and the hermit rather than to the bishop. Later it was the humble parish priest and the welfare-working monk whom he saw in his daily life who had the greatest hold over him. Such men understood the populace; they shared its sentiments and guided its views. The court, the hierarchy and the intellectuals might quarrel; the Emperor might depose officials and even Patriarchs. But in every Eastern city ultimate power has always lain with the mob, that is to say, with the demagogues who dominate the mob. In Byzantium these demagogues—and the word need not be understood in a pejorative sense—were the poorer priests and monks, men most of whom respected authority and education but who were swayed by an emotional and uncomplicated faith in the Holy Tradition that they had inherited. In spite of all the respect paid to the Emperor and the Patriarch, neither could count on the support of the people if he offended against their instinctive sense of right and wrong. If there seemed to be unrighteousness on high, the people would listen to the spiritual advisers whom they knew; and the discipline of the Church was not strong enough nor well enough organized to stifle opposition. The early Christian belief in religious democracy kept breaking through.

This elasticity in the organization was not altogether harmful to the Church. It might at times produce chaos and it might be injurious to the State. But it is significant that there was never in Byzantium a popular anticlerical movement; there was nothing to compare with the Waldensian or Lollard movements in the West or with Protestantism. The hierarchs might be attacked, but as persons. The lesser clergy, for all their insubordination, remained loyal to the idea of the Church. It is true that the Zealot movement in fourteenth-century Thessalonica appears at first sight to be anticlerical; for the Zealots hastened to confiscate episcopal and monastic property. But they claimed to be acting in the interests of the underpaid lesser clergy; they had no animosity against the Church but only against the disparity of its endowments. They wished to reform its details, not its structure. And their movement failed less from external pressure than from the loss of support from the priests and monks whom they professed to benefit.[1]

[1] See below, pp. 69–70.

When we contrast Church and State in Byzantium we must not think solely in terms of the Imperial government and the hierarchy. There was a third party in all the disputes, the people. And, if it is true that the Voice of the People is the Voice of God, in Byzantium the Voice of God was heard through the mouths of the humbler servants of His Church.

CHAPTER 3

CHURCH AND STATE

The chief practical problem that faces any organized Church lies in its relation to the State. It may be that the only complete answer is found in a Rule of the Saints, a theocracy, whether it be a government such as that of the Anabaptists at Münster or the *Plenitudo Potestatis* claimed by the later medieval Papacy. But a Christian Church must always bear in mind the words of Christ distinguishing between the things which are God's and the things which are Caesar's. To the early Christian, before the days of Constantine, the position was fairly clear. It was his business to be a good citizen. Peter bade him: 'Submit yourselves to every ordinance of man for the Lord's sake; whether it be to the king, as supreme; or unto governors...' and again: 'Fear God. Honour the King.'[1] The early Christian communities did their best to be law-abiding. Difficulty only arose when Caesar claimed to be God and demanded a token sacrifice to his divinity. That the Christian could not condone; and persecution might follow. The Triumph of the Cross ended such persecution; but it created other problems. For Ceasar claimed now not to be God Himself but God's representative on earth, a claim that was harder to refute.

In theory at least, the basic law of the Roman Empire was the *lex de imperio*, by which the people transferred their share of the sovereignty to the Emperor. By the days of Constantine the other partner in the sovereignty, the Senate, had for practical purposes lost its position.[2] As representative of the people the Emperor was Pontifex Maximus; it was his duty to conduct the sacrifices to the gods in the name of the people. When the people became the

---

[1] I Peter ii. 13, 17.

[2] See J. B. Bury, 'The Constitution of the Later Roman Empire', in *Selected Essays*, pp. 99–125.

Christian Oecumene he was still their representative and Pontifex Maximus. He was also the source of law. If the law had to be amended to include Christian principles no one else but he could do it. But the Church now possessed its own hierarchy, qualified to administer to its needs and preserve its discipline; and it was for a Council representing all the congregations of the Oecumene to assemble to receive divine inspiration on matters of Faith. How did a Christian Emperor fit into this? His soul was no more precious than other Christian souls. He was not a bishop nor even a priest; yet he was the trustee of the Oecumene before God and its High Priest and its law-giver. He could not be denied authority.[1] Constantine the Great, long before he had been baptized, considered it his duty to intervene in the Church to settle the Donatist question, which was more a matter of schism than of heresy, and the Arian question, where a fundamental dogma was concerned. His attempt to deal with Donatism through a commission failed; he was obliged to summon a Council of bishops to Arles to solve the problem. Warned by that experience, he summoned a Council of bishops from all over the Oecumene to deal with Arianism. For such a Council to be summoned by the head of State was a novelty; and Constantine copied the procedure from the old procedure of the Senate. He, or his deputy, acted as *princeps* or consul, taking the chair and arbitrating, while the Bishop of Rome as senior bishop, or his deputy, had the right, held by the *princeps senatūs*, of voting first. But the Emperor as chairman was not required to be neutral. He could intervene in the debates and make his views known. At this first Oecumenical Council, the Council of Nicaea, it was Constantine who proposed the compromise word ὁμοούσιον and forced it upon the unenthusiastic bishops. Then, as head of the State, he made it his business to see that the decisions of the Council were implemented and obeyed.[2]

---

[1] L. Bréhier, *Le Monde Byzantin*, II, pp. 54–62, for a good summary. See also L. Bréhier and P. Battifol, *Les Survivances du culte impérial romain*, p. 36.

[2] Eusebius, *Vita Constantini*, M.P.G., xx, coll. 1060ff. See F. Dvornik, *Early Christian and Byzantine Political Philosophy*, II, pp. 640ff.

The pattern set by Constantine at Nicaea was followed in the East until the fall of Byzantium. Whenever there was disagreement within the Church over a fundamental question of dogma, it was the Emperor's duty to convoke and preside over a Council to settle the problem and to give its decisions the force of law. It was a reasonable system, in theory and in practice. No bishop had greater charismatic authority than his fellows and none was therefore qualified to be chairman. The obvious chairman was the Emperor as representing the whole Oecumene. Moreover, as he was the source of law, the Council's canons could not be implemented without his help. Indeed, if the Church was to be a body united in doctrine and if its doctrine was to be guaranteed by the State, it was logical and practical that the head of the State should be head of the Church. Whether Constantine himself realized this consciously or whether he was merely taking the most efficient course for restoring unity, he established a precedent that was to last for eleven centuries. Some sixty years before the fall of Constantinople to the Turks, when the Emperor's power was dwindling into nothing, the Patriarch Antony IV wrote these words: 'The holy Emperor has a great position in the Church...and this is because the emperors from the outset established and confirmed the true faith in all the Oecumene. They convoked the Oecumenical Councils; they confirmed the pronouncements of the divine and sacred canons concerning true doctrine and the government of Christians, and they ordered them to be accepted.'[1]

The Patriarch Antony does not, however, specify what the 'great position' was. Could the Emperor pronounce on theology except before a Council? Both Zeno and Heraclius had tried to do so, from the highest motives and with the Patriarch's consent. But both failed.[2] Later Emperors went no further than to tell a Council what its pronouncements ought to be. The Emperor certainly commanded supreme respect as the head of the State. In the West Imperial authority collapsed; and Augustine could

[1] F. Miklosich and I. Müller, *Acta et Diplomata Graeca Medii Aevi*, II, pp. 188–92.
[2] J. B. Bury, *A History of the Later Roman Empire* (1923), I, pp. 402–4.

therefore contrast the decadent earthly Empire with the Kingdom of God. But in the East men followed Eusebius in believing that Christianity had purified and sanctified the Empire. It was the Holy Empire. The Emperor must therefore be tinged with holiness. When Diocletian instituted a coronation ceremony it was performed by the senior lay minister; and the first Christian Emperors continued the practice. Theodosius II, for example, was crowned by the Prefect of the City of Constantinople. But at his successor Marcian's coronation the Patriarch was present; and Marcian's successor Leo I was certainly crowned by the Patriarch.[1] The Patriarch was by now the official with the highest precedence after the Emperor; but his intervention turned the coronation into a religious ceremony. In the course of it the Emperor underwent a sort of ordination; he received charismatic powers. Henceforward the Imperial Palace was known as the Sacred Palace. Its ceremonies were liturgical ceremonies, in which he played the double role of God's representative on earth and representative of the People before God, a symbol both of God and of the Divine Incarnation. The acclamations to which he was entitled stressed his position. On Christmas Eve he was addressed in a prayer which begged that Christ would 'move all nations throughout the universe to offer tribute to Your Majesty, as the Magi offered presents to Christ'. The Whitsun hymns declare that the Holy Ghost descends in fiery tongues on to the Imperial head.[2] At the same time the Emperor paid homage to God in the name of the Christian commonwealth. In the words of the Emperor Constantine Porphyrogenitus it was through the Palace ceremonies that 'the Imperial power can be exercised with due rhythm and order and the Empire can thus represent the harmony and movement of the universe as it stems from the Creator'.[3] The Byzantines fervently believed in this interpretation of the Emperor's position. It did not prevent them from seeking to depose an Emperor whom

[1] Bury, *op. cit.* I, p. 236.
[2] Constantine Porphyrogenitus, *De Ceremoniis* (C.S.H.B. edition), I, pp. 59, 131.
[3] *Ibid.* pp. 3–5.

they thought unworthy or ungodly. His sanctity then might not preserve him from a violent death. It was the symbol, not necessarily the person, that they revered.

There was nevertheless a feeling that the Emperor's power over the Church was limited, though the extent of the limitation was uncertain. It was agreed that he had the final word in appointing the Patriarch. But could he therefore control the Church? Justinian I stated that 'the Sacerdotium and the Imperium', placing them in that order, 'are the greatest gifts that man has received from God...The Sacerdotium is concerned with divine matters, the Imperium presides over mortals...But both proceed from the same Principle.' He adds, though his actions belied his words, that the Emperor, although he is autocrat, cannot exercise a despotism over the Sacerdotium.[1] His friend Agapetus wrote to him that 'the Emperor is lord of all but is, like everyone else, the servant of God', adding that it is for the Church to interpret God's wishes.[2] John Chrysostom, most deeply venerated of all the Byzantine Fathers, said clearly that 'the domain of royal power is one thing and the domain of priestly power another; and the latter prevails over the former.'[3] When the Iconoclastic Emperor Leo III opened the introduction of his abridged lawcode, the *Ecloga*, with the words: 'Since God in His good pleasure has handed over to Us the Imperial authority...and has commanded Us, as He commanded Saint Peter, head and chief of the Apostles, to feed His faithful flock...',[4] and when he began his Iconoclastic decree by declaring himself to be a priest, John of Damascus, writing from the safety of the Caliph's dominions, replied in protest that 'it is not the Emperor's function to make laws for the Church' and that 'I cannot be persuaded that the Church is governed by Imperial decrees'.[5] Theodore the Studite

[1] Justinian, preface to *Novella* VI (ed. K. E. Zachariae von Lingenthal), I, pp. 44–5.
[2] Agapetus, Pope, *Epistolae*, *M.P.L.*, LXVI, coll. 38–40.
[3] John Chrysostom, *In Matthaeum*, *M.P.G.*, LVII, coll. 81 ff.
[4] *Ecloga Leonis*, in Zachariae von Lingenthal, *Collectio Librorum Juris Greco-Romani Ineditorum*, pp. 10–11.
[5] John of Damascus, *Opera*, *M.P.G.*, XCIV, coll. 1295–7, 1302.

maintained that issues concerning doctrine were properly entrusted
only to those to whom God had given the power to bind and
loose, that is, to the Apostles and their successors, who are the
Bishop of Rome and the four Patriarchs. 'This', says Theodore,
'is the pentarchical authority of the Church. These are they who
form the court of judgment on matters of holy doctrine. The
business of kings and rulers is merely to lend aid in a joint attesta-
tion of the Faith and to reconcile differences over secular affairs.'
'You are concerned with politics and war', he cried to Leo V.
'Leave the affairs of the Church to prelates and monks.'[1] The
Epanagoge, the law-code issued by Leo VI, says: 'the State, like
man, is formed of members, and the most important are the
Emperor and the Patriarch. The peace and happiness of the
Empire depends on their accord.' It then goes so far as to say that,
while the Emperor is the legal authority who must enforce and
maintain true doctrine as laid down by the Scriptures and the
Seven Councils, the Patriarch is 'the living and animate image of
Christ, typifying the truth by deeds and words...and alone is to
interpret the canons passed'. The code also forbids the Emperor to
give secular duties to the clergy, following the decrees enacted
by the Holy Councils. But it must be remembered that the
Epanagoge was drafted not by the Emperor but by the great
Patriarch Photius, and that it was never implemented, but was
the preface to a code which was never published.[2]

The views of these eminent churchmen seem only to have been
accepted by public opinion when, as in Iconoclastic times, an
Emperor's religious policy was rousing hot opposition. The
bishops assembled at the Council *in Trullo* had all loyally declared:
'We are the servants of the Emperor.'[3] Indeed, had Theodore of
Studium's theory of the Pentarchy been logically pursued, the
whole basis of the Oecumenical Councils would have been in-

[1] Theodore Studites, *Opera*, *M.P.G.*, xcix, col. 280 (*Vita Theodori*), and coll.
1417 ff.
[2] *Epanagoge*, ed. Zachariae von Lingenthal, *Jus Graeco-Romanum*, iv, pp. 181–4.
[3] J. D. Mansi, *Sacrorum Consiliorum nova et amplissima Collectio*, xi, col. 930.

validated. By the thirteenth century when for some centuries there had been no great doctrinal issue within the Church, the general attitude was that of the late twelfth-century canonist, Theodore Balsamon. He says, when comparing the Emperor with the Patriarch, that: 'the service of the Emperors includes the enlightening and strengthening of both body and soul. The dignity of the Patriarchs is limited to the benefit of souls, and that alone.' He adds that, though the clergy ought not to perform secular duties, the Emperor can by his Economy dispense with this ban, and can also, if need be, intervene in the elections not only of Patriarchs but of bishops as well.[1]

Leo III was wrong in claiming to be a priest. A century earlier Maximus the Confessor had shown at length that the Emperor was not one.[2] The coronation ceremony gave him certain priestly privileges. He could enter the sanctuary. He received communion in both kinds not by intinction, like the laity, but as priests do. On certain feasts he preached the sermon in Saint Sophia. He was acclaimed as *pontifex* or *sacerdos* or ἱερεύς, titles which even the Pope would give him if he considered him to be orthodox. But he was not in the full charismatic succession of the priesthood. In fact, he and the Patriarch were interdependent. He appointed the Patriarch; and the formula of appointment admitted his role as divine agent. 'I know here on earth two powers,' said John Tzimisces, when appointing Basil the Anchorite to be Patriarch in 970, 'the power of the priesthood and the power of the kingship, the one entrusted by the Creator with the cure of souls, the other with the government of bodies, so that neither part be lame or halt but both be preserved sound and whole.' But, having paid that tribute to the priesthood, he continued: 'As there is a vacancy on the Patriarchal throne I am placing there a man whom I know to be suitable.' The Synod had merely to endorse the Emperor's choice.[3]

---

[1] Theodore Balsamon, *Opera*, M.P.G., cxxxviii, coll. 93, 1017–18.
[2] *Acta Maximi*, M.P.G., xc, coll. 90, 117–18.
[3] Leo Diaconus, *Historia* (C.S.H.B. edition), pp. 101–2.

But the Emperor was crowned by the Patriarch; and it was generally held, though never legally stated, that it was the act of coronation that made him Emperor. The Patriarch received his declaration of orthodoxy and could refuse to perform the ceremony unless he amended his faith or his morals.[1] At the last resort the Patriarch could excommunicate the Emperor, though on the rare occasions when he did so public opinion seems to have been uncomfortable.[2] On the other hand the Emperor could and did sometimes obtain the displacement of the Patriarch. The method was either to oblige the Patriarch to abdicate of his own volition, which could usually be forced on him if there were a strong party in the Church opposed to him, or to depose him by a vote of the Holy Synod, on the ground that he had been appointed or had acted uncanonically; and, again, if he were unpopular within the Church it was easy for the Emperor to pack the Synod. But a deposition needed delicate handling. It often led to a schism within the Church, increasing rather than solving the Emperor's problem.[3]

The division between State law and Church law was similarly unclear. The Emperor, though he was under the law, was also the only source of law. He could and did legislate on all subjects, including ecclesiastical. He alone could give the decisions of Church Councils the force of law; and, though the Church could make its own rules, these were not legally binding unless he endorsed them. Canonists such as Balsamon and his younger contemporary, Demetrius Chomatianus, were positive about this. Chomatianus indeed held that only the Emperor could innovate ecclesiastical legislation.[4] As we have seen, the Emperor issued such laws in the form of a communication to the Patriarch, who circulated the contents round the Church. In practice Patriarchs occasionally legislated on their own authority. A difficult point

---

[1] Bury, *A History of the Later Roman Empire*, I, p. 431: Leo Diaconus, *op. cit.* p. 78.
[2] See below, p. 67.   [3] See below, p. 68.
[4] For Balsamon, see D. J. Geanakoplos, *Byzantine East and Latin West*, pp. 58–9; Demetrius Chomatianus, *Responsiones, M.P.G.*, cxix, coll. 948–9.

concerned marriage. By Roman law marriage was a civil contract, but to Christians it was also a religious union, a sacrament. Though the Emperor issued marriage laws, the Church performed marriages ' and could excommunicate those who contracted unions contrary to its laws. Imperial laws laid down the grounds for divorce; but suits for divorce were heard in ecclesiastical courts. The climax occurred in the reign of Leo VI. The Church had always disliked second marriages and positively forbade third marriages; and the Emperor had legally endorsed the ban. He then himself made not only a third but also a fourth marriage. This resulted in an excommunication of the Emperor, a dethronement of the Patriarch, a schism and eventually a compromise. The Patriarch was reinstated, fourth marriages were condemned, third marriages to be permitted only under special dispensation, but the Emperor's child by his fourth marriage, Constantine Porphyrogenitus, was legitimized and succeeded to the Empire. Thenceforward Patriarchs issued their own rules about marriages and grounds for divorce; and the Emperors did not intervene.[1]

Just as the Byzantines disliked hard and fast doctrinal pronouncements unless a need arose or a tradition was challenged, so they avoided a precise ruling on the relations between Church and State. These were decided by a mixture of tradition, of popular sentiment and the personalities of the protagonists. There was a limit which neither side ought to overstep. The Patriarch ought not to interfere in politics. Neither Nicholas Mysticus, hot from his triumph over fourth marriages, nor Michael Cerularius, hot from his triumph in blocking the Emperor's pro-Roman policy, could sustain an attempt to run the government. The former was displaced when he tried to act as Regent; the latter, after making and unmaking Emperors, was dethroned when he attempted to dictate purely secular policy.[2] The Emperor could not go far against the known wishes of the Church. He was supposed to take

---

[1] Bréhier, *op. cit.* II, pp. 492–3, for a good summary of the marriage laws.

[2] For a summary of the careers and aims of Nicholas Mysticus and Cerularius see R. Jenkins, *Byzantium: The Imperial Centuries*, pp. 212–43, 357–66.

an interest in theology. It was his duty to combat heterodoxy and to see to the punishment of incorrigible and antisocial heretics. His theological views were to be respected. When a lay courtier attempted to argue on doctrine with Manuel Comnenus, the Emperor's biographer, John Cinnamus, was shocked. Only doctors of the Church and the Emperor should discuss theology, he thought. But Manuel's other biographer, Nicetas Choniates, was inclined to mock at his ambition to be the new Solomon; and his bishops were kept busy trying tactfully to restrain his somewhat jejune contributions to doctrinal disputes.[1] The final arbiter between Church and State was public opinion, which tended to be swayed by the monks and lower clergy. The Iconoclastic Emperors succeeded for a while in forcing their controversial doctrine upon the Church by working through subservient Patriarchs and for a time controlling the whole upper hierarchy. They failed in the end because the people would not follow their views. Later Emperors were to face similar difficulties when they tried to enforce union with Rome.

After the Fourth Crusade the relations between Church and State began to change. There was an immediate constitutional problem, as on the fall of the city the Patriarch, John Camaterus, retired bewildered to Bulgaria, where after some hesitation he abdicated, giving no hint of his views about the succession. Theodore Lascaris, who had established himself as leader of the exiled Byzantines at Nicaea, then summoned a quorum of bishops to his capital. On his nomination they elected Michael Autorianus as Patriarch and the new Patriarch crowned Theodore Emperor. But could Theodore nominate a Patriarch before he was crowned Emperor? And could the Patriarch of Constantinople reside at Nicaea?[2] The other Greek succession states were doubtful. The Grand Comnenus of Trebizond refused to acknowledge either

---

[1] John Cinnamus, *Historia* (C.S.H.B. edition), pp. 251-5; Nicetas Choniates *Chronicon* (C.S.H.B. edition), pp. 274-8.

[2] D. M. Nicol, *The Despotate of Epiros*, pp. 76 ff.; A. Gardner, *The Lascarids of Nicaea*, pp. 97-9.

Emperor or Patriarch. He took the Imperial title himself and was crowned by his local metropolitan, whom he declared to be autonomous. It was only in 1260, on the eve of the recovery of Constantinople, that the authority of the Nicaean Patriarch was admitted by the Metropolitan of Trebizond, who remained in practice autonomous and who continued to perform the Imperial coronation of the Grand Comnenus.[1] The Despots of Epirus of the Angelus dynasty were equally unwilling to co-operate. There was nearly a schism when one of the family captured Thessalonica and there had himself crowned Emperor by the Metropolitan of Ochrid, the canon-lawyer Chomatianus, who tried to enhance his see by dubious historical claims and who now announced the theory that his newly crowned Emperor could dispose of the Patriarchate as he pleased.[2] But the Greeks in general began to accept the Nicaean Patriarchate, especially when the power of the Nicaean Emperor spread into Greece. After 1232 Epirote Church appointments were made from Nicaea; and in 1238 the Patriarch visited Epirus and was received with full honours there.[3] Up till the recovery of Constantinople he governed the churches in Epirus and the Greek peninsula through an exarch, usually the titular Metropolitan of Ancyra, who during this period seldom was able to visit his Turkish-held see.[4] This meant that already the Patriarch's authority was recognized over a wider area than the Emperor's. He was head of the hierarchy that survived in Turkish territory and of the hierarchy in Orthodox states which did not accept the Emperor's suzerainty. He, rather than the Emperor, was beginning to become the symbol of Orthodox unity. The practical effect of this could be seen when the Nicaean Emperors opened negotiations with the Latin Church. The Patriarchs feared that any compromise with Rome would lose for them the faithful that lived outside Nicaean territory. However much they officially

[1] Mgr Chrysanthos, Ἡ Ἐκκλησία τῆς Τραπεζοῦντος, pp. 177–8.
[2] Nicol, *The Despotate of Epiros*, pp. 80 ff.
[3] See diplomata in Miklosich and Müller, *op. cit.* III, pp. 59–65.
[4] *Ibid.* p. 65.

co-operated with the Emperor, they saw to it that no settlement was reached. The interests of Church and State were beginning to diverge.

The Nicaean Emperors were aware of the danger. They appointed worthy but unworldly men to the Patriarchal throne. When the dying Patriarch Germanus II recommended as his successor the learned but ambitious Nicephorus Blemmydes, the Emperor John Vatatzes offered the scholar the headmastership of the Imperial school. Blemmydes, who eagerly wished to be Patriarch, angrily refused the lesser post, saying that he only cared for a quiet life. This taste for quietude did not prevent him from trying again when his former pupil Theodore II had succeeded to the Empire. According to his own story he was begged to accept the dignity by Theodore, who offered him more power and glory than any Patriarch had ever possessed before. But he was suspicious because the young Emperor had already published a treatise maintaining that matters of faith and doctrine could only be decided by a General Council summoned by the Emperor and attended also by members of the laity. So he said that he would accept the Patriarchate only if he could put first the glory of God. 'Never mind about the glory of God', the Emperor replied crossly. Blemmydes, so he says, was so deeply shocked that he refused the post. It is possible that Theodore did discuss the appointment with his ill-tempered and irritating old tutor; but in fact he hastened to appoint an erudite and ascetic monk, Arsenius Autorianus of Apollonia, who was Patriarch when Michael VIII Palaeologus recaptured Constantinople.[1]

The recovery of the capital in the long run benefited the Patriarch more than the Emperor, re-establishing him as unquestioned head of a hierarchy whose sees stretched from the Adriatic to Russia and the Caucasus, while soon the Imperial territory began to shrink. The growing impoverishment of the Empire damaged the Emperor more than the Patriarch. For

[1] Nicephorus Blemmydes, *Curriculum Vitae et Carmina* (ed. A. Heisenberg), pp. 38–9.

reasons of economy the Palace ceremonies were curtailed and simplified. The Emperor began to lose his aura of mystery and splendour. The Turks, following the old tradition of the Persians and the Arabs, might still regard him as sovereign of the Orthodox, including the Orthodox communities within their dominions; but before the fourteenth century was out he had become the Sultan's vassal and his authority had been used to enforce his own free citizens of Philadelphia to submit themselves to the Sultan.[1] Politically he was becoming impotent; and his dwindling prestige could only be maintained by the loyal support of the Church.

The relationship between Emperor and Church had however suffered some severe shocks. The Emperor who reconquered Constantinople, Michael Palaeologus, was a usurper who had made himself in turn Grand Duke and regent for the child Emperor John IV, then co-Emperor and finally senior Emperor. The Patriarch Arsenius had grudgingly condoned each step, only when Michael swore to respect the boy-Emperor's rights. He was so suspicious of Michael's intentions that in 1260 he abdicated; but, when his successor died a few months later, Michael persuaded him to return, again promising not to harm John IV. But his triumphant recapture of the capital convinced Michael that he was divinely protected. He pushed the boy further and further into the background, and in 1262 he deposed and blinded him. Arsenius, who had been looking on with growing horror, thereupon excommunicated Michael.

The excommunication of an Emperor disquieted many even of the bishops. It had not occurred since the excommunication of Leo VI for his fourth marriage in 906. Michael's protests were in vain; but in 1265 he took his revenge. During the previous year he had interfered in Church affairs by trying to arrest some Patriarchal officials who had suspended a Palace chaplain for disobeying regulations about the registration of a marriage.

[1] See P. Charanis, 'The Strife among the Palaeologi and the Ottoman Turks, 1370–1402', *Byzantion*, XVI (1942/3), pp. 304 ff.

Arsenius had given his officials refuge, denouncing the Emperor more strongly than ever. Now even these officials turned against him, shocked by his intransigence and handsomely compensated by the Emperor. Michael felt strong enough to summon a Synod, attended also by the Patriarchs of Alexandria and Antioch, who were visiting him in search of financial aid. Arsenius was accused of omitting the Emperor's name from the services of the Church and of having permitted an exiled Turkish emir and his family to communicate although they were not Christians. The emir offered to give evidence of his conversion, even promising to eat a whole ham in front of the Emperor, to show that he was no longer a Muslim. His jocularity offended the Emperor; he was not called as a witness. Arsenius, who had indeed omitted the Emperor's name as the logical outcome of his excommunication, considered the Synod illegal and refused to appear before it. On that he was condemned, only the Patriarch of Alexandria and a small minority of bishops voting in his favour. He was deposed and sent as a prisoner to an island monastery, where he died seven years later. His successor as Patriarch, Germanus III, Metropolitan of Adrianople, was a worldly cleric whose only merit was to persuade the Emperor to found and endow schools for the liberal arts. As Patriarch he was so incompetent and soon so unpopular that the Synod insisted on his deposition two years later, on the excuse that he had been transferred from one see to another; which, though such transferences frequently occurred, was still against canon law. He was succeeded by the Grand Almoner of the Palace, Joseph of Galesia, a man of high ambition but a devoted servant of the Church. He agreed to absolve Michael on his own terms. Michael first signed a law giving Patriarchal decrees the same validity as Imperial decrees. He had to show that he was truly penitent of his treatment of John IV, to whom he gave a large pension; and, at a ceremony at which he appeared in penitential garb, confessing his crimes bare-headed on his knees before the Patriarch, he received absolution. The Church had triumphed.

But the Emperor's humiliation did not satisfy Arsenius's adherents. The ascetic element in the Church, based mainly on the monasteries, always suspicious of the court and the upper hierarchy, believing them to be sinfully luxurious and over-interested in secular learning, saw in Arsenius a saintly martyr who had dared to oppose the Emperor on a basic moral issue; and their party was joined by many even in the hierarchy who maintained the old Studite tradition that opposed Imperial control of the Church. The Arsenites, as they began to be called, would not accept Joseph's compromise. They continued to regard the Emperor as excommunicate, his hierarchy as illegitimate and his officials as the servants of a usurper. They were never very numerous; but their monkish connections gave them influence over the people. The hierarchy tried to rid the monasteries of such dissidents, but only drove them underground. Dismissed monks, poorly clad, and often called the *saccophoroi*, the wearers of sack-cloth, would go about the people preaching resistance. It is difficult to assess their power. They seem to have been suppressed in Constantinople but to have flourished in the provinces. Two leading churchmen wrote treatises against them. John Cheilas, Metropolitan of Ephesus, concerned himself with denouncing those who disobeyed the Councils of the Church; while the monk Methodius provided an interesting disquisition on the use of Economy by the Church, to explain when the rules may be modified in the interest of the whole community.[1]

The Emperor Michael's task in suppressing the Arsenites would have been easier if he had not divided the Church soon afterwards by his policy of union with Rome. The full story belongs to a later chapter; but it may be noted here that he could only find a small party of undistinguished clerics, led by the discredited ex-Patriarch Germanus, to represent him at the Unionist Council of Lyons. He subscribed to the Union of Lyons and used the full

---

[1] See L. Petit, 'Arsène Antoninus et Arsénites', in *Dictionnaire de théologie catholique*, by L. Petit, I, ii, coll. 1991–4; G. Ostrogorsky, *History of the Byzantine State* (trans. J. M. Hussey), pp. 411, 433.

power of the State to enforce it, deposing Patriarchs and imprisoning and maltreating priests, monks and laymen who opposed him. Yet he was powerless to make his people accept union, however much he might emphasize its political necessity.[1] As soon as he was dead his whole policy was reversed, in an atmosphere of popular enthusiasm. His successor, Andronicus II, though a poor administrator, was a man of high culture, a theologian and a peacemaker. He degraded the advocates of union, but showed far less harshness to his opponents than his father Michael had done. The Arsenites had been in the vanguard of the enemies of union. With Michael's death and the abandonment of unionism they began to fade away and to be reconciled with the hierarchy. But they left a party within the Church, known usually as the Zealots, who preached asceticism and contemplation and disliked the Imperial court and the intellectuals, lay and clerical, who frequented it. Their opponents, known as the Politicals, believed in co-operation with the State and the use, if need be, of Economy.[2]

These parties were inevitably involved in the civil wars of the mid-fourteenth century and in the simultaneous controversy over mysticism. Roughly speaking, the usurper John Cantacuzenus had the support of the landed aristocracy, the Church Zealots, the monks and the villages, while the legitimate dynasty, the Palaeologi, were backed by the upper hierarchy, by most, but not all, of the intellectuals and by the people of Constantinople. The people of Thessalonica went their own way, forming a party known as the Political Zealots, who advocated a democratic city-state and who disliked Cantacuzenus rather more than the Palaeologi.[3]

The Palaeologi won in the end; but it was a limited victory. The Emperor John V Palaeologus had learnt his lesson. Though he advocated union with Rome and himself submitted to the

---

[1] See D. J. Geanakoplos, *Emperor Michael Palaeologus and the West*, pp. 275–94.
[2] See Ostrogorsky, *op. cit.* pp. 432–3.
[3] Ostrogorsky, *op. cit.* pp. 459–61; O. Tafrali, *Thessalonique au quatrième siècle*, pp. 23–4. See also I. Ševčenko, 'Nicolas Cabasilas's "Anti-Zealot" Discourse: A Reinterpretation', *Dumbarton Oaks Papers*, XI (1957), pp. 81 ff.

Papacy when in Italy in 1369, he was careful not to involve his Church in his conversion. His tact was rewarded. Towards the end of his reign, probably in 1380 or soon afterwards, in circumstances that are unknown to us, he was able to make a concordat with the Patriarchate which clarified and restored much of the Imperial control over the Church. It contained nine points. The Emperor was to nominate metropolitans from three candidates whose names were submitted to him. He alone could transfer and promote bishops. He had to sanction appointments to high Church offices. He alone could redistribute sees. Neither he nor his senior officials nor members of the Senate, which was his advisory council, could be excommunicated except with his permission, 'because the Emperor is defender of the Church and the canons'. Bishops were to come to Constantinople and to leave it whenever he ordered. Every bishop must take an oath of allegiance to him on appointment. Every bishop must put his signature to acts passed by a Synod or Council. Every bishop must implement such acts and refuse support to any cleric or candidate for ecclesiastical office who opposed Imperial policy.[1]

As an Emperor John V was incompetent and almost impotent. The Turks were overrunning all his territory and exacting tribute from him. He himself in a reign of fifty years was three times driven into exile, by his father-in-law, by his son and by his grandson. Yet, as the concordat shows, he still retained prestige enough to reaffirm his theoretical control over a Church, many of whose dioceses lay far outside of his political control. It was soon after his death that the Patriarch Antony IV wrote the letter in which he talked of the great position of the Emperor. It was addressed to the Grand Prince of Muscovy, Vassily I, who had somewhat scornfully pointed out the actual weakness of the Emperor, hinting that some more powerful Orthodox ruler ought to lead the Oecumene. 'The Emperor', Antony wrote, 'is still the Holy Emperor, the heir of the Emperors of old and the

---

[1] V. Laurent, 'Les Droits de l'Empereur en matière ecclésiastique', *Revue des études byzantines*, XIII (1955), pp. 1–20.

6-2

consecrated head of the Oecumene. He, and he alone, is the King whom Saint Peter bade the faithful to honour.'[1]

The Patriarch's loyalty was greater than his realism. But the Emperor still had some power. About twenty years later, in 1414 or 1415, Manuel II, who was generally liked by his ecclesiastics, when in Thessalonica appointed a Macedonian bishop to the see of Moldavia and sent him to Constantinople for consecration by the Patriarch, Euthymius II. Euthymius refused to perform the service, on the out-of-date ground that a bishop could not be transferred. The case undoubtedly had deeper implications, of which we can only guess. It must be remembered the Emperor was actually nominating a bishop for a Christian country over which he had no control; and the Patriarch may have feared that his own good relations with the sovereign Prince of Moldavia might be endangered. He insisted that the transference be approved by the Holy Synod. But the Emperor referred him to the concordat. He had to yield.[2]

The existence of the concordat explains why John VIII was able to carry through the Union of Florence with greater success than Michael VIII had had with the Union of Lyons. John was able to appoint metropolitans who would be useful to him and to make all his delegation, whatever their views, subscribe with the majority to the document issued by the Council proclaiming union. The Metropolitan of Ephesus, who alone refused, was threatened with deposition and the loss of his see. John was helped by the fact that the Patriarch, Joseph II, was an old, weak and sick man, who died before the Council was ended. The Emperor could thus dominate his team at Florence unchallenged except by the conscience of the Metropolitan of Ephesus.[3]

At the end of the Byzantine Empire the Church was thus under the close control of the Emperor. But the control was more

[1] See above, p. 57.
[2] V. Laurent, *Revue des études byzantines*, XIII; Silvester Syropoulos, *Memoirs* (trans. and ed. R. Creyghton), pp. 1–2.
[3] See below, p. 109.

theoretical than real. The Emperor could not put pressure on bishops living in Turkish territory and still less on those who lived in the few still independent Orthodox countries; and, the greater his control over the Patriarch, the less could the Patriarch control the Church outside of the narrow bounds of the dying Empire. And, in spite of his domination over the hierarchy, the Emperor could not control public opinion or the monks and lesser clergy that were its mouthpiece. John could not make a reality of the Union of Florence. In spite of his support, unionist bishops found it wise to leave Constantinople; even the Unionist Patriarch whom he appointed found it prudent to retire to Italy. John's brother and successor, Constantine XI, the last Emperor, a man whom everyone personally respected, insisted that the Union should be formally proclaimed in Saint Sophia. But few clerics would serve at its altars. At the time of the fall of Constantinople the Patriarch and the bishops who supported him were in voluntary exile, and other sees stood empty because the Emperor could not find candidates who would accept his policy; while in bishoprics outside of his political control the union was flatly repudiated.[1]

The Orthodox Church has often been accused of Caesaropapism, of complete subservience to the secular ruler. With regard to the Russian Church the accusation is not unfounded. There the period of Mongol rule had given the prince an example of complete absolutism and had eliminated the old nobility, while the populace was ignorant and usually inarticulate. But even in Russia there were times when the Church dominated the Tsar.[2] In Byzantium, though the Emperor, particularly during these later years, had theoretical control of the hierarchy, his power was limited, partly by tradition and still more by public opinion. Byzantium was fundamentally a democracy. Not even the Emperor, though he was the legal and accepted representative of the people before God and Pontifex Maximus, could enforce a religious policy of which the people disapproved. Every Byzantine felt passionately about

[1] See below, pp. 109–10.   [2] See below, p. 333.

religion. If he were well educated he considered himself entitled to have his own views, whatever the Emperor or the hierarchy might say. If he were simple he depended upon his spiritual adviser; and the spiritual advisers of the humbler folk were the monks, over whom neither Emperor nor Patriarch could always exercise control. The Emperor was an august figure whose sacred rights were respected and who in a struggle with the Patriarch would usually have his way. But neither he nor the Patriarch, for all their splendour, could live securely in his high office if he lost the sympathy of the Christian people of Byzantium.

CHAPTER 4

THE CHURCH AND THE CHURCHES

THE EAST

It was in the sphere of foreign politics that the interests of Church and State in Byzantium were beginning to drift apart. The Emperor's chief concern was with the preservation of his tottering Empire, the Patriarch's with the unity and well-being of the Orthodox world.

Where the few remaining independent Orthodox states of the East were concerned, the Patriarch was prepared to work in harmony with the Emperor. The past had shown that independent Orthodox rulers had been far too eager to proclaim the autonomy of their Churches and to appoint, however uncanonically, their own Patriarchs. That had been the policy of the Kings of Bulgaria and Serbia when their kingdoms had been powerful. But by the end of the fourteenth century Bulgaria had been entirely overrun by the Turks; and all that was left of the Serbian kingdom was a small principality, vassal to the Turks and in no position to indulge ecclesiastical ambitions. The two upstart Patriarchates had disappeared, and their congregations were glad to keep in touch with Constantinople. Across the Danube the Princes of Wallachia and Moldavia were similarly placed and similarly unlikely to pursue an independent ecclesiastical policy. Further to the East the Metropolitan of Trebizond, so long as he enjoyed autonomy in practice, was ready to admit the Patriarch as his superior. The Christians of the Caucasus, encircled by infidels, clung eagerly to their connection with the Empire, even though it was obviously dying.[1] Indeed in 1453, when the news reached him that the Turks were massing to besiege the Imperial capital, the King of Georgia was preparing to dispatch his daughter, enriched with a handsome dowry, to be the bride of the Emperor

---

[1] L. Bréhier, *Le Monde Byzantin*, II, pp. 456–60.

Constantine.[1] The Orthodox Church of Cyprus, despite its historic claim to autonomy, anxiously sought help from Emperor and Patriarch alike in its struggle against the Latin rulers of the island.[2] Among the Orthodox a challenge to Patriarchal authority came only from Russia. The Grand Prince of Muscovy, having asserted his rule over his rival Russian princes and having virtually freed himself from Tatar suzerainty, showed a natural but inconvenient desire to run his Church himself. To curb this ambition the Patriarchate had recourse to the mystical prestige of the Empire. As the Patriarch Antony reminded the Grand Prince Vassily, the Emperor was still the Holy Emperor; he was still God's viceroy on earth. Vassily accepted the rebuke. To the Russians Constantinople was still a sacred city, a place of pilgrimage for the pious and the fountain of their faith and their culture. But it was doubtful how much longer the Russian Church and the Russian ruler would be content to have their chief hierarch nominated from Constantinople. In the old days there had been advantages in having a Greek archbishop. He could stand above the quarrels and intrigues of the rival Russian princes as no Russian could have done; and in the dark days of Tatar domination he could maintain a connection with the free Orthodox world and its great traditions. But such advantages were now out of date. Already the Russian ruler had insisted on appointing at least every alternate archbishop. The Patriarch had need to rely upon the ancient mystique of the Holy Empire to check further impertinence.[3]

This support would, however, be useless unless the Emperor himself showed tact. The quarrel between the Patriarch Euthymius and Manuel II over the Emperor's transference of a Macedonian bishop to the see of Moldavia, though the nominal issue was canonical, was almost certainly due to the Patriarch's fear of

---

[1] Georgius Phrantzes, *Chronicon* (ed. I. Bekker, C.S.H.B. edition), pp. 205 ff.
[2] G. Hill, *A History of Cyprus*, III, pp. 1041 ff.
[3] D. Obolensky, 'Byzantium, Kiev and Moscow: a study in ecclesiastical relations', *Dumbarton Oaks Papers*, XI (1957), pp. 21–78. See above, pp. 71–2.

offending the Moldavians.[1] A worse instance occurred when the Emperor John VIII, in his desire to have good intellectual support in his negotiations for union with the West, appointed the Greek Isidore as head of the Russian Church. Isidore's adherence to the union was angrily repudiated by the Russians, who insisted on his deposition as a heretic.[2] Therein lay the main problem. If the Emperor used his control of the Byzantine Church to enforce on it a policy which the Orthodox in general and in particular the Orthodox outside of his dominions detested, could the unity of the Patriarchate and its authority be maintained? As we shall see, opposition to union with Rome came not only from fanatical monks but from many thoughtful Byzantines who realized that it would mean the secession of the Russians and other independent Orthodox congregations. If we accept the figures given in 1437, union would mean that sixteen out of the sixty-seven metropolitan sees of the Patriarchate would almost certainly go at once into schism.[3]

There was a similar danger over the thirty-six metropolitan sees in Turkish territory. Even if their congregations were to favour union, it was unlikely that the Turkish authorities would approve of such a strengthening of ties with Western Europe. It would be risky for any Patriarch of Constantinople who wished to maintain his religious hold over the Sultan's Christian subjects to follow the Emperor on a policy which few of those Christians desired and which the Sultan would certainly oppose. Hitherto those Christians had not fared too badly, in comparison with their Orthodox brethren in Cyprus or in Latin Greece, where their masters tirelessly tried to drag them into the Latin net. They suffered from civil disabilities; but at least they were allowed to retain their own form of religion.

In the East it was traditional to group peoples not according to their nationality in any modern sense of the word, but according

[1] See above, p. 72.
[2] S. J. Pierling, *La Russie et le Saint-Siège*, I, pp. 56–9; H. Schaeder, *Moskau das dritte Rom*, p. 22: Obolensky, *loc. cit.*   [3] See above, p. 36.

to their religion; and members of a group with a distinctive religion differing from that of the paramount power were treated as an autonomous community under its religious head. The Persians had thus treated the Jews in Achaemenid days; and the Sassanids extended the system to include Christian communities. The Persian word 'melet' or 'milet', meaning a nation, was used to describe such a group. The Muslim Arabs adopted the practice, along with the word *milet*, when they overran lands where older religions were established. Each *milet*, so long as it was formed of 'people of the Book', that is to say, Christians and Jews, whose faiths the Prophet had emended but did not condemn, and, by courtesy, the Zoroastrians, was treated as a unit and governed itself according to its own laws, in all matters in which a Muslim was not concerned. The religious head of the group was responsible for its good behaviour. So long as its members paid their taxes and did not cause riots or indulge in treasonable activity, they were, at least in theory, left in peace. This worked well enough for such communities as were situated entirely or mainly within the Arab Caliph's dominions, such as the Monophysite Churches, the Copts and the Jacobites, or the Nestorian Church, or the Sephardic Jews. They might occasionally be oppressed by some fanatical local governor or have their homes sacked by a jealous Muslim rabble. But in general the Muslim rulers, though they taxed them highly and often arbitrarily, behaved justly and without rancour towards them. The Orthodox Christians were in a different position. The three Patriarchs whose sees were in the Caliph's territory, of Alexandria, Antioch and Jerusalem, might answer for them administratively; but to them the head of their community was God's viceroy on earth, the Emperor at Constantinople. They were thus potential traitors and had to walk warily. But the Emperor felt responsibility for them; it was his duty to intervene in their favour were they persecuted. The Caliph accepted this, so long as the Orthodox avoided open treason. If they were maltreated without due cause, the Emperor's protests were legitimate. When the Fatimid Caliph Hakim burnt down the Church of the Holy Sepulchre, his successor apologized to the Emperor; who was allowed to rebuild the shrine and to keep his own officials there. Earlier on, we find John of Damascus, who had been a civil servant in the Ommayad Caliph's administration, writing to the Emperor as though he were a citizen of the Empire—but one who was fortunately out of reach of the Emperor's fiercely iconoclastic arm.[1]

The Turks inherited the *milet* system. It seemed to them natural that the Orthodox in their dominions should continue to regard the Emperor as their ultimate sovereign; and they did not object to it, so long as the Orthodox *milet* did not take up arms against them in support of the Emperor. The Christians were more heavily taxed than the Muslims, on the ground that they were not required to join the Sultan's armed forces; though on an average they were less heavily taxed than their free brothers in the Emperor's territory. There were certain restrictions on their acquisition of landed property. If they were involved in a lawsuit against a Muslim it was unlikely that they would obtain justice. Their worst hardship was that, from the later fourteenth century onwards, their sons might be taken from them and forcibly converted to Islam, to be enrolled in the Sultan's corps of Janissaries; and if their daughters were coveted by a local Muslim magnate it might be difficult to preserve them from his seraglio. Inevitably a number of Christians passed over to the faith of their rulers, in order to enter the ruling classes; and these renegades were apt to be, as is the way of converts, fanatical and intolerant. But the Christian communities lasted on. Prudence taught them to be self-effacing; and by the end of the fourteenth century few of them had any hope left of regaining full freedom. Constantinople, however, remained to them the capital of their polity and of their Church.[2]

---

[1] See S. Runciman, 'The Byzantine "Protectorate" in the Holy Land', *Byzantion*, XVIII (1948), pp. 207–15.

[2] Bréhier, *op. cit.* II, pp. 472–3; A. Waechter, *Der Verfall des Griechentums in Kleinasien im XIVten Jahrhundert*, pp. 9–59, giving details of various sees.

The Emperor was conscious of his duty towards them. If at times he appeared to be unnecessarily subservient to the Sultan, it was often because the interests of these Christians were at stake. Indeed, when he submitted himself as vassal to the Sultan, it somewhat eased his position with regard to them. The Sultan was readier to let him intervene on their behalf.

To the Church they presented a special problem. As the Turks advanced the regular pattern had been for the Imperial civil administration to withdraw from each doomed city, leaving the bishop to make terms with the invaders. Muslim law held that, if a city surrendered to the Muslims, its Christian inhabitants might retain their churches and worship in them freely. If it were taken by storm, the Christians lost their rights. It was sometimes difficult to draw a distinction; and, if there were any great church building that the Turks especially desired, it was usually possible to find an excuse to justify its annexation. But in most cases the church buildings and the church organization were unharmed by the conquest, although, as we have seen, the consequences of the conquest involved movements of population and ecclesiastical reorganization. The Turks did not prevent the bishops of the conquered territories from keeping in touch with Constantinople. They were seldom forbidden to make the journey thither if they were summoned by the Emperor or the Patriarch to attend a Council, or if the business of their sees demanded their presence. But the business of their sees was changing its nature. In the absence of Christian civil officials they were left to administer the Christian communities. They had to enlarge their ecclesiastical courts to deal with all the litigation that concerned their congregations; they had to negotiate as administrators with their Turkish overlords. It was all haphazard and chaotic, and we have scant evidence to show how it worked. To many of such Christians, with their hope of liberty vanished, it seemed that the only chance of bettering their lives would be if the Sultan were to take over Constantinople and the Patriarchate.[1]

[1] Waechter, *op. cit.* pp. 60–5.

The Patriarch did his best to keep in touch. Bishops were summoned to Constantinople to report to him; but if they tried to avoid returning to their sees they were reprimanded, and the Emperor would be called in to put pressure on them. But, if the sees were to survive, the Patriarch had to maintain relations with the Sultan's court; and this might be difficult if the Emperor's foreign policy took a turn that the Sultan disliked, in particular if it veered towards union with the West.

There were also the Orthodox in other Muslim lands to consider. Hitherto the Patriarchs of Alexandria, Antioch and Jerusalem had not been entirely cut off from Constantinople. They had seldom been prevented from sending representatives to Church councils there; and each of them had occasionally been able himself to pay a visit to the Emperor. But would they continue to be allowed such facilities by their overlords if the Emperor tried to integrate himself with the militant Christian West?

It was the question of the union of the Church with Rome which presented the vital problem.

THE WEST

Every pious Christian must hope that the day will come at last when the Church of Christ will be united and whole and be in truth the Holy Catholic Church whose existence is an article of faith. The hope has so far been vain. Almost from the outset there has been schism and even heresy. As the Church on earth grew in size, so it grew in divisions. The jealous rivalries of hierarchs, the interference and resentment of the laity and the love of theologians to expose the damnable errors made by others of their craft have combined with differences in historical development and in spiritual temperament to break it into separate units; and even where cracks have been mended the line of the former breakage has always remained exposed.

The most serious division in the medieval Church was that which came to separate its two most important branches, the great Church of Old Rome and the great Church of New Rome which is Constantinople and of her sister Patriarchates. There had been differences in outlook from the earliest times. The Christological controversies of the fourth and fifth centuries had increased a spirit of rivalry between the Patriarchates, lasting until the Arab conquest of Syria and Egypt left Constantinople the one free Patriarchate of the East and the spokesman for Eastern Orthodoxy. Meanwhile the collapse of the Roman Empire in the West had made the Roman Church the surviving representative of unity and order. Western Christendom with its numerous rival lay rulers began to look on the Roman Pope as the head of the Christian commonwealth, whereas in the East the Emperor remained the Viceroy of God. There had always been a difference in language between the two halves of the old Empire; and language tends to influence thought. Greek, with its rich vocabulary, its subtlety and its flexibility, induced a different philosophical outlook from that induced by Latin, with its legalistic precision; and, as time went on, it became rare for anyone to speak or understand both tongues. Inadequate translations increased misunderstanding. Political needs and problems differed. Quarrels, even schisms, occurred from time to time throughout the Dark Ages; and, if none of them was final, it was because neither side wished for a definite breach and because contact between East and West was not too close, and divergencies could be tactfully ignored.[1]

It needed a series of political accidents to set off the sparks that flared into the final schism. The development of the Hildebrandine conception of the Papacy as the supreme power in Christendom coincided with the period of the Norman conquest of Byzantine Italy, with the expansion of Italian trade in the East and with the whole long, unhappy episode of the Crusades. The closer contact not only showed that the political interests of Eastern and Western Christendom were by no means the same and, indeed,

[1] For the rivalry between Rome and the Eastern Patriarchs see above, p. 21, n. 1. For the later disputes between Rome and Constantinople see S. Runciman, *The Eastern Schism*, pp. 1–27.

were often so far opposed as to lead to war; it also emphasized the differences that had grown up not only in ritual and ecclesiastical practice but also even in doctrine between the two great Churches. Even after the notorious quarrel between the Patriarch Michael Cerularius and Cardinal Humbert which led to their excommunication of each other in 1054, the ruling authorities on both sides were anxious to avoid schism.[1] Pope Urban II launched the First Crusade in a desire to bring help to the Eastern Christians. On the Eastern side the Emperors in particular were anxious to preserve good relations. After the Norman invasions and the launching of the Crusades they realized how dangerous a hostile West could be to them. Most leading Byzantine ecclesiastics, while unwilling to admit that they were wrong in their doctrine and their practices, believed that a judicious use of Economy might smooth over the difficulties. Until well into the twelfth century the ordinary Byzantine believed the ordinary Westerner to be a genuine fellow-Christian, however deplorable his habits might be.[2]

Unfortunately, the more that Eastern and Western Christendom saw of each other, the more, in general, they disliked what they saw. The simple Westerner, who had expected to find the Eastern Christians to be like himself, found instead a people with a strange language, strange customs and strange religious services, a people, moreover, which did not share his burning desire to go out and fight the infidel. The Byzantines on their side, though they were accustomed to variations in liturgical ways and language, with the Slavonic Churches nearby, found the Westerners to be crude, lawless and disrespectful, with a bellicosity that was ill timed and undiplomatic; and they were deeply shocked by the fighting priests in the Crusader armies. Dislike and distrust increased, to the genuine distress of the authorities. But conferences and debates only worsened matters, emphasizing the differences not only in political outlook and interests but also in religious practice and in theology.

[1] *Ibid.* pp. 49–51.　　　　[2] *Ibid.* pp. 124–44.

The failure to come together led to the Fourth Crusade, the sack of Constantinople and the establishment of Latin states in the Christian East. This was a disaster from which Byzantium never properly recovered and which it never forgave. So, though almost every Emperor, both while the Empire was in exile at Nicaea and after the recapture of Constantinople in 1261, tried to keep the door open for reunion, the vast majority of his subjects would now never countenance any compromise with the West. The opposition was strongest among the lesser clergy; for wherever the Latins had established themselves they had installed a Latin upper hierarchy which tried to force Latin practices and Latin doctrines upon the Orthodox congregations. Support for the union was limited. But there were Byzantines who shared with most of the Emperors the view that the Empire could not afford politically to risk the enmity of Western Europe, particularly when the Turkish menace loomed larger and larger; and there were others who felt that Byzantium, by cutting itself off from the West religiously, was cutting itself off also from its intellectual life and was being left in cultural isolation.

It was a difficult choice for a Byzantine. Had the Orthodox states of Eastern Europe ever been able to bring themselves together in a real alliance, they might have been able to hold out against the West and the Turks alike. But civil wars and the latent dislike of the Balkan Slavs for the Greeks prevented any such alliance. If the Turks were to be driven back it could only be with Western help. But how much help could the West provide? The Crusading movement was dissolving in disillusion. The Holy War had been preached too often against the personal and political enemies of the Papacy, regardless of their faith, to retain its spiritual appeal. If union were achieved the Pope might preach a Crusade to save Byzantium. But who would answer the call? The Venetians and the Genoese, with their great navies and their commitments in the East, would be far more useful allies. But they had always been singularly unresponsive to Papal exhortations; and, besides, they would never co-operate with each other.

Many Byzantine statesmen wondered whether the practical advantages of union would be large enough to outweigh the disadvantages. The theologians of Byzantium, however, were unconcerned with pragmatical issues. They saw the question *sub specie aeternitatis*; and it was they who conducted the debates.

Every attempt at union was accompanied by a number of theological debates and supported or opposed by a number of tracts and sermons. The debates make sterile reading; for they never got down to the fundamental issue. The real bar to union was that Eastern and Western Christendom felt differently about religion; and it is difficult to debate about feelings. Moreover, what was the ultimate authority which both sides would accept? It was admitted that this should be the Holy Scriptures, the findings of such Councils as both parties recognized as having been Oecumenical, and the writings of such Fathers of the Church as were generally admitted to have been orthodox and inspired. The debaters therefore spent their time in hurling texts at each other. The texts were often misquoted or mistranslated and were seldom conclusive. The Scriptures and the canons of the Councils sometimes had nothing relevant to say about the questions actually at issue; and, though the Fathers of the Church may have been divinely inspired, inspiration did not always produce consistency. They often disagreed with each other and occasionally even contradicted themselves. Some of the tracts and sermons are more profound. But they, too, were deliberately political. It is only by studying the writings intended, rather, for consumption within the Churches that we can appreciate the true differences between them. The whole question of mysticism and mystical theory, which was of fundamental importance to the Byzantines and on which the West held other opinions, was kept out of the debates, deliberately, it seems, in the case of the Union Council of Florence, because the issue could not be resolved by the methods used in the debates.

The debates were also sterilized by the avoidance of a direct discussion of the essential practical issue, which was the Pope's claim to supremacy over the whole Church. It barely needed discussion, because everyone knew that union meant in fact the submission of the Orthodox Church to the authority of Rome. Even the most extreme Latin apologists did not expect the Greeks to admit this authority without the opportunity of discussing theological and ritual differences at a Council. But the exact relations of the Pope with a Council, though it greatly exercised the Western theologians at the Council of Basle, was left untouched at these Union councils; nor was there discussion about the relations of the Emperor with the Pope. Yet the discussion of differences in doctrine and in practice was somewhat pointless when one side was determined to secure the total submission of the other. If the average Byzantine had no confidence in the value of a Union council, it was because he saw that its intention was to force his religious life under the control of a foreign potentate whose claims he thought to be uncanonical and whose doctrines faulty, and whose followers in the past had shown themselves to be hostile and intolerant. The most for which he could hope from such a council was to be graciously permitted to retain certain of his ritual usages.[1]

Outside the council-chamber the Pope's claim to supremacy was hotly discussed. To the Latins and the Unionists it was based on texts. They sought to show that the Fathers of the Greek Church as well as of the Latin had down the ages held that the Bishop of Rome was the legitimate heir of Peter, with the power to bind and to loose: that is to say, that he had supreme authority in the universal Church on matters of faith and of discipline. There were many texts to support them, even if some were used a little disingenuously. But here again the Fathers were not always consistent. The Roman see had in the past received special reverence. The Bishop of Rome, or his representative, acted as *princeps senatûs*, as tenant of the top-ranking see in Christendom. Except in

[1] See J. Gill, *The Council of Florence*, pp. 12–15; D. J. Geanakoplos, *Byzantine East and Latin West*, pp. 84–7; S. Runciman, *The Fall of Constantinople*, pp. 6–9, 16–21.

minor details his views had prevailed at them. No one who desired
the unity of Christendom wished rashly to break off relations
with its senior hierarch. On the contrary, to be in communion
with him had been, in many eyes, the outward sign of member-
ship of the undivided Church. Clerics who disagreed with their
local hierarchs were glad to appeal to him on matters of discipline
and doctrine. But could he, in such cases, do more than admonish
and advise? Could he interfere legally in the internal affairs of
another Patriarchate? The Council of Sardica in 343 had apparently
given him this right. But it was not an Oecumenical Council; and
the Second Oecumenical Council implicitly denied it, at least as
regards Constantinople. Again, were his pronouncements on
faith absolutely binding? He could be consulted as the highest
individual mortal authority; and his opinion would carry immense weight. When John of Damascus and Theodore of Studium each in turn found himself in opposition to an Iconoclastic
Emperor who had the Patriarch of Constantinople under his control, each demanded an appeal to Rome, protesting that Iconoclasm could not be introduced without the consent of its Bishop.
But, at the same time, John considered that it was ultimately for
an Oecumenical Council to settle the matter, while Theodore
believed that Rome must act with the co-operation of the four
other Patriarchs; no one put forward the theory of the Pentarchy
of Patriarchs more clearly than he.[1] Moreover, while Theodore
was still living, the Pope himself, in Byzantine eyes, broke the
unity of Christendom by crowning a rival Emperor in the West,
thus interfering, as it were, with the apostolic succession of Emperors. The Byzantine court saved its face by soon recognizing
Charlemagne as a co-Emperor, thus bringing him into line. But
the harm was done.[2] Consequently, when it appeared a little later
that Rome had countenanced an addition to the Creed without

---

[1] John of Damascus, *Orationes*, M.P.G., xciv, coll. 1296 ff.; Theodore Studites,
Epistolae, I, 28, M.P.G., xcix, col. 1001. The doctrine of the Pentarchy had been
put forward in the early seventh century by Maximus the Confessor, *Disputatio
cum Pyrrho*, M.P.G., xci, col. 352.
[2] See R. Jenkins, *Byzantium: The Imperial Centuries*, pp. 105 ff.

the permission or endorsement of an Oecumenical Council, faith in the unity of Christendom was not strong enough to prevent an angry reaction at Constantinople. The Patriarch of Constantinople may have been spurred on in his protest by jealousy and ambition, as Rome liked to claim. It naturally riled the bishop of the capital city of Christendom, who had already, despite Rome's protests, assumed the title of Oecumenical to emphasize his position as such, to find himself considered as a junior and subservient partner to the bishop of a revered but decaying city in Italy. He doubtless relished the triumph of catching his senior partner out in uncanonicity and heresy. But his indignation and that of his Church was perfectly genuine. Rome held that the addition to the Creed was legitimate in that it elucidated an accepted point of doctrine. To the Byzantines the acts and decisions of an Oecumenical Council were inspired by the Holy Spirit. To alter them for the purpose of elucidation could only be effected by another Oecumenical Council. Moreover, this addition seemed in the eyes of Byzantine theologians to alter the whole sense of the doctrine. For the Roman Church to make the change unilaterally was an insult to the Oecumenical Councils and to the Holy Spirit, the more so as the addition concerned the Holy Spirit. It was the word *Filioque*, placed after the words *ex Patre* in describing the procession of the Holy Spirit. The West might think the addition trivial. To Gibbon, as to many other historians, 'the reason, even of divines, might allow that the difference is inevitable and harmless'. But the Greek divines reasoned otherwise. The difference was in fact the expression of two opposing attitudes in religious thought.[1]

In the meantime the growing atmosphere of hostility led people to notice and complain of divergencies in ritual, to which hitherto no importance had been given. The Greeks accused the Latins of

---

[1] E. Gibbon, *Decline and Fall of the Roman Empire* (ed. J. B. Bury), VI, p. 368. For the dispute over the *filioque* clause in Photius's time see F. Dvornik, *The Photian Schism*, pp. 117ff., 196ff. (tending to play down the differences); F. Gavin, *Some Aspects of Contemporary Greek Orthodox Thought*, pp. 129ff.

Judaistic tendencies because they fasted on Saturdays, especially at Quadragesima. They remarked on the Latin omission to celebrate the Liturgy of Presanctified Gifts on fast days in Lent. They professed to be shocked that Latin priests shaved off their beards, though that was a complaint that better-educated Greek theologians dismissed as ridiculous. There was the question of the marriage of clergy, which the Latins now banned but which the Greeks allowed and even advocated in the case of priests who had not taken monastic vows. There was the question of divorce, which the Latins forbade but which the Greeks, to whom marriage was a civil contract as well as a sacrament, permitted on certain grounds. There was the doctrinal point of Purgatory, which seemed to the Greeks to be too precise. It was arrogant, they thought, to profess to know what God in his wisdom might choose to do with the souls of the departed; though they were prepared to believe that souls not actually condemned to Hell might yet be considered unworthy to be admitted at once into the presence of God, and that prayer might aid such souls on their upward path. The Latins on their side questioned two Greek practices in the celebration of the Eucharist, first, the use of the *zeon*, the warm water mixed into the chalice, and secondly, and more severely, the Epiklesis, the appeal to the Holy Spirit, without which, so the Greeks held, the change in the elements could not be completed.

Most of these differences were unimportant; and serious theologians were prepared to condone them. But there was one difference in ritual practice which was hotly contested. This was whether the bread used in the Sacrament should be leavened or unleavened. It seems that the use of unleavened bread only became general in the West in the ninth century, and, like the contemporary addition to the Creed, both were adopted first as a regular practice north of the Alps, though both had originated elsewhere. The argument in favour of unleavened bread was that Christ Himself had undoubtedly used it at the Last Supper. The Greeks admitted this; but they maintained that the Old Testament dispensation came to an end with Christ's death upon the Cross and the descent of the Holy Spirit at Pentecost. The leaven symbolized the presence of the Holy Spirit. The Latin usage seemed to them, as did the Latin refusal to admit the Epiklesis, an insult to the Holy Spirit. In the course of the controversy other arguments were adduced, some of them slightly absurd, as when some Greeks declared that not only did the word ἄρτος mean leavened bread but connected it, with the type of punning false etymology dear to the medieval mind, with ἄρτιος, 'perfected'. The Latins could retort that ἄρτος was used in the Gospel for the bread which Christ broke; but their plea that leaven was forbidden because Christ bade His disciples to 'beware of the leaven of the Pharisees and the Sadducees' was hardly convincing. In fact neither side was ready to abandon a cherished tradition. The Greeks felt so strongly on this issue that their popular pejorative name for the Latins was the Azymites, the unleavened, with the implication that they were untouched by the Holy Spirit.[1]

These ritual points, even that about the bread, need not have formed a bar to union. Tolerance, Economy and a willingness to admit that alternative practices might be permissible would have overcome the difficulty. Economy, the belief that a special grace or dispensation might be granted to condone minor error in the interest of the smooth running of the House of God, was a doctrine which the Greeks found sympathetic. But they could not bring themselves to apply it either to the Papal claim for complete supremacy or to the theological crime of the addition to the Creed.

To many pious persons, in the East as well as in the West, it has seemed strange that the unity of Christendom should have been split by a preposition. It should be equally possible to lead a holy life in the grace of God whether one believes that the Holy Ghost proceeds from the Father and from the Son or from the Father through the Son. The theologians of the West could not see that the difference was of importance. But to an Eastern theologian a

[1] For a summary of the differences in usage, see P. Evdokimov, *L'Orthodoxie*, pp. 249–52; Gill, *op. cit.* pp. 266, 277, 280–1.

vital principle is involved; the Latin addition upsets his notion of the Godhead. The inability of the Latins to appreciate the full implications of the addition that they made to the Creed showed how far the basic conceptions of Trinitarian theology in East and West had drifted apart.

The Scriptural text on which the Eastern view of the Procession of the Holy Spirit is based is St John xv. 26: 'But when the Comforter is come, whom I will send unto you from the Father, even the Spirit of truth, which proceedeth from the Father, he shall testify of me.' The verses in the next chapter (13 to 15) which say of the Spirit: 'he shall receive of mine', and later: 'all things that the Father hath are mine', did not, to the Easterners, affect the previous text, though Photius and his opponents were to spend much energy in discussing the word 'mine', ἐκ τοῦ ἐμοῦ, in the Greek, which Photius declared that the Latins interpreted as though it were τὰ ἐμοῦ; nor were Paul's rather vague references to 'the Spirit of Christ' relevant. The Fathers of the Second Oecumenical Council, when they had the duty of completing the Nicene Creed, were satisfied to pronounce that the Holy Spirit proceeds from the Father, without making mention of the Son. But the Spanish Fathers of the sixth century, busy combating the Arianism of the Visigoths, felt that greater precision was needed and added the word 'Filioque'. From Spain the addition moved northward, to Charlemagne's court, perhaps through the agency of the learned Spaniard Theodulphus, Bishop of Orleans; and by the middle of the ninth century it was in general use in Germany, and German missionaries working in Slav lands brought it to the notice of the Patriarch Photius. Pope Leo III had omitted the word when he had caused the Creed to be written out round the walls of St Peter's at Rome. His successors had however resented Photius's attack on the German Church, and by the early years of the eleventh century German-born Western Emperors had imposed its usage on Rome.[1]

[1] For the early history of the *filioque* see A. Palmieri, 'Filioque', in *Dictionnaire de théologie catholique*, v, ii, coll. 2309–17.

It is difficult to decide how far the difference in theological approach that developed was a matter of differing temperament and how far it was affected by historical circumstances. Certainly, while Eastern Orthodox churchmen from the fourth to the seventh centuries were occupied in fighting Christological heresies and concentrated therefore on emphasizing the hypostases in the Trinity, their contemporaries in the West were fighting the Arianism of the Goths and the polytheism of other Germanic peoples and concentrated therefore on the essential unity of God. Whatever the cause, the contrast in outlook has been summarized by the remark that Western thought tended to take as its starting-point the one nature and then passed to the consideration of the three Persons, but Greek thought followed the reverse course, from the three Persons to the one nature. Basil preferred the latter method. He considered that the Western approach too often led to Sabellianism; it was safer to start from the more concrete formula of Father, Son and Holy Ghost. There was nothing illegitimate in either approach. Ideally the Three and the One should be accepted simultaneously. 'No sooner do I conceive of the One', says Gregory of Nazianzus, 'than I am illumined by the splendour of the Three. No sooner do I distinguish them than I am carried back to the One.' But few theologians dwelt on so high a plane.[1]

The liking of the Greeks for the concrete approach was enhanced by their liking for apophatic theology, negative theology, based on what we cannot know. The three Hypostases of God are, so to speak, the relatively knowable parts of God. His essence is simple, unknowable and incommunicable. Any comprehension of the Divine is and can only be relative; and it is only by recognizing the reality of the unconfused distinctions between the three Hypostases in the Trinity that we can begin to understand how God with his unknowable essence can create, sustain and save the knowable world. The Latins did not reject apophatic theology; indeed, it has no finer exponent than Augustine. But they tended

[1] Basil, *De Spiritu Sancto*, M.P.G., xxxii, col. 136: Gregory Nazianzene, *Sanctum Baptisma*, M.P.G., xxxvi, col. 417.

to regard the essence of God in a more ontological light and to subordinate the Persons of the Trinity to it. Linguistic problems added to the difference in thought. While *essentia* is the only possible translation for οὐσία, the two words were not always understood in quite the same sense. *Persona* is not a perfectly exact translation for ὑπόστασις; yet if ὑπόστασις is translated as *substantia*, which is more accurate, and *persona* as πρόσωπον, further confusion arises. To call the Persons of the Trinity *Substances* seemed to the West to savour of tritheism, while πρόσωπον in Greek suggests the exterior rather than the personality. Translation constantly added to misunderstanding. Latins and Greeks honestly interpreted the same text in different ways because the words did not have the same connotation to them. The same words of John of Damascus, for instance, are quoted by each side as debating points, because each side read a different sense into the text.[1]

The Orthodox, with their apophatic tastes, preferred to avoid dogmatic definitions until the danger of heresy made them necessary. They would have been prepared to leave the question of the Holy Ghost unformulated. 'You ask', says Gregory of Nazianzus, 'what is the procession of the Holy Spirit. Tell me first what is the unbegottenness of the Father, and I shall then explain to you the physiology of the generation of the Son and the procession of the Spirit; and we shall both of us be stricken with madness for prying into the mystery of God.'[2] His was the Byzantine attitude. The Latins, however, with their legalistic minds, insisted on prying into the mystery and on explaining the procession of the Spirit; and the explanation that satisfied them

---

[1] A good summary of the Orthodox attitude is given in P. Sherrard, *The Greek East and the Latin West*, pp. 61–72. The difficulty of translating terms was noted by Theophylact of Bulgaria, *De iis in quibus Latini Accusantur*, M.P.G., CXXVI, coll. 228–9, excusing Latin errors because of the poverty of philosophical terms in Latin. The problem recurred at the Council of Florence. See Gill, *op. cit.* pp. 191–3.

[2] Gregory Nazianzene, *Theologica quinta: De spiritu sancto*, M.P.G., XXXVI, col. 141.

involved the addition to the sacred and accepted Creed. It was not mere factiousness on the part of the Patriarch Photius, though he set about the task with undoubted relish, when he took it upon himself to point out to the Pope that the Western Church was condoning a heresy. To him as a Greek the Dual Procession was heresy; but he was in consequence obliged to formulate the doctrine of the Orthodox.

Given its premise, each side had an unanswerable case. Both start from the basic dogma, expressed by John of Damascus, that: 'The Father, the Son and the Holy Spirit are one in all respects save those of being unbegotten, of filiation and of procession.'[1] But thereafter the approach is different. A learned Catholic divine has said: 'Latin philosophy first considers the nature in itself and proceeds to the agent; Greek philosophy first considers the agent and afterwards passes through it to find the nature.'[2] The Latin world was moving towards the idea of the *summum ens*. It identified God's essence with His being; God is absolute, perfect and simple Being. The Trinity has therefore one essence, one nature and one power. The hypostatic characteristics of the Three are absorbed in the essence of the One; and this essence, differentiated by relationships though it is, remains the principle of unity. The relationships become the hypostases instead of being their characteristics. The essence and the hypostatic powers of the Father cannot be distinguished. Hence He begets the Son essentially, and the Son is an essential hypostasis. As the cause and principle of Being in the Trinity is the essence, these two essential hypostases, having no distinction between them, together, according to their common nature, project the Spirit. The unity of God would be broken if we attributed to the Father alone the power to project the Spirit.

The Greek interpretation of οὐσία, for which word unfortunately 'essence' is the only translation, differs from the Latin

---

[1] John of Damascus, *De Fide Orthodoxa*, M.P.G., xciv, coll. 832–3, 849.
[2] T. de Regnon, *Etudes de théologie positive sur la Sainte Trinité*, I, pp. 433, quoted in V. Lossky, *The Mystical Theology of the Eastern Church*, p. 64.

interpretation of *essentia*. To the Greeks essence is entirely simple and unknowable; it is neither Being itself nor the cause of Being in others. It cannot enter into any form of relationship within itself or with anything else. The cause and principle of Being and of unity in the Trinity is therefore the hypostasis of the Father.

The distinctions of the hypostases within the Divinity are not according to essence; there is an indivisible division between the essence and the powers. There is one God because there is one Father Who through His hypostatic powers causes the Son by generation and the Spirit by procession. He is the πηγαία θεότης, the source of all divinity within the Trinity; He brings forth the Son and the Spirit by conferring on them His nature, which remains one and indivisible, identical in all three hypostases. The hypostases signify at the same time the diversity and the unity in reference to the Father, Who is principle as well as recapitulation —συγκεφαλαίωσις—of the Trinity. In the words of Dionysius of Alexandria: 'We extend the monad indivisibly into the triad and we recapitulate the triad without diminution into the monad.' To quote Gregory of Nazianzus once more: 'In my opinion we safeguard the one only God in referring the Son and the Spirit to a single Principle, neither commixing nor confounding them', and: 'The Three have one nature, God; and the union—ἕνωσις— is the Father.' Irenaeus goes even further when he calls the Son and the Holy Spirit the two arms of God; but the idea is the same. Some centuries later Theophylact, Archbishop of Bulgaria, gives the traditional Byzantine view when he compares the Father to the sun, the Son to the rays of the sun and the Spirit to the light or heat given by the sun. We can talk of the light of the rays, but the sun remains the principle.[1]

Holding such an interpretation of the Trinity the Greeks could not accept the Latin addition. Their Economy, though it might

---

[1] Irenaeus, *Contra Haereses*, M.P.G., VII, col. 975; Athanasius, *De Sententia Dionysii*, M.P.G., XXV, col. 505, quoting Dionysius of Alexandria; Gregory Nazianzene, *Oratio XX*, M.P.G., XXXV, col. 1073, and *Supremum Vale*, M.P.G., XXXVI, col. 476; Theophylact of Bulgaria, *Vita Clementis*, M.P.G., CXXVI, col. 1209.

enable them to overook differences in ritual, could not be stretched far enough to include an alteration in the Symbol of Faith as it had been laid down by the Fathers at an Oecumenical Council inspired by the Holy Spirit, and one which contradicted their conception of the Trinity. The Latins on their side could claim that the addition stemmed logically from the doctrine of the Trinity as they interpreted it, and had moreover been endorsed by the supreme doctrinal authority of the Papacy. Neither side would yield to the other's arguments, because the dispute was not so much about the addition itself as about whether any addition could be made to the Creed and, more fundamentally, the whole nature of the Trinity. It was futile for the Latins to think that they had scored a point when they quoted Greek Fathers from Paul onwards who used the phrase 'the spirit of Christ'. The phrase did not mean the same to the Greeks. John of Damascus indeed used the phrase, as the Latins gleefully pointed out; but what he said was: 'It should be understood that we do not speak of the Father as being derived from anyone; we speak of Him as the Father of the Son. We speak of the Son neither as cause nor Father; we speak of Him both as from the Father and Son of the Father. We speak likewise of the Holy Spirit as from the Father and call Him the Spirit of the Father. We do not speak of the Spirit as from the Son, yet we call Him the Spirit of the Son.' His attitude is somewhat apophatic and full of the Greek love for paradox. It was not so easy to support as was the clearer-cut attitude of the Latins.[1]

There were Greeks who were won over to the Latin view. Some of them were not theologians; they felt that the niceties of dogma should not outweigh the practical, cultural and moral advantages of union. But others were sincerely convinced by the Latin dogma, and among them were men with the finest philosophical brains in Byzantine history. But it was because they were philosophers that they found the rationalism of the Latins more sympathetic than the Greek apophatic tradition.

[1] John of Damascus, *loc. cit.*

The Greek Fathers had always allowed that the Holy Spirit proceeded through the Son. It was the coming of the Word that enabled the Spirit to penetrate throughout the world. For example, Theophylact of Bulgaria says that we must believe that the Spirit proceeds from the Father but is given to the created world through the Son.[1] The Latins argued with some reason that the phrase suggested that the connection between the Son and the Spirit was limited by time, beginning only at the historic moment of the Incarnation. Some Greeks hoped that, if a formula could be found which cleared up that difficulty, the Latins might be induced to drop the hated addition. Nicephorus Blemmydes the philosopher suggested, rather as Augustine had done, that the Holy Spirit proceeded from the Father and the Son as from one principle, but originally or principally from the Father alone. The compromise pleased nobody. But it suggested a possible line for compromise.[2]

Blemmydes's suggestion was made at a time when the Nicaean Emperors were holding out hopes of union to the Pope in order to dissuade him from trying to prop up the dying Latin Empire of Constantinople. Their sincerity was dubious; and in any case their Church was determined that they should not go too far. But after the recapture of Constantinople Michael VIII Palaeologus was seriously alarmed by the preparations made by the Papal protégé, Charles of Anjou, King of Sicily, to restore the Latin Emperor. To counter Charles he opened negations on union with the Papacy. In 1273, despite the protests of the Patriarch Joseph, he browbeat a synod into admitting the full primacy of the Roman see, the right of every churchman to appeal to it and the need for the Pope's name to be mentioned in the Liturgy. Next year he sent a delegation to announce his submission to the Council that Pope Gregory X was holding at Lyons. It was not an impressive delegation, particularly after one of the ships, carry-

---

[1] Theophylact of Bulgaria, *Enarratio in Ioannis Evangelium, M.P.G.*, cxxiii, col. 1224.
[2] See M. Jugie, *Theologia Dogmatica Christianorum Orientalium ab Ecclesia Catholica Dissidentium*, I, pp. 417–18.

ing two high court officials, a number of clerks and secretaries and all the Imperial gifts to the Pope, was wrecked with heavy loss of life off Cape Malea on the way to Italy. The most impressive member was the lay philosopher, George Acropolita, who attended as the Emperor's personal representative. Of the two ecclesiastical representatives, one was the discredited ex-Patriarch Germanus, the other Theophanes, Metropolitan of Nicaea, a man of no distinction. No bishop of quality would go on the Emperor's mission. There was no theological debate. The delegation merely handed to the Pope letters from the Emperor, his son and a few Greek clerics, accepting his authority. Five days later a religious service was held, attended by all the Council and partly sung in Greek, at which the Creed was recited with the addition. It was remarked that at the crucial moment the Metropolitan of Nicaea firmly closed his lips.[1]

Michael himself remained loyal to the Union of Lyons, even though he could not force it upon his Church and even though it was useless in stopping Charles's activities, which were only thwarted by the long and expensive diplomatic intrigue ending in the massacre of the Sicilian Vespers. His secretary Acropolita was a genuine convert to the Roman Church. But the tract explaining his conversion has not survived; it was destroyed by order of the Emperor Andronicus II. He had apparently been won over by a Franciscan monk of Greek origin, John Parastron, whose gentle charm made him well liked at Constantinople. Parastron was probably also responsible for the conversion of a man of finer intellect, John Veccus, who was to be the first pro-Unionist Patriarch of Constantinople. Veccus wrote several tracts to prove that the Greek Fathers, including Athanasius, Chrysostom and the Cappadocians, when they said: 'through the Son' really meant: 'from the Son'. His arguments were ably put; but he chose to interpret οὐσία as being the exact equivalent of the Latin *essentia*, and he blandly ignored the many texts, particularly in

[1] C. J. Hefele, *Histoire des Conciles* (trans. H. Leclercq), VI, I, pp. 153 ff.; D. Geanakoplos, *Emperor Michael Palaeologus and the West*, pp. 263 ff.

the Cappadocians' works, which were clearly opposed to his thesis.[1]

Amongst his opponents was a professor, George of Cyprus, who became Patriarch in 1283 as Gregory II. Gregory, though he disliked the Union of Lyons, genuinely sought for a formula which might satisfy Latin objections to the Greek doctrine by stressing the eternal relationship between the Son and the Holy Spirit. His attempts pleased no one. They were denounced by the Arsenites and their patron, Athanasius, Patriarch of Alexandria, by John Cheilas, who was both anti-Arsenite and anti-Latin, and by John Veccus, who pointed out that it depended on a senseless distinction between 'existing' and 'having existence'. Gregory's more extreme views were put forward in a book written by one of his disciples, a monk called Mark. The book is now lost, and Gregory himself repudiated it later. But the Council of 1285, held to abrogate the Union of Lyons and considered by later Greeks as being of almost Oecumenical authority, endorsed a *tomus* drafted by Gregory, which spoke of an 'eternal manifestation' of the Spirit by the Son; and went on to repeat Theophylact of Bulgaria's comparison of the Trinity to the sun, its rays and its light, which also suggests an eternal relationship.[2]

Veccus's pro-Latin views were supported by his friends, Constantine of Melitene and George Metochites, both of whom wrote tracts echoing his interpretation of the Greek Fathers. The historian George Pachymer, who disapproved of the Union of Lyons, tried to show in a treatise that the formula 'from the Father through the Son' did not exclude the Son from having some not clearly defined part in the procession. Like Gregory II, he was attacked from both sides for his pains.[3]

In the course of the fourteenth century the whole argument moved to a different plane. The political advantages of union

---

[1] Jugie, *op. cit.* I, pp. 418–21; K. M. Setton, 'The Byzantine background to the Italian Renaissance', *Proceedings of the American Philosophical Society*, c, 1 (1956), pp. 36–7.

[2] Jugie, *op. cit.* I, pp. 429–31.   [3] Jugie, *op. cit.* I, pp. 421–3.

were enhanced by the growing Turkish menace. The memories of the Latin Empire were losing some of their bitterness with the passage of the years; and Michael VIII's persecution of his opponents was gradually forgotten except in monastic circles. The presence of increasing numbers of Italian merchants in the Empire, though it aroused jealousy and resentment, at the same time created closer intellectual contacts. The discovery of Greek philosophy by the West, though it was mainly due to Arab intermediaries, led Italians who had some personal knowledge of Byzantium to realize what stores of ancient learning Byzantium contained and to take an interest in the cultural life of the Greeks among whom they lived. The Byzantines on their side began to discover that the Italians were no longer barbarians. Many Italians learnt to read Greek and began to visit and to correspond with Greek scholars. A few Byzantines began to study Latin literature. A turning-point was reached when a young scholar, Demetrius Cydones, learnt Latin from a Spanish Dominican friar living at Pera, the Genoese colony just across the Golden Horn, and then set himself the task of rendering into Greek the works of Thomas Aquinas. His translations were circulated among Byzantine intellectuals; and many of them were attracted by so complete a philosophical interpretation of Christian doctrine. Thomism is based on the Latin view of the Trinity. It emphasizes the unity of the Substance at the expense of the separateness of the Persons. Many Greeks hesitated to abandon the traditional Eastern outlook; and the translation of terms still caused problems. But intellectual circles in Constantinople were readier now to try to understand the Latin attitude.[1]

On the other hand this coincided with a movement within the Greek Church which developed and gave precision to the Greek attitude. Gregory Palamas's doctrine of the Divine Energies not only provided the dogmatic basis to the Greek view of mysticism.[2] It was also a restatement of the traditional interpretation of the Greek Fathers' theory of God's relation to man. It came to be

---

[1] Setton, *op. cit.* pp. 53–5.   [2] For Palamism, see below, pp. 145–54.

accepted by a series of fourteenth-century Councils as the official doctrine of the Greek Church. To Western theologians it seemed to be clear heresy. It could not be reconciled with Thomism, which many Greeks were beginning to regard with sympathy. This led many of the anti-Palamite intellectuals in Byzantium to come out openly in favour of union with Rome. Some of them, such as Manuel Chrysoloras, retired to Italy to make their careers there as lecturers, while Demetrius Cydones himself, after deeply involving himself in anti-Palamite controversy, ended his life as a member of the Roman Church in a monastery in the Venetian colony of Crete. Other unionists remained to fight for their cause at Constantinople.[1]

The Byzantines in favour of union always insisted that it could only be achieved if the doctrinal issues were discussed at a Council that could rank as Oecumenical. They also hoped that such a Council could be held in Byzantine territory, as otherwise the Easterners would certainly be outnumbered and subjected to political pressure. The failure of the union accepted at Lyons was held to be due to the inadequacy of the Greek delegation and the fact that they were operating so far from home. The Calabrian Greek Barlaam, whom we shall meet over the Palamite controversy, sent a well-thought-out memorandum along those lines to Pope Benedict XII in 1339. The Emperor John Cantacuzenus wrote a similar suggestion to Rome in 1350. But the Papacy was doubtful. In Roman eyes the Council of Lyons had been an Oecumenical Council, whose decisions should be binding. It would be wrong, in theory and in practice, to reopen the question. Moreover a Council held in Byzantine territory would in its turn put the Western delegation at a disadvantage. They might be outnumbered and be faced with majority decisions that they could not accept.[2]

The Emperor John V Palaeologus, son of a Latin mother and

[1] Setton, *op. cit.* p. 57; G. Mercati, *Notizie di Procoro e Demetrio Cidone, Manuele Caleca e Teodoro Meliteniota*, pp. 441–50.
[2] Setton, *op. cit.* pp. 28 ff.; Geanakoplos, *Byzantine East and Latin West*, pp. 90–2.

himself sympathetic to the West, in the first flush of his triumph over the usurping Cantacuzeni, opened direct negotiations with the Papacy. In 1355 he wrote to Innocent VI to say that, if the Pope would send him five galleys, 1,000 foot-soldiers and 500 horsemen, he would guarantee to convert all his subjects within six months. He offered to send his second son, Manuel, to be educated at the Papal Court, and offered to promise to abdicate in Manuel's favour should he not achieve union.[1] But the Pope had no troops to send. The dispatch of his blessing and a Papal legate was not the same thing. John V wrote again to say that under the circumstances he could not overcome the opposition to union among his people. But a few years later, in 1369, he himself journeyed to Rome, encouraged by his cousin Amadeus of Savoy, the 'Green Knight', to believe that his own conversion would produce military help. At Rome he publicly submitted himself to the Pope. But not one of his clerics would accompany him on the journey, and none of his officials followed his example; and he refused to put pressure on them. He seems to have expected, in vain, that the Pope would at least now agree to a Council at Constantinople. Meanwhile his Patriarch, Philotheus Coccinus, wrote anxious letters to the Orthodox throughout the East, warning them of the dangers of union.[2]

The Papacy was soon to be in no position to organize military help or even to negotiate on union. The Great Schism of the West began in 1378. But the Schism had the result that the Western Church itself began to feel the need for an Oecumenical Council and to review the Pope's relationship to such a Council; for if a Council was to end the Schism its authority must be superior to that of any of the rival Popes. If a Council were to be summoned, then the Greeks could and should take part in it. The Greeks were wooed, and were ready to be wooed if the supremacy of a Council was to be admitted. The Emperor Manuel, who succeeded to John V in 1390, was, however, cautious. He was himself a trained

---

[1] F. Dölger, *Regesten der Kaiserurkunden des oströmischen Reiches*, v, pp. 42–3.
[2] O. Halécki, *Un Empereur de Byzance à Rome*, pp. 335 ff.

theologian who personally disagreed with Latin theology. His advice, given in old age to his son John VIII, was not to break off negotiations over union but not to commit himself to it; Latin pride and Greek obstinacy would prevent it from ever being genuine, he thought.[1] He was not anti-Western. He encouraged the study of Western culture at Constantinople, and himself spent several years in the West, seeking for allies among its lay potentates, and, incidentally, debating on theology with the professors at the Sorbonne, for whose benefit he wrote a treatise refuting the Latin doctrine on the Holy Spirit. He was invited to send representatives to the Councils of Pisa and Constance. His unionist friend, Manuel Chrysoloras, with two noblemen from the Peloponnese, attended the latter Council as observers on his behalf. Chrysoloras, who made such a good impression on the assembled Fathers that they considered him a possible candidate for the Papacy, unfortunately died just as the sessions were beginning. But a Byzantine embassy, composed of diplomats, arrived at the Council of Constance and there interviewed the newly elected Pope, Martin V. We do not know what proposals they brought with them; but they were friendly enough for the Pope to name a delegation to go to Constantinople to arrange for what was called in the West the 'reduction of the Greeks'.[2]

Negotiations dragged on, held up partly by the Pope's difficulties with the leaders of the Conciliar movement and partly by the uneasy situation in the East. At one moment it seemed that a Council might take place at Constantinople; but the Turkish siege of the city in 1422 made it clear that it was no place for an international congress. Manuel II retired from active politics in 1423 and died two years later. His son, John VIII, was convinced that the salvation of the Empire depended upon union and tried to press for a Council; but he was unwilling at first to allow it to take place in Italy; while the Papacy still had problems to settle in the West. Delays continued. It was not till the beginning of 1438

[1] G. Phrantzes, *Chronicon* (ed. I. Bekker, C.S.H.B. edition), p. 178.
[2] Gill, *op. cit.* pp. 17–30, 46 ff.

that plans were completed and the Emperor arrived with his delegation at a Council recently opened at Ferrara and transferred to Florence in January 1439.[1]

We are fortunate in having full records of the debates at Florence; but their reading leaves one with a curious sense of unreality. The Latin delegates to the Council were a formidable team, all of them trained philosophers well read in the works of the Fathers. There were three learned Dominicans, the Greek-born Andrew Chrysoberges, Archbishop of Rhodes, John of Montenero, Provincial of Lombardy, and the formidable John Torquemada. They were led by Cardinal Cesarini; and in the background was the Pope himself, Eugenius IV, to see that their efforts were co-ordinated. It was less easy for the Emperor John to produce a first-class delegation to accompany him to Italy. Many of his bishops refused to attend, and those that came inherited the Eastern view, dear to the individualistic nature of the Greeks, that all bishops had an equal right to air their views. There was little team-spirit about them; and the Emperor remarked more than once that his best theologians were laymen. In fact the three most active delegates had been monks, consecrated as bishops only on the eve of the Council. These were Bessarion of Trebizond, Metropolitan of Nicaea, Mark Eugenicus, Metropolitan of Ephesus, and Isidore, Metropolitan of Kiev and All Russia. They were accompanied by the Patriarch Joseph II, a gentle, frail old man with no great mental powers, the illegitimate son of a Bulgarian Tsar and a Greek lady. The remaining Greek prelates who attended were even more mediocre. Of the lay delegates, besides the Emperor himself and his brother Demetrius, the most distinguished were four philosophers, all called George: George Scholarius, George Amiroutzes, George of Trebizond and the aged and eccentric neo-Platonist, George Gemistus Plethon. On the Emperor's insistence the Patriarchs of Alexandria, Antioch and Jerusalem nominated delegates to represent them from amongst the attending clerics; but they made it clear that

[1] Gill, *op. cit.* pp. 85 ff.

they would not necessarily be bound by what those representatives might decide. The Georgian Church sent a bishop and a layman.

George Scholarius, who at the time favoured union, though he changed his mind later, freely admitted that his compatriots were no match for the Latins in erudition and dialectic skill. Moreover, they disagreed with each other; and their task was not made easier by the Emperor. Despite his anxiety not to damage the dignity of his Imperial majesty or his Church, he was determined to achieve union. He was a shrewd enough theologian to see that there were issues on which agreement would be impossible. These were fundamental issues, the whole theory of the hypostases of the Trinity, and the particular doctrine of the Energies of God, approved by the whole Eastern Church and denounced as heresy by the West. He forbade his delegation to touch on them. When towards the end of the Council the Latins raised the question of the Energies, the Greeks had to reply with embarrassment that they were unable to discuss it. It is hard to see how a Council which shirked the main matters of discord could hope to achieve concord.

The issues that were allowed to be discussed were four: the procession of the Holy Ghost, the bread in the Sacrament and other liturgical differences, the doctrine of Purgatory and the position of the Pope. Matters such as the marriage of clergy and divorce were left to be settled later. It was agreed that the basis of discussion should be reference to the Holy Scriptures, the canons of the Oecumenical Councils and the works of those of the Fathers who were recognized as saints by the Universal Church. After some pressure the Greeks were induced to accept that the Latin Fathers were of equal standing with the Greek. This at once put them at a disadvantage, as they were very little acquainted with the Latin Fathers. To an objective observer the bandying of texts, however holy, hardly seems to be a satisfactory means for arriving at eternal truths. Moreover the teachings of the Fathers were often inconsistent and the canons of the Councils often deliberately vague and their Greek and Latin versions often completely different. The whole question of translation added difficulties. Of the issues discussed that of Purgatory caused the least trouble. The Greek Church held no definite dogma about Purgatory; and though Mark Eugenicus prepared a statement which opposed the Latin dogma he admitted that his views were purely personal. The Greeks in general held that the souls of the dead did not reach their final destination until the Last Judgment, but that it was not for us to know what happened to them between death and the Judgment. They had no specific objection to the Latin doctrine and were prepared to allow it, though they thought it oversure and they disliked the phrase in the Latin formula that 'the blessed see God', as it missed the distinction between His substance and His energies; but they did not press the point.

The ritual points, after some argument, were settled by compromise. The Latins agreed that the Greek use of the *zeon* was permissible. It was decided that the bread at the Eucharist might be leavened or unleavened, neither practice being wrong. The Greeks could continue to employ the Epiklesis, but they were required to admit that it was unnecessary, as it was the Dominical words that changed the elements. Many of the Greeks felt that they had been tricked, as the Emperor presented them with this decision as a *fait accompli*. They anyhow felt that over this, as over the permission to use unleavened bread, the Holy Spirit was being insulted.

It was the procession of the Holy Spirit that caused most trouble. Discussions on it took up more time than anything else at the Council; and its definition took up more space than anything else in the final Act of Union. Innumerable texts were brought up and disputed. Here the problem of translation was particularly acute. The Greeks at first rightly would not accept that ὑπόστασις and πρόσωπον should both be rendered as *persona*. Their yielding on this point weakened their arguments. The Latins later agreed to translate ὑπόστασις as *subsistentia*; but that made little difference. The crucial word αἰτία was translated by the Latins as *causa*.

Principium, which would have been closer in meaning, was equated with ἀρχή. These renderings led to genuine misunderstanding. The Latin argument was that the addition to the Creed was purely explanatory. They pointed out that the Second Oecumenical Council had made just such an addition to the Creed agreed at Nicaea. They then showed that not only the Latin Fathers but a number of Greek Fathers upheld the doctrine; and the saints must agree among themselves. The official Greek doctrine of the procession 'through the Son' must therefore mean the same as 'from the Son'. The texts which they quoted from Gregory of Nyssa, Athanasius, John Chrysostom and Symeon Metaphrastes seemed to support the Latin contention, but only because the Latins did not admit the distinction made by the Greeks between the οὐσία and the ὑποστάσεις in the Trinity; and they ignored texts from Basil and Gregory of Nazianzus and others which might have shown that, regrettably, the saints have not always agreed. They did however quote two texts, one from Epiphanius and one from Basil, which seemed definitely and fully to support the Dual Procession. Indeed, Epiphanius's words admit of no other interpretation, though Basil's were vaguer and, if compared with other of his statements, can be interpreted differently. Mark Eugenicus, supporting the extreme Greek view, claimed that the texts had been falsified, but he could not prove his case. Further, having accepted the sanctity of the Latin Fathers, he was obliged to suggest that their works too had been tampered with. Indeed, the very inconsistency of the Fathers could be used to support the Latin view; it suggested that they did not draw a nice distinction between 'through' and 'from'.

Indeed, in the arguments the Latins had the best of it. Bessarion, who was the most learned of the Greek prelates, allowed himself to be convinced by them, quite sincerely, though his desire for union was mainly from a desire to integrate Byzantine with Western culture. Isidore of Kiev followed his lead, as did the lay philosophers, with the exception of Plethon who had attended very few of the meetings, preferring to spend his time in Florence giving lectures on Plato to enthusiastic audiences. The old Patriarch Joseph wished for union and was prepared to admit that 'through' and 'from' meant the same thing. But he died before the Council was ended. George Scholarius scornfully remarked afterwards that after muddling his prepositions there was nothing left for the old man to do but die; but Scholarius himself at the time was ready to accept the Latin argument that, as the Persons of the Trinity were of the same substance, it did not matter whether one said 'through' or 'from' the Son, so long as it was clear that only one principle was involved. Only Mark of Ephesus continued to hold out. But, hampered by restrictions imposed by the Emperor, by difficulties of translation and ignorance of Latin and by his deep respect for the apophatic traditions of his Church, he proved an ineffectual debater.

The fundamental question of the Pope's supremacy was passed over rather quickly. If the Pope's claim to be the supreme doctrinal as well as disciplinary authority were admitted, then his views on doctrine should prevail without further argument. But even the Latins were shy of going so far, as it would logically have made the summoning of a Council superfluous; and the Conciliar movement was still strong in the West. Moreover they wished to prove by argument that their theology was correct. The Greeks were forbidden to bring up the question whether the Pope had any right to add to the Creed. The Latins demanded that the Pope should have full disciplinary powers over the whole Church and that as regards doctrine he should have the right on his sole authority to summon a Council to deal with doctrine and to bind the whole Church to its findings. The Emperor found this point hard to accept, as it was traditionally for an Emperor to summon an Oecumenical Council. He fought so hard for his right that in the end the question of the summoning of a Council was left vague. The Greeks tried in vain to have some mention made of the rights and privileges of the Eastern Patriarchates. The ultimate formula left much unsaid. It attributed to the Bishop of Rome full power to rule and govern the whole Church and all

Christians, 'as the acts of the Oecumenical Councils and the Holy Canons have laid down'. The Greeks protested at the word 'all' but had in the end to accept it. The word translated here as 'as' was a little equivocal. There is reason to believe that the original Latin text used the words *quemadmodum et*, 'as far as', but they were later changed to *quemadmodum etiam*, 'just as'. The Greek text says 'καθ᾽ ὃν τρόπον', 'according to the manner that', which can be regarded as a limitative clause or not, as the reader chooses.[1]

In the end, weary of it all, longing to get home and, it was said, deliberately kept short of food and comforts, the whole Greek delegation, under orders from the Emperor and in obedience to the concordat of their Church with John V, signed the decree of union, with the exception of Mark Eugenicus and, it seems, of Plethon, who disliked the Latin Church rather more than he disliked the Greek. Mark was threatened with deposition; and, after retiring for a while to his see of Ephesus, in Turkish territory, he submitted to pressure and abdicated.[2]

He was treated as a martyr by almost the whole body of the Greek Church. The Emperor soon found that it was easier to sign the union than to implement it. He remained personally loyal to it, but, influenced by his aged mother, he refrained from trying to force it on his people. He found it hard to persuade anyone to take the empty Patriarchal chair. Metrophanes II, whom he appointed in May 1440, died soon afterwards. His successor, Gregory Mammas, who was a sincere advocate of union, found it prudent to retire to Italy in 1451. Bessarion, liked and admired though he was personally, had already moved to Italy, shocked at the hostility that his actions had aroused at Constantinople and believing that he could best serve the Greek cause by remaining

---

[1] For the fullest account of the Council see Gill, *op. cit.* pp. 115 ff. See also Geanakoplos, *Byzantine East and Latin West*, pp. 88–109; G. Zonas, Περὶ τὴν Ἅλωσιν τῆς Κωνσταντινουπόλεως, pp. 9–70.

[2] Syropoulos, *op. cit.* p. 284. The lay delegates seem not to have been required to sign the union but to make statements supporting it, and Plethon managed somehow to avoid making a statement. The Georgian bishop left Florence early, to avoid signing the union decree.

among the Italians. Isidore of Kiev's adherence to union was angrily repudiated by the Russian Prince, Church and people, who deprived him of his see. He too went to Italy. The Eastern Patriarchs announced that they were not bound by anything that their representatives had signed and rejected the union. George Scholarius, though he had accepted the union and was devoted to the works of Thomas Aquinas, was soon convinced by Mark Eugenicus that he had been wrong. He retired into a monastery; and on Mark's death in 1444 he emerged as leader of the anti-unionist party. The lesser clergy and the monks followed him almost to a man.

The Emperor John VIII died weary and disillusioned in 1448. His brother and heir Constantine XI considered himself bound by the union; but he did not try to press it on his people till the very eve of the final Turkish siege. In the autumn of 1452 Isidore of Kiev, now a Roman cardinal, arrived at Constantinople with the union decree, which was solemnly read out in the Cathedral of Saint Sophia on 12 December. Isidore, who was anxious that everything should go smoothly, reported that it was well received. But his Italian assistant, Leonard of Chios, Archbishop of Mitylene, wrote angrily that few people were present and many officials boycotted the ceremony. Certainly, though during the last few months of the Empire's existence Saint Sophia was served by Latin and by a handful of unionist clergy, its altars were almost deserted. The vast majority of the clergy and the congregations of the city would have nothing to do with them.[1]

Had the Papacy been able to follow up union with effective material help, it is possible that the Byzantine populace would have accepted it. As it was, when Isidore arrived with a hundred soldiers there was at once a movement in his favour, though it faded away when it was seen that that was the full extent of Papal aid. A few officials at the court and a few scholars remained faithful to the union; and there were others who were prepared to condone it till the crisis should be over, so long as there was a

---

[1] Gill, *op. cit.* pp. 349 ff.; Runciman, *Fall of Constantinople*, pp. 18–21, 62–4, 68–72.

chance that then a new Council could be held, this time at Constantinople. The Emperor's chief minister, Lucas Notaras, seems
to have been of this view; but the intransigence of the Latin
clergy, led by Leonard of Chios, dashed any hopes that he might
have had and forced from him the bitter comment that he would
sooner see the Sultan's turban than the Cardinal's hat.[1]

It was in this atmosphere of unhappy controversy that the
Turkish siege of the city began. Only on the last night of the city's
freedom was there any union when clergy and congregation,
whatever they might feel about it, came together for a final
liturgy in Saint Sophia. By then it was clear to all that union had
not saved and could not save Byzantium. Whether they liked it or
not the Byzantines were to see the Sultan's turban in their midst.

---

[1] See Gill, *op. cit.* pp. 375–6, where Notaras's attitude is justly brought out.
Notaras's famous remark is reported by Ducas, *Historia Turco-Byzantina* (ed.
V. Grecu), p. 329.

CHAPTER 5

THE CHURCH AND THE PHILOSOPHERS

The chief strength of Western medieval civilization, at least in its ideal form, lay in its integration under the Church. It was the Church that had kept alive education and learning through the Dark Ages. It was the Church that continued to provide and organize schools and universities; and it was to the service of the Church that men of education dedicated their learning. Philosophy became the handmaiden of religion; and by its encouragement of philosophy the Church was able to develop its own theology and maintain its hold over intellectual life.

This integration was missing from the Byzantine world. There the tradition of lay education had never died out. It was the State rather than the Church which was responsible for providing educational facilities and which organized the great University of Constantinople. The leading scholars and philosophers were for the most part laymen or men who had taken orders long after their education was completed. Many even of the most celebrated theologians remained laymen all through their lives. In contrast to the West the lawyers tended to be laymen, operating in secular courts. The sphere of canon law was far smaller in the East; and even the canon lawyers were seldom members of the clergy. This inevitably led to a certain suspicion in clerical circles of lay learning and of philosophy, a fear that these lay philosophers might be lured by their admiration of ancient thought into overstepping the bounds of orthodoxy and carrying innocent disciples with them. The ecclesiastical organization as a body never disapproved of erudition and the use of the intellect. Public opinion in Byzantium had far too deep a respect for education and for the achievements of the mind, and there were far too many churchmen who were themselves highly cultured for religious obscurantism ever to triumph. The great fourteenth-century mystic, Nicholas Caba-

The Church and the Philosophers

silas, himself a layman, declared roundly that a priest who had received a secular education was far more valuable than one without secular learning.[1] Even Gregory Palamas, the theologian of mysticism, who thought that the true religious should lay aside his secular learning, was proud of his Aristotelian training, which enabled him to think clearly, though he feared that too eager a study of Aristotle might lead an unwary student to exaggerate the power of the intellect; and he himself was glad that he had not been tempted to delve into Platonism, as that was so attractive a philosophy that it often lured the unwary into paganism.[2]

There had, nevertheless, always been Byzantines who were suspicious of secular learning, including laymen such as the tenth-century author of the *Philopatris* who considered Platonism highly dangerous, or the rough soldier Cecaumenus in the early eleventh century, who maintained that knowledge of the Bible and a training in elementary logic were all that a boy needed.[3] Later in the eleventh century Psellus ran into difficulties and his pupil John Italus was dismissed from the university for teaching Platonic doctrines.[4] But that was at a period when the hierarchy was jealous of the university. Later hierarchs, right up to 1453, showed no such opposition. The enemies of secular learning were then to be found among the monks, especially those of the Arsenite and the later Church Zealot party; and their hostility was directed not so much against education as such, as against the wealth and worldliness of the cultured hierarchy. They also resented the control that the secular authorities wielded over higher education.

A child's education normally began at home, if the family

[1] For Cabasilas, see B. Tatakis, *La Philosophie Byzantine*, pp. 277–81.
[2] See J. Meyendorff, *A Study of Gregory Palamas* (trans. G. Lawrence), pp. 28–30, 129–32.
[3] *Philopatris* (C.S.H.B. edition), pp. 337 ff.; Cecaumenus, *Strategicon* (ed. B. Vassilievsky and V. Jernstedt), pp. 46, 75.
[4] For Psellus see Tatakis, *op. cit.* pp. 161 ff. For Italus, *ibid.* pp. 210–16, and A. Buckler, *Anna Comnena*, pp. 319–24.

could afford a private tutor. The tutor was often a monk, who would provide basic religious instruction together with the elements of the *trivium* and the *quadrivium*. This involved, first, Grammar, which meant reading, writing, grammar and syntax and a study of the classical authors, especially Homer, and occupied the child roughly from the ages of six to fourteen. He then moved on to study Rhetoric, the study of pronunciation and composition and of authors such as Demosthenes and Thucydides, and Philosophy, which at this stage meant a study of Aristotelian methodology. Close on their heels came the four Liberal Arts, Arithmetic, Geometry, Music and Astronomy. At this stage the pupil would probably be attending a school run either by some lay scholar or by some monastery. The *trivium* and the *quadrivium* completed the ἐγκύκλιος παιδεία, which constituted the general basic education which every Byzantine was supposed to possess. So far the lay and the monastic schools worked in concert, though the latter probably placed a greater emphasis on Biblical studies. For his higher studies, Law, Medicine, Physics and higher Philosophy, which included the study of the Platonic and other philosophical systems, he went to the university, unless he was already destined for the Church. In that case he was probably already studying at the Patriarchal Academy, which seems to have taken boys at a fairly early age and kept them on to do their specialist studies in Theology.[1]

This was the general pattern throughout the Byzantine period, though there were times when the university was in a decline or had completely faded out, as under the later Iconoclastic Emperors or in the reign of Basil II. At such times higher education was carried on by individual professors and even by the Patriarchal Academy. It is remarkable that the only occasions on which the high ecclesiastical authorities tried to curb the philosophers teaching at the university were when the university was in a

---

[1] For a summary of the educational course see L. Bréhier, *Le Monde Byzantin*, III, pp. 474–6: Buckler, *op. cit.* pp. 165 ff. For the Patriarchal Academy see Bréhier, *op. cit.* III, pp. 492–7.

The Church and the Philosophers

flourishing condition, in the mid-ninth and later eleventh centuries. At other times the Church schools appear to have been perfectly enlightened. We even find an early eleventh-century archbishop, John Mavropus of Euchaita, writing poems in praise of Plato.[1]

Higher education was entirely reorganized under the Emperor Andronicus II, inspired by his learned Grand Logothete, Theodore Metochites. The old disciplines were revived, each with a professor at its head, but under the supreme authority of the Grand Logothete. The professors' salaries were, as before, paid by the State; but, as an innovation, the parents of students were now charged a small fee to supplement them. There seems to have been no central university building; professors taught in various parts of the city, some of them, such as the grammarian Maximus Planudes, using monastic buildings.[2] It is probable that private schools, such as that founded by Nicephorus Gregoras in a building attached to the monastery of the Chora, were in some way connected with the university. They could be closed on the orders of the Grand Logothete; this was the fate of Gregoras's school.[3] The Patriarchal Academy had been reorganized a little earlier, under Michael VIII. It seems at this time to have covered much the same ground of instruction as the university, though always with a greater insistence on theology. About the year 1400 the Emperor Manuel II gave the university its final form. The office of Grand Logothete had declined; and higher education was placed under one of the four judges-general. Under John VIII the judge-general who held this post was George Scholarius, who was also a member of the Senate, an Imperial secretary and the professor of philosophy. The university was now called the *Catholicon Museion*; and Manuel concentrated its buildings in one

[1] Johannes Mauropus, *Poemata*, *M.P.G.*, cxx, col. 1156.
[2] F. Fuchs, *Die Höheren Schulen von Konstantinopel im Mittelalter*, pp. 56ff; Bréhier, *op. cit.* III, pp. 482–4.
[3] R. Guilland, *Essai sur Nicéphore Grégoras*, pp. 13–15. George Scholarius opened a private school in about 1420. It was closed when he became judge-general. Fuchs, *op. cit.* pp. 70–1.

place, round the monastery of Saint John the Baptist in Petra, where there was an excellent library which was placed at the disposal of the students. This move was doubtless made possible by the fact that the number of students had declined in proportion to the decline in the population of the city. About the same time Manuel moved the Patriarchal Academy to buildings round the monastery of Saint John the Baptist in Studion, where also there was a good library, and placed it under the Studite monk, Joseph Bryennius. The two institutions seem to have co-operated and even to have shared professors. Joseph Bryennius, who was head of the Patriarchal Academy and its professor of scriptural exegesis, seems also to have given lectures on philosophy at the university as well as at the academy. The two institutions commanded great respect even in Italy; and many Italians came to study at them. It was there, at one or other of them, that the last generation of Byzantine intellectuals was educated. Bessarion and George Scholarius both attended courses at the university, while Mark Eugenicus studied at the academy.[1] However, the most famous school of the time was not situated in Constantinople but at Mistra, in the Peloponnese, where George Gemistus Plethon taught his own brand of Neo-Platonism, far away from the eyes of the Church hierarchy, which could not well condone such frank leanings towards paganism. Both Bessarion and George Scholarius went on from Constantinople to sit at his feet.[2]

The Church was thus in partnership with the State in the field of education; and on the whole the partnership ran smoothly. There was certainly an element of anti-intellectualism amongst the followers of the Arsenite school and the religious Zealots; but though their attitude might sway public opinion on particular issues it never succeeded in damaging the general Byzantine respect for education. Gregory Palamas, indeed, disapproved of monks indulging in higher intellectual studies; but he had no desire to suppress them. He merely considered that, like marriage

[1] Fuchs, *op. cit.* pp. 70–5.
[2] For Plethon's school, see Tatakis, *op. cit.* pp. 281–93.

and the eating of meat, they were unsuitable for anyone who aimed to lead the contemplative life. His view was by no means accepted by all the mystics. As we have seen, his friend and admirer Nicholas Cabasilas felt differently, as did his patron, the highly cultured Emperor John VI Cantacuzenus. Moreover he himself would never have been able to express his views so effectively had he not been well trained in logic and in Aristotelian methodology.[1]

Trouble only occurred when the philosophers began to meddle in theology. The apophatic tradition was very strong in Byzantium. Its accepted theologians based their attitude on the consciousness that God is unknowable. They fought shy, wherever possible, of dogmatic definitions, unless a basic doctrine were involved; when they would fight passionately over the correct wording. There had been no attempt to systematize theology since John of Damascus had published his great work on the Faith; and he had left much unsaid. The prudent philosophers kept away from theological controversies. The father of fourteenth-century learning in Byzantium, Theodore Metochites, Grand Logothete under the pious Emperor Andronicus II, was interested in every branch of the humanities and sciences. He did not claim to be an original thinker; for, he said, the great thinkers of the past had covered everything and had left nothing for us to add. This was far too often the Byzantine attitude. But in fact Metochites modifies it by providing in his commentaries reflections derived from his own experience. He recommends his pupils to read all the ancient philosophers, including the Sceptics; for, he remarks, all human wisdom that is based on experience can be challenged by arguments based on contrary experience. The study of history, which he warmly advocates, shows how varied human experience can be. But, though his recommendations could lead to heterodoxy in the eyes of the Church, he carefully reserves his interest in philosophy to matters of human experience. When he touches upon theology he is apophatic. He recognizes the limits of the

---

[1] See Meyendorff, *A Study of Gregory Palamas*, pp. 129–32.

human intellect and believes it to be impossible for human judgment, unless inspired by Grace, to be impartial and free from error. He quotes with approval Plato's verdict that it is difficult to conceive of God and impossible to put such a conception into words intelligible to others.[1]

Metochites's most celebrated pupil, Nicephorus Gregoras, was not so cautious. He shared his master's wide range of interests; but, as we shall see, he let himself be involved in theological discussions, and thus ruined his career.[2] A little later we find Demetrius Cydones making his translations from Thomas Aquinas and introducing to Byzantium the conceptions of Scholasticism. There were Byzantine scholars who were attracted by so remarkable a blending of philosophy with theology, even though it was opposed to the long tradition of their Church. Most of them, such as Cydones himself and his pupil Manuel Chrysoloras, found themselves in the end more comfortable in the bosom of the Roman Church. But, so long as they avoided active controversy, they were never in any way penalized by the Byzantine Church authorities. The troubles that beset Cydones's career were political, not religious, in origin.[3] The Emperor Manuel II and his learned contemporary, Joseph Bryennius, though both of them disagreed with Latin theology, encouraged Latin studies.[4] George Scholarius, who was to be the fiercest enemy to union with Rome, was an ardent admirer of Aquinas all his life. In his later years he was, indeed, somewhat embarrassed in trying to reconcile his taste for scholasticism with the traditional theology of his Church.[5] His opponent Bessarion, on the other hand, was a Platonist by temperament and training, to whom the full paraphernalia of Scholasticism were not particularly attractive. But, out of respect for Italian scholarship and in the interests of cultural unity, he was ready to be convinced by Roman theology. His conversion to

---

[1] Tatakis, *op. cit.* pp. 249–56.
[2] See below, pp. 144–5.   [3] See above, pp. 100–1.
[4] M. Jugie, *Theologia Dogmatica Christianorum Orientalium ab Ecclesia Catholica Dissidentium*, I, pp. 451–4.
[5] *Ibid.* pp. 459–69; Tatakis, *op. cit.* p. 298.

Rome was of great value to the West; for his influence helped to free the Roman Church from its scholastic bonds.[1]

It is true that the most distinguished Greek philosopher of the time, George Gemistus Plethon, perhaps the most original thinker that Byzantium produced, would have fallen foul of the Church had he not established himself away in the provincial capital of Mistra, under the enlightened patronage of the cultured Despots of the Morea.[2] He represented a new movement connected with the appearance, a generation before his time, of the word 'Hellene' to describe a citizen of Byzantium. The word had been in disgrace for a thousand years. After the Triumph of the Cross it had been used to denote a pagan Greek, particularly in law-codes and commentaries. It was only as regards language that it was permissible. The average Byzantine, just as he called himself a Roman, called the language that he spoke 'Romaic'. But in polite society 'Romaic' was employed to describe the vulgar language of the people. A man of education was expected, as Anna Comnena says, to 'hellenize' his tongue. The Council of 1082 which condemned the Neo-Platonist John Italus pronounced that Hellenic studies formed a valuable part of education but anathematized anyone who held Hellenic doctrines. For a man to call himself a Hellene was as if he denied himself to be a Christian. Suddenly in the fourteenth century Byzantine intellectuals began to speak of themselves as Hellenes. The fashion seems to have started not in the oecumenical city of Constantinople but in Thessalonica. The humanist mystic, Nicholas Cabasilas, writing as a young man in about 1345 to his father at Thessalonica, hesitates to send him one of his sermons for fear that the style might shock 'your Hellenes' —τοὺς ἐν ὑμῖν Ἕλληνας. In later works he refers to 'this community of Hellas'. The Cypriot Lepenthrenus, writing in about 1351 to Nicephorus Gregoras, talks of 'all the Hellenes here', and, when comparing Syria with Byzantium, adds 'or everywhere

---

[1] Jugie, *op. cit.* I, pp. 483–6; Tatakis, *op. cit.* pp. 299–301. On Bessarion in general see L. Mohler, *Kardinal Bessarion als Theologe, Humanist und Staatsmann.*

[2] See above, p. 116, n. 2, and below, pp. 121–5.

where Hellenes dwell'. Demetrius Cydones in his later works uses Hellas as the equivalent of Byzantium. Gregoras himself still contrasts 'Hellene' with 'Orthodox', but writes with admiration of Hellas. By the fifteenth century most Byzantine intellectuals alluded to themselves as Hellenes. John Argyropoulus even calls the Emperor 'Emperor of the Hellenes' and describes the last wars of Byzantium as a struggle for the freedom of Hellas. We have moved far from the days when a Western ambassador who arrived with letters addressed to the 'Emperor of the Greeks' was barely received at court.[1]

There were various reasons for the new attitude. The Empire had shrunk by now to lands that were traditionally Greek, the Peloponnese, a few Aegean islands and coastlands early colonized by the Greeks. Much of the Greek-speaking world was under alien domination; and the Emperor, though still the legal heir of the Caesars, was no longer a supra-national potentate. The old term for the Empire, the Oecumene, had become absurd, and the epithet 'Roman' was hardly appropriate when New Rome was dying and Old Rome reviving in majesty. Moreover, the renewed interest in Classical culture involved a reassessment of Classical authors. They were admired more than ever, and they were Hellenes. They were especially admired in Italy; and Byzantine scholars, whether or not they favoured union with the West, found that it added to their prestige and the prestige of their people if they emphasized their descent from the venerated Greeks of old, whose language they spoke and whose works they had never ceased from studying. As Hellenes they were guardians of a precious heritage, whether or not they wished to share it with the Western world.

The traditionalists found it hard to accept the new term. To them it meant an abandonment of the Oecumenical idea, if the Emperor were no longer to be Roman Emperor. As the Patriarch Antony wrote in his letter to the Grand Prince of Moscow, 'even

[1] See S. Runciman, 'Byzantine and Hellene in the fourteenth century', Τόμος Κωνσταντίνου 'Αρμενοπούλου.

though the heathen now encircle the government and the residence of the Emperor, he is still anointed with the holy myrrh and appointed Emperor and Autocrat of the Romans, that is, of all Christians'.[1] That proud boast, placing the Emperor above all other earthly potentates, would be empty if he were merely the monarch of the Hellenes. Still more, to the pious among them it seemed to give too great a sanction to pagan philosophy. They could not forget the older meaning of the word. Even George Scholarius, humanist though he was, and though he himself often spoke of his compatriots as Hellenes, when he was asked, on the eve of the fall of the Empire, what was his nationality replied: 'I do not call myself a Hellene because I do not believe as the Hellenes believed. I might call myself a Byzantine because I was born at Byzantium. But I prefer simply to call myself a Christian.'[2] His was the voice of tradition. Was it out of date? As a practical concept the Oecumenical Christian Empire had long since become unreal. Was Orthodoxy also to give up its oecumenicity? was it to survive merely as the guardian of Hellenism?

It was George Gemistus Plethon who was the greatest advocate of Hellenism. He was born in Constantinople about the year 1360. As a young man he spent time at Adrianople, then the capital of the Sultan. There he learnt something, or so he claimed, about Islam and about Judaism and Zoroastrianism as well. Back in Constantinople he soon began to air his Neo-Platonic views, giving himself the surname of Plethon, a synonym of Gemistus, because of its resemblance to the name of the ancient philosopher. This caused offence in many quarters; and Manuel II advised him to retire from the capital. Soon after 1400 he established himself at Mistra, where he enjoyed the friendship of the young Despot of the Morea, Manuel's second son, Theodore, a somewhat neurotic intellectual, and of Theodore's charming Italian wife, Cleope Malatesta. He remained there till his death in about 1450, only

[1] See above, p. 71.
[2] Georgius Scholarius Gennadius, 'Contre les Juifs', in *Œuvres Complètes*, III, 252.

emerging to attend the Councils of Ferrara and Florence. Mistra suited him. The Peloponnese had recently been almost entirely reconquered from the Franks and represented now the one solid piece of Byzantine territory. It was consciously Greek in sentiment. To Plethon it seemed that it was on the Peloponnese, the Despotate of the Morea, that the reformed Empire that he passionately desired could best be based. He had little use for Constantinople, 'New Rome'. 'We are Hellenes by race and culture', he wrote.

He outlined his proposals for reform in memoranda addressed to the Emperor Manuel. He advocated a monarchy, the monarch being advised by a council, not too small, of his best-educated subjects. Otherwise his constitutional programme copied that of Plato; and like Plato he approved of slavery, at least of helots to work on the land. He gave what he considered to be practical advice about the nationalization of land, the recruitment and organization of the army, reform of the coinage, control of trade and penal reform. But he realized that religion was all-important. As a theologian Plethon was frankly Platonist. He owed much to the eleventh-century Neo-Platonist Psellus, though Psellus succeeded in refuting the charge of heresy. He owed much, too, to the Alexandrian Neo-Platonists and to the Pythagoreans and the Stoics; and he envisaged Moses and Zoroaster as having been among Plato's spiritual ancestors. His main venom was directed against Aristotle.

According to Plethon Christianity had gone wrong because Christian theology had accepted Aristotle's principle that generation according to cause involves generation according to time. Aristotle was a physicist, not a philosopher; his God was not a metaphysical principle but a hypothesis introduced to account for the setting in motion of the cosmic machine and for the generation and corruption of temporal things. If the Christians see God not as the First Mover but as a creator *ex nihilo*, then either the essence of things must be considered to be contained in God's essence and so to lack any ontological roots, which seems to make God's essential nature plural; or one must take the Scholastic view that forms subsist only in their sensible objects, a view which, to Plethon, led straight to materialism and atheism, whatever reservations might be made about divine revelation. By confusing a physical principle with a metaphysical principle Christian theologians were now obliged to fall back upon either subtle Trinitarian distinctions within God or distinctions between essence and energy. Plethon demanded a return to the full metaphysical tradition, the tradition inherited and transmitted by Plato. As he rejected revelation he sought to find authority first in 'common consent', 'the doctrines and words of the wisest men of antiquity' and, above that, the reason. He had no use for apophatic theology. Reason in itself is able to investigate the divine; why else did God give it to us and with it the desire to study His nature? 'Divine things', he remarks, 'do not contain anything evil which would oblige God to conceal them from us.' Plethon's practical object was the rebirth of Greece. But the political order must be rooted in the intellectual order. For there to be order everything must be produced by a cause; and from that it follows that the supreme principle must act in a determined way. God cannot have created the world at a historic moment, nor can He intervene in time with new decisions. Plethon's God is the creator of the eternal essences, the Ideas of perishable things. He Himself is beyond all essence or Idea. 'In the superessential One, since He is absolutely one, we cannot distinguish essence nor attribute nor energy nor power.' From this One emanates the *Nous*, the eternal and unchangeable principle of the intellectual world, after the pattern of which the sensible world is made. In the world of the *Nous* essence may be distinguished from attributes but not energy from power. The *Nous* produces the Soul of the world in which essence, power and energy can be distinguished. This Platonized Trinity manifests itself in gradually descending degrees, through the intelligibles of the ideal world, which are angels or minor deities, then through immaterial substances and finally through bodily things. If we can grasp the nature of this κόσμος νοητός, then we have, so to speak, the blue-print for the κόσμος πολιτικός, the government which will regenerate Hellas.

Plethon cannot be called a Christian; and he further offended Christian taste by frequently referring to God as Zeus and talking of 'the Gods' in the plural. But his book *On the Laws*, in which he aired his theological views, was never in general circulation; and his contemporaries did not for the most part realize how heterodox he had become. Had he remained in Constantinople he would doubtless have provoked action against himself. As it was, he was allowed to run his Platonic Academy at Mistra without hindrance, and many pious young scholars sat at his feet. When he went to the Council of Florence many of his fellow-delegates professed to be shocked by his conversation. The Aristotelian George of Trebizond accused him of advocating an entirely new and entirely pagan religion. He himself disapproved of the Council, which seemed to him to be a case of bargaining about spiritual things in order to secure material advantages. He seems to have had no sympathy with either side in the controversies, though of the two he slightly preferred the Eastern viewpoint. But he acquired an enormous reputation in Italy. Manuel Chrysoloras, who had been one of his pupils, had already been giving successful lectures on Plato at Florence. The coming of the Master himself and the lectures that he himself gave made a profound impression. It was in his honour that Cosimo de' Medici founded the Platonic Academy at Florence. He was, in fact, the real originator of Platonic studies in the West. Some years after he had died and had been buried in a church at Mistra, the Italian soldier of fortune, Sigismondo Malatesta, who was in temporary occupation of the town, removed his remains and transported them to a church in Rimini, where they are to this day.[1]

In Byzantium his fate was different. Soon after his death and soon after the fall of Constantinople the Despot Demetrius of the

[1] See above, p. 109 and n. 2; also F. Masai, *Plethon et le Platonisme de Mistra*, *passim*; M. V. Anastos, 'Pletho's Calendar and Liturgy', *Dumbarton Oaks Papers*, IV (1948), pp. 183 ff.; Tatakis, *op. cit.* pp. 281–94.

Morea discovered the manuscript of *On the Laws* and sent it to Constantinople, to George Scholarius, who was now Patriarch. George, who had been his pupil and his friend, read it with growing fascination and growing horror, and eventually ordered it to be burnt. Considering the temper of the times, when the Greeks had little left but their faith, we cannot wholly blame him. In consequence only such fragments of the work as were published elsewhere survive. They are sufficiently daring to explain the Patriarch's horror. We cannot tell what further outrages were contained in the pages that perished.[1]

Plethon thus had little effect on the immediate course of Greek thought; though his spirit survived and reappeared three centuries later, among thinkers who equally sought to revive Greece by an appeal to the Classical past and who equally caused embarrassment to the Church.

George Scholarius himself did not strike all his contemporaries as being fully Orthodox. Though he inherited from Mark Eugenicus the leadership of the anti-Unionist party, he remained an admirer of Aquinas and disagreed with Mark on many theological points. Mark had been of the school of Nicholas Cabasilas, a humanist Palamite, with a loyalty to the apophatic tradition which rendered him ineffective at the debates at Florence. Had he never attended the Council he would probably have been as irenical as his contemporary Symeon, the beloved Metropolitan of Thessalonica, whose death even the Jewish community mourned sincerely, and whose theology was close to his own. As it was, his failure at Florence made him bitter and fanatical against Rome.[2] He persuaded Scholarius to change his mind over union. Scholarius began, like Plethon, to see the union as an unworthy bargain for material benefits, which were anyhow unlikely to be effective; and he began to believe that steadfastness in the faith would preserve Byzantium far better than political aid. An enforced union would merely weaken and confuse the spiritual life

---

[1] See Plethon, *Traité des Lois*, ed. C. Alexandre, app. xix, pp. 412–21.

[2] Tatakis, *op. cit.* pp. 295–7.

of the Greek people, which alone could ensure their salvation. Antichrist might be coming. It was more essential than ever to keep the faith unsullied. He therefore recanted and accepted the traditional Orthodox view of the Trinity. But though he followed Mark so far he disagreed with him on other things. He would not accept the full Palamite doctrine of the Energies but evolved a compromise which he considered, not very accurately, to follow the views of Duns Scotus and therefore to be acceptable to the West. He rejected Palamas's distinction between essence and energies or operations. The latter, he says, are formally finite but really infinite because they have the same existence as essence, which is infinite. This nice contrast between formality and reality pleased no one else. The Orthodox Church continued to follow the unadulterated Palamite doctrine. His other disagreement with Mark concerned determinism. Mark drew a distinction between prescience and predestination in God. The first is absolute, the second relative. Only good actions are predetermined as well as foreknown by God because they conform with His will. Mark follows Cabasilas in maintaining that only the righteous man is truly free because his will is God's will. Scholarius answered that prescience precedes predestination, and predestination must be subdivided into true predestination, which concerns the elect, and reprobation, or the withdrawal of grace, which concerns the rest. Created beings are free to act, and the initiative for good or evil comes from the created will. But good actions are performed by the grace of God, and the grace is withdrawn concurrently with an evil action. In this controversy Scholarius rather than Mark represents the general view of the Orthodox Church, in so far as its attitude towards predestination was subsequently defined.[1]

It was only after 1453 that Scholarius wrote his final treatise on predestination. But the controversy was typical of the liveliness of intellectual life during the last centuries of Byzantium and of the complicated cross-currents, personal, political, philosophical and theological, in which the disputants were caught. It is impossible

[1] See below, pp. 280-1.

to draw a clear line between the Church and the philosophers. It is impossible to say that the humanists favoured union with the West and the anti-intellectuals opposed it. In the Palamite controversy, as we shall see, many humanists supported Palamas along with the anti-intellectual party within the Church. In the civil wars between John V Palaeologus and John VI Cantacuzenus the latter had the support of the monks and the country nobility as well as that of most of the leading intellectuals. The question of union with Rome cut across party lines. Palamas himself was far better disposed towards Rome than was his opponent Nicephorus Gregoras, whose theology on that point was far nearer to the Roman. Manuel II and Joseph Bryennius were keen students of Western culture though both opposed union. In the final struggle over union the Platonist pupil of Plethon, Bessarion, longed for union, while the Aristotelian Scholastic George Scholarius led the opposition. The debates were passionate and bitter; but they followed no pattern.

Many of the issues were ephemeral. Only two were of lasting importance. The one was the question of union with Rome and all that that entailed. The other was concerned with the whole theology of mysticism and is connected with the name of Gregory Palamas.

CHAPTER 6

THE THEOLOGY OF MYSTICISM

The drifting apart of the Eastern and Western branches of Christendom is clearly marked in their respective attitudes towards mysticism. Since the later middle ages the Church in the West, with its superb organization and its taste for philosophical systems, has always been a little suspicious of its mystics. The career of a Master Eckhart or of a Saint Teresa of Avila shows the alarm felt by the ecclesiastical authorities for men and women who took a personal short-cut in their relations with God. Care was needed to see that the mystic's experiences were genuinely Christian and did not lead outside of the proper bounds of doctrine. In the Eastern tradition theology and mysticism were held to be complementary. Outside of the Church personal religious experience would have no meaning; but the Church depended for its very life on the experience granted in varying degrees to each one of the faithful. This is not to say that dogma is unnecessary. Dogma is the interpretation of the revelation that God has chosen to give us. But, within the framework thus provided, each man and woman can work out his or her own way towards the ultimate end which transcends all theology and which is union with God. 'God became Man that men might become Gods.'[1]

In this aspiration the East outdistanced the West. It has been said with some truth that in the West the mystic seeks to know God and in the East he seeks to be God.[2] It is largely a question of semantics. Eastern mystics often speak of 'knowing God'. But to them the knowledge involves participation. The aspiration of Teresa (of Avila or of Lisieux) to be the bride of Christ is a little

[1] For the best account of the Eastern mystical outlook see V. Lossky, *Mystical Theology of the Eastern Church*, esp. pp. 7–22. See also P. Sherrard, *The Greek East and Latin West*, pp. 31–4.
[2] Aldous Huxley, *Grey Eminence* (1st edition), p. 52.

shocking to the Orthodox, to whom the Church is the only bride of Christ. The Eastern mystic must entirely lose his personality. It was therefore harder for him than it was for the later Western mystics to recount his experiences. Deification, 'becoming God', can never be adequately described in human terms.

But deification raises theological problems. On the one hand there is the tradition of apophatic theology. God from His nature cannot be known. If His essence could be understood He would be brought down to the level of His creatures. Man would become God by nature. On the other hand owing to the Incarnation God has revealed Himself in Jesus Christ in a revelation that is total, establishing between God and man an intimacy and a unity that is complete, so that men can become, in Peter's words, 'partakers of the Divine nature', θείας κοινωνοὶ φύσεως.[1] Orthodox theology thrives on such antinomies which the theologians prefer to leave as antinomies. But the moment sometimes comes when the unwritten tradition is challenged and the antinomy must be resolved.

To the Fathers of the Greek Church, as to Augustine in the West, apophatic theology was fundamental. It alone could rid human beings of the concepts proper to human thought and could raise them step by step to the point from which it might be possible to contemplate a changeless reality which the created intelligence cannot contain. It was not a theology of ecstasy nor was it an intellectual quest for abstractions. As with the Neo-Platonists it involved a catharsis, an inward purification. But, while the Neo-Platonists sought an intellectual catharsis, to rid the mind of multiplicity, to the Orthodox the catharsis should be a complete renunciation of the realm of created things, an existential liberation. The mind must learn to refuse to form concepts about God. It must reject all intellectual and abstract theology and all attempts to adapt the mysteries of God to human ways of thought. According to Gregory of Nazianzus, anyone who imagines that he has come to know what God is has a 'depraved

[1] II Peter i. 4.

spirit'. It is only by entering into the Divine Darkness, the Cloud of Unknowing, that man can hope to penetrate into the Light. In one of his mystical poems Gregory tries to describe how he succeeded in escaping from the things of the world and by heavenly contemplation was carried into the secret darkness of the heavenly tabernacle to be blinded by the Light of the Trinity, a light that surpasses all that the mind can conceive.[1]

Apophatic theology inevitably encourages a renunciation of the world. It can easily lead to so great an exaltation of the life of contemplation over the life of action that the latter is regarded as being undesirable; and from there it is only a short step into dualist heresy, into a disowning of material things and into a belief that they are therefore the creation of the Devil or the Demiurge. The Fathers were well aware of the danger. While extolling the mystical life they insisted at the same time on the fact of the Incarnation. By sending the Son into the world the unknowable God became communicable to His creation. They sternly opposed any doctrine which seemed to deny to God the Son His complete humanity. By the Incarnation the body of a man, as well as his soul, was capable of becoming a receptacle for grace. There was nothing wrong in leading an active life in the world, so long as it was led according to Christ's precepts and so long as the active man kept himself perpetually refreshed by partaking of the Holy Sacrament. Men and women who had received grace by baptism and renewed it by participation in the Mysteries and who lived godly lives would in the end attain blessedness and deification. But, all the same, it was a higher thing to aim at deification before the grave. To medieval man, in the West as in the East, there was a permanent attraction away from the sordid world of everyday life into the life of contemplation; but, while in the West the ecclesiastical authorities tried to keep some check over contemplatives, in the East the memories of the desert were stronger. It is true that vast numbers of monks and nuns in Byzantium had led active lives before their retirement. It is true that the monk in the

---

[1] Gregory Nazianzene, *Poemata*, M.P.G., xxxvii, coll. 748, 984-5.

literal sense of the word, the 'solitary', was not encouraged; the Fathers thought that some sort of community life was best and that the contemplative hermit should have his cell attached to some monastery to which he could go to take part in the Liturgy. It is true that many monks moved in the world as welfare workers, and others were scholars and others farmers. But the mystic ranked above them all.

The way to deification was through prayer. The anchorites of the desert had given up even preaching, teaching and good works, and even regular participation in the Mysteries, in order to concentrate upon prayer. These early Christian mystics held that only by prayer would they realize the fruits of baptism and penetrate into the Light of God.

Their doctrine was first codified by Evagrius of Pontus in the fourth century. Prayer, he said, was the conversation of the intellect with God. It involved a complete catharsis; we must pray first for the gift of tears, that is to say, for true repentance, and for escape from the passions, then from ignorance and then from all temptations and distractions. The state of prayer is an impassive state which by the strength of love can carry the intellect high above all intellectual peaks into the realm of wisdom. 'Do not think', he wrote, 'of the divinity in you when you pray nor let your intellect have the impression of any form. You must go as immaterial into the immaterial, and you will understand.' Evagrius gave the mystics their vocabulary. It was a Neo-Platonic vocabulary; for that was the existing language of religious thought. But Evagrius himself was a trifle too Neo-Platonic. He seemed to ignore the Incarnation and to accept the Neo-Platonic concept of the intellect and to see prayer as a disincarnation of the intellect and its movement into its proper activity. His works were condemned after his death and passed out of circulation. But his language lasted on.[1]

[1] I. Hausherr, 'La Traité de l'Oraison d'Evagre le Pontique', *Revue d'ascétique et de mystique*, XV (1934), pp. 34–93, 162–70; J. Meyendorff, *A Study of Gregory Palamas*, trans. G. Lawrence, pp. 135–6.

It was to check the Neo-Platonic slant which Evagrius had inherited from Origen that mystical writers began to advocate that
prayer should consist only of the Prayer of Jesus. In its original
form this consisted simply of the words *Kyrie eleison*, repeated
again and again. The next great mystical writer, usually known
as Macarius, though he was certainly not the historical Saint
Macarius, held that prayer should be only a repetition of the
word *God, Lord* or *Jesus*. Macarius was rather nearer to the Stoics
than to the Neo-Platonists. He believed that owing to the Incarnation man as an entire being could enter into contact with God.
The heart, he said, was the focal point of the body and the seat of
the intelligence and of the soul. When grace entered into a man it
dwelt in his heart and so dominated the body as well as the mind
and soul. It is not therefore as a disembodied soul or intellect that
we reach out to God. Macarius has been accused of being allied to
the heretical sect of Messalians or Euchites, the Praying People,
who believed that by ardently repeating the Lord's Prayer they
could enter into union with the Holy Spirit and see or be God.
The accusation is unjust; for the Messalian creed was based on a
dualist conception of matter, which was considered to be the
creation of an evil power, though it might be sanctified. Macarius's
firm belief in the Incarnation implies an orthodox view about the
Creation; but he did, like the Messalians, give a somewhat
materialistic slant to the ultimate contact with God. Henceforward the taunt of Messalianism was periodically to be raised
against the Greek monastic tradition.[1]

This tradition was carried on, later in the fifth century, by
Diadochus of Photice, who combined the Christocentric doctrine
of Macarius with the cathartic practices of Evagrius. To quote a
typical sentence of his, he says: 'The intellect demands of us
absolutely that we close all its outlets by the memory of God, an
activity which should satisfy its need for activity. It is therefore
necessary to give it the Lord Jesus as the sole occupation which

---

[1] Meyendorff, *A Study of Gregory Palamas*, pp. 137–8; Lossky, *op. cit.* pp. 68,
115–16.

fully answers this aim.'[1] Still more influential in the tradition was John Climacus, who as a boy entered the newly founded monastery of Saint Catherine on Mount Sinai in the middle of the sixth century and eventually became its abbot. He owes his surname to his book, the Ladder, or Climax, of Perfection. His monastery, at the foot of the mountain on which Moses saw the sight of the Lord like devouring fire, had been from its foundation a centre for monastic mysticism, where hesychast, or quietist, monks sought to see the Light. John spent some time as a solitary, but he considered, as his career showed, that the hesychast need not be a hermit. The hermit's task was harder because he had no brother to support and strengthen him, but his reward was greater, for if he strove he would receive the support of an angel. John's Ladder was a series of rules to guide contemplation. He recommended the Prayer of Jesus, which should be the shortest and simplest invocation of the name of the Lord. Like Evagrius he insisted that the memory of God should be without distraction. When remembering God we should not meditate upon episodes in the life of Christ; for that at once involves the creation of exterior images in the mind. God should enter into us really and existentially, without the help of the imagination. The vision of Light that is the ultimate goal is not a symbol nor a product of the imagination, but a reality, as was the fire that Moses saw on Sinai and the shining whiteness that the Apostles saw on Mount Thabor.[2]

While apophatic theology leads naturally towards ascetic mysticism, the attempts of Macarius and his disciples to avoid Neo-Platonism seem to defeat the apophatic tradition. If we believe that man in his body can see the Light of God, can God be unknowable? The Cappadocian Fathers were conscious of the problem. Gregory of Nyssa makes use of the antinomic expression 'luminous darkness' to illustrate how the Unknowable can make

---

[1] Meyendorff, *A Study of Gregory Palamas*, pp. 135–7.
[2] Lossky, *op. cit.* pp. 200, 205, 210–12; Meyendorff, *A Study of Gregory Palamas*, pp. 128, 212.

Himself known while remaining unknowable. When a man has climbed the spiritual ladder so high that he sees God, he is at once all the more aware of God's transcendence. Gregory therefore makes use of the alternative words 'energies' 'ἐνέργειαι' or 'powers' 'δυνάμεις', to describe the manifestations which make divinity accessible without destroying its inaccessibility.[1] Basil puts it in simpler terms. 'It is by His energies that we can say that we know God', he writes. 'We cannot claim that we come near to the essence itself. His energies descend to us, but His essence remains unapproachable.'[2] Rather more than a century later Maximus the Confessor says that: 'God is communicable in what He imparts to us, but He is not communicable in His essence.'[3] John of Damascus expresses the same idea when he says that: 'All that we can say positively—cataphatically—of God shows not His nature but things about His nature.' John is chary of using the word 'energies', but he talks of the 'movement' or the 'rushing forth'—'ἔξαλμα'—of God and often speaks, as do other Fathers, of the rays of divinity that penetrate into creation.[4]

There thus developed a tradition in Eastern Christendom which combined apophatic theology with the use of prayer and which resolved the paradox between the knowable and the unknowable by distinguishing between the essence and the energies or powers of God. The doctrine was not defined because it was not challenged. Many centuries later Mark Eugenicus was to defend Palamas against the charge of having introduced a novel doctrine by saying that: 'It would have been inopportune to impose the distinction in the operations of God upon those who even had difficulty in admitting the distinction in the hypostases.' In those early days, he says, it was important to insist on the simplicity of God, but 'by a wise discretion the divine teachings became clarified

---

[1] Gregory of Nyssa, *Vita Moysis*, M.P.G., xliv, coll. 297 ff.; Lossky, *op. cit.* pp. 34–5.

[2] Basil, *Epistolae*, M.P.G., xxxii, col. 869.

[3] Quoted by Euthymius Zigabenus, *Panoplia*, M.P.G., cxxx, col. 132.

[4] John of Damascus, *De Fide Orthodoxa*, M.P.G., xciv, col. 800.

in due course of time'.[1] Mark's excuses were needless; no one had felt the need to clarify the doctrine. It lasted as an unwritten tradition in the East, while Western theologians, though they studied the works of the Cappadocian Fathers, paid no attention to it. The search for the Light was carried on in the eleventh century by the monk Symeon, known as the New, or Young, Theologian. He was perhaps the greatest of the Byzantine mystics and one of the few who attempted to describe mystical experience. For a time the ecclesiastical authorities viewed him with some suspicion; he seemed too independently personal. Though he made no particular contribution to doctrine, the burning sincerity of his writings had an enormous influence. He stressed the need for self-discipline. The contemplative must purge himself by tears, that is, by true repentance, and by the active abandonment of the passions. He must seek love; for love is the link between God and man, a lasting possession, whereas even the divine illumination itself is only, so to say, a temporary experience. He was aware of the theological problem. 'Do you say', he asks, 'that there can be no vision nor knowledge of Him Who is unseen and unknowable?' and he answers: 'How can you doubt? He Himself, Who is above all being and before all time and uncreated, became incarnate and appeared to me and miraculously deified me whom He received. If God, Who, as you believe, was made man, adopted me, a human being, and deified me, then I, a god by adoption, perceive Him Who is God by nature.' In many images he seeks to express the climax of Christian experience, communion with the incommunicable, made possible through the incarnation of the Logos. The end of experience is Light, not, he says, in the likeness of fire which can be perceived by the senses, but Light which is eternal, the splendour and glory of everlasting happiness, the Light that transforms into light those whom it illumines, the Light that is uncreated and unseen, without beginning and with-

[1] M. Jugie, 'Palamas', *Dictionnaire de théologie catholique*, XI, coll. 1759 ff., quoting Canon Oxoniensis.

out matter, but that is the quality of the grace by which God makes Himself known.[1]

Symeon's example was keenly followed on Mount Athos. In the monasteries of the Holy Mountain monks sought continually to experience the Light. In the course of their search they learnt the value of physical exercises. This was an old tradition. John Climacus had recommended breathing exercises. The memory of Jesus, he said, should be united to the breath; and he was not speaking in symbols. By the breath the spirit enters into the body and by control of the breath the body can be controlled. We are close here to the psycho-physiological tradition of the further East, the *yoga* of the Hindus and the *dhikr* of the Muslims. It may be that influences from such Eastern sources penetrated into Byzantine monasticism. The great traditional home of monastic meditation was the monastery of Sinai, which from its geographical situation was in intimate touch with the Muslim world; and Muslim mysticism probably received influences through Persia from India. There was also a more direct route to Byzantium through Anatolia. The greatest of Persian mystics, Jelal ad-Din ar-Rumi, came in the thirteenth century to Konya, the ancient Iconium, where he wrote and taught and founded his sect of the Mevlevis, the Whirling Dervishes, who by the gyrations of the dance reach a state of ecstasy. Attitudes suitable for contemplation as well as breathing exercises were known to the Muslim Sufis. It is likely that there was an informal and unwritten interchange of practices between Christian and Muslim mystics. There was however a difference. The Indian and, to a lesser extent, the Muslim mystic sought to induce a state of auto-hypnosis in which he could become the passive recipient of divinity. The Byzantine teachers were anxious to maintain that such exercises were not an end in themselves but an unessential though helpful discipline.[2]

The first teacher in Byzantium to advocate them in his writings

[1] Symeon the New Theologian, *Divinorum Amorum Liber*, M.P.G., CX, coll. 592–3. See Lossky, *op. cit.* pp. 218 ff.

[2] See Meyendorff, *A Study of Gregory Palamas*, pp. 139–40.

was a late thirteenth-century monk known as Nicephorus the Hesychast. He was Italian by birth, probably a Calabrian Greek, and came to Constantinople under Michael VIII, whose policy of union he fiercely opposed. He therefore retired to Athos, where he issued a short book called *On Sobriety and the Guardianship of the Heart*. It is a somewhat careless compilation of quotations from the Fathers, with an appendix recommending certain physical exercises as helping to induce concentration and banish distraction. He preferred that aspiring mystics should follow the counsels of a spiritual adviser; but, if there was none at hand, there were physical movements and attitudes which would assist them. He considered that body, soul and spirit formed a unity and that every psychical activity had a somatic repercussion. He suggested that the repetition of the Holy Name should be combined with rhythmical breathing. He maintained, in perhaps dangerously simple language, that thus the Holy Spirit could enter through the nostrils into the heart.[1] Another treatise of which he may have been the author, but which later ages wrongly attributed to Symeon the New Theologian, described the proper attitude for prayer. The mystic was to sit alone in a corner of his cell and to bend forward, turning his eyes towards the centre of his body, in the region of the navel, and search for the place of his heart. There was nothing really new in this. Breathing exercises had certainly been practised for centuries, and the bent, seated attitude for concentrated prayer goes back to the earliest times.[2] Elijah on Mount Carmel, when he prayed for rain, 'cast himself down upon the earth and put his face between his knees'.[3] A miniature in a twelfth-century manuscript of John Climacus shows a monk praying in a similar posture, though his eyes are closed and not looking inward.[4] Doctrinally there was no essential difference

---

[1] Nicephorus the Hesychast, *De Sobrietate*, M.P.G., CXLVII, coll. 945–66. For him see G. Palamas, *Défense des saints hésychastes* (ed. and trans. J. Meyendorff), I, pp. 331–3.

[2] This treatise, called *The Method of Holy Attention*, is edited by Hausherr in *Orientalia Christiana Periodica*, IX, 2 (1927).

[3] I Kings xviii. 42.

[4] MS of John Climacus, Vatican, Graec. 1754.

between such attitudes and the raising of the hands in prayer or the regulated movements in the Liturgy or in the ceremonies of the Sacred Palace. But in the hands of ignorant monks the exercises could take on a disproportionate importance.

By the end of the thirteenth century there was a strong wave of mysticism flooding Byzantine religious life. The mystics were to be found most of all in the cells on Mount Athos; but there were ecclesiastics, such as the Patriarch Athanasius I and Theoleptus, Metropolitan of Philadelphia, who felt that contemplation, helped by physical exercises conducted in moderation, could be practised without isolation from the world. Athanasius, who was an eager and stern reformer of monastic life, held that contemplation could well be fitted in with the active good works and regular liturgical practices of a monastery.[1] Even laymen were affected by the movement. Gregory Palamas's biographer tells us how once his father, Constantius Palamas, was attending a meeting of the Senate; but, when suddenly asked a question by the Emperor Andronicus II, he was too deeply absorbed in spiritual contemplation to pay any attention to the Imperial inquiry. So far from being annoyed, the pious Emperor only respected him the more highly.[2] Other Byzantines, however, found this attitude somewhat exaggerated. While the Empire was falling to pieces far too many of its citizens seemed only to be concerned with their own souls. For it happened that the growing interest in mysticism coincided with a renewed interest in Byzantium in the application of philosophy to religion, an interest that was stimulated and encouraged by Cydones's translations of the works of Thomas Aquinas. Many of the philosophers longed to escape from the limitations of apophatic theology and follow the West down a more cataphatic path. A clash was inevitable.

The clash actually came half-accidentally. Among the many Calabrians in Constantinople was a philosopher called Barlaam,

---

[1] See J. Meyendorff, *Saint Grégoire Palamas et la Mystique Orthodoxe*, p. 140, and his preface to Palamas, *Défense*, pp. xxxix–xli.
[2] Philotheus, *Encomium Gregorae Palamae*, M.P.G., CLI, col. 553.

who had been educated in Italy. He arrived in the capital in about the year 1330 and soon acquired a reputation as a mathematician and an astronomer and a logician. John Cantacuzenus, who was then Grand Domestic, greatly admired him and gave him a chair of philosophy at the university. He became a devoted member of the Orthodox Church. He was appointed a spokesman for the Greeks against two Dominican fathers who came to Constantinople in 1333-4. In 1339 he led an embassy to Avignon, to Pope Benedict XII, to whom he explained clearly and sensibly why the Greeks in general were opposed to union. He seemed to be an admirable servant of Orthodoxy. Unfortunately he had his own ideas. It has been suggested that in his youth in the West he had studied the works of William of Occam. Certainly he had been affected by the same intellectual atmosphere. He attacked the Latin Church along the lines of Occam's nominalist attack on Thomism; and he combined the attack with a devotion to apophatic theology, derived from the study of the works of the Areopagite, on which he had given a series of lectures. He particularly disliked Thomism. 'Thomas', he said, 'and those who follow his reasoning believe that nothing can exist that is inaccessible to the intelligence. But we believe that such an opinion can only be held by a soul affected by a proud and malicious demon; for nearly every divine thing lies beyond human knowledge.' The Latins, he maintained, were guilty of presumptuous pride when they declared that the Holy Spirit descended from the Father and the Son. As God was unknowable, how could they profess to know such a thing? But Barlaam carried his apophatic tastes almost too far. He implied that the Greeks were almost as bad in saying that the Holy Spirit descended from the Father only; but at least they were supported by the Creed as laid down by the Oecumenical Councils.

As a result Barlaam began to find himself unappreciated by the Greeks whom he championed. He offended the philosophers, such as Nicephorus Gregoras, who, in a public debate, was able to show flaws in his knowledge of Aristotle; while to the orthodox theologians his views seemed to make no allowance for the Incarnation and to lead straight to agnosticism. As has been said, he fled from the intellectual realism of the Scholastics in the West to come up against the mystical realism of the monks in the East.[1]

The monk who made it his business to point out Barlaam's errors was Gregory Palamas. He was born in 1296, the son of the noble who meditated during meetings of the Senate, and received a good basic education under Theodore Metochites at the university. But his father died while he was still young; and, instead of pursuing secular studies further, he decided, under the influence of Theoleptus of Philadelphia, to enter the monastic life and persuaded his whole family to follow him. At about the age of twenty he went with his brothers to Mount Athos, eventually attaching himself to the Grand Lavra there. After nearly ten years on the Mountain he planned to visit the Holy Land and Mount Sinai. The voyage proved not to be practicable. He spent some time at Thessalonica, where he was ordained a priest, then organized a community of hermits near Berrhoea in Macedonia. Serbian invasions disrupted the hermits' life; and in about 1331 he returned to Athos, settling in a cell known as Saint Sabbas, not far from the Grand Lavra, to which he would repair weekly to partake of the Sacraments. For a few months in 1335–6 he was abbot of the monastery of Esphigmenou; but the monks there resented his stern discipline, and he returned gladly to his hermitage.[2] Soon afterwards Barlaam's writings came into his hands, sent to him by a disciple of his called Akyndinus. He was shocked by them and wrote a series of letters both to Barlaam and to Akyndinus, courteously pointing out his objections.[3]

---

[1] For Barlaam's career and philosophy see his own writings in *M.P.G.*, CLI, coll. 1239–342; B. Tatakis, *La Philosophie Byzantine*, pp. 263–6; Meyendorff, *Saint Grégoire Palamas*, pp. 42–4; M. Jugie, *Theologia Dogmatica Christianorum Orientalium ab Ecclesia Catholica Dissidentium*, I, pp. 470–3; K. M. Setton, 'The Byzantine Background to the Italian Renaissance', *Proceedings of the American Philosophical Society*, C, I, pp. 40–1. Meyendorff, *op. cit.* p. 90, for his words about Thomas Aquinas.

[2] Meyendorff, *Saint Grégoire Palamas*, pp. 28–41.   [3] *Ibid.* p. 44.

Akyndinus replied in a mediatory spirit; but Barlaam was furious. 'I will humiliate that man', he declared.[1] He decided to attack the hesychast teaching which Palamas represented and went to Thessalonica, where he began to move in hesychast circles. His acquaintances were somewhat ignorant monks who followed the injunctions of Nicephorus the Hesychast and other such teachers without any real understanding of their teaching. With obvious relish Barlaam issued a number of treatises showing up the absurdity of the practices which he had witnessed in their company. 'They have informed me', he wrote, 'of miraculous separations and reunions of the spirit and the soul, of the traffic which demons have with the soul, of the difference between red lights and white lights, of the entry and departure of the intelligence through the nostrils with the breath, of the shields that gather together round the navel, and finally of the union of Our Lord with the soul, which takes place in the full and sensible certitude of the heart within the navel.' He said that they claimed to see the divine essence with bodily eyes, which was sheer Messalianism. When he asked them about the light which they saw, they told him that it was neither of the superessential Essence nor an angelic essence nor the Spirit itself, but that the spirit contemplated it as another hypostasis. 'I must confess', he commented, 'that I do not know what this light is. I only know that it does not exist.'[2]

The attack was effective. In the hands of ignorant monks such as he had encountered, the psycho-physical teaching of the Hesychasts could produce dangerous and ridiculous results. Many of the Byzantine intellectuals who had disliked Barlaam's exaggeratedly apophatic teaching welcomed an exposure of doctrines that seemed to be even more shockingly anti-intellectual. The attack moreover appealed to the sardonic humour of the Byzantines. The Hesychasts were given the nickname of Omphaloscopoi, the navel-gazers; and the nickname has stuck to them and has coloured the tone of most subsequent Western writing about the

[1] *Ibid.* p. 45.   [2] Quoted by Palamas, *Défense*, II, pp. 401-3.

Byzantine mystics.[1] But Barlaam himself gained little advantage out of his venom. The intellectuals might cheer him at first but they still mistrusted him; and Byzantine opinion in general respected mysticism even when it did not understand it. Moreover in Palamas Barlaam found an opponent far more profound than himself.

Palamas replied to the attack in a great work called *Triads for the Defence of the Holy Hesychasts*, and composed a summary of it which was signed by representatives of all the monasteries on the Holy Mountain and forwarded to Constantinople.[2] John Cantacuzenus, much as he had admired Barlaam, was impressed by the opinion of the Holy Mountain.[3] The Patriarch John Calecas was less enthusiastic and sought to avoid a controversy, but he was overruled. Late in 1340 Palamas and a party of Athonite monks arrived in Constantinople; and early the next year a council was held at which Barlaam's doctrines were attacked from all sides and condemned, and the Palamite manifesto was accepted as embodying Orthodox doctrine. After making one more attempt to renew his attack Barlaam saw that he was defeated and retired to Italy.[4] There he was received back into the Roman Church, presumably abandoning much of his former theology, and spent his time trying vainly to teach the poet Petrarch Greek. For this arduous task he was rewarded with the bishopric of Gerace, a see where the Greek rite was still practised. He returned to Constantinople as Papal ambassador in 1346. It was scarcely a tactful choice. His mission was a failure. He returned to Gerace, where he died in 1348.[5]

Barlaam was removed from the scene; but Palamas's troubles were not ended. His former friend and pupil Akyndinus now

[1] Barlaam's own name for the Hesychasts was *Omphaloscopoi*.
[2] Palamas, *Défense*. I use Meyendorff's edition (see Bibliography), which is the only complete edition. Other of Palamas's works are published in *M.P.G.*, CL.
[3] J. Cantacuzenus, *Historiarum Libri IV* (ed. L. Schopen, C.S.H.B. edition), I, pp. 551–2.
[4] Meyendorff, *Saint Grégoire Palamas*, pp. 50–67.
[5] For Barlaam's later career see Setton, *op. cit.* pp. 44–5. Setton is remarkably kind to Barlaam.

turned against him. Akyndinus had tried to put forward a compromise solution, demanding that old formulae should not be discussed and that the difference between essence and energy should not be emphasized. A synod in August 1341 condemned this compromise, though out of friendship Palamas saw to it that Akyndinus's name was omitted from the condemnation.[1] But Akyndinus was unrepentant and ungrateful. He returned to the attack, with the support of a number of intellectuals, led by Nicephorus Gregoras. The civil war that broke out a few months later gave him his chance. The Emperor Andronicus III had died in June 1341, leaving a son of nine, John V, to succeed him under the regency of the Empress, Anna of Savoy. John Cantacuzenus remained in power as chief minister; but in October, when Cantacuzenus was away on a campaign in Greece, a *coup d'état* gave the control of Constantinople to a rival minister, Alexius Apocaucus, and his friend, the Patriarch John Calecas. Cantacuzenus retorted by open rebellion against the new government. Palamas, who condemned the *coup d'état* but was on friendly terms with the Empress, tried to keep aloof from the contest. But the Patriarch disliked him. At first he did not dare to touch so venerated a figure; but early in 1343, urged on by Akyndinus, he arrested Palamas, putting him first under house-arrest in a monastery in the suburbs and then imprisoning him in the capital, while a packed synod in 1344 condemned his views. Akyndinus, who had been ordained by the Patriarch, was rewarded with the post of Metropolitan of Thessalonica, though, owing to the Zealot revolt there, he was never able to visit his see. In 1345 Apocaucus was murdered. Soon afterwards the Empress quarrelled with the Patriarch, deposing him on 2 February 1347. But their joint government had been so bloodthirsty and incompetent that John Cantacuzenus was able to enter Constantinople next day. He was accepted as co-Emperor and married his daughter Helena to the boy John V.[2]

---

[1] Meyendorff, *Saint Grégoire Palamas*, pp. 57–60.
[2] *Ibid.* pp. 63–80.

As the Empress's relations with the Patriarch worsened she began to show favour to Palamas, releasing him from prison when she deposed Calecas. He then acted as the mediator between her and Cantacuzenus. His triumph was now complete. He was named Metropolitan of Thessalonica in place of Akyndinus, though it was not till 1350, on the collapse of the Zealots, that he was able to settle in the city. Meanwhile a number of synods reinstated his doctrines; and in July 1351 a Council attended by representatives of all the Orthodox Churches, and therefore ranking in Orthodox eyes as Oecumenical, published a Synodal Tome approving all his views. After various local synods had confirmed the Tome, it was reproduced in a Synodicon of Orthodoxy, which was appended to the liturgical books of the Church.[1]

As Metropolitan of Thessalonica Palamas was deeply respected. His efforts to right social injustices helped to reconcile the supporters of the Zealots and to bring peace to the city. During a voyage to Constantinople in 1354 he was captured by the Turks and was obliged to spend a year in detention at the Ottoman court. He was well treated there. In the course of several frank conversations on religion with members of the Sultan's family he is reported to have expressed the hope that the time would soon come when Christians and Muslims would reach an understanding with each other.[2] He was equally well disposed towards the Latins, maintaining a friendly correspondence with the Genoese at Galata and the Grand Master of the Hospitallers at Rhodes. Indeed, Nicephorus Gregoras accused him of favouring them.[3] It was only in 1355, when a Papal Legate, Paul, Archbishop of Smyrna, arrived in Constantinople and was present at a discussion between Palamas and Gregoras, that difficulties arose. Paul, influenced perhaps by Barlaam, whom he had known in Italy, was from the

---

[1] Meyendorff, *Saint Grégoire Palamas*, pp. 86–101. Gregoras's anti-Palamite account of the Council is given in his *Historia*, ed. L. Schopen and I. Bekker (C.S.H.B. edition), II, pp. 898–978. The *Tome* of the Council is published in *M.P.G.*, CLI, coll. 721 ff. Palamas's Confession of Faith, which the Council accepted, *ibid.* coll. 763–8.

[2] Meyendorff, *Saint Grégoire Palamas*, pp. 102–7.

[3] *Ibid.* p. 81, quoting MS letter of Akyndinus.

outset hostile to Palamas and reported unfavourably on his doc-
trines to Rome; even though John Cantacuzenus, now ex-Emperor
and a monk, did his best to explain that there was nothing in
Palamite teaching that was in opposition to the traditions of the
Fathers. But Paul seems to have realized that Palamism and
Thomism were mutually exclusive. Of the discussion with
Gregoras, Gregoras's version frankly admits to omitting most of
Palamas's speeches as being unworthy of record, whereas he reproduces what he claims to have said at such length that Palamas
drily remarked that had his account been accurate the debate
would have lasted not one evening but many days and nights.
The official record, drawn up by the Protostrator George Phacrases,
is more impartial, though it omits a philological digression in which,
according to Gregoras, Palamas made some unfortunate errors.[1]

Palamas died at Thessalonica on 27 November 1359. Nine
years later he was canonized by the Patriarch of Constantinople,
his friend and disciple Philotheus Coccinus. After Demetrius, the
legendary patron of the city, he has remained to this day the best-
loved saint of the Thessalonians.[2]

The theological controversy had been embittered by the civil
war. But the religious and political parties did not coincide. John
Cantacuzenus gave his support to Palamism; but so did his
opponent Apocaucus, while Anna of Savoy remained Palamas's
friend. Nicephorus Gregoras and Demetrius Cydones were both
supporters of Cantacuzenus and both strongly anti-Palamite.
While Cantacuzenus sought for an understanding with Rome
and Cydones was to join the Roman Church, Gregoras remained
Latinophobe; and, as we have seen, it was only Paul of Smyrna's
logical mind and his dislike of Palamas that drove the Palamites
into the anti-Latin camp.[3] Palamas himself never believed that he
was an innovator. He merely sought to defend what he held to be

---

[1] Gregoras, *op. cit.* III, pp. 324 ff. See also M. Candal, 'Fuentes Palamíticas:
Diálogo de Jorge Facrasi', *Orientalia Christiana Periodica*, XVI (1950).
[2] Meyendorff, *Saint Grégoire Palamas*, pp. 111–12.
[3] *Ibid.* pp. 80–6.

the orthodox tradition; and he defended it in writing because he had been attacked in writing. It is characteristic that he entitled his main work a *Defence*. If he seems in his later works to develop his doctrine, it is because he had to meet further attacks.[1]

Barlaam's first attack had been against the Hesychasts' methods of prayer. Palamas replied by first stressing the importance of prayer. Here he was in the old Eastern tradition. Gregory of Nyssa had called prayer 'the leader in the choir of virtues'.[2] To Isaac of Nineveh, who had greatly influenced the Sinaitic school, prayer was 'the conversation with God which takes place in secret'.[3] 'The power of prayer', Palamas wrote, 'fulfils the sacrament of our union with God.'[4] In this fulfilment perfection is reached. But first there must be penitence, then purification. The need for the 'gift of tears' was fully accepted by the Orthodox. Purification was a more difficult process. It involves the abandonment of earthly passions and distractions but not of the body itself. When we speak of a man, says Palamas, we mean his body as well as his soul. When we speak of the Incarnation we mean that God the Son became man. It would be Manichaean to hold that in purifying ourselves we must try to escape from the body. According to Holy Writ man was made by God in His image. Though we cannot know exactly what that means, it certainly means that man in his entirety is the creation of God, just as man in his entirety was sullied by the Fall. In the hard task of purification we need what help we can obtain. That is the value of what Palamas and his contemporaries called 'scientific prayer'—the adjective in Greek is 'ἐπιστημονική'. As the body is not essentially evil but was created by God to be the temple of the indwelling spirit, we should use its help. Of the two methods that the Hesychasts recommended and that Barlaam criticized, Palamas first noticed the connection of prayer with the intake of breath.

[1] See above, p. 135, n. 1.
[2] Gregory of Nyssa, *De Instituto Christiano*, M.P.G., xlvi, col. 301.
[3] Isaac of Nineveh, Homily xxxv, Greek version, W. N. Theotoki, p. 229.
[4] G. Palamas, *De Hesychastis*, M.P.G., cl, col. 1117.

This can aid anyone who is praying to retain his mind within himself, in the region of the heart, which Palamas and his contemporaries held to be the centre of man. 'It is not valueless', he says, 'particularly in the case of beginners, to teach them to look into themselves and to send their minds inwards by means of breathing.' His physiological ideas may seem a little crude to us today. But there is no doubt that rhythmical breathing helps to induce contemplation. Moreover Palamas was careful not to go too far. Experience proves the method to be valuable, but its value is purely supplementary. A man should only use it until 'with God's help he has perfected himself in what is better and has learnt how to keep his mind immovably fixed within itself and distinct from all else, and so can gather it perfectly into one whole.' His attitude is similar towards the other method, which the opponents of Hesychasm called omphaloscopy. 'How should it not be helpful', he asks, 'for a man who is trying to keep his spirit within him if, instead of letting his eye wander here and there, he keeps it fixed upon his breast or on his navel as a fixed prop?' Here again he shows his belief that the heart is the centre of the entire man; it is particularly useful to gaze at the area where the heart is situated. But again he emphasizes that the discipline of prayer will come easily and without conscious thought to those who have progressed along the path. It is the beginner, to whom the path is difficult and tiring, who needs what help he can obtain.[1] Palamas was aware that there were some so foolish as to confuse the means with the end. He admits that there were simple-minded Hesychasts who fell into the error; and it was from such folk, he says, that Barlaam procured his information. Indeed, Cantacuzenus tells us that Barlaam's chief informant was a novice of six months standing, notorious for his stupidity.[2] Like Nicephorus the Hesychast, Palamas preferred that a beginner should consult a spiritual adviser, to avoid such risks. Indeed, while it is easy for us today to make fun of omphaloscopy, there is nothing heretical or unchristian in making use of physical exercises to

---

[1] Palamas, *Défense*, I, pp. 87–93.   [2] Cantacuzenus, *op. cit.* I, pp. 544–6.

induce concentration. Palamas and his disciples were following an ancient tradition that had long proved its worth. Nor is it fair to assume that the Hesychasts were substituting an easy and mechanical way of prayer for the hard way of keeping the commandments. The Hesychast Fathers took it for granted that unless the commandments were kept it was profitless to start upon the way of prayer. It was because that way was so difficult that mechanical aids could be used.

To Palamas purification was not the ultimate end. In one of his homilies he says: 'It is impossible to be united with God unless, besides purifying ourselves, we come to be outside, or, rather, above ourselves, having abandoned everything that pertains to the sensible world and having risen above all ideas and reasoning and even above all knowledge and reason itself, until we are entirely under the influence of the sense of the intellect and have reached the unknowing which is above all knowledge and every form of philosophy.' By the intellect, or understanding (αἴσθησις νοερά), he means nothing mental but the spiritual image of God in man, seated not in the brain but in the heart. That is to say, enlightenment is only achieved by bringing the mind into the heart. Then 'the intellect, purified and illumined, enters manifestly into possession of the grace of God and perceives itself...not only contemplating its own image but the clarity formed in the image by the grace of God...and this accomplishes the incomprehensible union with the Highest, through which the intellect surpasses human capacities and sees God in the spirit'. Palamas adds specifically that 'He who participates in this grace becomes himself to some extent the Light. He is united to the Light and by that Light he is made fully aware of all that remains invisible to those who have not this grace...The pure in heart see God, Who, being Light, dwells in them and reveals Himself to those that love Him.'[1]

What is this Light? The Hesychasts identified it with the light that shone on Mount Thabor. The divine reality which is manifested to the holy mystics is identical with the light that appeared

[1] Palamas, *Défense*, II, pp. 407-9, 421-3.

to the Apostles at the time of the Transfiguration. But there is a difference. 'Since the Transfiguration of the Lord on Thabor was a prelude to the visible apparition of God in glory that is yet to come, and since the apostles were thought worthy to see it with their bodily eyes, why should not those whose hearts are purified be able to contemplate with the eyes of the soul the prelude and pledge of His apparition in the spirit? But, since the Son of God, in His incomparable love for man, deigned to unite His divine hypostasis with our nature in assuming an animate body and a soul dowered with intelligence, in order to appear on earth and live among men, and since, too, He unites Himself with human hypostases themselves, mixing with each of the faithful by the Communion of His holy body, and since He thus becomes one body with us and makes of us a temple of the entire divinity "for in Him dwelleth all the fullness of the Godhead bodily", how shall He not illuminate those who communicate worthily with the divine ray of His body which is in us, giving light to their souls as He illuminated the bodies of the disciples on Thabor? At that time His body, the source of light and grace, was not yet united with our bodies. He illuminated from outside those who approached in worthiness, and sent the light to their souls through their sensible eyes. But now that He is immixed with us and exists in us, He illuminates the soul naturally within us.'[1] That is to say, Palamas believes that it is the historic fact of the Crucifixion and of Pentecost which gives reality to the Sacrament of Communion and so enables man to experience the Light without the help of an exterior miracle. But, though man's ability to see the Light is thus, so to speak, dependent upon history, the Light itself is transcendental and eternal; and no one who has not experienced it can know what it is, since it is above knowledge. Palamas compares it to the white stone in Revelation, 'and in the stone a new name written, which no man knoweth saving he that receiveth it'.[2]

---

[1] Palamas, *Défense*, I, p. 193.
[2] *Ibid.* I, p. 195, quoting Book of Revelation ii. 17.

God is Light. Therefore the Light is uncreated and everlasting, a part of God. This was a traditional view, expressed in icons of Christ in Glory by the *mandorla*, the light that rays out from Him. But to Barlaam and Akyndinus and the other opponents of Hesychasm this savoured of heresy. How can man in his body see the Light if the Light is God? It was sheer Messalianism to say that man can see the divine essence with bodily eyes. Many later theologians have assumed that Palamas and his school must have been affected by the Bogomils, with their Messalian heritage, who were still flourishing in the Balkans and had even penetrated on to the Holy Mountain.[1]

To Palamas such an attack seemed absurd. He answered that Barlaam and his supporters were themselves in danger of heresy by their definition of essence. They seemed to equate essence with God in His entirety, or at least to suggest that it is in His essence that God possesses in unity and uniquely all His powers. But God is not essence. He is, in the divine words, what He is: 'I am who I am.' He Who Is does not derive from His essence. His essence derives from Him. Palamas quotes the words of the Areopagite: 'If we name the superessential Mystery "God" or "Life" or "Essence" or "Light" or "Word", we are thinking of no more than the deifying powers which come to us.' If therefore Barlaam says that only the essence of God is a reality without beginning, he means that only the essence-making or substance-making power of God is eternal. His other powers must belong to the temporal sphere. Not only does this limit God but it implies a mental knowledge of Him Who is not only above all knowledge but also above all unknowing. Yet, owing to the Incarnation, there is a relation between us and God, a reality between creatures and the imparticipable superessentiality, and not one reality but many. These realities are the powers of that superessentiality, which, in a unique and unifying fashion, possesses eternally and takes back into itself all the multitude of participable realities. 'If', Palamas

---

[1] This accusation is made by both Akyndinus and Nicephorus Gregoras. See Meyendorff, *Saint Grégoire Palamas*, pp. 35–7; Jugie, *op. cit.* I, pp. 431 ff.

says, 'you suppress that which is between the Imparticipable and the participants, you separate us from God and destroy the link between us, creating a vast impassable abyss between God on the one side and creation and created beings on the other...We shall have to find another God if we are to participate in divine life.'[1]

According to Palamas the participable realities of God are provided by His energies. Neither the term nor the doctrine was novel; but hitherto no one had felt the need for defining it. Palamas gives a clear definition. 'Creation', says Cyril of Alexandria, 'is the task of energy.' If we deny a distinction between essence and energy there is no frontier between the Procession of the divine hypostases and the creation of the world. Both would equally be acts of the same divine nature; and the being and action of God would be identical and of the same character. We must therefore distinguish in God His nature, which is one, the three hypostases in His nature, and the uncreated energy which proceeds from and is inseparable from the nature.[2] But energy, though it is the creative force, does not exist solely for that purpose. It is an eternal attribute. The metaphor most often used by the Hesychast Fathers is based on the sun and its rays. The solar disk is compared with God in His essence and the rays of the sun to His energies. The rays cannot exist without the sun, and we cannot conceive of the sun without its rays; for they are what can penetrate to us and give us light and warmth. But the rays are as everlasting as the sun. They would emanate from it even if there was no one to perceive them. At the same time, though the energies are eternal the created world does not therefore become co-eternal. The act of creation is effected *ex nihilo*, determined by the common will of the Triune Godhead.[3]

God, inaccessible in His essence, is omnipresent in His energies, remaining invisible yet seen. Palamas likens this to the manner in

---

[1] Palamas, *Défense*, II, pp. 685–7. The passage from Dionysius the Areopagite can be found in his *De Divino Nomine*, M.P.G., CL, col. 916.

[2] Palamas, *Capita Physica*, M.P.G., CL, coll. 1189, 1220.

[3] See Lossky, *op. cit.* pp. 67–90.

which we can see our faces in a looking-glass though they are invisible to us. The energies are the uncreated and deifying grace which can become the portion of the saints in their life of union with God. We cannot comprehend the distinction between the energies and the essence, and we cannot conceive of them in separation from the Trinity, of which they are the common and eternal manifestation. They are not hypostases themselves, nor is it possible to attribute any particular energy to any one of the three Hypostases. Barlaam misquoted Palamas, declaring that he went so far as to call the energies by the name of 'lesser or down-going divinity'—'ὑφειμένη θεότης'—while the essence is called the 'greater or transcendent divinity'—'ὑπερειμένη θεότης'. Palamas himself never used the words in this sense, and indignantly denied the latter phrase, while showing that the former phrase occurs in the Areopagite.[1]

It must be repeated that Palamas was only seeking to explain a doctrine that is implicit in the works of the Cappadocian Fathers, of Maximus the Confessor, of John of Damascus and of other saints of the Eastern Church. That it should have aroused so much opposition in Constantinople is surprising. This was due to the lively interest in philosophy among the intellectuals trained by Theodore Metochites, an interest illustrated by the welcome that they gave to the works of Thomas Aquinas when they were translated by Cydones. To traditional Eastern thinkers Thomism was revolutionary in a way that Palamism was not. The knowledge that Thomas regards as being the highest accessible to man has nothing to do with the gnosis of the Eastern Fathers; and he debars the traditional Orthodox notion of deification by his conception of beatitude, which, where man is concerned, is created and human and only to be attained after death, an imperfect form alone being accessible to man on earth. His distinction between the active and the passive intellect, though it logically provides man with a power to know of the Divine by a process of abstraction from sensible objects, cannot well fit into Orthodox tradition.

---

[1] Meyendorff, *Saint Grégoire Palamas*, pp. 218–19.

Thomas indeed respects the apophatic theology of the Areopagite. He is fully conscious of the limits of human knowledge. But to him apophatic is little more than a corrective to cataphatic theology. Barlaam when he first attacked Palamas had no love for Thomism; but Palamas's later opponents, such as Akyndinus and Nicephorus Gregoras, were more profound. To them Palamite doctrine destroyed the unity of God. Palamas agreed that God must be simple; but to Gregoras, as to most Western theologians, simplicity must mean essence and nothing more. The light with which God illumines the faithful, the light of Thabor or the light of God's glory, cannot be God because it is not of God's essence. As only God is uncreated, this light must be created. By introducing uncreated energies Palamas was introducing additional Gods. In his desire to avoid Messalianism he had fallen into the Neo-Platonic error of producing a multiplicity of minor deities. To accepted Western thology God is simple essence—*Deus est substantia spiritualis omnino simplex*. As the twelfth-century Council of Rheims which condemned Gilbert de la Porrée declared: 'We believe and confess one God, the Father, the Son and the Holy Ghost, to be eternal, and nothing else to be eternal, whether they be called relations or properties or singularities or unities; nor can other things of this sort be part of God since they ware taken out of the eternal and are not God.' In particular the opponents of Palamism could not accept that grace was uncreated or could be equated with the divine light. The gifts of the Holy Spirit are, to the West, created gifts. To Western theologians, if ever man can see God with bodily eyes, which few Catholics outside of the ranks of the Calced Carmelites have maintained, he sees God in His essence by some supernatural added gift.[1]

Palamas had no difficulty in answering the question of the simplicity of God. What is simplicity, he asked? We confess the Trinity in God, which might logically seem to be dissonant with simplicity. Do we damage His simplicity further by saying

[1] For Aquinas's thought see E. Gilson, *The Philosophy of Saint Thomas Aquinas* (trans. E. Bullough), *passim*. See also Sherrard, *op. cit.* pp. 145–54.

that there are rays or sparks perpetually emanating out from Him?[1]

A few opponents of Palamism, feeling that the doctrine had to be defined, sought a compromise. The monk Isaac Argyrus, for example, suggested that the Light was not uncreated but was the first-created light and beauty with which the first man was made and into which redeemed man can return. But it was difficult to find texts to support such a view. Of the adherents of Palamism John Cantacuzenus tried nevertheless to lessen the emphasis on the distinction between essence and energy, in the vain hope of making the doctrine more acceptable to the Latins.[2] The most distinguished mystic of the time, Nicholas Cabasilas, seems to have hesitated a little before admitting the doctrine, but was entirely convinced by it, even though his views on mysticism differed from the Hesychasts'. He was a humanist and a philanthropist; he did not feel that the mystic should necessarily retire from the world of men. To him the supreme mystical experience was to be obtained by participation in the Liturgy and the Sacrament. The participant should certainly prepare himself by repentance, prayer and meditation. But, he says, there is no need for weariness or sweat, no need to retire into a solitary place and to wear a strange habit. You may stay in your house, you may keep your worldly goods; for God is everywhere around us and will come to us if we open the door by meditating upon His goodness and on the link that He has provided between Himself and man. Then we can reach him by sharing in the divine drama of His life and death and resurrection, which is the Holy Liturgy; and He will fill us with love, love of God and love for His creatures. Cabasilas considered the eremetical life too egocentric. The true Christo-centric life is to be found in the world, not by fleeing from it. Of all the Byzantine theologians Cabasilas is the most attractive. His writing, though with the elegance and classi-

[1] Palamas, *Capita Physica*, col. 949.
[2] For Isaac Argyrus see H.-G. Beck, *Kirche und theologische Literatur im Byzantinischen Reich*, pp. 729–30.

cal echos of all good Byzantine writing, is at the same time fresh and simple; his works are, said George Scholarius, 'a jewel of the Church'. On the few occasions when he ventured into theological controversy he showed himself to be opposed to Latin theology and to Latin Scholasticism. The West, he thought, paid too little regard to the economy of the Holy Spirit. But he was not by nature a controversialist. His influence was great. He provided a link between mysticism and the world, between the humanism of his time and the old Orthodox tradition.[1]

The noblest of his pupils was Symeon, Metropolitan of Thessalonica, who died in 1429. Symeon never claimed to be a mystic himself; but, like his master, he believed that the highest mystical experience was to be found in the Liturgy. He was the author of the fullest symbolical interpretation of the church building. In controversy he was remarkable for his irenical tone. Though he argued against the Latins he clearly longed to reach an understanding with them. With it all he was a vigorous and kindly administrator, so well beloved in his diocese that when he died, six years after the city had been sold to the Venetians, not only did the Italians mourn him along with the Greeks, but the Jews, a race that seldom had cause to love Byzantine hierarchs, joined sincerely in the mourning. The ease with which the Turks captured Thessalonica the following year was attributed by many to the feeling of despair in the city which followed the great Metropolitan's death.[2]

Cabasilas and Symeon represented the humanist tradition in Eastern mysticism. But their humanism depended on the existence of a cultured lay society at Constantinople, such as existed up till 1453. A sterner tradition was to be more influential in the future. This was represented at its most extreme by Gregory of Sinai,

---

[1] For Cabasilas's mystical teaching see M. Lot-Borodin, *Un Maître de la spiritualité Byzantine au XIVe siècle: Nicolas Cabasilas, passim*; Tatakis, *op. cit.* pp. 277–81.

[2] For Symeon of Thessalonica, see M. Jugie, 'Symeon de Thessalonique', *Dictionnaire de théologie catholique*, XIV, 2, coll. 2976–84: Beck, *op. cit.* pp. 952–3. His personal popularity is recorded by Anagnostes, *De Excidio Thessalonicae* (ed. I. Bekker, C.S.H.B. edition), pp. 487–8.

who was born in Asia Minor in 1255. He spent his youth on Mount Sinai, from where he derived his surname, then moved to Crete and from Crete to Mount Athos. He harked back to the literal monasticism of the desert; to him Hesychasm involved a life of solitude and a hermit's existence was far more commendable than life in a coenobitic establishment. For a true mystic, he maintained, participation in the Liturgy was unnecessary and even harmful. 'Psalmody', as he called it, was too exterior to bring men to the real memory of God. He told his disciples to attend the Liturgy seldom. 'Frequent psalmody', he said, 'is for active men... but not for hesychasts who are content to pray to God alone in their hearts and to protect themselves from all thought.' Partly because of piratical raids which made a hermit's life on the Mountain unquiet, partly, too, because he was disliked by the monks there, Gregory moved in about 1325 to Bulgaria, to a cell at Paroria, in the Strandja mountains, where he died aged 91 in 1346.[1]

Gregory's example resulted in a revival of eremite life on the Holy Mountain and elsewhere in Greece; but his views were too extreme to have much influence among the Greeks. Palamas seems never to have known him and would not have sympathized with his attitude about the Liturgy. But Gregory's pupil, Isidore Boukheras, who was to succeed John Calecas as Patriarch, was a friend of Palamas and may well have influenced him; Palamas echoes Gregory's insistence on the mystic's need not to delude himself with easily obtained exterior visions.[2] It was amongst the Slavs that Gregory's legacy was greatest. From his retreat in Bulgaria his disciples went out northward across the Danube into Russia. Eminent among them was Cyprian of Tirnovo, who became Metropolitan of Kiev in 1390. He carried Gregory's views still further, preaching against the possession by monasteries of landed property and demanding complete monastic poverty, and even discouraging monastic communities in general. In his view

[1] For Gregory of Sinai, see Tatakis, *op. cit.* pp. 261–3; Lossky, *op. cit.* pp. 209–10.
[2] Meyendorff, *Saint Grégoire Palamas*, pp. 70–1, 136.

hermits and mendicant monks were nearer to God. His teaching
and that of his followers of the next two or three generations,
notably Nil Maykov of Sor, who lived from 1433 to 1508, led to
the emergence of the *starets* as a familiar and deeply respected
figure in Russian life. The *starets* was a hermit, often nomadic
and usually solitary, though sometimes a group of disciples would
cluster round him, seldom attending any church service but enjoying a prestige far greater than that of any bishop or abbot. His
position was not unlike that of the hermit of early Byzantine
times, though he was more consciously dedicated to mystical
exercises. It may be doubted whether the *starets* really enriched
the spiritual life of Russia. He was apt, being an ignorant man
amongst a superstitious peasantry, to become a magician as well
as a meddler in local and sometimes in national politics, and an
enemy to education and reform: till at last we come to the most
famous of all the *staretsi*, Grigor Rasputin. Meanwhile for centuries Russian ecclesiastical history was dominated by the struggle
between the hierarchy, allied with the large, orderly monasteries,
and the advocates of religious poverty.[1]

The Byzantine Church was to be spared such a struggle, owing
to the cruel fact of the Turkish conquest. Byzantium was full of
religious activity right up to the fall of the Empire; but in such
troubled times the contemplative life was difficult to follow except
in the isolation of the Holy Mountain. Soon after the Turkish
occupation of Thessalonica in 1430 Mount Athos was obliged to
admit the suzerainty of the Sultan. But he left the monks alone to
form an autonomous monastic republic; and they were able to
retain most of their endowments and mainland estates, and to
keep in touch with the Patriarchate. Hesychasm was steadily
practised there. Many centuries later, in 1782, an Athonite monk,
Nicodemus the Haghiorite, published a collection of extracts from
the Fathers of the Church, Western as well as Eastern, beginning
with the fifth century, all dealing with the theory and practice of

[1] For Cyprian of Tirnovo and Nil of Sor, see V. Ikonnikov, *Cultural Importance of Byzantium in Russian History* (in Russian), pp. 72–83. See also below, p. 326.

mysticism. Nicodemus cannot be rated highly as a scholarly editor or textual critic; but his compilation, known as the *Philokalia*, is a work of great importance not only because it includes many unpublished and some otherwise unknown texts, but also because it shows the continuity of Christian mystical thought. The Hesychast theologians, with Gregory Palamas at their head, were only defining doctrines that had long been part of the Orthodox tradition and that still survive in the Orthodox world to this day, though weakened by the stress of modern life.[1]

Mystical experience lies at the heart of Orthodoxy. To many onlookers the Orthodox Churches have sometimes seemed too ready to turn their backs upon the material world and to escape into an unreal world of the spirit, submitting too readily to infidel governments and too readily condoning their godless practices. It may be so. Byzantium inherited from Rome so deep a respect for the Law that the Byzantines too willingly left it to the State to punish wrong-doing and to right social injustice, only protesting when their Faith and their Liturgy were impugned. There were, indeed, great churchmen who sought to see that the laws of God prevailed in daily life; but in general it was held that the business of divines was to see to the welfare of the soul, not that of the body. This attitude may have worked against philanthropy. But it was also a strength to the Church, enabling her to survive the humiliation and the demoralization that political captivity brought in its train. The Christian of the East might have to bow down to Antichrist in his daily life; but his soul remained in communion with God.

[1] The *Philokalia*, compiled by Macarius of Corinth and Nicodemus of the Holy Mountain, is printed in full in a Russian translation by Feodor, Bishop of Vladimir-Suzdal. There is a shorter Greek version, Ἡ Φιλοκαλία τῶν ἱερῶν Νηπτικῶν.

THE END OF THE EMPIRE

By the middle of the fifteenth century it was clear to any impartial observer that the sands of the ancient Empire were running out. Its territory consisted now only of the city of Constantinople itself, half in ruins and with its population dwindling, a few towns strung along the Marmora and Black Sea coasts of Thrace, and the islands of Tenedos and Imbros off the entrance to the Dardanelles. Cadets of the Imperial house maintained the Despotate of the Morea, which now consisted of the whole Peloponnese, apart from two or three Venetian fortresses. In the East the Empire of the Grand Comnenus of Trebizond lingered on. There were still a few precarious Latin principalities on the Greek mainland and in the islands; and Venice and Genoa held other islands and a few mainland ports. Elsewhere, from the Danube to the Taurus mountains everything was in the hands of the Ottoman Turks. The Ottoman Empire was ably and vigorously governed; and the Ottoman army was the finest and most up-to-date in all the world. When in 1451 the Ottoman throne passed to a brilliant and ambitious boy of nineteen, Mehmet II, it was not to be expected that he would long be content to allow the great city to last on as an alien island in the very centre of his dominions.

Life was tense in the threatened city. The philosophical and theological debates that had excited the Byzantines of the previous century were subordinated now to the urgent political issue: could the Empire still be saved? But this issue involved a religious issue. If the Empire were to be saved it could only be through help from outside; and help from outside meant help from the West, for which the price was the union of the Churches under Rome.

At this supreme moment of the Empire's agony, the Church of Constantinople could provide little help for the people. Its provincial administration had been disorganized by the Turkish advance. Now, in Constantinople itself the official policy of union had produced chaos. There was no Patriarch. The last occupant of the post, Gregory Mammas, had fled to Italy. As bishoprics fell vacant the Emperor could find no one to fill them who would support his work for union. The clergy and the congregations of the city held aloof from the ceremonies in the Great Church of Saint Sophia, going instead for guidance to the monastery of the Pantocrator, where the monk Gennadius, the former George Scholarius, fulminated against the union. Was it right for the Byzantines to seek to save their bodies at the cost of losing their souls? and, indeed, would they save their bodies? To Gennadius and his friends it was all too clear that the help provided by the West would be pathetically inadequate. Holy Writ maintained that sooner or later Antichrist would come as a precursor of Armageddon and the end of the world. To many Greeks it seemed that the time was near. Was this the moment to desert the purity of the Faith?

Yet, when the crisis came, there was scarcely a man or a woman in Constantinople who did not rally to its defence. The Western allies were few; but, whether they were Venetian or Genoese merchants whose chief motive was self-interest, or gallant adventurers like the brothers Bocchiardi or the Spaniard Don Francisco of Toledo, or the clergy in the suite of Cardinal Isidore, all fought with courage till the fatal moment when the ablest of them, the Genoese Giustiniani, mortally wounded, deserted the battlefield. The Greeks, depressed though they were by omens and prophecies, realistically aware that the city could not hold out for long, and some of them convinced that by now the Turkish conquest would provide the only solution for their problems, joined whole-heartedly in the struggle. Old men and women came night after night to repair the damaged stockade. Even monks patrolled the walls as watchmen, and, forgetting the ancient injunctions of the Fathers, took up arms against the assailants. There was jealousy and bitterness between the allies, between the Venetians and the Genoese, between the Greeks themselves and between Greeks and

Latins in general. But the quarrels never seriously impaired the defence. Pride and loyalty to the Emperor and to Christendom transcended their differences; and on the last night before the final assault everyone who could be spared from the walls, whatever his allegiance, came to the final Liturgy in the great Cathedral, to pray for a deliverance that all knew that only a miracle could produce.

The Empire ended in glory. It was only when the news sped through the city that the Emperor was slain and the Sultan's banner was waving over the Sacred Palace that the Greeks gave up the struggle and sought to adjust themselves as best they could to a life of captivity.[1]

[1] For the story of the fall of the Empire see S. Runciman, *The Fall of Constantinople*.

BOOK II

THE CHURCH UNDER THE
OTTOMAN SULTANS

CHAPTER I

THE NEW PATTERN

On Tuesday, 29 May 1453, an old story was ended. The last heir of Constantine the Great lay dead on the battlefield; and an infidel Sultan had entered in triumph into the city which Constantine had founded to be the capital of the Christian Empire. There was no longer an Emperor reigning in the Sacred Palace to symbolize to the Faithful of the East the majesty and authority of Almighty God. The Church of Constantinople, for more than a thousand years the partner of the Orthodox State, became the Church of a subject people, dependent upon the whims of a Muslim master. Its operation, its outlook and its whole way of life had abruptly to be changed.

It was a fundamental change; and yet it was not quite as complete as it might seem at first sight. For centuries past the historic Patriarchates of the East, Alexandria, Antioch and Jerusalem, had been, but for brief interludes, under the political power of Muslim authorities. Ever since the Turks had first occupied parts of Asia Minor in the eleventh century congregations belonging to the Patriarchate of Constantinople had been living under Muslim rule. In recent decades the rapid spread of the Ottoman Empire, in Europe as well as in Asia, had added to their number, till by 1453 the majority of the Patriarch's flock dwelt in the Sultan's dominions. There were also many Greek lands which had been for some time past under Latin masters and which were to remain under them for some time to come. Though the Genoese were to lose the greater part of their Greek colonies immediately after 1453, they retained the island of Chios till 1566.[1] The Venetians held fortresses in the Peloponnese and a number of Aegean islands till well into the sixteenth century; they held Crete till 1669 and

---

[1] See P. Argenti, *The Occupation of Chios by the Genoese*, I, pp. 651 ff., and *Chios Vincta*, pp. cxlviii–cl, cxcii–cxciii.

Tinos till 1715. Cyprus, still an independent kingdom at the time of the fall of Constantinople, was in Venetian hands from 1487 to 1570.[1] The Italian Duchy of the Archipelago lasted till 1566, when the Turks imposed a Jewish vassal Duke.[2] The Knights of St John held Rhodes till 1522.[3] The Ionian islands off the west coast of Greece never passed under Turkish rule. They remained in Venetian hands until the end of the eighteenth century, when they were taken over by the French and then passed to the British, who ceded them to the Kingdom of Greece in 1864.[4] Thus there were still a few provinces where the Patriarch's authority could not always be implemented. Nevertheless, from the narrow viewpoint of ecclesiastical control and discipline the Patriarchate gained from the conquest because the vast bulk of its territory was reunited under one lay power.

But the lay power was infidel. So long as the Christian Empire lasted on at Constantinople, Church and State were still integrated there in one holy realm. The Emperor might in fact be pathetically feeble, but in theory he was still the transcendent head of the Christian Oecumene, the representative of God before the people and the people before God. Now the Church was divorced from the State. It became an association of second-class citizens. Here again, as the only association that these second-class citizens were permitted to organize, its powers of discipline over its congregations were enhanced. But it lacked the ultimate sanction of freedom.

The Conquering Sultan was well aware of the problems that faced the Church; and he was not hostile to its well-being. He had been a truculent enemy until Constantinople was conquered; and the conquest had been accompanied by bloodthirsty and destructive violence. But, having conquered, he was not ungenerous. He had Greek blood in his veins. He was well read and

---

[1] See W. Miller, *Essays on the Latin Orient*, pp. 265-8.
[2] See C. Roth, *The House of Nasi: the Dukes of Naxos, passim.*
[3] See D. M. Vaughan, *Europe and the Turk 1350-1700*, pp. 11-12, 109-10.
[4] See Miller, *op. cit.* pp. 199-230.

deeply interested in Greek learning. He was proud to see himself as the heir of the Caesars and was ready to shoulder the religious responsibilities of his predecessors, so far as his own religion permitted. As a pious Muslim he could not allow the Christians any part in the higher control of his Empire. But he wished them to enjoy peace and prosperity and to be content with his government and an asset to it.[1]

His first duty to the Christians was to establish the new pattern for their administration. His solution followed lines traditional in Muslim dominions. Muslim rulers had long treated religious minorities within their dominions as *milets*, or nations, allowing them to govern their own affairs according to their own laws and customs, and making the religious head of the sect responsible for its administration and its good behaviour towards the paramount power. This was the manner according to which the Christians in the Caliphate had been ruled, amongst them the congregations of the Eastern Orthodox Patriarchates. The system was now extended to include the Orthodox Patriarchate of Constantinople. For practical purposes it had already been followed in the districts of the Patriarchate that were within the Turkish dominions. Where their lay officials had been ejected or had fled the Christians had naturally looked to their hierarchs to negotiate with the conquerors on their behalf; and it was the hierarchs who carried on the day-to-day administration of their flocks as best they could. But hitherto for them, as also for the Orthodox Patriarchs of the East, there had been in Constantinople an Orthodox Emperor to whom they owed ultimate allegiance and whose duty it was to protect them, even if he could no longer administer them. In recent years the protection that he was able to provide, in his impotent and impoverished state, had been merely nominal; but nevertheless it gave them prestige; it raised them above the heretic Churches, such as the Coptic and the Jacobites, who had no lay protector and were entirely the servants of the Muslim monarch.

[1] For Mehmet II and his interest in Greek culture see F. Babinger, *Mehmed der Eroberer und seine Zeit*, pp. 449 ff.

But now, with the Emperor gone, even this nominal protection disappeared. The Orthodox were reduced to the status of the heretic Churches, in theory at least. In practice they were better off; for they formed the largest, the richest and the best-educated Christian community in the Sultan's dominions; and Sultan Mehmet with his sense of history was inclined to pay them special attention.

The Sultan was well aware, also, that the Greeks would be of value to his Empire. The Turks would provide him with his governors and his soldiers; but they were not adept at commerce or industry; few of them were good seamen; and even in the countryside they tended to prefer a pastoral to an agricultural life. For the economy of the Empire the co-operation of the Greeks was essential. The Sultan saw no reason why they should not live within his dominions in amity with the Turks, so long as their own rights were assured and so long as they realized that he was their overlord.

If the Greek *milet* was to be organized, the first task was to provide it with a head. Sultan Mehmet knew well of the difficulties that the attempt to force union with Rome had produced in the Greek Church; and, after the conquest, he soon satisfied himself that the average Greek considered the Patriarchal throne to be vacant. The Patriarch Gregory Mammas was held to have abdicated when he fled to Italy in 1451. A new Patriarch must be found. After making some inquiries Mehmet decided that he should be George Scholarius, now known as the monk Gennadius. Gennadius was not only the most eminent scholar living in Constaninople at the time of the conquest. He was everywhere respected for his unflinching probity; and he had been the leader of the anti-Unionist, anti-Western party within the Church. He could be relied upon not to intrigue with the West. Within a month of the conquest the Sultan sent officials to bring Gennadius to his presence. He could not at first be found. Eventually it was discovered that he had been taken prisoner at the time of the fall of the city and had passed into the possession of a rich Turk of

Adrianople, who was deeply impressed by his learning and was treating him with honours seldom accorded to a slave. He was redeemed from his buyer and was conveyed honourably to Constantinople and led before the Sultan. Mehmet persuaded him to accept the Patriarchal throne; and together they worked out the terms for the constitution to be granted to the Orthodox. The main lines were probably arranged before the Sultan left the conquered city for Adrianople at the end of June, though six months elapsed before Gennadius actually assumed the Patriarchate.[1]

The enthronization took place in January 1454, when the Sultan returned to Constantinople. Mehmet was determined to play in so far as his religion permitted the role played in the past by the Christian Emperors. We know nothing about the necessary meeting of the Holy Synod; but presumably it was formed by such metropolitans as could be gathered together and it was their task to declare the Patriarchate vacant and, on the Sultan's recommendation, to elect Gennadius to fill it. Then, on 6 January, Gennadius was received in audience by the Sultan, who handed him the insignia of his office, the robes, the pastoral staff and the pectoral cross. The original cross was lost. Whether Gregory Mammas had taken it with him when he fled to Rome or whether it disappeared during the sack of the city is unknown. So Mehmet himself presented a new cross, made of silver-gilt. As he invested the Patriarch he uttered the formula: 'Be Patriarch, with good fortune, and be assured of our friendship, keeping all the privileges that the Patriarchs before you enjoyed.' As Saint Sophia had already been converted into a mosque, Gennadius was led to the Church of the Holy Apostles. There the Metropolitan of Heraclea, whose traditional duty it was to consecrate, performed the rite of consecration and enthronization. The Patriarch then emerged and, mounted on a magnificent horse which the Sultan had presented to him, rode in procession round the city before returning to take up his residence in the precincts of the Holy

---

[1] G. Phrantzes, *Chronicon*, C.S.H.B. edition, pp. 304–7; Critobulus (Kritovoulos), *History of Mehmed the Conqueror*, trans. C. T. Riggs, pp. 94–5.

Apostles. He had also received from the Sultan a handsome gift of gold.[1]

It is unlikely that the new constitution was ever written down. The general lines along which a Christian *milet* in Muslim territory was administered were well enough known not to need a general restatement. The Imperial *berat* which gave the Sultan's approval of every appointment to episcopal office usually stated the duties of the incumbent, following the traditional customs. We only hear of two specific documents issued by the Conquering Sultan. According to the historian Phrantzes, who was at that time a captive with the Turks and was in a position to know about it, Mehmet handed to Gennadius a firman which he had signed, giving to the Patriarch personal inviolability, exemption from paying taxes, freedom of movement, security from deposition, and the right to transmit these privileges to his successors. There is no reason for doubting this. It is indeed probable that the Sultan would give to the Patriarch some written guarantee about his position. It should, however, be noted that the freedom from deposition clearly was not held to interfere with the traditional right of the Holy Synod to depose a Patriarch if his election was held to have been uncanonical or if he were demonstrably unfitted for the office. Patriarchal chroniclers writing nearly a century later claimed that the Sultan had signed another document in which he promised that the customs of the Church with regard to marriage and burial should be legally sanctioned, that Easter should be celebrated as a feast and the Christians should have freedom of movement during the three Easter feast-days, and that no more churches should be converted into mosques.[2] Unfortunately, when

[1] Phrantzes, *loc. cit.*; Critobulus, *loc. cit.*: *Historia Politica Constantinopoleos* (C.S.H.B. edition), pp. 27–8: *Historia Patriarchica Constantinopoleos* (C.S.H.B. edition), pp. 80–2. For the actual date of the enthronement see T. H. Papadopoullos, *Studies and Documents relating to the History of the Greek Church and People under Turkish Domination*, p. 2 n. 2.

[2] Phrantzes, *loc. cit.*; Critobulus, *loc. cit.*; *Historia Politica, loc cit.*; *Historia Patriarchica, loc. cit.*; Hierax, Χρονικόν, in C. Sathas, Μεσαιωνικὴ Βιβλιοθήκη, I, p. 267; D. Cantemir, *The History of the Growth and Decay of the Othman Empire*, trans.

the last point was disregarded by later Sultans, the Church authorities could not produce the document, which they said, no doubt correctly, had been destroyed in a fire at the Patriarchate. But, as we shall see, they were able to produce evidence to substantiate their claim.[1]

Whatever might have been written down, it was generally accepted that the Patriarch, in conjunction with the Holy Synod, had complete control over the whole ecclesiastical organization, the bishops and all churches and monasteries and their possessions. Though the Sultan's government had to confirm episcopal appointments, no bishop could be appointed or dismissed except on the recommendation of the Patriarch and the Holy Synod. The Patriarchal law-courts alone had penal jurisdiction over the clergy; the Turkish authorities could not arrest or judge anyone of episcopal rank without the permission of the Patriarch. He also, in conjunction with the Holy Synod, had control over all matters of dogma. His control was almost as complete over the Orthodox laity. He was the Ethnarch, the ruler of the *milet*. The Patriarchal courts had full jurisdiction over all affairs concerning the Orthodox which had a religious connotation, that is, marriage, divorce, the guardianship of minors, and testaments and successions. They were entitled to try any commercial case if both disputants were Orthodox. Though the Christian laity were heavily taxed, the clergy were free from paying the taxes, though on occasions they might of their own consent agree to pay special taxes; and it was not difficult for the Sultan to exert pressure to secure this consent. The Patriarch could tax the Orthodox on his

N. Tindall, pp. 101 ff.; A. K. Hypsilantis, Τὰ μετὰ τὴν Ἅλωσιν, pp. 3–6. For modern discussions of the rights and privileges of the Patriarchate and the Greek *milet* see N. P. Eleutheriades, Τα Προνόμια τοῦ Οἰκουμενικοῦ Πατριαρχείου *passim*: C. G. Papadopoulos, *Les privilèges du patriarcat œcuménique dans l'Empire Ottoman*, *passim*; P. Karolidis, Ἱστορία τῆς Ἑλλάδος ἀπὸ τῆς ὑπὸ τῶν Ὀθωμανῶν ἁλώσεως τῆς Κωνσταντινουπόλεως, pp. 212–21. C. Amantos, 'Οἱ Προνομιακοὶ Ὁρισμοὶ τοῦ Μουσουλμανισμοῦ ὑπὲρ τῶν Χριστιανῶν', in Ἑλληνικά, ΙΧ (1936), Papadopoullos, *op. cit.* pp. 1–39; V. Laurent, 'Les Chrétiens sous les sultans', in *Echos d'Orient*, XXVIII (1929), pp. 398–406, quoting Turkish sources. [1] See below, p. 189.

own authority to raise money for the needs of the Church. Complaints against the Patriarch could only be heard by the Holy Synod, and only if it agreed unanimously to listen to them. The Patriarch could call in the Turkish authorities to see that his wishes were carried out by his flock. In return for all this, the Patriarch was responsible for the orderly and loyal behaviour of his flock towards the ruling authorities and for ensuring that the taxes were paid. He did not collect the State taxes himself. That was the duty of the head-man of the local commune, who was responsible for keeping the registers. But, if there was any difficulty over the collection, the Government could ask the Church to punish recalcitrants with a sentence of excommunication.[1]

The Patriarchal courts administered justice according to the canon law of the Byzantines and according to Byzantine civil and customary law. Customary law grew rapidly in volume, owing to changed circumstances for which the codified law did not allow, and which varied from place to place. In civil cases the judgment was in the nature of an arbitration award. If either party were dissatisfied with it he could have recourse to the Turkish courts; and, if either party insisted, the case could be brought before the Turkish courts in the first instance. This was seldom done, as the Turkish courts were slow, expensive and often corrupt, and heard cases according to Koranic law. The Patriarchal courts were considered to be remarkably free from corruption, though rich Greeks on whose financial support the Church depended could undoubtedly exercise some influence. A feature of the courts was that a statement taken on oath counted as valid evidence; and so seriously were oaths regarded that this was seldom abused. Criminal offences, such as treason, murder, theft or riot, were reserved to the Turkish courts, unless the accused was a priest.[2]

---

[1] A full discussion of the powers of the Patriarchal court is given in Papadopoullos, *op. cit.* pp. 27–39.

[2] Karolidis, *op. cit.* pp. 215–17; N. Moschovakis, Τὸ ἐν Ἑλλάδι δημόσιον δίκαιον ἐπὶ Τουρκοκρατίας, pp. 52–4; D. Petrakakos, Κοινοβουλευτική Ἱστορία τῆς Ἑλλάδος, pp. 212–15. For local customary law see *Jus Graeco-Romanum*, ed. J. and P. Zepos, VIII, *passim*.

In theory the structure of the Great Church, as the Greeks called the Patriarchal organization, even though the Great Church itself, Saint Sophia, was no longer a Christian temple, was not altered by the conquest. The Patriarch was still officially elected by the Holy Synod consisting of his metropolitans, and the election was confirmed by the lay suzerain. As in Byzantine times the lay suzerain almost invariably indicated the candidate whom he wished to be elected; and the old custom of submitting three names to him, which had fallen into disuse in late Byzantine times, was formally abandoned. But the increased administrative duties of the Patriarchate inevitably led to changes. The Holy Synod had originally consisted of the metropolitans alone, though the high officials of the Patriarchate seem sometimes to have attended its meetings. Soon after the conquest they were officially added to it; and there was a general enhancement of the constitutional importance of the Synod. It retained its right to depose a Patriarch by a unanimous vote. In addition Patriarchal decrees were not now binding unless they had the support of the Synod. The Patriarch became little more than its president. In theory this was a reaffirmation of the democratic principles of the Church. In practice it meant that, while a strong and popular Patriarch would meet with no difficulties, Patriarchal authority could always be undermined. Turkish officials, without seeming openly to interfere in the internal affairs of the Church, could exercise what influence they desired through intrigues with individual members of the Synod.[1]

The high officials of the Great Church continued to bear the same names as before the conquest and in theory to exercise the same duties; but in practice their duties were enlarged. Constitutional lawyers now arranged them into nine groups of five, known as *pentads*. The first *pentad* was composed of the senior officers: the Grand Economus, who, as before, controlled the finances of the Patriarchate and acted if necessary as the Patriarch's deputy; the Grand Sacellarius, who was in charge of all the

---

[1] Papadopoullos, *op. cit.* pp. 39–41.

monasteries and convents throughout the Patriarchate; the Grand Skevophylax, in charge of all liturgical possessions, icons and relics; the Grand Chartophylax, the secretary-general of the Patriarchate, in charge of all its registers and archives; and the minister of the Sacellion, who was distinct from the Sacellarius but whose functions were somewhat vague; he had been in charge of the Patriarchal prison in the old days and now was responsible for ecclesiastical discipline. Not long before the conquest a sixth office had been added as an appendage to the first *pentad*, that of the Protecdicos, who originally had the duty of examining and pronouncing upon all appeals for justice or for aid brought before the Patriarchal court and who after the conquest became the chief judge. The Grand Economus and the Grand Sacellarius ranked slightly above their fellows in the *pentad*. As a symbol of their special authority each carried a sacred fan at religious ceremonies.

In the second *pentad* the Protonotary and the Logothete assisted the Chartophylax as his chief clerk and his keeper of the Seal; the castrinsius acted as personal aide-de-camp to the Patriarch; the Referendarius carried the Patriarch's communications to the lay authorities; and the Hypomnematographer acted as secretary to the Holy Synod, recording its meetings for the Patriarchal registers.

The remaining *pentads* were composed of officials whose duties were purely clerical or purely liturgical. There were many other functionaries who were not given places in the official lists of the *pentads* but who were nevertheless important, in particular the judges, who worked in the office of the Protecdicos and who were competent to give decisions of minor importance. All major legal decisions had to be pronounced by the Patriarch sitting in the Holy Synod.[1]

Metropolitans and bishops had their own local officials, based on the pattern of the Patriarchal court. In the provinces civil

---

[1] Papadopoullis, *op. cit.*, pp. 41–85. The system was slightly reorganized in the eighteenth century when several of the posts formerly held by clerics had fallen into the hands of the laity. See below, p. 376.

lawsuits were heard before the head of the commune, the *demogeron*. But matters with a religious significance, such as marriage and inheritance, came before the bishop's own court. In all cases there was a right of appeal to the Patriarchal court.[1]

The significant difference brought by the new pattern of things to the Patriarchate was that it was now obliged to concern itself with a number of lay affairs. The Patriarch as head of the Orthodox *milet* was to some extent the heir of the Emperor. He had to become a politician, able to plead and to intrigue for his people at the Sublime Porte, as the seat of the Sultan's government came to be called. He had to use his religious authority to see that the Orthodox accepted the Sultan's authority and abstained from disorders. Though he was not himself the tax-collector for the Sultan he had to see that the taxes were forthcoming. Above all, in practice the new system involved the Great Church in legal and financial activities far greater than it had known before. Not only did the Patriarch have to employ skilled financiers to advise him on the raising of taxes from the Faithful and on all matters of expenditure, but he also needed the services of lawyers trained in secular law. It was difficult and, indeed, doubtfully correct for ecclesiastics to go deeply into the study of civil law. Inevitably laymen began to enter the administrative offices of the Church. In Byzantine times the high offices had all been reserved for clerics. Now lay judges had to be appointed and had to be given proper authority, while it proved impossible to obtain the advice of lay financiers unless they too were given official rank. Laymen were soon brought into the lower *pentads* and gradually worked their way upwards. The first lay Grand Chartophylax appears in 1554, 101 years after the conquest, and the first lay Grand Skevophylax ten years later. The Protecdicos was invariably a priest until 1640; but by then almost the whole of his department was staffed by laymen. The laity were already beginning to occupy other offices

---

[1] See N. Vlachos, 'La Relation des Grecs asservis avec l'Etat Musulman souverain', in *Le Cinq-centième anniversaire de la prise de Constantinople, L'Hellénisme Contemporain*, fascicule hors série (1953), pp. 138–42.

and to increase their importance. The office of Logothete, which from 1575 onwards was held as often by a layman as by a priest, began to take over many of the duties of that of the Grand Economus; and by the seventeenth century the Logothete was called Grand Logothete and ranked above the first *pentad*. The Ecclesiarch, who had been chief sacristan of the Patriarchal church and had ranked only in the eighth *pentad*, was usually a layman after the beginning of the seventeenth century, and soon took over the functions of the Skevophylax and enjoyed the title of Grand Ecclesiarch. A new high office, reserved for the laity, emerged early in the sixteenth century, that of Grand Orator, or official spokesman of the Great Church. These new or amended offices owed their high precedence to the fact that they were considered to be *basilikoi*, that is to say imperial, the assistants of the Patriarch in his role as Ethnarch, heir to functions that had been the Emperor's. It has been suggested that the growing importance of the laity in the Church organization was due to the influence of the great Trapezuntine families, such as the Ypsilanti, whom the Conquering Sultan brought to Constantinople; for the Church of Trebizond had for some time past made use of lay officials. But, as the name *basilikos* indicates, it was the inevitable result of the Patriarch's enlarged powers. In the course of the eighteenth century measures had to be taken to prevent the metropolitans' powers being overridden by the powers of the lay magistrates.[1] Further powers were added when the Ottoman Empire expanded southwards. In the course of the sixteenth century the Sultan acquired dominion over Syria and Egypt, thus absorbing the lands of the Orthodox Patriarchates of Alexandria, Antioch and Jerusalem. The Sublime Porte wished to centralize everything at Constantinople; and the Great Church followed its lead. As a result the Eastern Patriarchates were put into a position of inferiority in comparison with that of Constantinople. The Eastern Patriarchs lost in theory none of their ecclesiastical rights or autonomy, and they continued to administer the Orthodox within their sees. But

[1] Papadopoullos, *op. cit.* pp. 48–50.

in practice they found that they could only negotiate with the Sublime Porte through their brother of Constantinople. When a vacancy occurred on any of the Patriarchal thrones it was the Patriarch of Constantinople who applied to the Sultan for permission to fill it; and, as the Sultan himself was seldom much interested in naming a successor, it was easy for the Constantinopolitan Patriarch to secure the appointment of the candidate whom he advocated. The Eastern Patriarchates were moreover relatively poor. The Patriarch of Jerusalem, though his see was the smallest, was the richest, as the prestige of the Holy City led to endowments from all over the Orthodox world, and pilgrimage brought in a steady income. The Patriarch of Antioch, resident since the time of the Crusades at Damascus, was the poorest, being dependent for most of his income on Syrian Orthodox merchants who were not always well disposed towards the Greeks of Constantinople. The Patriarch of Alexandria was a little better off, owing to the number of Greek merchants that began to settle in Egypt after the Ottoman conquest. The Church of Cyprus retained its nominal historic autonomy, but in fact during the Venetian occupation of the island it depended for support on the Patriarch of Constantinople; and after the Turkish conquest the Constantinopolitan influence remained paramount. The autonomous Archbishop of Sinai had jurisdiction only over the monks of his monastery.[1]

The Slav Orthodox Churches posed a greater problem. It usually suited the convenience of the Turkish government that they should be under the control of Constantinople, though they retained their Slavonic liturgy and usages. But occasional Turkish ministers with Balkan affiliations were occasionally persuaded to increase their autonomy. It was not until the eighteenth century that the Patriarchate firmly established its authority; and by then it had to contend with growing forces of nationalism. The Russian Church was in a special position. It regarded Constantinople with greater and more sincere respect than did the Balkan Churches.

[1] *Ibid.* pp. 86–9: N. Jorga, *Byzance après Byzance*, pp. 72–7.

But Russia was far away and independent. It was unthinkable that the Russian ruler would allow his Church to be in practice dependent upon a hierarch who was the servant of the infidel Sultan.[1] The structure of the hierarchy within the Patriarchate remained as it had been in Byzantine times, with certain archbishops without suffragans depending directly upon the Patriarch but more generally with metropolitan sees dependent on the Patriarch and episcopal sees dependent on the metropolitan. As in Byzantine times bishops were elected by the priests of the diocese and the metropolitan by the bishops, and elections were confirmed by the Patriarchate; and, as in Byzantine times, confirmation by the lay authorities was required. Applications were now made through the Patriarchate to the Sublime Porte; and the Sultan issued a document, known as a *berat*, formally appointing the elected candidate to the see. In the case of bishops these *berats* were usually simple documents which merely announced the elections; but the *berats* that appointed Patriarchs and, in some cases, metropolitans might contain not only a confirmation of the specific rights of the see but also additional privileges or a promise by the lay authorities to take action on behalf of the see. For instance, a *berat* appointing an eighteenth-century Patriarch of Alexandria promises aid in the suppression of Roman Catholic propaganda in the province. Such *berats* provide valuable historical evidence. Unfortunately few have survived. The earliest that is extant and can be dated appoints a metropolitan of Larissa in 1604. It is uncertain whether the *berat* possessed the same overriding and everlasting authority as an Imperial *firman*. It is probable that the rights and privileges that it mentions were intended only to apply *ad personam*, a new *berat* being required for each subsequent appointment. But a hierarch was entitled to the advantages that his predecessor had enjoyed, so long as he could produce a *berat* that listed them.[2]

[1] See below, pp. 231–4.

[2] No early *berats* appointing high ecclesiastical officials have survived. N. Beldiceanu, *Les Actes des premiers sultans*, II, p. 137, reproduces a *berat* (no. 47), apparently dating from the sixteenth century, appointing a certain Mark to an unnamed metropolitan see. The Sultan confirms the dignity because Mark has

On the whole, in theory at least, the Orthodox Church of Constantinople survived the shock of the Ottoman conquest better than might have been expected. The Christians were not allowed to forget that they were a subject people. They could not build new churches without special permission, which was seldom granted unless the proposed site was in a purely Christian locality. Permission had also to be granted for the repair of churches; and no church was to be permitted near a Muslim shrine. The Christians had to wear a distinctive costume. With the exception of the Patriarch none of them might ride on horseback. No Christian could officially serve in the armed forces, though in fact they were sometimes press-ganged into the navy, and in Christian districts local Christian militia bands, known as the Armatoles, were formed. Christian families had to submit to the arbitrary seizure of their young sons, to be converted to Islam and enrolled in the Janissary regiments. A Christian who was converted to Islam, even involuntarily as a child or as a captive, was liable to the death penalty if he reverted to his old faith. Any lawsuit involving a Christian and a Muslim was heard in a Muslim court, according to Koranic law; and few Muslim judges were prepared to give a judgment in favour of an unbeliever. Finally, all the rights and privileges of the Christians depended on the good will of the Sultan. Even *firmans* signed by a Sultan, though they were held to be binding upon his successors, might be ignored. The Court lawyers could state that it had contravened Islamic law and was therefore invalid.[1]

paid a gift (*peshtesh*) to the Imperial Treasury. He is to be exempted from local taxes, such as the tax for the repair of fortresses (*cherakhor*), and from the *kharadj*. The earliest surviving *berat* concerning a Patriarch is that confirming Dionysius III's election in 1662, given in J. Aymon, *Monuments authentiques de la réligion en Grèce et de la fausseté de plusieurs confessions de foi des Chrétiens* (published in 1708), p. 486. Dionysius has paid 900,000 *aspres* (equal to 12,000 *écus*, according to Aymon), and is accorded the traditional privileges. See also Laurent, *art. cit.*

[1] The books of Smith and Ricaut (see below, pp. 204–5, 272–3), and other seventeenth century travellers illustrate the difficulties undergone by the Christians; but it must be remembered that they were writing at a time when the Turkish

In spite of all that, and in spite of the destruction and misery that accompanied the fall of the city, the Orthodox *milet* did receive a constitution which enabled it not only to exist but also to increase its material prosperity. The Greeks benefited from the rebirth of Constantinople which the conquest brought about. At the time of the conquest the Greek population in the city did not number more than about 50,000. Several thousand perished during the siege and capture, and several thousand more were scattered in captivity. But the Conquering Sultan not only left certain quarters to the Greeks, but also encouraged the immigration of Greeks there. Sometimes the immigration was forced. The wealthier citizens of Trebizond were all moved to Constantinople. Others were brought in from Adrianople, others from Lesbos when it was occupied in 1462; and we are told that two thousand families were transported from Argos. By the middle of the sixteenth century it was estimated that there were no fewer than 30,000 Greek families living in the city. If we allow five or six persons to each household—which is probably too few—the Greek population had risen to over 150,000, and was rising; and money was to be made in this busy new Imperial capital.

Many of the villages in the suburbs, particularly along the European shores of the Bosphorus and the Marmora, were soon repeopled by Greeks. Some of them, such as Therapia or Yediköy, were almost exclusively Christian.[1]

administrative machine was beginning to run down. The position was always worse in the provinces where the central government could not supervise things closely. Crusius, *Turco–Graecia*, writing in the later sixteenth century, notes that the Christians of Constantinople 'do not want any other domination in preference to the Turks' (p. 250). In the sixteenth century it was probably only the wealthier Christians who suffered from the arbitrary actions of the Porte. In some Balkan districts the Christian peasants were probably better off than under their previous landlords (see Vaughan, *op. cit.* pp. 24–6). This applies particularly to Bosnia and may help to explain why so many Bosnians became willing converts to Islam.

[1] Jorga, *Byzance après Byzance*, pp. 45–56, for a general conspectus. The Spanish traveller de Villalon (*Viaje de Turquia*, 1557, in M. Serrano y Sanz, *Autobiograpfías y Memorias*, p. 146) says that official lists give 40,000 Christian houses in the city, of which the vast majority were Greek, with 10,000 Jewish houses

The Sultan was wise enough to see that the welfare of the Greeks would add to the welfare of his Empire. He was anxious to provide them with a government that would satisfy their needs without infringing upon the privileges of the ruling race of Turks. The constitution that he gave them was workable so long as they were prepared to abandon political ambitions and to lead orderly lives according to the pattern permitted to them. In the meantime their *milet* was united and their freedom of worship was guaranteed. Indeed, in one respect they were better treated than might have been expected. By Islamic tradition the Christians in a city taken by storm had no right to retain their church buildings. But in captured Constantinople not only did they still possess the second greatest church, that of the Holy Apostles, but also a number of churches in other parts of the city, in particular in the Phanar and Petrion districts by the Golden Horn and in Psamathia on the Marmora. It seems that the hasty submission of these quarters to the Turkish troops that had entered the city was allowed to count as an act of voluntary surrender; and the churches were therefore not forfeited. The Sultan had the sense to see that if his new Christian subjects were to accept his rule peacefully they must be allowed places of worship.[1]

The integrity of the Orthodox *milet* was guaranteed by the new powers accorded to the Patriarch. The Muslim conquest had not resulted in the disestablishment of the Church. On the contrary, it was firmly established with new powers of jurisdiction that it had never enjoyed in Byzantine times. With the conquest of the capital and the subsequent conquest of other districts, practically the whole of the Patriarchal territory was united once more, and, though there was an alien power superimposed, it was its own master. The Byzantine thinkers who had rejected Western help, which at best could only have rescued a small proportion of

and 60,000 Turkish houses. There were 10,000 Greek houses in the suburbs. The numerous Greek villages in the suburbs are listed in Evliya Celebi, *Seyahal-name*, ed. N. Asim, I, p. 452.

[1] For the legal excuse for allowing the Christians to keep some of their churches see S. Runciman, *The Fall of Constantinople*, pp. 199–204.

Orthodox territory and which involved the union of the Church with Rome and a consequent deepening of the divisions within the Church, were justified. The integrity of the Church had been preserved, and with it the integrity of the Greek people.

But the enhanced powers of the Patriarchate involved new and difficult problems. The Byzantine Church had hitherto been essentially a body concerned only with religion. Could its organization and its spiritual life stand the strain of an involvement in political administration? And there were deeper problems. Could the Church sincerely accept Turkish rule in perpetuity? At the back of the mind of every Greek, however faithfully he might collaborate with his new Turkish masters, there lurked the belief that one day the power of Antichrist would crumble and that then the united Greek people would rise again and recreate their holy Empire. How far could a Patriarch, who was a high official in the Ottoman polity and had sworn allegiance to the Sultan, encourage this ambition? It might be politic to render under Caesar the things which were Caesar's; but was not his higher loyalty to God? Could he ever be whole-heartedly loyal to the infidel Sultan? and would the Sultan ever be certain of his loyalty? Moreover, his ambition involved a second problem. The Byzantine Empire had been, in theory at least, oecumenical, the holy Empire of all Christians, regardless of their race. Its decline had reduced it to an empire of the Greeks; and the Orthodox *milet* organized by the new constitution was essentially a Greek *milet*. Its task as the Greeks saw it was to preserve Hellenism. But could Hellenism be combined with oecumenicity? Could the Patriarch be Patriarch of the Orthodox Slavs and the Orthodox Arabs as well as of the Greeks? Would there not inevitably be a narrowing of his vision? The events of the following centuries were to show how difficult these problems were to be.

For the moment, when once the horror of the conquest was over, the prospect for the Orthodox seemed less dark than had been feared. The Sultan was known to like and respect the new Patriarch Gennadius, with whom he had friendly discussions on religion; and at his request Gennadius wrote for him a brief objective statement of the Orthodox Faith for translation into Turkish.[1] News of his interest reached Italy. The Philhellene Francesco Filelfo, whose mother-in-law, the Italian widow of the Greek philosopher John Chrysoloras, had been captured at Constantinople, when writing fulsomely to the Sultan to beg for her release, suggested that His Majesty would be even more admirable if he were to join the Catholic Faith.[2] Soon afterwards Pope Pius II, fearing lest Mehmet might be attracted to the schismatic doctrines of the Greeks, sent him an admirably expressed letter pointing out the truth and wisdom of the Holy Catholic Church.[3] At Constantinople the Greek philosopher George Amiroutzes went so far as to suggest that Christianity and Islam could be blended into one religion. He presented to the Sultan a study which showed that they had much in common. It might be possible to devise a synthesis; or at least each faith could recognize the other as a sister. The difference between the Bible and the Koran had always been exaggerated by bad translations, he maintained; and the Jews were to be blamed for having deliberately encouraged misunderstandings. Unfortunately, his enlightened arguments carried no weight. The Muslims were uninterested; and the Greeks resented the duplicity that he had shown at the time of the Turkish capture of Trebizond; nor did his subsequent behaviour reassure them.[4] But, though such optimism was doomed to disappointment, the atmosphere at the Sultan's court was not intolerant. There were fanatics amongst his ministers, such as Zaganos Pasha and Mahmud Pasha, both of

---

[1] *Historia Patriarchica* (C.S.H.B. edition), pp. 83 ff. Gennadius's treatise is given in his *Œuvres Complètes* (ed. L. Petit, X. A. Sidérides and M. Jugie), III, pp. xxx ff.

[2] E. Legrand, *Cent-dix Lettres Grecques de Fr. Philelphe*, pp. 62–8.

[3] Pius II, *Lettera a Maomitto II*, ed. G. Toffanin.

[4] *Historia Politica* (C.S.H.B. edition), pp. 38–9: *Historia Patriarchica* (C.S.H.B. edition), pp. 96–101. A kindlier judgment on Amiroutzes is given in N. B. Tomadakis, ''Ετούρκευσεν ὁ Γεώργιος 'Αμιρούτзης; ', 'Επετηρὶς 'Εταιρείας Βυзαντινῶν Σπουδῶν, XVIII (1948), pp. 99–143.

them converts to Islam; but their influence was countered by men such as the admiral Hamza Bey, the friend of the Greek historian Critobulus. The Sultan deeply respected his Christian stepmother, the Lady Mara, daughter of George Branković, Despot of Serbia, and his Greek wife, Irene Cantacuzena, and widow of Murad II. She lived now in retirement at Serres in Macedonia; but any wish that she expressed was promptly fulfilled by her stepson. Not all the converts to Islam were fanatical. Many whose conversion had been for political rather than religious motives were ready to help their former co-religionists. Even among the officers of the Janissaries there were numbers who remembered their Christian homes and families and were anxious to do them services. Had the Sultan not been tolerant these converts would not have dared thus to create doubts about their sincerity. But Mehmet seemed to favour collaboration.

Nevertheless there were clouds on the horizon. Gennadius himself was the first to notice them. A few months after his installation he asked permission of the Sultan to move the Patriarchal headquarters out of the church of the Holy Apostles. The district in which it stood was now colonized by Turks who resented the presence of the great Christian cathedral. One morning the corpse of a Turk was found in the courtyard. It had obviously been planted there; but it gave the neighbouring Turks the excuse for demonstrating against the Christians. Had the church building itself been in a better condition Gennadius might have tried to ride out the storm; but it was structurally unsound. Its repair would have been costly; and there might well have been objections from the Turks had he sought permission for the work. He collected all the treasures and relics that the church contained and moved with them into the Phanar quarter, which was inhabited by Greeks. There he installed himself in the convent of the Pammacaristos, transferring the nuns to the neighbouring monastery of St John in Trullo; and the small but exquisite church of the Pammacaristos became the Patriarchal church. It was in its side-chapel that the Sultan came to visit him to discuss religion and politics, carefully refusing to enter the sanctuary itself lest his successors would make that an excuse for annexing the building for Islam. His precautions were in vain.[1]

Deeply respected though Gennadius was, his task was not easy. He roused opposition from religious purists by his use of Economy uncanonically to confirm or annul marriages which Christians taken prisoner at the time of the capture of Constantinople had contracted during their captivity. In particular he was criticized for allowing marriages of boys under the canonical age of twelve; which he permitted because a married boy was not liable to be taken by the Turks for the Janissary corps, to be brought up as a Muslim, according to the system known as the *devshirme* in Turkish and the *paidomazoma* in Greek. Wearied by such illiberal opposition, Gennadius resigned the Patriarchate in 1457 and retired first to Mount Athos, then to the monastery of St John at Serres, under the patronage of the Lady Mara, Murad II's Serbian widow. He was not left in peace. Twice more he was summoned back to the Patriarchal throne. The date of his death is unknown. We may hope that he was spared the sight of the scandals that were to come.[2]

[1] *Historia Politica* (C.S.H.B. edition), p. 28. When Murad III converted the Pammacaristos into a mosque (see below, p. 190), it was on the excuse that the Conqueror had worshipped there.

[2] For the obscure history of the Patriarchate up till 1466 see below, pp. 192–3. Gennadius's use of Economy is reported by his disciple, Theodore Agallianos. See C. G. Patrineli, ''Ο Θεόδωρος 'Αγαλλιανὸς καὶ οἱ 'Ανέκδοτοι Λόγοι του', pp. 146–8, and preface, pp. 69–70.

CHAPTER 2

THE CHURCH AND THE INFIDEL STATE

The constitution arranged between the Conquering Sultan and the Patriarch Gennadius for the Orthodox *milet* soon proved to be more effective on paper than in fact. The Turks could not forget that they were the ruling race, the conquerors of the Christians; and it irked them that the Greeks should retain privileges that no conquered infidel race ought to enjoy. Mehmet himself and his advisers, who were most of them older men than he, had been brought up at a time when Constantinople was a great cultural centre and Greek learning was renowned throughout the world. They could not fail to feel some respect for Greeks. Mehmet was proud to see himself as the heir of the Caesars, Roman Emperor as well as Sultan; and he wished his Christian subjects to accept him as such. Subsequent generations of Turks did not share the same feelings. Mehmet's son Bayezit II was five years old when his father captured Constantinople. By the time that he was a young man all the Greek scholars that had given lustre to Constantinople were scattered, some in Italy and the West, others in the safe obscurity of a monastic cell. All the Greeks that he met were either merchants or clerks or artisans, or priests chosen for their tactful and often obsequious demeanour. He had no special intellectual tastes, such as his father had possessed; to him Greek culture meant nothing.[1] His son, Selim I, actively disliked the Christians. The triumph of his reign was the completion of the conquest of Syria, Egypt and Arabia; and his main ambition was gratified when he took the title of Caliph, Commander of the Faithful.[2]

[1] W. J. Perry, 'Bāyazīd II' in *Encyclopaedia of Islam* (new edition), I, pp. 1119–21; J. von Hammer-Purgstall, *Geschichte des Osmanischen Reiches* (1st edition), II, pp. 250 ff.; N. Jorga, *Geschichte des Osmanischen Reiches*, II, pp. 230 ff.

[2] J. H. Kramers, 'Selim I', in *Encyclopaedia of Islam* (1st edition), IV, pp. 214–17; von Hammer-Purgstall, *op. cit.* II, pp. 350 ff.; T. W. Arnold, *The Caliphate*, pp. 137, 164 ff.

The Church and the Infidel State

With Sultan Suleiman the Magnificent there was once more a Sultan who was interested in the intellectual currents of the world; but by then the Greeks within his dominions were in no position to make any great contribution to them. He himself tried to deal justly with them; but to him and to the average Turk they had become a servile race, useful at times for financial or secretarial or even diplomatic work, but essentially untrustworthy and intriguing, and undeserving of privileges.[1] With the accession of Suleiman's son, Selim II, the Drunkard, decline set in at the top of the Ottoman structure. The Sublime Porte began to be controlled by ministers who, with a few distinguished exceptions, were greedy and unscrupulous; while usually the Sultana Valide, the Sultan's mother, pulled the strings from behind the curtains of the seraglio.[2]

The fate of the Ottoman Sultanate is perhaps an example of the corruption of absolute power. But the corruption of absolute impotence began to show itself amongst the Greeks. As they found themselves less and less able to rely on good treatment from above and less and less certain that their rights would be regarded, they inevitably took refuge in intrigue. In their hopelessness they began to forget the need for mutual loyalties. Each man began to plot for his own benefit; and it was to the interest of the Turks to encourage jealousy and intrigue and the demoralization of the *milet*.

The outward symptom of the worsening condition of the Greeks was the steady annexation of their churches and their conversion into mosques. The Conquering Sultan had been remarkably indulgent on this point. The only church that he had formally annexed had been Saint Sophia. Its annexation was hardly surprising; for the Great Church was more than a church; it was a symbol of the old Christian Empire. Its conversion set a seal on

[1] For Suleiman see A. M. Lybyer, *The Government of the Ottoman Empire in the time of Suleiman the Magnificent*, esp. pp. 34, 151, 160, 163.
[2] Von Hammer-Purgstall, *op. cit.* II, pp. 354 ff.; N. Jorga, *Geschichte des Osmanischen Reiches*, III, pp. 137 ff.

the new dispensation. Yet for many years to come little attempt was made there to alter the old Christian decoration, apart from the covering or destruction of the faces of Christ and the saints in the mosaics.[1] Other churches, such as the New Basilica and Our Lady of the Lighthouse in the old Imperial Palace quarter, had been so badly damaged in the looting of the city that they were abandoned and either demolished or allowed to fall down. Others again, such as the Pantocrator or Saint Saviour in Chora, had been sacked and desecrated; and the Greeks made no attempt to retain them. As they were structurally sound it was not surprising that they were soon transformed into mosques. Some churches were taken over at once and put to secular uses. Saint Irene, close to Saint Sophia, became an armoury; Saint John in Dippion, near to the Hippodrome, housed a menagerie.[2] In these cases the churches were in districts settled by Turks, and the Christians were prudent enough to make no protest. The Holy Apostles, though preserved for the Christians at the time of the fall of the city, was given up, as we have seen, within a few months; and, in view of its dilapidated condition, the Sultan was not un-

---

[1] In 1550 Nicolas de Nicolay remarked on the mosaic figures in Saint Sophia but noted that the Turks had plucked out the eyes (*Les Navigations, Peregrinations et Voyages*, p. 104). A manuscript account of an Italian's visit to Constantinople in 1611 (British Museum, MS. Harl. 3408) reports that the Turks had covered everything inside the church with whitewash. But sixty years later Grelot was able to sketch many of the mosaics and found that only the faces of the figures had been covered or removed. The mosaics that the Turks could not reach were barely spoiled; but he saw men with long poles trying to daub plaster over the figures (G. J. Grelot, *A Late Voyage to Constantinople* (trans. J. Philips), pp. 111 ff., esp. pp. 125–6). Lady Mary Wortley Montagu (*Complete Letters* (ed. R. Halsband), I, pp. 398–9), eager to defend the Turks from any charge of vandalism, declares that if the faces have vanished it is because of the ravages of time. She does not explain why the rest of the figures were in a better condition. Gerlach saw unspoiled frescoes in St John of Studium, though it was already converted into a mosque, as well as in St Theodosia (at that time used as a warehouse) and other former churches (S. Gerlach, *Tagebuch*, pp. 217, 358–9).

[2] For the fate of these churches see S. Runciman, *The Fall of Constantinople*, pp. 199–200. Arnold von Harff, visiting Constantinople in 1499, declares more than once that many churches were being used as menageries (*The Pilgrimage of Arnold von Harff* (Hakluyt edition), pp. 241–2, 244).

reasonable in destroying it in order to erect a great mosque which should bear his name on the site. But a number of other churches were left in Christian hands.[1] These churches remained inviolate so long as Sultan Mehmet II lived. His son, Bayezit II, had other ideas. In 1490 he demanded the surrender of the Patriarchal church, the Pammacaristos. But the Patriarch Dionysius I was able to prove that Mehmet II had definitely bestowed the church upon the Patriarchate. The Sultan gave way, merely ordering the removal of the cross from the summit of the dome. At the same time he forbade his officials to annex other churches, as they were proposing to do.[2] His ban, however, was soon disregarded, no doubt with his own connivance. The church of the Panachrantos was annexed before 1494 and that of Saint John in Studium about 1500. It was about this time that Turkish officials turned the abandoned churches of the Chora and the Pantocrator into mosques; and they no doubt wished to extend their operations to churches still in use.[3]

In about 1520 Sultan Selim I, who disliked Christianity, suggested to his horrified vizier that all Christians should be forcibly converted to Islam. When he was told that this was impracticable, he demanded that at least all their churches should be surrendered. The vizier warned the Patriarch, Theoleptus I, who engaged the services of a clever lawyer called Xenakis. Theoleptus admitted that he had no *firman* protecting the churches. It had been burnt in a fire at the Patriarchate, he said. But Xenakis was able to produce three aged Janissaries who had been present when the Conquering Sultan entered Constantinople. They swore on the Koran that they had seen a number of notables from the city come to the Sultan as he was waiting to make his entrance and offer him the keys of their respective districts. In return he

---

[1] See above, p. 181.

[2] A. C. Hypsilantis, Τὰ μετὰ τὴν Ἅλωσιν (ed. A. Germanos), pp. 62, 91, based on Patriarchal records.

[3] A. van Millingen, *Byzantine Churches in Constantinople*, pp. 128, 304; R. Janin, *Constantinople Byzantine*, I, iii, 'Les Eglises et les monastères', pp. 224, 447, 533, 550. For the Chora, P. Gyllius, *De Constantinopoleos Topographia*, p. 201.

promised them that they could retain their churches. Sultan Selim accepted this evidence and even allowed the Christians to reopen some of their churches which his officials had closed. All the same, several more churches were annexed during his reign.[1] In 1537, under Suleiman the Magnificent, the question was raised again. The Patriarch Jeremias I referred the Sultan to Selim's decision. Suleiman then consulted the Sheikh ul-Islam, as the highest Muslim legal authority; and, after going into the matter, the Sheikh pronounced that 'as far as was known Constantinople was taken by force; but the fact that the churches were untouched must mean that the city surrendered by capitulation'. Suleiman accepted this decision.[2] For the rest of his reign no more churches were taken over. Later Sultans were less indulgent. More conversions were made under Selim II; and in 1586 Murad III, just back from a successful campaign in Azerbaijan, announced that he was going to transform the Patriarchal church of the Pammacaristos into a Mosque of Victory—Fethiye Cami. Had the Patriarch Jeremias II, whom Murad liked, been still on the throne, the annexation might have been averted. But Jeremias had been recently ousted by an intrigue in the Holy Synod; and the incumbent at the moment, Theoleptus II, was a nonentity. Murad was doubtless glad to be able to justify his annexation as a punishment to the intriguers. The Patriarch of Alexandria put the small church of Saint Demetrius Kanavou, which he owned, at the disposal of Jeremias II, when he returned to the Patriarchate a few months later, until new accommodation could be arranged. Finally the Patriarchate was allowed to rebuild the church of Saint George, in the

---

[1] *Historia Patriarchica* (C.S.H.B. edition), pp. 158 ff.; Demetrius Cantemir, *The History of the Growth and Decay of the Othman Empire* (trans. N. Tindal), pp. 102–3. See following note.

[2] *Historia Patriarchica, loc. cit.*; Cantemir, *loc. cit.* The *Historia Patriarchica* combines the two episodes into one; but the janissaries clearly took part in the earlier episode, as they could not have been alive in 1537, eighty-four years after the fall of the city. Dr R. Walsh, two and a half centuries later, heard a garbled version of the story (*Residence in Constantinople during the Greek and Turkish Revolutions*, II, pp. 360–1).

heart of the Phanar quarter, to serve his needs. The new church was ready early in the next century and buildings were erected nearby to house the Patriarchal residence and offices. Like all the churches that the Greeks were permitted to build to replace those that they had lost, the new church was kept deliberately drab on the exterior, and the erection of a dome visible from outside was forbidden.[1]

By the eighteenth century there were some forty Greek churches in Constantinople; but only three of these had been built before the conquest. These were Saint George of the Cypresses, in Psamathia, which was destroyed by earthquake early in the century; Saint Demetrius Kanavou, which was destroyed by fire a few years later; and Saint Mary of the Mongols. This church owed its preservation to the fact that Mehmet II had employed a Greek architect to build for him the mosque that was erected on the site of the Holy Apostles; and the architect, Christodulos, was rewarded with the gift of the street in which the church, to which his mother was deeply attached, stood. He transferred the title-deeds, which guaranteed the integrity of the church, to the church itself. At the end of the seventeenth century the Muslims attempted to confiscate the building. Demetrius Cantemir, who was then legal adviser to the Patriarchate, was able to show the Sultan's original *firman* to the vizier Ali Köprülü, who kissed it reverently and gave orders that the church was to be unmolested. It still remains a church, though it was badly damaged in the anti-Greek riots of 1955.[2]

A fourth church, the Perivleptos, was in Christian hands, though not in the hands of the Greeks. It had been transferred to the Armenians by Sultan Ibrahim at the request of his Armenian

---

[1] M. Gedeon, Πατριαρχικοὶ Πίνακες, p. 530.

[2] M. Baudrier, *Histoire générale du serrail et de la cour du Grand Seigneur*, published in 1623, says (p. 9) that the Greeks possessed forty churches in the city. For St George of the Cypresses and St Demetrius Kanavou see Janin, *op. cit.* I, iii, pp. 75, 95. For St Mary of the Mongols, Cantemir, *op. cit.* p. 105. Evliya Celebi, *Seyahalname* (ed. N. Asim), I, p. 452, lists a large number of Greek churches in the suburbs.

favourite, a lady of ample charms known as Şekerparce, or 'lump of sugar', who was said to weigh more than 300 pounds.[1] The same process went on in the provincial towns. In Thessalonica the great church of Saint Demetrius and the churches of Saint Sophia and Saint George were converted in the middle of the sixteenth century.[2] In Athens, the church of Our Lady, which earlier ages had known as the Parthenon, became a mosque about the same time, with a minaret rising jauntily by its side; and, when the Parthenon was wrecked in 1687 by a Venetian shell landing on an armament store kept in its precincts, a little mosque was built within the ruins.[3] In any town in which Turks settled, it was the same story. Only in purely Christian districts were the churches left unmolested. The annexations were not only humiliating, but they caused grave legal and economic problems. Many of the annexed churches possessed considerable property, whose disposal involved endless lawsuits and intrigue. Nor was it easy for the Greeks to obtain permission to erect churches to replace those that they had lost. If they did not meet with active hostility they had to face the blank wall of Turkish officialdom. Bribery was usually the only method for securing a quick answer to any such request. All too soon the Greeks learnt that their masters must be manipulated through gifts of money.

[1] Janin, *op. cit.* p. 328: A. D. Alderson, *The Structure of the Ottoman Dynasty*, xxxvii, n. 4: Van Millingen, *Byzantine Constantinople: The Walls of the City*, p. 20.

[2] O. Tafrali, *Topographie de Thessalonique*, pp. 150 ff., shows that some of the churches were converted immediately after the Turkish occupation. St Demetrius was converted in Bayezit II's reign. The conversion of St Sophia is dated by an inscription as 993 A.H. (A.D. 1545). The Venetian ambassador Lorenzo Bernardo, who passed through the city in 1590, says that it was already a mosque, but the mosaic of the Pantocrator in the dome had not been covered over. *Viaggio a Constantinopoli di ser Lorenzo Bernardo*, in *Miscellanea pubblicata dalla Deputazione Veneta di Storia Patria*, p. 33. N. Jorga, *Byzance après Byzance*, p. 46, wrongly supposes that Bernardo refers to Sophia in Constantinople.

[3] It is uncertain when the Parthenon was converted into a mosque. Mehmet II seems himself to have converted the church of Our Lady of Salvation, which had been the Orthodox cathedral in Frankish times. See D. Sicilianos, *Old and New Athens* (trans. R. Liddell), p. 96. See also F. W. Hasluck, *Christianity and Islam under the Sultans*, I, pp. 13–16, II, p. 755.

This might not have been so harmful if the organization of the Church itself had remained uncorrupted. There the Greeks helped to bring on their own troubles. They could not abandon their love for politics; and, with the open exercise of power now denied to them, they revelled in underground intrigue. Gennadius had been a figure that commanded universal respect. In their despair after the conquest the Greeks were glad to follow a leader who was ready and able to act on their behalf. But soon factions arose, and when he retired there was no one of equal calibre to succeed him. Of his successor as Patriarch, Isidore II, we know little beyond his name. He died on 31 March 1462. The next Patriarch, Joasaph I, was reigning in 1463, when an incident occurred which illustrated the dangers of the new régime. The scholar George Amiroutzes, who was living in Constantinople and enjoyed the favour of the Sultan because of his learning, wished to contract a marriage with the widow of the last Duke of Athens, though his own wife was still alive. According to another version of the story the would-be bigamist was a noble from Trebizond called Kavazites, on whose behalf Amiroutzes was agitating. Whoever was the petitioner, Joasaph refused to bless the bigamous union. Amiroutzes then worked on the Holy Synod, threatening its members in the name of his powerful cousin, the Muslim convert Mahmud Pasha, to have Joasaph deposed. Joasaph tried in vain to commit suicide. Gennadius seems to have been summoned to restore order.[1] Of the next Patriarch, Sophronius I, nothing is known; indeed, his reign may have occurred between Isidore II's and Joasaph I's. Certainly Gennadius was back on the throne for a while in 1464. With his successor, Mark Xylocaraves, worse trouble began. Mark was elected early in 1465; but he had enemies, led by Symeon, Metropolitan of Trebizond, who coveted the Patriarchal throne. Early in 1466

---

[1] *Historia Politica* (C.S.H.B. edition), pp. 38–9; *Historia Patriarchica* (C.S.H.B. edition), pp. 96–101; *Ekthesis Chronica* (ed. S. Lambros), p. 36. More precise information is provided in the memoirs of Theodore Agallianos, in Ch. G. Patrineli, Ὁ Θεόδωρος Ἀγαλλιανὸς καὶ οἱ Ἀνέκδοτοι Λόγοι του, which gives the date of Isidore's death (p. 118). See Patrineli's preface, pp. 61–8.

The Church and the Infidel State

Symeon raised the sum of 2,000 pieces of gold, 1,000 from his own resources and 1,000 from his friends, and presented the money to the Sultan's ministers, who then obligingly ordered the Holy Synod to depose Mark and elect Symeon. News of the simoniacal transaction reached the ears of Murad's Christian widow, the Lady Mara. She hastened from Serres to the Sultan's court, prudently bringing with her another 2,000 pieces of gold. The Sultan greeted her with the words: 'What is this, my mother?' She begged him to solve the problem by having both Mark and Symeon deposed in favour of her own candidate, the saintly Dionysius, a Peloponnesian who was Metropolitan of Philippopolis. Her request was granted. But Symeon was undefeated. In 1471 he accused Dionysius before the Synod of having been circumcised as a Muslim when as a child he had spent some time in captivity. Though Dionysius was able to provide visible proof that the charge was false, the Synod deposed him; and a further payment of 2,000 gold pieces to the Sublime Porte secured Symeon's re-election. Sultan Mehmet seems to have watched it all with cynical amusement, while the Lady Mara was too badly disillusioned to interfere, though she offered Dionysius protection near her own residence at Serres.[1] But Symeon three years later was outbid by a Serbian candidate, Raphael, who offered to make an annual payment of 2,000 pieces of gold to the Sublime Porte. The Metropolitan of Heraclea refused to consecrate him; and, though the Metropolitan of Ancyra was more obliging, there were doubts of the legality of his enthronement, and many of the Synod refused to communicate with him. He had, moreover, difficulty in raising the money that he had promised. Eventually, probably early in 1477, the Sultan, urged again by his stepmother, intervened to restore order and secured the election of Maximus III Manasses. Maximus, whose real name was Manuel Christonymus, had been Grand Ecclesiarch and had quarrelled with Gennadius over his use of Economy and later had offended the Sultan by

[1] *Historia Politica* (C.S.H.B. edition), pp. 39–42; *Historia Patriarchica* (C.S.H.B. edition), pp. 102–12.

supporting Joasaph I against Amiroutzes. He had now recaptured the Sultan's respect, and died honourably in office a few months after Mehmet himself died. Symeon then bought his way back to the throne and was now generally accepted.[1] The Council which he held in 1484, in order formally to abrogate the Union of Florence and to fix the procedure for the readmission of unionists into the Church, was attended by representatives of all the Orthodox communities.[2]

Henceforward it was rare for a Patriarch not to represent some party or faction. Influence to control the appointment was exercised from various quarters. The Lady Mara died in about 1480; but her role was carried on by her niece, the Princess of Wallachia, who secured the appointment of Symeon's successor, Niphon II. This marked the entry of the Danubian rulers on the Patriarchal scene. The Princes of Wallachia and Moldavia had submitted voluntarily to the Sultan and thus preserved their autonomy; and they were wealthy. Their subjects, the ancestors of the Roumanians of today, were consciously not Slavs, though their Church formed a part of the Serbian Church and employed the Slavonic liturgy. Their upper classes felt themselves far nearer to the Greeks than to the Slavs. As the most exalted lay personages within the Ottoman Empire the Danubian princes sought continually to place their candidates on the Patriarchal throne.[3] The King of Georgia, as the only independent monarch, apart from the distant Russian Grand Prince, to rule within the area of the Patriarchate, tried now and then to intervene. But the Georgian Church was semi-autonomous, with its own liturgy in its own

---

[1] *Historia Politica* (C.S.H.B. edition), pp. 43–4; *Historia Patriarchica* (C.S.H.B. edition), pp. 113–15; Gedeon, *op. cit.* pp. 490–1. See also V. Steplanidou, Συμβολαὶ εἰς τὴν Ἐκκλησιαστικὴν Ἱστορίαν καὶ τὸ Ἐκκλησιαστικὸν Δίκαιον, pp. 104, 113.

[2] See below, p. 228.

[3] *Historia Patriarchica* (C.S.H.B. edition), pp. 128–40. See Jorga, *Byzance après Byzance*, pp. 84–6. It was through Wallachian influence that Niphon returned to the Patriarchal throne in 1497–8. He was re-elected in 1502 but refused. Pachomius I, who took his place, also had Wallachian support. See N. Popescu, *Patriarhii Ţarigradului prin ţerile româneşti in veacul al XVI-lea*, pp. 5 ff.

vernacular; and Georgia had its own political troubles. But, if the Georgian monarch chose to exert it, his influence could be formidable.[1] More constant and more effective was the influence exerted by the monks of Mount Athos. The Holy Mountain was still full of rich monasteries and still a centre of intellectual and spiritual activity. Its autonomy was respected by the Turks, though, later, a Turkish official, condemned to temporary celibacy, resided there as the Sultan's representative. Until they declined in the late seventeenth century a candidate for the Patriarchate with the backing of the Athonite monasteries enjoyed great prestige.[2] But the Princes of the Danubian states and the King of Georgia and even the monks of the Mountain lived at a distance from Constantinople. Far more effective pressure was soon to be exercised by the rich Greek merchants of the Sultan's capital.

One of the unforeseen consequences of the Ottoman conquest was the rebirth of Greek mercantile life. For some centuries past the Italians had dominated the trade of the Levant, enjoying privileges denied to local merchants. Now their privileges were gone and their colonies dwindled away. Few Turks had any aptitude or any taste for commerce; and trade within the huge and expanding dominions of the Sultan passed into the hands of his subject races, the Jews, the Armenians, and, above all, the Greeks. The Greek genius for commerce always flourishes in areas where the Greeks are debarred from political power and are thus ready to direct their ambition and enterprise to commercial ends. It was not long after the conquest that Greek merchant dynasties emerged at Constantinople. Some of the dynasties claimed to be descended from well-known Byzantine families; and, though the claims were seldom justified, for few of the old families survived in the male line, it helped the prestige of a rising merchant if he bore a grand Imperial surname such as Lascaris, Argyrus or Ducas.

---

[1] Joachim I in 1504 had Georgian support. *Historia Patriarchica* (C.S.H.B. edition), pp. 140–1.

[2] Maximus IV (1491–7), had Athonite support, as, later, had Metrophanes III (1565–72, and 1579–80). See Jorga, *Byzance après Byzance*, pp. 70, 84–5.

The noble families forcibly imported by the Conquering Sultan from Trebizond had a better claim to ancient lineage, such as the Ypsilanti, kinsmen to the Imperial Comneni. A little later when the Turks occupied Chios, Chiot families migrated to Constantinople and showed a particular genius for business. Amongst them it was fashionable to claim a high Italian descent, preferably with Roman origins.[1] In the sixteenth century the leading Greek family was that of the Cantacuzeni, perhaps the only family whose claim to be in the direct line from Byzantine Emperors was authentic. By the middle of the century the head of the family, Michael Cantacuzenus, whom the Turks surnamed *Shaitanoglu*, or the Devil's son, was one of the wealthiest men in all the East. He earned 60,000 ducats a year from his control of the fur-trade from Russia, for which the Sultan had given him the monopoly. He was able to pay for the fitting-out of sixty galleys for the Sultan's navy. His wife was the daughter of the Prince of Wallachia and the granddaughter of the Prince of Moldavia. He seldom came to Constantinople, preferring to live at Anchialus, on the Black Sea coast, a city inhabited almost exclusively by Greeks, where the sight of his wealth would not offend Turkish eyes. But even so he aroused envy. In the end, in 1578, the Turks arrested him on a nominal charge and put him to death. His possessions were confiscated and put up for sale. Their splendour amazed everyone. Most of his precious manuscripts were bought by the monasteries of Mount Athos.[2]

Such magnates, called by the Greeks of the time *archontes*, or rulers, inevitably became the dominant influence at the Patriarchate. They were at hand; they had plentiful ready money, for

[1] See below, p. 367.

[2] For the Cantacuzeni see N. Jorga, *Despre Cantacuzini—Genealogia Cantacuzinilor —Documentele Cantacuzinilor, passim,* and, for Michael in particular, *ibid.* pp. xxii–xxxv; Jorga, *Byzance après Byzance,* pp. 114–21. There are numerous references to him in the Patriarchal History and in Gerlach, *op. cit.,* esp. pp. 55, 60, 223 ff. Gerlach believed that he was not really a member of the old Imperial family of the Cantacuzeni but the son of an English ambassador. Crusius, *Turco-Graecia,* p. 509, tells of the sale of his books, his informant being Gerlach.

supplementing church funds or for bribing Turkish officials. When the Patriarchate needed laymen to fill its administrative offices, it was from their class that the officials were drawn. The power of an *archon* was shown in 1565, when Michael Cantacuzenus secured the deposition of the Patriarch Joasaph II, one of the most distinguished and learned of Patriarchs, personally popular among all the Orthodox and fully supported by the monks of Mount Athos, after a successful reign of ten years, because he would not further one of Michael's ambitious family-marriage schemes, on the ground that it infringed canon law.[1]

These intrigues were complicated by the presence of Turkish officials in the offing, all eager to make what money they could out of the difficulties of the Patriarchate. It had become the regular custom now that the Patriarch had not only to pay a sum to the Sublime Porte to have his election ratified, but also had to provide a regular annual offering. When the Patriarch Symeon died intestate and without any close relative, the Turkish authorities confiscated his possessions even though he had only a life-interest in them and they should have passed to his successor. Niphon, who succeeded him, tried clumsily to recover them by inventing a hitherto unknown nephew of Symeon's; but the imposture was discovered and punished by further confiscations. Niphon proved altogether to be a foolish and unsatisfactory Patriarch, and, despite his backing by the Prince of Wallachia and the Athonite monasteries, public opinion insisted on his deposition and his replacement by the saintly Dionysius I, who came out of his retirement at Serres. The Athonite monks were annoyed, and after two years obtained his retirement and the election of their candidate, Maximus IV, who reigned from 1491 to 1497. Maximus was an estimable man whose main efforts were concentrated on securing, not unsuccessfully, better treatment for the Orthodox living in Venetian territory. On his death Niphon II returned to power for a year, but was then displaced by an able young priest, Joachim I, who was backed by the King of Georgia. His reign was interrup-

---

[1] Crusius, *op. cit.* p. 274; Gerlach, *op. cit.* p. 30.

ted by an attempt to replace Niphon and by the temporary elevation of Pachomius I, to whom the Wallachians transferred their
favour. Joachim died in Wallachia in 1504, when trying to reconcile himself with the Prince; and Pachomius then occupied the
throne for nine years.[1] On his death Sultan Selim himself intervened to order the election of a Cretan whom he liked, Theoleptus I. It was fortunate that Theoleptus was in power when Selim
made his abortive attempt to take over the Christian churches, as
the Sultan respected him. But his attempt to deal with the difficult
case of Arsenius of Monemvasia made him a number of enemies,
who in 1522, soon after Selim's death, accused him of gross
immorality. He died before the case was heard by the Synod.[2]
His successor, Jeremias I, was in Cyprus when he was elected,
where he had managed to make a concordat with the Venetian
authorities on behalf of the Orthodox. His reign of twenty-one
years is the longest in Patriarchal history, though he nearly lost
the throne in 1526, when he was on a pilgrimage to Jerusalem; a
certain Joannicius persuaded the Holy Synod to depose him in his
own favour, but the transaction was not ratified, though Jeremias's friends had to pay 500 gold pieces to the Sublime Porte to
have the ratification held up. On the whole Jeremias enjoyed the
support of the Sultan, Suleiman the Magnificent, an orderly man
who was glad to see his Christian subjects enjoying some stability.[3]

On Jeremias's death, it was decided, under the influence of
Germanus, Patriarch of Jerusalem, to lay it down clearly that only
the full Synod could elect a patriarch. But Dionysius II, whom
Jeremias designated as his successor, was elected against the wishes
of the Holy Synod, which only gave way when there were
popular demonstrations in his favour. He reigned for nine years,
and his successor, Joasaph II, for ten, until he was deposed through
the machinations of Michael Cantacuzenus. The next two

[1] See above, p. 195, n. 3.
[2] *Historia Patriarchica* (C.S.H.B. edition), pp. 141–52. For Arsenius of Monemvasia see below, p. 229.
[3] *Historia Patriarchica* (C.S.H.B. edition), pp. 153–72; Gerlach, *op. cit.* pp. 502, 509.

Patriarchs, Metrophanes III and Jeremias II, both reigned for seven years. Metrophanes was deposed in 1572 because he was believed to have pro-Roman tendencies, and promised never to try to return to the Patriarchal throne.[1] Jeremias II, who like Dionysius II owed his election to noisy demonstrations by the Greek congregations, was probably the ablest man to sit on the Patriarchal throne during the Captivity. He was a sound theologian, an ardent reformer and a fierce enemy to simony. His virtues irritated the Holy Synod, who deposed him in 1579, bringing back Metrophanes III, in spite of his promise. But Jeremias still enjoyed popular support. After nine months the Synod was forced to re-elect him. Three and a half years later he was again deposed; but once again, after two years, his popularity, backed by the personal good will of the Sultan, secured his return, and he reigned for another nine years, till his death in 1595.[2]

The period that followed was chaotic. Ever since Symeon of Trebizond had introduced the practice, each election to the Patriarchate involved the payment of money to the Sublime Porte; and the price was rising. An annual subvention was also expected. Dionysius II paid a *peshkesh* of 3,000 gold pieces to have his election ratified, but succeeded in having the yearly tribute paid by the Church reduced to a maximum of 2,000 pieces of gold. In return, the Patriarch was permitted to add to the Patriarchal residence and offices. Joasaph II succeeded in reducing the *peshtesh* to 2,000 pieces; but his success was short lived. Disputed elections began to involve an auction sale, the Sublime Porte naturally favouring the candidate who could pay most. A

[1] *Historia Patriarchica* (C.S.H.B. edition), pp. 173–91; Dorotheus of Monemvasia, *Chronicle* (1818 edition), pp. 440–3. Metrophanes had visited Venice and Rome before his elevation and therefore was suspect.

[2] *Historia Patriarchica* (C.S.H.B. edition), pp. 191–204; Dorotheus of Monemvasia, *op. cit.* pp. 439–40. Dorotheus disliked Jeremias II and accused him, unreasonably, of being dull-witted. For a full account of Jeremias's career see C. Sathas, Βιογραφικὸν Σχεδίασμα περὶ τοῦ Πατριάρχου Ἱερεμίου Β'; also L. Petit, 'Jérémie II Tranos', in *Dictionnaire de théologie catholique*, VIII, 1, coll. 886–94. For his relations with the Lutherans and with Russia see below, pp. 247–56.

Patriarch like Jeremias II, who was elected by the will of the congregations, was thus at a disadvantage compared with a candidate backed by the rich rulers of the Principalities or by the rich mercantile families of Constantinople. Not unnaturally, the Turkish authorities welcomed frequent changes on the Patriarchal throne. A few Turkish statesmen, such as Suleiman the Magnificent, tried to ensure greater stability among the Greeks. But the quarrels and intrigues in which not only the Holy Synod but the whole Greek community indulged offered too tempting an opportunity for Turkish greed to ignore.[1]

In the century from 1595, when Jeremias II ended his last Patriarchal reign, to 1695, there were sixty-one changes on the Patriarchal throne, though, as many Patriarchs were reinstated after deposition, there were only thirty-one individual Patriarchs. Some enjoyed short spells of office. Matthew II reigned for twenty days in 1595, then for nearly four years, from 1598 to 1602, and finally for seventeen days in 1603. Cyril I Lucaris, the most celebrated of all the seventeenth-century Patriarchs, enjoyed seven different spells on the throne. One of his rivals, Cyril II, reigned once for one week only, and later for twelve months. The average length of reign was slightly less than twenty months. Occupational risks were higher: four Patriarchs, Cyril I, Parthenius II, Parthenius III and Gabriel II, were put to death by the Turks on the suspicion of treason. Occasionally a candidate had such powerful friends among the authorities that he achieved his ambition without a specific money-payment; but such men were rare.[2] By the end of the seventeenth century the usual price paid by a Patriarch on his election was in the neighbourhood of 20,000 piastres—roughly 3,000 gold pounds. At the same time the Patriarchate had been paying to the Porte from early in the century an annual tax of 20,000 piastres, as well as various minor

---

[1] *Historia Patriarchica* (C.S.H.B. edition), p. 179. See Jorga, *Byzance après Byzance*, pp. 82 ff.

[2] S. Vailhé, 'Constantinople (Eglise de)', *Dictionnaire de théologie catholique* III, 2, coll. 1418–26.

taxes, which included the obligation to provide the mutton required daily by the Palace Guard, men of voracious appetite.[1] The climax was reached early in the eighteenth century, in 1726, when the Patriarch Callinicus III paid no less than 36,400 piastres for his election—roughly 5,600 gold pounds. As he died of joy, from a sudden heart attack, the following day, the transaction proved expensive for the Church.[2] Such scandals produced in the end a greater stability. The Greek community began to realize that the Church, which their members had increasingly to subsidize, simply could not afford such frequent changes; and the Turks realized that things had gone too far. In the century from 1695 to 1795 there were thirty-one Patriarchal reigns, and twenty-three individual Patriarchs. This was bad enough, if we compare it with the century from 1495 to 1595, when there had been only nineteen reigns; but at least it was an improvement on the seventeenth century.[3] Nevertheless the debts of the Patriarchate rose steadily. In 1730 they amounted to 100,769 piastres, that is to say, rather more than 15,000 gold pounds, while the Patriarchal revenues, for which we have no definite figures, seem seldom to have been adequate to cover regular expenses.[4] It was inevitable that the whole Church should become dependent upon the

[1] Vailhé, *art. cit.* coll. 1430-2. According to J. Aymon, *Monuments authentiques de la religion des Grecs et de la fausseté de plusieurs confessions de foi des Chrétiens*, p.486, Dionysius III paid 12,000 écus in 1662. Sir Paul Ricaut, *The Present State of the Greek and Armenian Churches, Anno Christi, 1678* (published in 1680), says that the Patriarch used to pay 10,000 dollars on his election, but the price had risen now to 25,000 (p. 107). Grelot says that, when he was in Constantinople in the 1670s, two successive Patriarchs paid 50,000 and 60,000 crowns (*op. cit.* p. 138). This is confirmed by Pitton de Tournefort, *Relation d'un voyage du Levant*, 1700, p. 118, who says that the Patriarchal dignity is now sold for 60,000 écus.

[2] Vailhé, *art. cit.* col. 1432.   [3] *Ibid.* coll. 1432-3.

[4] *Ibid. loc. cit.* See also T. H. Papadopoullos, *Studies and Documents relating to the History of the Greek Church and People under Turkish Domination*, pp. 132, 160. After 1763 Patriarchal candidates had to pay the *peshtesh* out of their own pockets (Hypsilantis, *op. cit.* p. 397), which helped to improve the financial position of the Church, but made candidates all the more dependent on rich friends. However, on the eve of the Greek War of Independence the debts of the Patriarchate amounted to 1,500,000 Turkish piastres. See M. Raybaud, *Mémoires sur la Grèce* (historical introduction by A. Rabbé), p. 80.

richer members of the laity, the semi-independent Orthodox princes and the merchants of Constantinople. Meanwhile another disruptive factor had appeared. The Ottoman Empire had entered upon regular diplomatic connections with Western Europe; and Western ambassadors to the Sublime Porte began to seek for influence within the Empire. It would be worth while to capture the sympathy and support of the Christian communities. The Embassies therefore fostered new intrigues. France and Austria, though not in unison, employed Catholic missionaries to work among the local Christians, for political rather than for religious ends; while England and Holland, similarly not in unison, countered by encouraging opposition to the Catholics and by trying to build up a connection between the Orthodox and the Protestant Churches. Western agents were added to the elements that pulled strings whenever there was a Patriarchal election; and, while money provided from the Western embassies was welcomed, the Turkish authorities could not be expected to look upon such transactions with favour. The execution of four Patriarchs for treason was the indirect outcome of these ambassadorial intrigues. Here again the situation was improved in the eighteenth century, when the Western powers began to realize that such intrigues produced no valuable results. But their place was taken by a power that the Turks were soon to regard with far greater aversion and fear, the revived and growing Russian Empire.[1]

With such a situation in the Patriarchate it was difficult for the Church to maintain its constitutional rights against its Turkish masters. Individual Sultans or viziers might occasionally be friendly. The mother of Sultan Murad III was a Greek; and he was said to have secretly bought and to worship an icon of the Holy Virgin.[2] Suleiman the Magnificent's vizier, Söküllü, a Bosnian converted to Islam, used sometimes to attend Orthodox

---

[1] See below, chapter 6.
[2] Gerlach, *op. cit.* pp. 335, 361. According to Dorotheus of Monemvasia (*op. cit.* pp. 453–5), Murad III later became violently anti-Christian.

services, accompanied by his two nephews; though he offended the Greeks by insisting in 1557 on the reinstitution of the Serbian Patriarchate of Peć, for the benefit of one of his Christian relatives. However the Serbian Patriarch was ordered to be subservient to his brother of Constantinople. The Turks had no desire to encourage local separatism.[1] The great Albanian family of the Köprülü, which provided four Grand Viziers in the seventeenth century, was consistently favourable towards the Christians.[2] But the average Turk, whether he were Sultan, commander, official or even labourer, regarded the Christians as people to be exploited. Sir Paul Ricaut, an Englishman of Spanish descent, who had travelled widely in the East, wrote at the request of King Charles II a book entitled *The Present State of the Greek and Armenian Churches, Anno Christi 1678*. In it he states that the election to the Patriarchate was vested 'rather in the hands of the Turks than of the bishops'. He was deeply moved by the position of the Greeks. 'Tragical', he writes, 'the subversion of the Sanctuaries of Religion, the Royal Priesthood expelled from their Churches, and these converted into Mosques; the Mysteries of the altar concealed in secret and dark places; for such I have seen in Cities and Villages where I have travelled, rather like Vaults and Sepulchres than Churches, having their roofs almost levelled with the Superficies of the Earth, lest the most ordinary Exsurgency of Structure should be accused for Triumph of Religion, and stand in competition with the lofty Spires of the Mahometan Mosque.' Ricaut well understood the difficulties that faced the Greek Church. Indeed, knowing what he did, he was amazed that it should survive at all. 'It is no wonder', he wrote, 'to human reason that

---

[1] Gerlach, *op. cit.* p. 88. For the Patriarchate of Peć, see Vailhé, *art cit.* col. 1444; also L. Hadrovice, *Le Peuple Serbe et son église sous la domination turque*, pp. 49, 149.

[2] According to Demetrius Cantemir, *The History of the Growth and Decay of the Othman Empire*, p. 368, Mehmet Köprülü deserved to rank with Justinian for the number of churches that he allowed to be built. It was his son Ahmet who appointed Panayoti Nicoussios and after him Alexander Mavrocordato to the post of Grand Dragoman. See below, pp. 364, 368. He was on intimate terms with both of them.

considers the Oppression and the Contempt that good Christians are exposed to, and the Ignorance in their Churches occasioned through Poverty in the Clergy, that many should be found who retreat from the Faith; but it is, rather, a Miracle, and a true Verification of those Words of Christ, *That the Gates of Hell shall not be able to prevail against his Church*, that there is conserved still amongst so much Opposition, and in despite of all Tyranny and Arts contrived against it, an open and public Profession of the Christian Faith.'[1]

Sir Paul was well informed. The priests were indeed poor; for the Patriarchate, with its burden of debt, could not afford any generosity towards its servants. Instead it all too often extorted from them and from their congregations whatever money was available. Nor, as we shall see, was it able to provide them with an adequate education. The conversions to Islam noted by Sir Paul were largely due to the ignorance of this impoverished clergy. They were due, too, to a natural desire to escape from the ignominy of being for ever a second-class citizen. It was a one-way traffic. No Muslim would demean himself by accepting a religion that was politically and socially inferior; and had he done so he would have incurred the death-penalty. As late as the 1780s a Greek boy who had been adopted by Muslims and brought up in their faith was hanged at Janina for reverting to the faith of his fathers. Sir Paul was tactful enough not to dwell too harshly upon the manifest weaknesses of the Patriarchate itself. He was well aware of them, but he was shrewd enough to understand why things had come to such a pass; and his censure was mitigated by real sympathy. But he was almost alone among Western writers of the seventeenth and eighteenth centuries in showing such sympathy. Most of them believed with Robert Burton that the Greeks 'be rather semi-Christians than otherwise', or with Lady Mary Wortley Montagu that, as to their priests, 'no body of Men were ever more ignorant'.[2]

---

[1] Ricaut, *op. cit.* pp. 12–13.
[2] For Burton see below, p. 290. Lady Mary Wortley Montague, *op. cit.* pp. 318–19.

Paradoxically, the weaknesses of the Patriarchate may have afforded the Church some protection. For the Turks grew accustomed to treat the whole ecclesiastical organization with easygoing contempt. They might subject it to petty persecution, extortion and oppression, but at other times they left it alone. They were never sufficiently alarmed by it to take measures that would have threatened its existence. Its secret spirit could survive.

This political background must be realized before we criticize the Greek Church under the Turks for not having made a larger contribution to religious life and religious thought. We must remember how cruelly servitude restricts enterprise. The Church had been very much alive right up to the last days of independent Byzantium. Amongst its prelates had been many of the best brains of the time. Even in the fifteenth century it was still producing works on theology of the highest calibre. Its officials could concentrate on the things which are God's, because there was a Christian Caesar to look after the things which were Caesar's. The conquest altered all that. The Patriarch had to become a lay ruler, but the ruler of a state that had no ultimate sanction of power, a state within a state, depending for its existence on the uncertain good will of an alien and infidel overlord. Many new and costly cares were imposed upon him. His court had to concern itself with fiscal and judicial problems that in the old days had been the business of the secular arm. It had no traditions of its own to help it in this work; it had to borrow what it could remember of the old Imperial traditions. And all the while it was conscious of its exigent suzerain. Even the great Papal monarchy of the West had found the combination of secular with religious power an intolerable strain. It was far harder for the Patriarchate to support the burden so suddenly imposed upon it, with no training in the past and no ultimate freedom of action in the present. It was not surprising that few Greek ecclesiastics now had the time to devote themselves to theological discussion or the spiritual life. It is, rather, remarkable that the Church still managed for two centuries to come to produce a number of lively theologians who could hold their own with theologians in other parts of Europe. But these luminaries belonged to a small intellectual aristocracy. Among the vast body of the clergy and among their congregations standards of learning rapidly declined. It was no longer possible to provide them with adequate means for education.

CHAPTER 3

THE CHURCH AND EDUCATION

No Church, except perhaps the most evangelical, can flourish without some standard of culture among its clergy and among its laity. It was in the sphere of education that the Greek Church was to feel the effects of servitude most profoundly and most disastrously.

At the time of the Turkish conquest of Constantinople the university was still in existence. Many of its best professors had already migrated to the greater security of Italy, where their learning was appreciated and their salaries more regularly paid. Its head in 1453 was an able youngish scholar, Michael Apostolis, who was in favour of union with Rome but whose views do not seem to have lost him pupils. He was taken prisoner when the city fell, but later escaped to Italy, where he had a distinguished career.[1] At Thessalonica, at Mistra and at Trebizond there seem to have been academies which depended on the State for support. When each city was in turn captured by the Turks, all these centres of higher learning inevitably disappeared.[2]

At Constantinople all that was left out of the wreckage was the Patriarchal Academy. It had worked in co-operation with the university and shared professors with it; but it took boys at a younger age, and it concentrated on theological rather than lay studies. Now, more than ever, it had to devote itself to the training of clergy. Higher secular studies, including philosophy except for its rudiments, were abandoned. Martin Kraus, or Crusius, who became Professor of Greek at Tübingen about 1555 and was almost the only Western scholar to concern himself with the state

---

[1] For Apostolis see E. Legrand, *Bibliographie Hellénique: description raisonnée des ouvrages publiés en Grec par des Grecs aux 15e et 16e siècles*, pp. lvi–lxx; D. J. Geanakoplos, *Greek Scholars in Venice*, pp. 73–110.

[2] For Plethon's Academy at Mistra see above, p. 121. Little is known about the academies at Thessalonica and Trebizond.

of the Greeks of his time and kept up an active correspondence with the Greek clergy at Constantinople, was deeply distressed by what he learnt about their lack of schools. 'In all Greece studies nowhere flourish', he writes. 'They have no public academies or professors, except for the most trivial schools in which the boys are taught to read the Horologion, the Octoëchon, the Psalter, and other books which are used in the liturgy. But amongst the priests and monks those who really understand these books are very few indeed.'[1]

Crusius was unfair to the Patriarchal Academy, which was struggling to do its best, though badly in need of reform. On the whole such higher education as survived among the Greeks in Greek lands was provided by private teachers. A few teachers who had been educated in the old days before 1453 managed to keep the tradition of learning alive and to teach pupils. But the results were meagre. We know of not a single Greek of intellectual distinction living within the bounds of the Ottoman Empire during the later fifteenth century and the first years of the sixteenth. There were distinguished Greeks alive at the time; but they were to be found in the West, mainly at Venice. Indeed, we can only tell that the tradition was not lost by the fact that towards the middle of the sixteenth century a number of Greek scholars begin to emerge who had never travelled abroad. Manuel of Corinth, Orator and Chartophylax of the Great Church, who died in 1551 after having written a number of works against the Latins and against the Neo-Platonism of Plethon and Bessarion, was a man of wide erudition, with a good knowledge of Latin, who never travelled outside of the Ottoman Empire. He must have received his education either at his native Corinth or somewhere in the Peloponnese—he is sometimes surnamed Peloponnesiacus—or else at Constantinople.[2] Damascenus the Studite, who wrote

---

[1] M. Crusius, *Germanograecia*, p. 18.

[2] M. Crusius, *Turco-Graecia*, pp. 90 ff., giving a genealogy of scholarship provided by Zygomalas, says that Manuel was the pupil of Matthew Camariotes, one of the last scholars of free Byzantium, and was the teacher of Arsenius of Monem-

homilies which are still admired by the Greek Church, was born at Thessalonica and died as Metropolitan of Arta, without having travelled farther afield. It is likely that he studied on Mount Athos.[1] His contemporary, Manuel Malaxus, who wrote a history of the Patriarchs which Crusius translated, seems to have lived all his life at Constantinople, where he ran a small school in a hut full of fish hanging up to dry.[2] The Patriarch Jeremias II, who was born at Anchialus and educated at Constantinople, probably at the Patriarchal Academy, in which he always took a deep interest, was a philosopher and a historian, as well as a theologian of real merit.[3] The rich layman Michael Cantacuzenus must have been a scholar of some standing, to judge from the excellence of his library.[4] But such men were rare; and we do not know who were their teachers.

By one of the few happy ironies of history, it was Venice, the state which by its part in the Fourth Crusade had done more than any other to destroy Byzantium, that now came to the rescue of Greek culture. There had been for some time past a Greek colony at Venice, originally composed of merchants and technicians. Recently it had been swelled by refugees from Constantinople, some of them cultured aristocrats, such as Anna Notaras, daughter

vasia, the heretic, for whom see below, p. 229. For Manuel see Legrand, *Bibliographie Hellénique au 15e et 16e siècles*, I, p. cvi, and M. Jugie, *Theologia Dogmatica Christianorum Orientalium ab Ecclesia Catholica Dissidentium*, I, pp. 493–4.

[1] Jugie, *op. cit.* I, p. 496. Damascenus also wrote a history of Constantinople which has never been published (MS. 569 formerly in the Metoechia of the Holy Sepulchre at Constantinople, now in the Patriarchal library).

[2] The chronicle known as the *Historia Patriarchica* (published in the C.S.H.B., 1849, ed. J. Becker) is traditionally attributed to Malaxus and was reproduced as such by Martin Crusius in his *Turco-Graecia*, though his friend Gerlach, the Lutheran chaplain at Constantinople (see below, p. 256), says that Malaxus was only the copyist (S. Gerlach, *Tagebuch*, p. 448). For Malaxus's school, Crusius, *op. cit.* p. 85. Jugie, *op. cit.* I, p. 496, wrongly attributes to him the edition of the Nomocanon in modern Greek, which was actually compiled by Nicholas Malaxus, a cousin of his, and by the priest Zacharias Skordylius. M. Gedeon, Πατριαρχικοὶ Πίνακες, p. 515.

[3] For Jeremias II see above, pp. 200–1, and below, pp. 247–56.

[4] See above, pp. 197–8.

of the last Emperor's chief minister, Lucas Notaras,[1] others scholars such as Apostolis, last Rector of the University.[2] In addition ambitious boys from the Greek territories owned by Venice, in particular from the island of Crete, collected there to be educated and to advance their careers. By the end of the fifteenth century Venice had become a lively centre of Greek culture. Eminent Greek-born philosophers and teachers, such as Mark Musurus, Janus Lascaris, George of Trebizond and Andronicus Callistus, made their homes there.[3] Cardinal Bessarion had bequeathed to the city his incomparable library of Greek manuscripts.[4] Cretan students were employed there to copy such manuscripts; and it was there, in the amicably rival presses of Aldus Manutius and the Greek Calliergis that the printing of Greek texts was first undertaken on a large scale.[5] It was to Venice that Erasmus travelled when he wished to perfect his Greek.[6]

To any ambitious young Greek of Constantinople who had intellectual tastes a visit to Venice was infinitely desirable. It was not so difficult to make the journey. The Turks seldom troubled themselves to prevent young Greeks from going abroad; and, if the student could raise enough money to reach Venice, he would find there a number of hospitable compatriots who would probably see him through his studies or would advance him the money that he needed. His religion need not embarrass him. Though the leading Greek scholars in Venice had all joined the Roman Church, and though Venice in the past had shown no friendliness towards the Orthodox, now there was far less intolerance, partly because the Venetians realized that they could not afford to offend their Greek subjects, partly because they had a large number of Greek soldiers of fortune in their armed forces, and partly because of their general spirit of enlightenment and independence, which

---

[1] For Anna see D. J. Geanakoplos, *Byzantine East and Latin West*, pp. 117–18.
[2] See above, p. 208.
[3] D. J. Geanakoplos, *Greek Scholars in Venice, passim*, especially chs. 4–6.
[4] *Ibid.* p. 145.
[5] *Ibid.* pp. 116ff., 201ff.
[6] *Ibid.* pp. 256–78.

made them refuse to allow the Inquisition to operate within their territory without a licence from the government.[1] The Patriarch Maximus IV had been able to secure freedom of worship for the Orthodox in the Ionian Islands, and soon afterwards a Greek church was founded at Venice. It was at first supposed to be Uniate and under the authority of the Patriarch of Venice. In 1577 the Venetian government allowed it to be transferred to the authority of the Orthodox Patriarch of Constantinople. He appointed as its bishop the Metropolitan of Philadelphia, whose titular see in Asia Minor was now a half-ruined village.[2]

Venice had a further advantage to offer. Nearby was the University of Padua. It had been founded in 1222 and from the outset had been famed for its medical and its philosophical studies. The Venetians occupied Padua in 1405; and the Venetian Senate had promptly confirmed the autonomy and the privileges of the university. This autonomy, guaranteed by a government that would permit of no interference from the Papacy or the Inquisition, enabled the university to indulge in religious speculation to an extent impossible elsewhere in Western Europe. The University of Padua was one of the first to encourage the study of Greek; and Greeks who could lecture on Greek texts were especially welcome. A Chair of Greek was founded there in 1463 and given to the Athenian Demetrius Chalcondylas.[3] One of his successors, Nicholas Laonicus Thomaeus, an Epirot by birth, gave in 1497 a course of lectures on Aristotle, using only the Greek text and a few Alexandrian commentaries. His course seemed to the future

---

[1] There were only six occasions on which the Inquisition was allowed to prosecute in Venice. See P. G. Molmenti, *Venice*, pt. II, *The Golden Age* (trans. H. Brown), I, pp. 23–4.

[2] For the history of the Greek church in Venice see Geanakoplos, *Byzantine East and Latin West*, pp. 116–21. A Greek school seems already to have been founded on a modest scale. In 1626 a rich Venetian Greek, Thomas Flanginis, presented the colony with a large sum of money to be spent on education; and the school was developed into a much admired academy, known as the Flanginion. For Maximus's concordat with Venice see F. Miklosich and J. Müller, *Acta et Diplomata Graeci Medii Aevi Sacra et Profana*, V, p. 284.

[3] See G. Camelli, *Demetrio Calcocondilo*, pp. 50–5.

Cardinal Bembo to mark the coming of a new era in philosophical studies.[1] Aided by the printing-presses at Venice, which made Greek texts readily available, Greek studies at Padua won a high renown. It was not surprising that Greek students should wish to go there. Young men who desired to enter the Church and who found the education provided by the Patriarchal Academy inadequate could study up-to-date philosophy there and thus equip themselves to deal with the hostile propaganda with which their Church was faced; and if they were intelligent they were welcomed there as native authorities on the Greek language. Boys who felt no special religious vocation gravitated towards its famous medical schools. Medicine offered a promising career in the Ottoman Empire; for few Turks would demean themselves to do the hard work that a medical training involved, and thus became dependent upon Greeks or Jews for their physicians; and the Greeks soon discovered how influential a family doctor can become. They would study philosophy also; and a class arose of doctor-philosophers, of whom it was said that if they failed to cure their patients' bodies they could at least provide their souls with the consolations of philosophy.

One of the first of the Greeks born in Ottoman territory to go to the West for his education was the Epirot Maximus, known later as the Haghiorite. He was born at Arta in 1480 and as a boy he journeyed in search of learning as far as Paris, then went to Florence, and finally to Venice and Padua. On his return to the East he became a monk on Mount Athos, at the monastery of Vatopedi; he seems to have had some influence in keeping education alive on the Mountain. He was deeply conscious of the value of good libraries and acquired fame as a librarian. Consequently when the Grand Prince of Muscovy, Vassily III, sent in 1518 to Constantinople to ask the Patriarch Theoleptus I to send him a

---

[1] Bembo's speech on what Venice owed to the Greeks is given in J. Morelli, 'Intorno ad un orazione greca inedita del Cardinale Pietro Bembo alla Signoria di Venezia', *Memorie del Regale Istituto del Regno Lombardo-Veneto*, II, pp. 251–62.

good librarian and translator, Maximus was selected for the post. The rest of his career belongs to Russian history.[1]

Most of the Greek scholars of his and the following generation who were educated in the West had the initial advantage of having been born in Venetian-held territory, so that it was easy for them to go to Venice. There was Pachomius Rhusanus of Zante, the exact dates of whose life are unknown. He studied at Padua and other Italian cities, and was a good grammarian as well as a theologian. His chief theological works were directed against the Latins and against a heretic called Joannicius Kartanus, who taught fanciful Neo-Gnostic doctrines about God and the angels.[2] In the next generation there was the Cretan, Meletius Pegas, who died in 1601 after a distinguished career in Orthodox ecclesiastical politics.[3] There was another Cretan, Maximus Margunius, who died in 1602. He also had been educated at Padua. In later life, as Bishop of Cythera, he attempted to find a compromise acceptable to both East and West on the disputed *filioque* clause and was accused by the Metropolitan of Philadelphia, the head of the Greek Church at Venice, of harbouring Latin ideas. He was obliged to send an apologia to Constantinople to prove that he was sound on the doctrine of the Procession of the Holy Ghost; and he wrote a number of tracts, as yet unedited, against the Jesuits and the Franciscans. As a result the Inquisition twice attempted to prosecute him; but he was protected by the Venetian government. His will has been preserved; and it is interesting to note how anxious he was about the proper disposal of his books, a vast number of which were in Latin. Most of his Greek library was to go to the Cretan monastery at which he learnt to read as a child, but one book which had somehow come from the monastery of Saint Catherine on Sinai was to be returned there. In the end his library was scattered.[4] His manuscript copy of the

[1] E. Dénissoff, *Maxime le Grec et l'Occident, passim.*
[2] Legrand, *Bibliographie Hellénique au 15e et 16e siècles*, I, p. 231; Jugie, *op. cit.* I, pp. 495–6.   [3] See below, pp. 261–6.
[4] Legrand, *Bibliographie Hellénique au 15e et 16e siècles*, II, pp. xxiii–lxxvii; Geanakoplos, *Byzantine East and Latin West*, pp. 165–93. See below, pp. 260–1.

ancient Greek tragedians is now in the monastery of Iviron on Mount Athos, as are most of his Latin books.[1] His former critic, Gabriel Severus, Metropolitan of Philadelphia, was born in Monemvasia in 1541, just after its capture by the Turks. He too was an alumnus of Padua. He had spent most of his career at Lesina in Dalmatia, where there was a Greek colony, before taking charge of the Greek community in Venice. He wrote works attacking both the Latins and the Lutherans. He died in 1616.[2] His friend, the Athenian Theodore Karykis, who became Metropolitan of Athens and in 1596, in rather dubious circumstances, was elected Patriarch as Theophanes I, seems to have studied with him at Padua.[3]

Almost all these theologians, whether they came from Venetian or Ottoman territory and whether or not they studied in Italy, were strongly anti-Latin. It was only towards the end of the sixteenth century that the Church of Rome took counter-measures. In 1577 Pope Gregory XIII founded the College of Saint Athanasius at Rome for the education of Greeks in the proper faith. Its pupils came almost entirely from islands which were or had recently been under Italian domination, Corfu, Crete, Cyprus and, especially, Chios. It provided an excellent training; amongst its alumni was the great Chiot scholar, Leo Allatius. It also admitted boys from Orthodox families, in the hope of converting them, a hope that was not always gratified.[4]

In the meantime it had become easier to obtain a good education at Constantinople. From about 1550 onwards, owing to the influence of scholars educated at Padua, there had been attempts to reform the Patriarchal Academy. Higher studies were introduced, particularly the study of philosophy. In 1593 the learned Patriarch Jeremias II summoned a synod which gave a new constitution to

---

[1] Geanakoplos, *Byzantine East and Latin West*, pp. 183–93, gives a personally verified list of Margunius's books that are still in the library at Iviron.

[2] Legrand, *Bibliographie Hellénique au 15e et 16e siècles*, II, pp. 144–51; A. C. Demetracopoulos, 'Ορθόδοξος 'Ελλάς, pp. 143–6. See below, p. 257.

[3] D. Sicilianos, *Old and New Athens* (trans. R. Liddell), pp. 191–2.

[4] Jugie, *op. cit.* I, pp. 522 ff.

the academy. Various departments, to include higher philosophy and certain of the sciences as well as theology and literature, were set up, each under a *scholarch* appointed by the Patriarch. The first *scholarchs* seem all to have been graduates of Padua.[1] Thus by the end of the sixteenth century there were several courses open to an intelligent and enterprising Greek boy who wanted a higher education. But for a boy who did not live at Constantinople or who had not the opportunity of going to Italy, things were not too easy; and even places at the Patriarchal school were not so very plentiful. The synod of 1593 which reformed the Patriarchal Academy also urged metropolitans to see to the foundation of academies in their cities. It is doubtful how many metropolitans followed this advice. Academies were expensive to organize and to maintain; and the supply of good teachers was limited. Academies seem to have been founded within the next few decades at such large cities as Thessalonica and Trebizond and Smyrna, which were presumably under the care of the local metropolitan; but the evidence about them is very scanty.[2] The only academy which achieved some renown and produced pupils of some distinction was founded not by a metropolitan but by an Epirot priest, Epiphanius the Higoumene, who was attached to the Greek church at Venice. He collected a sum of money, presumably from the richer members of his congregation, which he deposited in the treasury of Saint Mark, the interest from which was to pay for the salaries of teachers at an academy which was set up at Athens. In the first years of the seventeenth century the Athenian academy counted amongst its

---

[1] For Jeremias see C. Sathas, Βιογραφικὸν Σχεδίασμα περὶ τοῦ Πατριάρχου Ἱερεμίου Β΄ (1572–94), *passim*. Jeremias tried to persuade Margunius to come and teach at the Patriarchal Academy: See Legrand, *Bibliographie Hellénique au 15e et 16e siècles*, II, pp. xxviii–xxx; Geanakoplos, *Byzantine East and Latin West*, pp. 167–8. For Margunius's letters to Jeremias, Sathas, *op. cit.* pp. 98–135.

[2] See P. Karolides, Ἱστορία τῆς Ἑλλάδος, p. 531; J. Z. Stephanopoli, 'L'Ecole, facteur du reveil national', in *Le Cinq-centième anniversaire de la prise de Constantinople*, *L'Hellénisme contemporain*, fascicule hors série (1953), pp. 242–3, 253–4.

professors Theophilus Corydalleus, the Neo-Aristotelian, his pupil, Nicodemus Pherraeus, and Demetrius Angelus Benizelos.[1] Amongst its pupils was Nathaniel Chychas, who achieved some fame as a polemical writer. But as Chychas went on from Athens to the College of Saint Athanasius at Rome, it may have been to the Catholic Fathers there that he owed his training. They converted him to Catholicism; but he moved to Venice and Padua and reverted to his ancestral faith. In the words of Dositheus of Jerusalem who subsequently edited an anti-Latin tract of his, 'at Rome he drank of the troubled waters of schism and heresy, but going later to Venice he was set right by the late Gabriel Severus, Metropolitan of Philadelphia.'[2] But Epiphanius's endowment was too small and local Turkish suspicion too great for the Academy of Athens to survive. A Peloponnesian boy called Christopher Angelus went there in 1607, only to be arrested almost at once on the improbable charge of being a Spanish spy. He was stripped of his books and his money and only with difficulty escaped with his life. His later career was spent in England. Soon afterwards the academy closed its doors.[3]

In Asia Minor outside of the larger towns there seem to have been practically no Greek schools. Thomas Smith, writing towards the end of the seventeenth century, noted that the Turkish authorities in the Asiatic provinces were far more intolerant than those in Europe.[4] In Europe a school was founded at Janina by Epiphanius the Higoumene, before he went to Athens. One was founded at Arta some time in the seventeenth century, and several in Macedonia, and, a little later, in the islands of Myconos, Naxos and Patmos. At Dimitsana in the Peloponnese there was by the end of the seventeenth century a celebrated academy at which no less than six Patriarchs of the following century were educated.

---

[1] *Ibid.* pp. 254–5: Sicilianos, *op. cit.* pp. 258–9.
[2] Sicilianos, *op. cit.* pp. 193–4: Demetracopoulos, *op. cit.* p. 142.
[3] See below, pp. 293–4.
[4] P. Ricaut, *The Present State of the Greek and Armenian Churches, Anno Christi, 1678* (1680), p. 23.

The Church and Education

There was already a school at Nauplia.[1] The school at Athens was refounded about 1717 by a monk, Gregory Sotiris, and was given a new endowment by an Athenian, George Anthony Melos, who had made a fortune in Spain; and this was supplemented by an Athenian living in Venice, Stephen Roulis. Its most famous headmaster was a Cretan, Athanasius Bousopoulos of Dimitsana, amongst whose pupils was the future Patriarch Gregory V. But it seems that this school was thought to be old-fashioned in its curriculum. A more up-to-date school was founded in 1750 by another Venetian Greek, John Deka.[2]

Though the Sublime Porte never interfered with the Patriarchal Academy at Constantinople, provincial governors were free to be as oppressive as they pleased; and many of them regarded the education of the minority races as being most undesirable.

The most effective academies of the eighteenth century were situated in districts that were not under direct Turkish control, in the two capitals of the Danubian principalities, Bucharest and Jassy, and in the island of Chios, which enjoyed a limited self-government. In Chios there had been a tradition of good schools since the days of the Genoese occupation, when the Greco-Italian Hermodorus Lestarchus had conducted a famous establishment, attended by Catholics and Orthodox alike.[3] In the Ionian

---

[1] Gedeon, Χρονικὰ τοῦ Πατριαρχικοῦ Οἴκου καὶ Ναοῦ, p. 131, and Πατριαρχικοὶ Πίνακες, pp. 491, 511, 594, 599, 622, 625. See Stephanopoli, *op. cit.* pp. 254–8. R. Pococke gives an unflattering picture of the 'University' at Patmos in about 1730 (*A Description of the East*, II, 2, p. 31).

[2] Sicilianos, *op. cit.* pp. 261–2.

[3] The academy at Bucharest was created by the *stolnic* Constantine Cantacuzene, uncle of the Prince Constantine Brancovan (see N. Jorga, *Byzance après Byzance*, pp. 203–5, 216, and the article by C. Tsourkas, 'Autour des origines de l'Academie grecque de Bucarest', in *Balkan Studies*, VI, 2 (1965), which dates the foundation in about 1675, some fifteen years earlier than Jorga). Its first eminent professor was John Caryophylles, who had been Director of the Patriarchal Academy and Grand Logothete at the Patriarchate but left Constantinople after an ugly scene when he had insulted the Patriarch and been knocked down by Alexander Mavrocordato, then Grand Skevophylax as well as Grand Dragoman. The Patriarch Dositheus of Jerusalem, who was present, managed to restore order, but Caryophylles was soon afterwards suspended for heresy

Islands, under Venetian rule, Greek schools had been permitted since 1550; and their standards were higher than any on the mainland, because many of the teachers had been trained at Venice or Padua. In Crete, equally controlled by the Venetians but inclined to be rebellious, schools were not encouraged.[1]

The average Greek provincial boy was thus not well served, particularly if he belonged to the poorer classes from which most of the monks and village priests were drawn. Many children remained uneducated and illiterate. A boy who wished to be a priest would go to the local monastery to learn to read and write and to memorize the religious works that he would need later on. But that was about the extent of his education. The monasteries were required to maintain libraries; but only a few were wealthy enough to keep them up to date and to buy new books; and in the poorer monasteries the monks began to lose the taste for reading. Only a few well-thumbed Gospels and Psalters and liturgical books, the Horologion and the Octoëchon to which Crusius refers, were ever in circulation. Once the future priest had learnt the words of the Liturgy his education was finished.

(K. Daponte, *Chronicle*, p. 39). The Academy at Jassy seems to have been founded before 1660 (see Jorga, *op. cit.* p. 205). Additional schools at Bucharest and Jassy were founded in the later eighteenth century (*ibid.* pp. 236–7). The Academy at Chios, the Χία Σχολή, dates from the Genoese occupation. Lestarchus, who came from Zante, taught for a time at Ferrara, but was established in Chios before 1560 (*Gedeon*, Πατριαρχικοὶ Πίνακες). It seems to have been for a time under Jesuit control about the end of the sixteenth century. It was noted for its chemistry laboratories and its library. By the end of the eighteenth century it had 700 pupils. In the early nineteenth century the French professor was the son of the painter David. See P. Argenti, *Chios Vincta*, pp. ccxvi–ccxviii: Stephanopoli, *L'Ecole, facteur du reveil national*, pp. 257–8.

[1] In the Ionian Islands the Greek schools seem to have all been privately run. Zante, not Corfu, was the chief intellectual centre. A. Drummond (*Travels*, pp. 94–5), who visited Zante in 1744, was struck by the high level of culture there. He found the inhabitants, including Greek priests, reading Locke and other philosophers, but thought that they disregarded mathematics. For Crete see Geanakoplos, *Byzantine East and Latin West*, pp. 140–2. The one eminent school in the island was that attached to the monastery of St Catherine, where Cyril Lucaris studied as a boy and to which Margunius left part of his library. See above, p. 214, and below, p. 260.

He outshone his parishioners because he could read and could perform the Mysteries. But higher learning was beyond his reach, and he was suspicious of it. Amongst women illiteracy was even more widespread. A few girls might have lessons at the local convent; but many nuns could barely read. A richer farmer or a merchant might engage a literate monk to give his children, girls as well as boys, a smattering of education; but it did not go very far.

The decline in literacy was even felt in such great monasteries as the Athonite houses. In the sixteenth century they cared for learning sufficiently to buy up the library of Michael Cantacuzenus; and their catalogues show that they were still acquiring books, printed and in manuscript, on secular as well as on religious subjects throughout most of the seventeenth century. In the eighteenth century there was a decline. In 1753 the Patriarch Cyril V made a determined effort to restore the Holy Mountain to its proper place as a centre of religious culture. He founded an academy there for the monks and appointed as its professor one of the leading philosophers of the time, the Corfiot Eugenius Vulgaris. But Vulgaris was a modernist who had been largely trained in Germany; and his philosophical theories so horrified the monks that after a few years he was removed to become head of the Academy at Constantinople. Even there his modernism was considered somewhat extreme. He retired in 1765 to Germany, where he was better appreciated, and ended his life in Russia under the patronage of Catherine the Great.[1]

The story of the Athonite Academy showed how inadequate the new centres of learning were for the Church as a whole. There was a complete cultural cleavage between the cultivated hierarchs of Constantinople and the rich laity amongst whom they

[1] For the Academy on Athos see the contemporary account in S. Macraios Ὑπομνήματα Ἐκκλησιαστικῆς Ἱστορίας, in Sathas, Μεσαιωνικὴ Βιβλιοθήκη, III, p. 219: also Sathas's introduction to the volume, pp. οʹ–οβʹ. See also T. H. Papadopoullos, Studies and Documents relating to *The History of the Greek Church and People under Turkish Domination*, pp. 190 ff.; also T. Ware, *Eustratios Argenti*, pp. 6–7.

lived on the one side and the ordinary priest and monk on the other, who, even if he was well grounded in the traditional theology of the Church, found the new learning of the academies unfamiliar and shocking, and who more often was too ill educated to begin to understand it. Indeed, the type of philosophy that was fashionable amongst the Greek intellectuals of the seventeenth and eighteenth centuries fitted badly with the traditions of the Church. The Greek scholars who had gone to Padua and had taught the professors there to study the ancient philosophers in their original tongue had helped to give birth to a new school of philosophy, a school of Neo-Aristotelians, whose chief spokesmen were Pietro Pomponazzi, who lectured at Padua and Bologna in the early sixteenth century, and Cesare Cremonini, who was professor of philosophy at Padua not quite a century later. The doctrine that they taught was a type of philosophical materialism. Matter is the permanent basis of everything. It contains in itself the germ of each form as a potential or active cause. Forms, or their Ideas (in the Platonic sense), pre-exist within matter and emerge from matter, determining it in the multiplicity of sensible objects. There is thus a purely natural and organic causality. God's existence was not denied; but to Pomponazzi God does not and cannot intervene in the natural order of things. His nature consists of knowing everything but not of immixing in natural laws. The soul is purely mortal, a part of the form of the body, neither immaterial nor immortal. Cremonini carried the doctrine further, in that he was quite uninterested in the soul. Under his influence Neo-Aristotelianism concentrated on the exterior phenomena of nature and on empirical knowledge. The philosophy had its practical merits. It prepared the way towards notions of evolution and progress. It was a corrective against the medieval treatment of everything as being *sub specie aeternitatis*, a viewpoint that could lead politically to defeatism and intellectually to stagnation. But it was ill-suited for members of a Church whose strength lay in its fidelity to ancient tradition and its emphasis on the mystical life. The Greek intellectuals who fell under its spell had either to move

The Church and Education

towards Natural Religion or else make an arbitrary divorce between religion and philosophy.[1]

The Patriarch Jeremias II, when he reformed the Patriarchal Academy, seems to have been conscious of this. Though he encouraged the study of sciences such as physiology and chemistry, he did not include the new philosophy in the courses.[2] The next generation was more advanced. The remarkable Cretan, Cyril Lucaris, who reigned as Patriarch, with a few short interruptions, from 1620 till his execution in 1638, was an eager patron of up-to-date thought. His career will be discussed later. Here it should be first noted that he managed to provide the Patriarchate with a Greek printing-press, procured from England, which proved a great asset for Greek learning during the short period that the Turks permitted its existence. Secondly, he continued the reform of the Patriarchal Academy. In 1624 he installed as its Chief Director his friend Theophilus Corydalleus, then head of the Academy at Athens. Corydalleus had come under the influence of Cremonini at Padua and was deeply interested in Neo-Aristotelianism. He instituted courses on it, and, more valuably, courses on physics and generation and corruption. Henceforward students at the Academy could obtain as good a scientific education as many of the Western universities provided. Corydalleus was removed from his post in 1639 because of his support of Cyril Lucaris's doctrines, which had been condemned as heresy. He was later rehabilitated and became for a while Metropolitan of Arta. But the curriculum that he had started survived, the courses being revived by his pupil, John Caryophylles, who was appointed Director in 1642. Caryophylles in his turn was removed for heresy and rudeness; but the courses were now well enough entrenched not to be abandoned.[3] Later Directors encouraged them, above all Alexander Mavrocordato, of whose remarkable

[1] For a summary of this Neo-Aristotelianism and its effect on Greek thought see P. Sherrard, *The Greek East and the Latin West*, pp. 174 ff.
[2] See above, p. 200, n. 2, and p. 216, n. 1.
[3] See Meletios, Ἐκκλησιαστικὴ Ἱστορία (ed. G. Vendotis), III, pp. 471–2.

career more will be said later. He became Director of the Academy at the early age of twenty-four in 1666, and himself gave lectures there on philosophy, medicine and Classical Greek. As he was at the same time Grand Orator of the Patriarchate and was a member of one of the wealthy families of Constantinople on which the Patriarchate depended, no one would venture to accuse him of heresy. He had studied both at the College of Saint Athanasius and at Padua and his early training made him sympathetic towards some understanding with Rome, which he seems to have hoped to reach on the basis of the new philosophy.[1] When he retired from the Academy to become Grand Interpreter at the Sublime Porte, his successor was Sevastus Kymenites, who came from Kymena, near Trebizond. He too was an alumnus of Padua, but belonged to an older tradition. Indeed, he wrote a tract in support of Palamite doctrines. But he seems to have disliked life at Constantinople and soon went back to take over the Academy at Trebizond. He was a professor at Bucharest when he died in 1702.[2]

The study of these new-fangled sciences at Constantinople and at the academies at Bucharest and Jassy had its use. It enabled a Greek of education to keep up with the currents of thought that ran in the West. But Greeks of education were by now only to be found in the big cities, among rich merchant dynasties, and, in particular, the great families of Constantinople, usually known collectively as the Phanariots, as their houses clustered round the Patriarchate in the Phanar quarter. The Phanariots genuinely admired learning, and they were ready to spend money on it. It was thanks to them more than to anyone else that Hellenism was able to survive. But they were not interested in the education of the clergy. Their money enabled them to control the Patriarchate. They liked to secure the election of a Patriarch who was sympathetic to their ideas and who would appoint their sons to posts at

[1] A. A. C. Stourdza, *L'Europe Orientale et le rôle historique des Maurocordato*, pp. 35 ff.; E. Stamatiades, Βιογραφία τῶν ῾Ελλήνων μεγάλων διερμηνέων τοῦ ᾽Οθωμανικοῦ Κράτους, pp. 65 ff.
[2] Jugie, *op. cit.* I, p. 519.

his court. But they were quite uninterested in the provincial Church. A Patriarch with reforming zeal who attempted to face the problems of the education of the clergy lost their support, which he needed both for financial reasons and for the influence that they wielded at the Sublime Porte. As a result, the Patriarchate began to lose touch with the provincial Church. It was difficult to find among the well-educated bishops any who would go to a remote provincial see and devote himself to its needs. The provincial hierarchy was mainly composed of men of little learning, appointed because they were on the spot and willing to remain there. They were often devoted pastors to their flock, but often, too, narrow and ignorant men, with no use for the sophisticated circles of the Patriarchate and its Phanariot courtiers. The monasteries, in their reaction against the new learning, tended to turn against learning of any sort. Even on Mount Athos, with very few exceptions, monastic libraries were left neglected, the monks carelessly using pages of old manuscripts as wrappings for their victuals or, even more gladly, selling them to visitors who were ready to pay for such things. The village priest had no encouragement to interest himself in things of the mind. Travellers from the West in the eighteenth and early nineteenth centuries were horrified at the low standards of the Greek clergy. The decadence must not be exaggerated. There were still a few establishments where the old traditions were maintained, such as the monastery of Saint John on Patmos or the Great Lavra on Mount Athos. There were still provincial bishops who could discuss theology with erudition and intelligence. But the overall picture was drab and depressing.

It was in its failure to provide a proper education for its flocks and, in particular, for its clergy that the Orthodox Church of the captivity committed its worst fault. Yet the failure would have been difficult to avoid. Schools need money; and the Patriarchate was always short of money. Even if the Patriarchs themselves had not begun the habit of paying huge sums to the Turks for their own personal advancement, it is unlikely that the Turks would ever have allowed the Church to accumulate enough wealth for it to endow many schools. And, even if the money had been forth-coming, it was extremely doubtful whether the Turkish authorities in the provinces would have allowed Greek schools to operate on any large scale. There was never any official ban. But school buildings could be confiscated and individual pupils harried, so that in the end it was not worth while to keep the schools open. Moreover, the longer education is neglected the harder it is to revive it; for it will be impossible to find a sufficiency of trained teachers. And, even if teachers are available, it is never easy to induce them to leave the big cities to work in distant provinces.

It was only in the Ionian Islands that the level of education did not fall. They were comparatively rich; Corfu and Zante, in particular, contained prosperous communities; and the Venetian government, once it decided in 1550 to permit the existence of Greek schools, put no restrictions on them. Venice rescued Greek intellectual life by welcoming Greek students to its own libraries and to its University of Padua. It performed perhaps an even greater service in allowing the continuation of Greek provincial education in the islands. Elsewhere, the failure of the Church to provide proper schooling for any but its aristocracy of talent and of money was to cause a lack of sympathy and understanding between the hierarchy at Constantinople and the struggling churches of the provinces, which was to have serious consequences when the moment came for liberation.

CHAPTER 4

THE CHURCH AND THE CHURCHES: CONSTANTINOPLE AND ROME

The Turkish conquest left the Greek Church with a sense of despair and of isolation. In the struggle for survival, with practical difficulties in the field of education, it had no time and no energy for theological adventures. The Patriarch Gennadius had indeed continued to write on theology during the few remaining years of his life. But with the following generation the Church began to turn in on itself. The educated laity whose philosophers and scholars provoked discussion were gone. The Orthodox with their apophatic tradition never desired new developments in doctrine. Their doctrine and tradition embodied eternal truths. It was only when these were challenged that they felt the need to establish fresh formulae. But now, in their isolation, they received no new challenge. For about a century after the fall of Constantinople their learned clerics merely repeated opinions and arguments that had already been given to the world by earlier and greater theologians.

The one challenge that continued from the past was provided by the Church of Rome. Rome still earnestly desired to bring the Eastern Churches into her fold. The union signed at Florence, whether or no it could ever have been implemented, had been cut short as far as Constantinople and the Patriarchate were concerned by the fall of the city. But there were still many Greek lands that were under Latin rule, Naxos and the Duchy of the Archipelago, the Genoese island of Chios, Rhodes, under the Knights of Saint John, the Kingdom of Cyprus, soon to pass to the Venetians, and their possessions, Crete and the Ionian Islands and ports round the coasts of the Greek peninsula. In time the Ottoman Empire would absorb them all, except for the Ionian

Islands; and they would return into the authority of the Patriarchate. But, until they won religious liberation by passing into the dominion of an infidel master, the Orthodox in these districts had to submit to varying degrees of persecution. In most of them the Orthodox congregations were obliged to admit the authority of the Roman hierarchy but otherwise were allowed to follow their own ritual and customs without interference. It was in the larger islands, where there was an established Orthodox hierarchy, that trouble occurred. In Cyprus, where the Orthodox had suffered many disabilities, their situation had been improved in the fifteenth century by the passionately Orthodox queen of John II, Helena Palaeologaena; but after the Venetian occupation of the island in 1489 there was continuous trouble between the authorities and the Greek clergy. There was similar trouble in Crete, where the Venetian authorities considered that the Greek clergy fomented resistance and therefore laid heavy fiscal burdens on them, confiscating much of their property. Relations between the Greek and Latin hierarchies in Genoese Chios were always strained. On the other hand, in the Ionian Islands the Venetian policy was far more lenient, while by the end of the fifteenth century the Greek colony in Venice was allowed complete freedom of worship. In the Ionian Islands the Greek and Latin clergy were on remarkably cordial terms. The hierarchies remained separate; but intermarriage and even inter-communion were not infrequent.[1]

The Patriarchate of Constantinople, with so many members of its flock under Latin domination, could never forget the rivalry of Rome. Yet it was forty-five years after the meeting of the Council of Florence before the union signed there was officially repudiated at Constantinople. Anti-Western feeling ran high there during those years. The bitterness of the controversy and the failure of the West to send help when it was needed were unforgotten. Many practical-minded Greeks feared, also, that any

---

[1] For relations between the Orthodox and the Catholics in the Greek provinces see T. Ware, *Eustratios Argenti*, pp. 16–21, who provides many examples of friendly co-operation.

gesture of friendship towards the West might worsen their relations with their new masters. But the Church authorities, with
more pressing problems on their hands, did not trouble to legalize
a situation that everyone accepted. It was only in 1484 that the
Patriarch Symeon, in his third and most stable period of office,
summoned a Council to meet in the Patriarchal Church of the
Pammacaristos, to which the Patriarchs of Alexandria, Antioch
and Jerusalem sent representatives. To judge from what survives
of the Acts of this Council, its immediate object was to decide upon
the correct ritual for the reception into the Orthodox Church of
converts from Rome. The Turkish conquest of territories that
had been under Latin rule meant that many Greeks who had been
obliged to submit to the authority of Rome could now revert to
the faith of their fathers and their compatriots. There seems to have
been some controversy over the proper procedure and over the
question whether Greeks who had admitted Papal supremacy but
had retained their own ritual required the same treatment as
Greeks who had followed the Latin ritual. But, as this was the first
Council of an Oecumenical status to meet since the Council of
Florence, its first action was to declare that the Council of
Florence had not been canonically summoned or composed, and
that its decrees were therefore invalid. The attendant bishops then
settled down to discuss the ritual problem. It was decided that in
all cases rechrismation, together with a solemn abjuration of
Roman heresies, would suffice. It was not considered, at this time,
that rebaptism was necessary.[1]

As the sixteenth century advanced the bitterness began to die
down. Partly this was due to the Greek students who went to
study at Venice, many of whom travelled to other parts of Italy
and found themselves, so long as they behaved with tact, perfectly

[1] The Acts of the Council of 1484 in so far as they concern the admission into the
Church of ex-Latins are published in J. N. Karmiris, Τὰ Δογματικὰ καὶ Συμβολικὰ
Μνήματα, II, pp. 987–9. A fuller version of the Acts exists in manuscript in the
University Library, Cambridge, Additional 3076. It has been described by
P. E. Easterling, 'Handlist of the Additional Greek Manuscripts in the Univer-
sity Library, Cambridge', *Scriptorium*, XVI (1952), p. 317.

welcome in Catholic circles. Partly it was due to the glamour
attached to the position, if not to the unromantic person, of the
Emperor Charles V, who seemed to be the one potentate able and
willing to lead a Crusade that would rescue the Greeks. Orthodox
Greeks in Venice, such as Antony the Exarch, believed that
nothing should be done to alienate Charles, who was known to
be a staunch Catholic.[1] The Peloponnesian scholar, Arsenius
Apostolis—or Aristobulus, which was probably his name before
he took holy orders—the son of Michael Apostolis, who, after a
scholarly career at Venice, had himself consecrated as Archbishop
of Monemvasia by two unqualified priests, and then tried to make
terms with the Patriarchate to be recognized as holder of this
Greek see, and who wrote alternately flattering and abusive letters
to the hierarchs of both Churches, became a leading advocate of
Habsburg intervention. He elaborated his scheme in a long epistle
to Charles, at the end of which he signed himself: 'Your Majesty's
dog', adding that he barked for his supper. But Charles was never
in a position to embark upon an aggressive war against the Turks.[2]

By that time the Greeks were no longer so isolated. As the
sixteenth century advanced West European statesmen began to
realize that the Ottoman Empire could not be regarded as a
transitory phenomenon. It had to be recognized as a European
power with which diplomatic contact must be maintained. A
number of books began to appear describing the Turks and the
organization of their state. The Christian minorities were
numerous; it might be worth while to cultivate their good will.
Trade between the West and the Ottoman ports began to expand;
and the Western merchants demanded protection from their own
government. At the same time, as the ruling Turkish classes took
little personal interest in commerce, it was with Christian or
Jewish merchants that the Westerners had to deal, especially with

[1] For Anthony the Exarch see below, pp. 240–1.
[2] For an account of the career of Arsenius of Monemvasia see E. Legrand,
*Bibliographie Hellénique: description raisonnée des ouvrages publiés en Grec par des
Grecs au 15e et 16e siècles*, pp. clxv ff., and D. J. Geanakoplos, *Greek Scholars in
Venice*, pp. 167–200.

the Greeks, who were beginning to control the export trade. There was a revival of interest in the Greek problem. The Society of Jesus was founded in 1540. Within a few years Jesuits were working in Ottoman territory. These well-trained, cultivated and courteous men, taking a sympathetic interest in the difficulties of the minorities, could not fail to find a welcome in many Greek households and even to make friends with members of the hierarchy. They soon found an ally in the learned and saintly Metrophanes, Metropolitan of Caesarea; and, thanks to him, they made contact with the Patriarch Dionysius II (1546–55), who seems to have been anxious to reopen negotiations with the Papacy. Nothing came of it at the time; but, when Metrophanes himself was elected to the Patriarchate in 1565, he began to make cautious appoaches to Rome. Metrophanes was generally admired and loved; and no one wished to take action against him. But at last, in 1572, the Holy Synod felt that he had gone too far along the path towards reunion. He was solemnly excommunicated and deposed, swearing that he would never attempt to mount the throne again. He did not keep his promise. In 1579, seven years after his deposition, popular pressure restored him to the Patriarchate. But he had learnt his lesson. During the nine months that elapsed before his death he refrained from further negotiations. The hierarchy was alarmed. Though his successor Jeremias II accepted gifts from Pope Gregory XIII and thanked him cordially, for some time to come any ecclesiastic who was suspected of Romanizing tendencies was promptly reprimanded.[1] When the scholar Maximus Margunius, Bishop of Cythera, was found to be wavering on the doctrine of the Procession of the Holy Spirit, he was advised by his superior, Gabriel Severus, head of the Orthodox

---

[1] M. Crusius, *Turco-Graecia*, p. 211; Philip of Cyprus, *Chronicon Ecclesiae Graecae* (Latin trans., ed. H. Hilarius), pp. 413–17: Busbecq met Metrophanes before his first elevation to the Patriarchate and found him sympathetic towards Rome (O. G. Busbecq, *Legationis Turcicae Epistolae*, IV, p. 231). See also G. Cuperus, *Tractatus historico-chronologicus de Patriarchis Constantinopolitanis*, p. 233. For Jeremias II and Gregory XIII, see E. Legrand, *Bibliographie Hellénique: description raisonnée des ouvrages publiés en Grec par des Grecs au 17e siècle*, II, pp. 212, 377.

Church at Venice, to send a statement to Constantinople to assure the Holy Synod that he had not deviated from Orthodoxy.[1] But the Jesuit influence continued. It was helped by the foundation of the College of Saint Athanasius at Rome by Pope Gregory XIII in 1577 for the higher education of Greek boys.[2] Though most of the students came from Catholic families in the Aegean islands, the Jesuits at Constantinople were able to persuade some Orthodox parents there to send their sons to it. Not all of them were converted to Catholicism in the course of their studies; but almost all of them returned with a kindlier feeling towards Rome and a readiness to work for some sort of union. Soon the Jesuits founded schools within the Ottoman Empire. Well before the end of the century their establishment at Pera was running schools where boys could receive an excellent education at almost nominal fees; and similar schools were set up at Thessalonica and Smyrna. Not all these establishments were successful. The one founded at Athens in 1645 met with very little sympathy there and was soon moved to the friendlier atmosphere of Chalcis.[3] It was not until the end of the eighteenth century that there was a Catholic school in Athens, the school run by the Franciscans at the Lantern of Demosthenes, where Lord Byron lodged in 1810.[4]

In Constantinople itself these schools were very successful. Of the Orthodox boys who attended them many became Catholics, and in some cases their whole families were also converted. They had the useful effect of stimulating the Orthodox authorities into making greater efforts over education.[5]

[1] D. J. Geanakoplos, *Byzantine East and Latin West*, devotes a chapter to Margunius (pp. 165–93).
[2] For the College of Saint Athanasius, see L. Pastor, *History of the Popes from the Close of the Middle Ages*, XIX, pp. 247–9, XX, pp. 584–5. See also P. de Meester, *Le Collège Pontifical Grec de Rome, passim*.
[3] For the Jesuit school at Pera see G. Hofmann, *Il Vicariato Apostolico di Constantinopoli, Orientalia Christiana Analecta*, CIII, pp. 40–4, 70. For the schools at Naxos, Paros, Athens and Smyrna, see A. Carayon, *Relations inédites des missions de la Société de Jesus à Constantinople*, pp. 111 ff., 122 ff., 138–47 and 159 ff.
[4] D. Sicilianos, *Old and New Athens* (trans. R. Liddell), pp. 227–8.
[5] See above, p. 215.

It was owing to their friendship with Jesuit fathers that two Patriarchs in the early seventeenth century, Raphael II and Neophytus II, showed an interest in union and even started a correspondence with the Papacy. Raphael kept his correspondence secret; but in 1611 his successor Neophytus, then in his second term of office, thought that the time had come to test public opinion. That spring a Greek priest from Southern Italy preached under Patriarchal licence a lenten sermon in which he openly advocated union with Rome. Cyril Lucaris, the future Patriarch, was in Constantinople at the time and was asked by angry members of the Synod to preach a counterblast. Neophytus himself seems to have repudiated the over-eager Italian. But the Synod was highly suspicious; and the atmosphere was strained for some months, until Neophytus died the following January. But his successor, Timothy II, was reported to be friendly to Rome and in 1615 wrote a letter to Pope Paul V, acknowledging him as his superior; but he never made any open declaration of submission. The career of Cyril Lucaris showed that there was a powerful party within the hierarchy which was prepared to accept Roman supremacy. Cyril's opponents, the Patriarchs Gregory IV, Cyril II and Athanasius III, all declared themselves for Rome. Of his successors Parthenius II, when Metropolitan of Chios, wrote to Pope Urban VIII to render obedience to him, though he seems not to have continued the correspondence after his accession to the Patriarchate. Joannicius II kept up a correspondence with Rome but prudently avoided any act of submission.[1]

Roman missionaries had many successes in the provinces. In 1628 Ignatius, Abbot of Vatopedi on Mount Athos, visited Rome and there suggested that a priest should be sent to establish a school for monks on the Holy Mountain. In response to his request a former student at the College of Saint Athanasius, Nicholas Rossi, arrived on the Mountain at the end of 1635 and opened a school

---

[1] The relations of these Patriarchs with Rome have been fully described, with the relevant documents, by G. Hofmann, *Griechische Patriarchen und Römische Päpste, Orientalia Christiana*, XIII, no. 47; XV, no. 52; XIX, no. 63; XX, no. 64; XXV, no. 76; XXX, no. 84; XXXVI, no. 97.

at Karyes. The Turkish authorities, however, were not pleased to see Western influences infiltrating into the Mountain. In 1641 they obliged Rossi to move his school to Thessalonica. On his death there the following year the school faded out. But in 1643 the Holy Synod of the Mountain wrote to Rome to ask whether a church there could be handed over for the use of visiting Athonite monks. In return they would offer a *skete* or *kellion* for the use of Basilian monks from Italy.[1]

A number of distinguished seventeenth-century provincial prelates announced their submission to Rome, including three Metropolitans of Ochrid, one of Rhodes and one of Lacedaemon. Conversions continued into the eighteenth century. The great monastery of Saint John at Patmos twice announced its submission, in 1681 and in 1725; and other monasteries did likewise: though sometimes the motives were diplomatic rather than spiritual.[2] But in Constantinople itself Roman propaganda grew less effective. The Anglican chaplain John Covel tells of a visit that he received soon after his arrival at Constantinople from a young Greek priest from Venice who, believing Covel to be a Catholic, revealed to him a plot organized by the French Embassy and the Jesuits to remove the actual Patriarch, probably Methodius III, and replace him by the more sympathetic Metropolitan of Paros. Nothing seems to have come of it.[3] Athanasius V, a distinguished musicologist who was Patriarch from 1709 to 1711, was suspected of Roman tendencies; and similar suspicions were harboured against one or two of his successors.[4] The growing

---

[1] G. Hofmann, *Athos e Roma, Orientalia Christiana,* v, no. 19, esp. pp. 5–6, and *Rom und Athosklöster, Orientalia Christiana,* VIII, no. 37.

[2] G. Hofmann, *Patmos und Rom, Orientalia Christiana,* XI, no. 37, esp. pp. 25–7, 53–5. See also Ware, *op. cit.* pp. 27–8.

[3] *Extracts from the Diary of Dr John Covil,* in J. T. Bent, *Early Voyages and Travels in the Levant,* Hakluyt Society, LXXXVII, pp. 149–50. Bent erroneously dates the entry 'Feb. 7, 1667': whereas Covel did not arrive in Constantinople until 1670. 1671 is a more probable date.

[4] For Athanasius V see S. Vailhé, 'Constantinople, Eglise de', in *Dictionnaire de théologie catholique,* III, 2, col. 1432. His musical gifts are mentioned in Meletius, Archbishop of Athens, *op. cit.* IV, p. 5.

influence of Russia made the Orthodox less eager to seek for friends in the West. Even the works of the great Greek Catholic scholar, Leo Allatius, had very little effect on Orthodox readers at Constantinople.

It was in the Patriarchate of Antioch that Rome enjoyed its greatest success. While the Patriarchs of Alexandria and Jerusalem seemed to have worked well during the sixteenth and seventeenth centuries with their brothers of Constantinople, the Patriarchs of Antioch seem to have felt some jealousy and preferred to go their own way. It was an area in which Catholic missionaries had worked since the time of the Crusades and in which they were well established. In 1631 the Patriarch Ignatius II of Antioch made an informal act of submission to Rome. His successors, Euthymius II and Euthymius III, were both on the friendliest terms with Roman missionaries; and Euthymius III's successor, Macarius III, who reigned from 1647 to 1672, not only sent his secret submission to Rome in 1662 but also publicly toasted the Pope as his Holy Father at a dinner at the French Consulate at Damascus later that year. The Patriarch Athanasius III was said to have sent a secret submission to Rome in about 1687; but if he did so he repented of it, probably under the influence of his formidable brother of Jerusalem, Dositheus, whose anti-Latin activities he imitated. Cyril V similarly submitted in 1716. In 1724 when Athanasius III, who had returned to the Patriarchate, died, the pro-Roman hierarchs at Damascus hastily elected a certain Serapheim Tanas, who had been educated at Rome, to succeed him as Cyril VI, while the anti-Roman party, with the approval of the Holy Synod at Constantinople, elected a young Greek monk, Sylvester. For the next three decades there were two rival Patriarchs of Antioch, neither of them able to control the whole of the Patriarchate, or even to remain for long at the Patriarchal palace at Damascus. Cyril VI predeceased Sylvester, who therefore won in the end, but only when a large portion of his congregation left the fold to form a separate Uniate Church.[1] Similar tactics were attempted

---

[1] The struggle at Antioch is described in Ware, *op. cit.* pp. 28–30.

in about 1750 in Egypt, where an Arab priest called Joseph Babilas, consecrated as Bishop of Alexandria by Seraphim Tanas, claimed to be Patriarch, with the support of the Roman missionaries. He attracted a number of followers for a time; but his movement faded out, largely owing to the energy of the Orthodox Patriarch, Matthew Psaltis, and his friend the lay theologian Eustratiuos Argenti.[1]

Books and tracts were still written by the Orthodox condemning the doctrines and usages of Rome. But the controversialists merely repeated arguments that had frequently been put forward before. On the procession of the Holy Spirit they added little to the views given by Photius in the eighth century and frequently repeated ever since. Their attack on the use of unleavened bread at the Sacrament followed similarly traditional lines. The Greek theologians tended now, however, to be more critical of the Roman doctrine of Purgatory than their predecessors had been. Even Mark of Ephesus had been unwilling at the Council of Florence absolutely to condemn the doctrine, though he maintained that man cannot know what God intends to do with the souls of the departed. But to Maximus the Haghiorite and to Meletius Pegas it seemed unlawful and arrogant to assert the existence of Purgatory. Meletius introduced a newer note when he condemned the refusal of the Latin clergy to administer communion in both kinds to the laity. This refusal, though it was totally contrary to Orthodox tradition, had been curiously ignored by his predecessors. It may be that Meletius, most of whose polemical writing was for the benefit of the Ruthenians, felt it necessary to provide elucidation on a subject that the more staunchly Orthodox took for granted. The main bone of contention remained the Papal claim to supremacy. But there again nothing new was added to the arguments.[2]

Perhaps the chief cause of bitterness between the Churches,

---

[1] Ware, *Eustratios Argenti*, pp. 52–4.
[2] M. Jugie, *Theologia Dogmatica Christianorum Orientalium ab Ecclesia Catholica Dissidentium*, I, pp. 495, 499–500.

particularly in the eighteenth century, concerned the ownership of the Holy Places in Palestine. This long and complicated story lies outside of our scope; but it has to be remembered that, ever since the Crusades, and even before that, there had been angry disputes over the custodianship of the shrines, disputes in which not only the Greeks and the Latins but also the Monophysite Churches, the Armenians, Copts and Jacobites, were involved; and the disputes have continued to this day. On the Orthodox side it was the Patriarch of Jerusalem, rather than his brother of Constantinople, who led the Greek cause. But, after the conquest of Palestine by the Ottoman Sultan, it was at his court at Constantinople that decisions were made. This was the source of endless intrigues at the Sublime Porte and continually fomented ill will between the Churches. Towards the end of the seventeenth century the Greeks obtained from the Sultan orders that gave them the leading position both at Jerusalem and at Bethlehem. Their triumph was due to the advocacy of the great Patriarch of Jerusalem, Dositheus and his nephew and successor Chrysanthus, who were aided at the Porte by the Grand Dragoman, the Phanariot Alexander Mavrocordato. Mavrocordato had been a pupil of the Jesuits at the College of Saint Athanasius, and, in theory at least, he was no enemy of reunion. But, when the question of the Holy Places was in dispute, his Greek blood asserted itself, and he secured a settlement that greatly distressed his Catholic friends. The Holy Places played a permanently unholy role in destroying any atmosphere in which the idea of union or even of mutual tolerance and understanding could breathe.[1]

In spite of all the Jesuit efforts it is difficult to see how union with Rome could have been achieved. The differences in dogma and in ritual may have been in many ways trivial and even unintelligible to humbler folk. But, even if they could have been overlooked in a spirit of mutual tolerance, yet they did represent a difference in religious outlook. Even if the Patriarch of Constantinople could

---

[1] A picture of the issues in Palestine can be obtained from U. Heyd, *Ottoman Documents on Palestine, 1552–1615*, pp. 174 ff. See below, pp. 355, 369.

have humbled himself and admitted the Roman pontiff not only as his senior but also as his superior, he would in so doing have betrayed the traditions of his Church. The theory of the Pentarchy of Patriarchs might not be so ancient as many of the Orthodox believed, but the theory of the charismatic equality of bishops and of the right of a General Council alone to pronounce on doctrine went back to early Christian days. The Greeks could move a long way towards compromise, with the judicious use of Economy, but they could not accept the idea of Papal supremacy; and Rome, however far she might be willing to condone divergencies in doctrine and usages, could never yield on that. Moreover, though some Patriarchs, like some Emperors before them, might decide in all sincerity that union with the West was necessary for the welfare of the Orthodox world, in simpler circles, where the monks swayed opinion, below the ranks of the upper hierarchy, there was still too much bitterness. Memories of the Latin Empire lingered on, constantly fed by the persecution of the faithful in districts where Latins ruled. To these congregations, particularly in the provinces, Rome seemed the enemy. To them the Sultan's turban was slightly less objectionable than the Cardinal's hat. Then there was the Russian Church, the daughter grown wealthier than her mother, to whom the mother in her old age looked for sustenance. The Russians had their own good reasons for hating the Catholic West. They were more bitterly Orthodox than the Greeks. They would angrily repudiate any attempt at union, just as they had repudiated the attempted Union of Florence. Union would bring a schism in the heart of Orthodoxy. And, anyhow, would the Sultan allow his Greek subjects to ally themselves so intimately with the West? He would suspect every Greek as a traitor; and the results might well be disastrous for the Orthodox *milet*.

But there were other Churches in the West now, which had thrown off the domination of Rome. Might it be possible to reach some sort of inter-communion with them?

CHAPTER 5

THE CHURCH AND THE CHURCHES: THE LUTHERAN APPROACH

It was inevitable that, sooner or later, the Protestant Churches, protesting against Roman autocracy, should seek to find out about a Church which had made such a protest from the earliest times. Even before the great Reformation movement the Hussites had made overtures to the Orthodox. In 1451 a Bohemian whom the Greeks called Constantine Platris and surnamed the Englishman—he was probably the son of a Lollard refugee settled in Bohemia—came to Constantinople with letters to the Orthodox authorities. There was no Patriarch in the city at the time, Gregory Mammas having retired a few months previously to Rome, as his bishops would not support his policy of union. The Englishman was received by the dissident bishops, who formed a body known as the Synaxis, as they could not, without the Patriarch, call themselves the Synod. Friendly messages, full of denunciations of Roman pretensions, were exchanged. But the fall of the city little more than a year later prevented further negotiations.[1]

Martin Luther's chief interest in the Eastern Question lay in the belief, which he shared with many of his evangelical contemporaries, and with many of the Greeks themselves before the fall of Constantinople, that the end of the world was near and that the Grand Turk was Antichrist: though he had an alternative candidate in the person of the Pope. The Turks were a scourge sent from Heaven to punish Christendom for its sins and its lapses from the true faith. Consequently, though he sincerely dreaded their advance, he had no compunction in causing political trouble to

[1] See M. Pavlova, 'L'Empire Byzantin et les Tchèques avant la Chute de Constantinople', *Byzantinoslavica*, XIV (1953), pp. 203–24.

the Emperor Charles V, who alone in Europe, had he been allowed, might have dealt with the scourge. Nor did he feel any sympathy with the Greeks, with their decadent and idolatrous Church, who were already undergoing the scourging. Much as he loathed Rome, he did not consider that Constantinople had any better right to claim a primacy over the Christian hierarchy. The true mother-Church was that of Jerusalem, the city of which Christ Himself had been bishop. It alone was entitled to claim world allegiance. Divine retribution, helpfully provided by the Devil, had seen to the punishment of Constantinople at the hands of the Muslims; and the sack of Rome in 1527 should be a warning to the Papacy. But Luther had a dual personality. When he was swayed by his powerful mind and not by his powerful emotions he felt more kindly about the Greeks. He was a devoted student of the early Greek Fathers; and, after all, Greek was the language of the New Testament. In his disputation with Eck, when Eck declared that the Greek Church was schismatic because of its repudiation of Roman authority and that it had been the breeding-ground of heretics such as Nestorius, Eutyches and Achatius, Luther answered sternly that the Greeks were not schismatic as they had never from the earliest days admitted the supremacy of Rome, and that the Western Church itself had produced its heretics, its Pelagians, its Manichaeans and its Jovinians. He was unimpressed by Eck's reference to the Union of Florence, the unreality of which he clearly saw. The Greek Church, he concluded, represented the true tradition of early Christianity far better than did the theologians of Rome.[1]

Luther himself was a reactionary in temperament, disliking the spirit of the Renaissance. But his leading disciples were children of the Renaissance. The most distinguished of them, Philip Melanchthon, had been professor of Greek at Wittenberg and was deeply interested in Hellenism. His interest extended to the contemporary

---

[1] M. Luther and J. von Eck, *Der authentische Texte der Leipziger Disputation (1519). Aus bisher unbenutzten Quellen* (ed. O. Seitz), pp. 60 ff. See also M. Luther, *Von den Consiliis und Kirchen* (Weimar edition, 1914), pp. 576–9. His attitude towards the Turks is given in his *Vom Kriege wider die Türcken* (1529).

Greeks; and he thought that it would be valuable to establish a friendly understanding with the Greek Church.[1]

The difficulty was to find out how to make contact with the Greeks. The only European powers in diplomatic relations with the Ottoman Empire were Catholic: Venice, France, and the Habsburg dominions. It was, he thought, through Venice, with its colony of Greek scholars, its Greek possessions and its lack of religious intolerance that an approach could best be made, particularly if a Greek scholar could be found there who was in touch with the East and had not joined the Roman faith.

There was among the intellectuals at Venice a man known as Antony the Eparch. He was a Corfiot of good family who had gone to Venice as a boy, when Turkish attacks on Corfu made life there difficult, and had been educated at a school organized by the Roman Church for the benefit of Greek refugees and directed by Arsenius Apostolis. Antony became for a time professor of Greek at Milan. But, though he moved in Catholic circles he seems never to have joined the Catholic Church. It was with him that Melanchthon decided to get into touch. In about 1542 Melanchthon either wrote to him or sent him a message through a friend, to ask for his sympathy with the Reforming movement. In 1543 Antony replied in a long letter addressed to Melanchthon. It was a courteous but not a very sympathetic reply. We do not know what Melanchthon had said. Antony's letter showed only a slight interest in theology but a passionate devotion to the cause of Greek freedom. On the theological issues he merely indicated that he considered some of the Lutheran doctrines to be wrongheaded. It was the political side of the Reformation that concerned him; and he thought that to be dangerous and disastrous. The Lutherans were encouraging intrigue and even rebellion against the authority of Charles V, whom he believed, as did many others, to be the only man who might be able to drive the Turks out of Europe. The letter, which was lengthy and ornamented, in the

---

[1] For Melanchthon's attitude towards the Greeks see E. Benz, *Die Ostkirche im Lichte der Protestantischen Geschichtsschreibung*, pp. 17–20.

true Renaissance style, with quotations from Hesiod, Sophocles, Aristophanes, Hippocrates, Plato, Demosthenes and the Greek Anthology, accused the Reformers of being trouble-makers at a time when peace in the Church was desperately needed to defeat the forces of Antichrist. Melanchthon was politely but firmly told to read the lessons of history.[1] Melanchthon was disappointed. He told one of his pupils, Matthew Irenaeus Francus, to ask his friend Joachim Camerarius, the professor of Greek at Leipzig, to compose a reply. Later in 1543 Camerarius sent to Irenaeus the draft for a letter to Antony. In it Camerarius maintained, with equal verbosity but fewer Classical quotations, that no one was more eager for concord than Melanchthon and his followers, but that the Papists had made concord impossible by the corruption of their hierarchy and the distortions that they had introduced into the True Faith and their neglect and misinterpretation of the Scriptures. Camerarius might have gone further and pointed out a basic flaw in Antony's argument. For when the Catholic powers of France and Venice and the Papacy itself were united in an aggressive alliance against Charles, as happened in that year 1543, it was scarcely fair to put all the blame on the Lutherans if Charles was unable to take effective action against the Turks.[2]

In fact it seems that no reply was sent to Antony the Eparch. After all, he only represented the Greeks of Venice. It was with the Patriarchate of Constantinople itself with which the Reformers of Wittenberg wished to make contact. They had to wait for more than ten years before an opportunity arose.

In 1555 Melanchthon made friends with a Greek-born adventurer, James Basilicus Marchetti, self-surnamed the Heraclid. James Basilicus was a remarkable character even for that age of

---

[1] E. Legrand, *Bibliographie Hellénique: description raisonnée des ouvrages publiés en Grec par des Grecs aux 15e et 16e siècles*, I, pp. 259 ff., with the text of Antony's letter. See also E. Benz, *Wittenberg und Byzanz*, pp. 4–29.

[2] Camerarius's letter is given among Melanchthon's correspondence in *Corpus Reformatorum* (ed. C. G. Bretschneider), v, p. 93. See also Benz, *Wittenberg und Byzanz*, loc. cit.

adventurers. He was the subject of much speculation in his lifetime, and his biography was later written by his court-poet, Johann Sommer, and by an angry Papal Legate in Poland, Antonio Maria Graziani, and, more shortly, by a Hungarian bishop, Heinrich Forgach. He was born about the year 1515. According to his own story he was the son of the hereditary Prince of Samos and Paros, who belonged to the ancient family of the Heraclids, descended from the Kings of Epirus and from the hero Heracles himself. His parents and brother were killed by order of Sultan Selim I; but his nurse rescued him and took him to Crete. There he studied at the school run by the scholar Hermodorus Lestarchus: or so he told Melanchthon. His biographer Sommer says that he was educated in Chios, which is more convincing, as Lestarchus did run an academy there for a while. There was no future for the boy in Greece; so he went to the West and took service in Charles V's army. His Catholic biographers gave him a humbler origin. Graziani says that he was the son of a Cretan sailor attached to the Heraclid lord of Samos. His master found him clever and attractive and had him well educated, and eventually employed him as secretary. When the Heraclid died in exile at Coron in the Peloponnese, James Basilicus so effectively controlled the household that he could threaten its members to withhold the legacies due to them from the dead man unless they all signed a declaration that he was really the Heraclid's nephew. Forgach varies the story by making the young man abscond on his master's death with all the family papers. Charles V's troops were temporarily occupying Coron at the time; and, when they abandoned it in 1533, James Basilicus went with them. He spent twenty-two years in Charles's army, serving in Germany under Count Wolrad of Mansfeld and later, in France, under Count Gunther of Schwarzburg, fighting with distinction. In 1555 he was at Charles's court at Brussels. There he showed the Imperial chancery his papers and a family tree that he had compiled. Charles, who wished to reward him for his military prowess, was sufficiently impressed to award him the title of Count Palatine. This carried with it the right to nominate a poet laureate; he gave the post to his future biographer Sommer. But he was unpopular in Catholic circles because he dabbled in necromancy and prophesied with the aid of numerology disasters for the new Pope, Paul IV. When Charles V abdicated later that year, it was time for him to move. Armed with introductions from the Counts of Mansfeld and Schwarzburg, both of them Protestants, and from a friend of his, Justus Jonas, whom he had met on the French campaign and who was the son of one of Luther's closest associates, he appeared at Wittenberg. Melanchthon was delighted by this distinguished, cultivated Greek, who persuaded him that an alliance between the Lutherans and the Church of Constantinople could be easily achieved. James Basilicus had a talent for finding eminent relatives. He now claimed that the Patriarch, Joasaph II, was his cousin; and he assured Melanchthon that Joasaph would be most sympathetic, and that he himself would help in every possible way.

Melanchthon sent him on with a cordial introduction to King Frederick II of Denmark, who received him amiably and encouraged him to visit various Protestant lords in Lettonia and Poland. But his ambitions were growing. He learnt that the Prince of Moldavia, Alexander IV Lapuchneanu, was a savage and moody man, more interested in his cattle and pigs than in his subjects, and consequently very unpopular. James Basilicus's researches now proved to him that Alexander's wife Roxandra was another of his cousins. He arrived in Moldavia in 1558 to pay her a cousinly visit and was made welcome at her court at Jassy. But after a few months Alexander discovered that his wife's new cousin was plotting to displace him. James Basilicus had to flee, first to Cronnstadt in Transylvania, where he consoled himself by publishing his remarkable family tree, and then to Poland to see his Protestant friends there. After an unsuccessful attempt in 1560, in 1561 he invaded Moldavia with a force of Polish auxiliaries. Alexander was defeated and fled to Constantinople; and James Basilicus took over the Principality of Moldavia under the title of John I.

James Basilicus, or John I, saw himself as an enlightened and progressive ruler. His reign started well. An embassy laden with gifts and composed of boyars who had suffered under Alexander secured the good will of Moldavia's suzerain, the Sultan, and the confirmation of his title. King Sigismund Augustus of Poland, who had hitherto disapproved of him, now sent to congratulate him and permitted him to propose marriage to a noble Polish lady, Cristina Zborowska, daughter of the Governor of Cracow. The Emperor Ferdinand suggested to him that they might make a joint campaign against the Turks. But the new Prince's views on enlightenment did not please his staunchly Orthodox subjects. James Basilicus was Orthodox by birth. He may, like many Greeks who had migrated to the West, at some time have submitted to Rome. But he had been greatly impressed by the Lutherans. He may have been sincere when he encouraged Melanchthon to attempt to ally the Lutheran and Orthodox Churches; but his own method of doing so in Moldavia was to try to reform the Orthodox Moldavian Church along Lutheran lines. Without any reference to his cousin, the Patriarch of Constantinople, he appointed a Polish Protestant, Jan Lusinsky—or John Lusinius—to be Archbishop of Moldavia. Lusinsky not only shocked the Moldavians by possessing a wife, whom he brought with him to Jassy; but he began his attack on the Church by ordering a reform of its practices over the annulment of marriages. The Orthodox Church in general permits divorce through ecclesiastical courts, though it frowns on more than one subsequent remarriage. But divorce and dispensations for additional remarriages were easily obtainable in Moldavia and Wallachia; and Lusinsky was determined to root out what seemed to him to be sheer polygamy. He also had plans to dissolve monasteries and remove icons from churches. But in 1562 he died, almost certainly poisoned. James Basilicus did not long survive. The Moldavians were angry at his reliance on Protestant Poles; and, when it was learnt that his future bride, Cristina Zborowska, was the daughter of a man who, while Governor of Cracow, was also the leader of an anti-Trinitarian sect, there was horrified dismay. But the

Prince's downfall came when he began to confiscate money and precious objects from the monasteries. His finances were in a bad way. The ex-Prince Alexander had made off with much of the national treasure; and the revenue of the Principality, large though it was, was not large enough to pay for the expensive administration that he set up, as well as the tribute and bribes demanded by the Sublime Porte. The last straw was his attempt to confiscate holy relics. Riots broke out in which Archbishop Lusinsky's wife was murdered, as was a bastard daughter of the Prince; and the poet laureate Sommer was forced, he tells us, to live for three weeks hidden in orchards and woodlands. The Prince vainly summoned help from over the border. His Catholic neighbours would not intervene, and the Polish Protestants were too few. He held out for three months against the rebels in one of his fortresses; then, in 1563, he surrendered and was put to death. So ended the attempt to introduce Lutheranism into south-eastern Europe.[1]

Calvinism was later to achieve a certain success over the Carpathians, in Transylvania, but at the expense of Catholicism, not of Orthodoxy, the converts being Hungarians rather than Roumanians.

The strange career of James Basilicus did not help future relations between the Lutherans and the Orthodox. There is no direct reference to him in any contemporary Greek source. But his 'cousin', the Patriarch Joasaph, must have known of his efforts and cannot have liked them. Abundant evidence shows that the Patriarchate was worried by missionary work in the Principalities; and the missionaries were not all Catholic.

Melanchthon did not live to hear of his friend's fate in Moldavia.

[1] J. Sommer, *Vita Jacobi Despotae*, and A. M. Graziani, *De Joanne Heraclide Despota*, are printed with Forgach's, in E. Legrand, *Deux Vies de Jacques Basilicus*. An Italian version of Graziani's life, and some of James's correspondence are given in N. Jorga, *Nouveaux Matériaux pour servir à l'histoire de Jacques Basilikos l'Héraclide*. His history roused interest in England. See *Documents concerning Rumanian History, collected from British Archives* (ed. E. D. Tappe), pp. 33–6, which deal with 'the Despot's' adventures. See also Benz, *op. cit.* pp. 34–58.

He died in 1560. But rather more than a year earlier he had received at Wittenberg an elderly cleric from Montenegro called Demetrius, who came with an introduction from James Basilicus. Nothing is known of Demetrius's early history. He was already an old man when he met James in Moldavia in 1558. Demetrius made an excellent impression in Lutheran circles. Melanchthon liked him; and Nicholas Hemmingius wrote in a letter that he was an old man of exemplary piety and admirable morals, whose claim to be a deacon was undoubtedly genuine, though the Lutherans could not check up on this; he was certainly full of erudition about his Church. Here was a heaven-sent agent for achieving the desired contact with Constantinople. In order that the Orthodox might be properly informed about the Reformed religion, the Confession of Augsburg, which summarized Lutheran belief, was hastily but ably translated into Greek by a learned Hellenist, Paul Dolscius of Plauen; and a copy was given to Demetrius to deliver to the Patriarch, together with a personal letter from Melanchthon, which barely touched upon doctrine but suggested that the Lutheran and Greek Churches had much in common.[1]

Demetrius left on his journey late in 1559. Melanchthon died before an answer could have easily been returned; but his fellow-divines waited for many more months for news from Constantinople. At last they decided that Demetrius could not have delivered the letter. In fact he arrived at Constantinople at the end of 1559 and was received by the Patriarch. But the documents that he brought embarrassed Joasaph and the Holy Synod. A brief glance at the Confession of Augsburg showed that much of its doctrine was frankly heretical. But it would be undesirable to spoil relations with a potential friend. The Patriarch and his advisers took refuge in the favourite device of oriental diplomacy. They behaved as if they had never received the communication, which they carefully mislaid.[2] Demetrius waited for two or three

---

[1] Benz, *Wittenberg und Byzanz*, pp. 94 ff., giving the text of Melanchthon's letter.
[2] *Ibid.* pp. 71–2: J. N. Karmiris, Ὀρθοδοξία καὶ Προτεσταντισμός, p. 36.

months for a reply to carry back to Wittenberg. When none was forthcoming he did not venture to return to Germany. He moved to Transylvania, where he spent three years trying to introduce Lutheranism into its villages, encouraged by James Basilicus. After James's fall he carried on his propaganda in the Slav dominions of the Habsburg Emperor. The date of his death is unknown.[1]

The subsequent events in Moldavia must have confirmed Joasaph in his suspicion of the Lutherans. Some fifteen years later the atmosphere improved. The Habsburg Emperors employed a number of Lutheran officials. In about 1570 an Imperial Ambassador arrived at Constantinople who was a Protestant, David von Ungnad; and he brought with him as chaplain an eminent Lutheran scholar, Stephen Gerlach, who was in close touch with the Lutheran universities in Germany. Gerlach soon made friends with the learned Protonotary of the Great Church, Theodore Zygomalas, who introduced him to the Patriarch Jeremias II, then in his first term of office. In return he put Zygomalas into touch with the leading professor of Greek in Germany, Martin Kraus, or Crusius, of Tübingen, a man interested not only in Classical Greek but also in the Greek world of his time. Through Zygomalas Crusius entered into correspondence with the Patriarch Jeremias, whom he greatly admired.[2]

When such friendships were established it was natural for the Lutherans to press again for closer ecclesiastical relations with the Greeks. In 1574 Ungnad was prompted by Gerlach to write to Germany to ask for fresh copies of the Confession of Augsburg. In reply six copies were sent out by Crusius and Jacob Andreae, Chancellor of the University of Tübingen. One was to be given

---

[1] Benz, *Wittenberg und Byzanz*, pp. 73 ff.

[2] For Ungnad and Gerlach see E. Benz, *Die Ostkirche im Licht der Protestantischen Geschichtsschreibung*, pp. 24–9. Gerlach's very discursive *Tagebuch* was not published until after his death; but Crusius in his *Turco-Graecia* frequently cites Gerlach as the source of information. Jeremias II spoke no Western European language. When Philippe Du Fresne visited him in 1573, Theodore Zygomalas and his father were present to act as interpreters. P. du Fresne Canaye, *Voyage du Levant* (ed. M. H. Hauser), pp. 106–8.

to the Patriarch, one to Zygomalas, one to Metrophanes, Metropolitan of Berrhoea, one to the scholar Gabriel Severus, and one to the rich layman, Michael Cantacuzenus, who had promised to have it translated into vernacular Greek. A copy translated into Georgian was dispatched a little later, for transmission to the Orthodox Church of Georgia in the Caucasus. To the Patriarch's copy the Lutheran divines added a letter, in which they said that, though because of the distance between their countries there was some difference in their ceremonies, the Patriarch would acknowledge that they had introduced no innovation into the principal things necessary for salvation; and that they embraced and preserved, as far as their understanding went, the faith that had been taught to them by the Apostles, the Prophets and the Holy Fathers, and was inspired by the Holy Spirit, the Seven Councils and the Holy Scriptures.[1]

What the Georgians thought of the Confession of Augsburg, if their copy ever reached them, is unrecorded. To the Greeks it was as embarrassing as it had been fifteen years previously. Cantacuzenus did nothing about its translation into the vernacular. But Jeremias could not ignore the Confession as Joasaph had done. Von Ungnad and Gerlach were close at hand, pressing for an answer. After a little hesitation Jeremias wrote a polite letter of thanks to Tübingen, promising to send a statement on doctrinal points a little later. These delaying tactics were vain; Gerlach continued to ask for his views. At last, after consulting with the Holy Synod, the Patriarch, with the help of Zygomalas and his father John, composed a full answer to the various points in the Confession. The letter was dated 15 May 1576.

The Confession of Augsburg contains twenty-one articles. Jeremias replied to each in turn, stating wherein he agreed or disagreed with the doctrines contained in them. His comments are valuable, as they add up to a compendium of Orthodox theology at this date.

---

[1] Benz, *Wittenberg und Byzanz*, pp. 94 ff. For the text of the correspondence, see below, p. 256, n. 3.

The first article states the Nicene Creed to be the basis of the true faith. The Patriarch naturally concurred, but pointed out that the Creed should be accepted in its correct form, omitting the Dual Procession of the Holy Ghost, an addition which, as he explains at length, was canonically illegal and doctrinally unsound.

In the original Confession the second article proclaims original sin, the third is a summary of the Apostles' Creed and the fourth declares that man is justified by faith alone. In the Greek version the second and third articles change place: which is more logical. The Patriarch's second chapter therefore deals with the Creed. While approving of the Germans' summary he adds for their benefit twelve amplifying articles which, he says, contain the traditional doctrine of the Church. Three concern the Trinity, six the Incarnation, the Crucifixion and the Redemption, and three the life hereafter. He gives further glosses to these and appends a list of the seven cardinal virtues—he actually gives eight—and the seven deadly sins.

On original sin the Patriarch takes the opportunity of pointing out that baptism should be by triple immersion and not by aspersion, and should be followed up by chrismation. The baptismal practice of the Latins is, he says, incorrect.

In his fourth chapter, on justification by faith alone, the Patriarch points out, quoting Basil, that grace will not be given to those who do not live virtuous lives. He amplifies his views in his fifth and sixth chapters. In the Confession the fifth article says that faith must be fed with the help of the Holy Scriptures and the Sacraments, and the sixth that faith must bear fruit in good works, though it repeats that good works alone will not bring salvation. Jeremias takes for granted the doctrine given in the fifth article, and uses the chapter to continue his previous argument. The Sermon on the Mount lists virtues that will bring salvation without any reference to faith. Faith without works is not true faith. In the sixth chapter he warns the Germans not to presume on grace nor despair of it. He makes it clear that he disapproves.of anything that might suggest predestined election.

The seventh article of the Confession declares that the Church is one and eternal, and the sign of its unity is that the Gospel shall be rightly taught and the Sacraments rightly administered. So long as this is fulfilled, differences in ritual and ceremonial do not impair its unity. Jeremias agrees; but he goes on to talk about the Sacraments. Suspecting that the Lutherans held baptism and the eucharist to be the only Sacraments, he insists that there are seven Sacraments, baptism, chrismation, ordination, marriage, penitence and extreme unction. These are what Isaiah means when he speaks of the seven gifts from the Lord.

Jeremias concurred with the eighth and ninth articles in the Confession. The former says that Sacraments do not lose their validity even when administered by evil priests. The latter recommends infant baptism, so that the child may be at once qualified to receive grace.

The tenth article was more controversial. It says that the body and blood of Christ are truly present at the Lord's Supper and are distributed to those who participate in it; and those who teach otherwise are condemned. So far the Patriarch could agree. But he may have learnt that the original German version of the Confession added the words 'unter der Gestalt des Brods und Weins' —'in the form of the bread and the wine'—words omitted in the Latin and Greek versions. He asks for further details, saying: 'for we have heard of certain things about your views, of which it is impossible for us to approve'. The doctrine of the Holy Church, he maintains, is that at the Lord's Supper the bread is changed into the very body of Christ and the wine into His very blood. He adds that the bread must be leavened, not unleavened. He points out that Christ did not say 'This is bread', or even 'This is the figure of my body', but 'This is My body'. It would indeed be blasphemy to say that the Lord gave to His disciples the flesh that He bore to eat or the blood in His veins to drink, or that He descends physically from heaven when the mysteries are celebrated. It is, he says, by the grace and invocation of the Holy Spirit, which operates and consummates the change, and by our sacred prayers and by the Lord's own words that the bread and wine are transformed and transmuted into the very flesh and blood of Christ.

Jeremias is here making three points. In two of them he considered that the Lutherans were following the errors of the Latins. The Greeks, faithful to the traditions of the early Church, had long disapproved of the Latin use of unleavened bread, which seemed to them to mar the symbolism of the Sacrament; for the leaven symbolizes the new dispensation. Then Jeremias touches delicately on the Epiklesis, the invocation of the Holy Ghost which to the Greeks completed the change in the elements. They could not condone the Latin omission of the Epiklesis. On the actual question of the change in the elements Jeremias is cautious. He avoids the word μετουσίωσις, which is the exact Greek translation of 'transubstantiation'. The words that he uses, μεταβολή and μεταποίησις, do not necessarily imply material change. He does not explain the exact nature of the change, leaving it, rather, as a divine mystery. But the Lutheran view that though Christ's body and blood were present at the Sacrament there was no change in the elements seemed to him inadequate.

The eleventh article of the Confession advocates the use of private confession, though it is not absolutely necessary; nor can one enumerate all one's petty sins. The Patriarch agrees but thinks that more should be said about the value of confession as spiritual medicine and as leading to true acts of penitence. It must be remembered that to him the act of penitence ranked as a sacrament.

The twelfth article teaches that sinners who have lapsed from grace can receive it again if they repent. It disavows both the Anabaptist view that the saved can never fall from grace and the Novatian view that the lapsed can never recover it. The Patriarch concurs but adds that repentance must be shown by works.

The thirteenth article declares the Sacraments to be proofs of God's love for men and should be used to stimulate and confirm faith. This seems a little crude to Jeremias, who stresses the need for the Liturgy as providing the necessary framework for the

Sacraments, a re-enactment of the whole divine drama which gives them their spiritual value.

To the fourteenth, which states that only ordained priests should preach or administer the Sacraments, the Patriarch agrees, so long as the ordination has been correctly performed and the hierarchy canonically organized. He clearly doubted whether this was the case with the Lutheran Church.

The fifteenth article pleased him less. It approves of such rites and festivals as are conducive to giving peace and order to the Church but denies that any of them are necessary for salvation or provide the means for acquiring grace. To the Greek Church, with its full calendar of feasts and fasts, such teaching was distressing. The Patriarch, quoting at length from the early Fathers, emphasizes that these holy days and the ceremonies attached to them are lasting reminders of the life of Christ on earth and of the witness of the saints. To deny them any spiritual value is narrow-minded and wrong.

He concurs with the sixteenth article, which says that it is not contrary to the Gospel to obey civil magistrates or to engage in warfare if they should order it. He adds that one should remember, all the same, that obedience to the laws of God and to His ministers is a higher duty, and that no true Christian seeks for worldly power.

He concurs also with the seventeenth article, which foretells the coming of Christ to judge the world and to reward the faithful with eternal life and punish the wicked with eternal torment. He seems to have been unperturbed by the implied denial of the doctrine of Purgatory.

The eighteenth article deals with free will. The Lutherans maintained that, while a man may by the exercise of free will lead a good life, it will avail him nothing unless God gives him grace. This is too close to the doctrine of complete predestination for the Patriarch, who points out, with long quotations from John Chrysostom, that only those freely willing to be saved can be saved. Good deeds conform with the grace of God, but that grace is withdrawn concurrently with an evil deed.

The nineteenth article, declaring that God is not the cause of evil in this world, is perfectly acceptable. The twentieth returns to the problem of faith and works, repeating that, though good works are necessary and indispensable, and it is a libel to say that the Lutherans ignore them, yet they cannot purchase the remission of sins without faith and its accompanying grace. The Patriarch agrees about the dual need for faith and works; but why, he asks, if the Lutherans really value good works, do they censure feasts and fasts, brotherhoods and monasteries? Are these not good deeds done in honour of God and in obedience to his commands? Is a fast not an act of self-discipline? Is not a monastic fraternity an expression of fellowship? Above all, is not the taking of monastic vows an attempt to carry out Christ's demand that we should rid ourselves of our worldly entanglements?

The Patriarch was especially shocked by the twenty-first and last article, which says that, while congregations should be told of the lives of the saints as examples to be followed, it is contrary to the Scriptures to invoke the saints as mediators before God. Jeremias, after citing the special powers given by Christ to the disciples, answers that true worship should indeed be given to God alone, but that the saints, and, above all, the Mother of God, who by their holiness have been raised to heaven, may lawfully and helpfully be invoked. We can ask the Mother of God, owing to her special relationship, to intercede for us and the archangels and angels to pray for us; and all the saints may be asked for their mediation. It is a sign of humility that we sinners should be shy of making a direct approach to God and should seek the intervention of mortal men and women who have earned salvation.

Jeremias ended his letter with a supplementary chapter, stressing five points. First, he insists again that leavened bread should be used at the Eucharist. Secondly, while he approves of the marriage of secular clergy, the regular clergy should take vows of celibacy and should keep to them. Thirdly, he emphasizes once more the importance of the Liturgy. Fourthly, he repeats that the remission of sin cannot be attained except through confession and the act of penitence, to which he attaches sacramental importance. Finally, and at great length, he gives arguments in support of the institution of monasteries and the taking of monastic vows. Many mortals, he admits, are unfitted to bind themselves to a life of asceticism; and if they lead good lives according to their abilities, they too can reach salvation. But it is, he thinks, a better thing to be ready to forswear the world and to devote one's life to the disciplined service of God; and for this end monasticism provides the proper means.

His final paragraph is written in a mixture of humility and condescension. 'And so, most learned Germans,' he writes, 'most beloved sons in Christ of Our Mediocrity, as you desire with wisdom and after great counsel and with your whole minds to join yourselves with us to what is the most holy Church of Christ, we, speaking like parents who love their children, gladly receive your charity and humanity into the bosom of our Mediocrity, if you are willing to follow with us the apostolic and synodical traditions and to subject yourselves to them. Then at last truly and sincerely one house will be built with us...and so out of two Churches God's benevolence will make as it were one, and together we shall live until we are transferred to the heavenly fatherland.'[1]

This reply reached Germany in the summer of 1576. The German divines detected in it a certain lack of enthusiasm. Crusius arranged a meeting with the theologian Lucius Osiander; and together they composed an answer in which the points to which the Patriarch seemed to object were elucidated and justified. They confined themselves to doctrines mentioned in the Confession of Augsburg and therefore did not touch on matters such as leavened bread, the Liturgy or even monasticism. They attempted to show that their view on justification by faith was not really so very

---

[1] It was this letter, which gives Jeremias II's fullest statement on doctrine together with the Lutheran arguments that he was answering, that the Jesuit Sokołowski published in 1582, thus obliging the Lutherans to publish the whole correspondence. See below, p. 256 and n. 2.

different from the Patriarch's; and they repeated at some length the Lutheran view that, though Christ's flesh and blood were present at the Lord's Supper, there was no material change in the elements. They made it clear that they believed in only two Sacraments and that they could not admit the propriety of invoking the saints.[1]

Their letter was written in June 1577, but it probably only reached Constantinople in the course of the following year. Once again Jeremias tried to avoid sending an answer. But Gerlach was still in Constantinople, pressing for one. Gerlach left to return to Germany in the spring of 1579. In May Jeremias sent off at last a further statement of his views. His tone was now a little less conciliatory. He pointed out clearly and at greater length the doctrines which the Orthodox Church could not accept. It could not admit the Dual Procession of the Holy Ghost. In spite of what the Lutherans claimed, their views on free will and on justification by faith were not Orthodox and were in the Patriarch's opinion too crude. While admitting that the Sacraments of baptism and the eucharist ranked above the others, the Patriarch insisted that there were seven sacraments. He repeated that it was correct to invoke the saints and added that respect should be paid to holy images and relics.[2]

A committee of Lutheran divines, including Crusius, Andreae, Osiander and Gerlach, met at Württemberg to compose a further reply, which was dispatched in June 1580. Its tone was very conciliatory. When not yielding on any points it tried to suggest that the doctrinal differences between the Churches on justification by faith, on free will and on the change in the elements at the Lord's Supper were only matters of terminology, and that other differences could perhaps be treated as differences in ritual and usage.

The Germans had to wait for an answer. Jeremias had been deposed in November 1579, and did not return to office till September 1580. Some months elapsed before he could settle down to compose an answer. It was eventually sent in the summer

---

[1] See below, p. 279.   [2] See below, p. 280.

of 1581. He briefly recapitulated the points of disagreement, then begged for the correspondence to cease. 'Go your own way', he wrote, 'and do not send us further letters on doctrine but only letters written for the sake of friendship.' In spite of this, the Lutheran committee sent one more letter, almost identical with their last. The Patriarch did not reply to it.[1]

In 1584 the whole correspondence was published at Wittenberg. The Lutherans might have preferred to keep silence about their failure to achieve union. But a Polish Jesuit, Stanislas Sokołowski, obtained a copy of the Patriarch's letter of 1576, which he translated into Latin and published in 1582, adding notes to correct Greek doctrines that differed from the Roman.[2] The Lutherans felt that they must therefore present the full story.[3]

The friendly relations continued nevertheless. Jeremias and Theodore Zygomalas kept up their correspondence with Crusius on matters such as Greek linguistic usages and the present state of the great Greek cities of the past. It was in 1581 that Zygomalas sent to Crusius most of the material, including a copy of the Patriarchal Chronicle of Malaxus, that enabled the German scholar to write his great book, *Turco-Graecia*, which is our main source of information about the Greek world in the sixteenth century.[4] But Gerlach's successor as chaplain to the Imperial

---

[1] See below, p. 339.

[2] S. Sokołowski, *Censura Orientalis Ecclesiae—De principiis nostri seculi haereticorum dogmatibus—Hieremiae Constantinopolitani Patriarchae, judicii & mutuae communionis caussa, ab Orthodoxae doctrinae adversariis, non ita pridem oblatis. Ab eodem Patriarcha Constantinopolitano ad Germanos Graece conscripta—a Stanislao Socolovio conversa* (Cracow, 1582; dedicated to the Pope).

[3] *Acta et Scripta Theologorum Wirtembergensium et Patriarchae Constantinopolitani D. Hieremiae* (Wittenberg, 1584), *passim.* See Legrand, *op. cit.* II, pp. 41–4, for a list of the various letters.

[4] It is to Crusius that we owe the publication of the so-called *Historia Politica* and *Historia Patriarchica*, of which the editions published in the Bonn Corpus are a reproduction. The relation of the former to the *Ekthesis Chronica* (published by S. Lampros in *Byzantine Texts*, ed. J. B. Bury) and to the 'Chronicle of 1570', described by T. Preger in *Byzantinische Zeitschrift*, XI, needs still to be elucidated. The *Historia Patriarchica* is also related to the 'Chronicle of 1570' as well as to the chronicle of 'Dorotheus of Monemvasia'; but here again more

embassy, Salomon Schweigger, was unsympathetic. On his return home he wrote a travel-book in which the Orthodox were accused of idolatry and ignorance, even though he admits that the Patriarch entertained him most hospitably and fed him on caviare.[1] On the Greek side Gabriel Severus, when resident at Venice, published a work attacking the Lutherans for their doctrine on the Sacraments: though, as with Antony the Eparch some decades earlier, it was their political rather than their doctrinal activities that he really deplored.[2]

It is difficult to see how any real union between the Orthodox and Lutheran Churches could have been achieved. The Lutherans had not rid themselves of the superstitions of Rome in order to unite with a Church whose devotion to saints and images and monastic vows must have seemed quite as idolatrous. To the Orthodox the Lutherans seemed to combine certain Roman errors with an unsound evangelism and a regrettable taste for iconoclasm. The chief common-ground was a mutual dislike of the Papacy; and that was hardly a sufficient bond.

Nevertheless Greek theological students were always welcomed in Lutheran Germany. Early in the eighteenth century a small theological seminary was endowed for them at Halle in Saxony, which enjoyed a certain success.[3] Metrophanes Critopoulos

work needs to be done on the relationship. See T. H. Papadopoullos, *Studies and Documents relating to the History of the Greek Church and People under Turkish Domination*, pp. xviii–xx. It is interesting to note that Margunius, who was also in correspondence with Crusius, reported to Jeremias II that the *Turco-Graecia* was secretly anti-Orthodox. See G. Fedalto, 'Ancora su Massimo Margounios', *Bolletino dell'Istituto di Storia Veneziano*, v–vi (1964), pp. 209–13.

[1] S. Schweigger, *Ein newe Reyesteschreibung auss Teutschland nach Constantinopel und Jerusalem.* See Benz, *Die Ostkirche im Licht der Protestantischen Geschichtsschreibung*, pp. 29–38.

[2] Gabriel Severus, Πόσαι εἰσὶν αἱ γενικαὶ καὶ πρῶται διαφοραὶ καὶ ποῖαι, ἃς ἔχει ἡ 'Ανατολικὴ 'Εκκλησία τῇ 'Ρωμαικῇ; printed in a volume of treatises by Nicodemus Metaxas, for which see below, p. 279, n. 1. It was principally an attack on Roman doctrines, but incidentally mentioned Lutheran errors.

[3] For the Halle seminary, which lasted from 1728 to 1729, see E. Wolf, 'Halle', in *Die Religion in Geschichte und Gegenwart*, III. The inspiration for the seminary came from the orientalists J. H. and C. B. Michaelis, and from the former's son J. D. Michaelis.

lectured in Germany in 1629 on his journey home from England; and among the earlier students who remained in Germany was a certain Zacharias Gerganos, of whom we know little except that he was invited to Germany in 1619 by the Elector of Saxony and published at Wittenberg in 1622 a treatise dedicated to his patron and intended to bring the two Churches together. He was more Lutheran than Orthodox. The Holy Scriptures, he said, contained all that was necessary for the definition of faith and were fully intelligible and easy to interpret. He denounced the doctrine of Purgatory and vehemently attacked the Bishop of Rome's claim to primacy. But, unlike the Orthodox and the strict Lutherans, he said that a sinful priest was robbed of grace and therefore could not administer the Sacraments. His book made little impression in Germany, though it seems to have circulated in the East; and we would scarcely have heard of it had it not provoked an angry reply from a Greek educated at Rome at the College of Saint Athanasius, John Matthew Caryophyllus, in a work published at Rome in 1631.[1] But John Matthew had family reasons for his horror of such an attitude; for he had a cousin at Constantinople, John Caryophyllus, whose views on transubstantiation and grace showed undoubted Protestant influences.

This cousin had fallen under the spell of one of the most remarkable of all Greek ecclesiastics, Cyril Lucaris.

---

[1] Z. Gerganos, *Catechismus Christianus*, published in 1622. See E. Legrand, *Bibliographie Hellénique: description raisonnée des ouvrages publiés en Grec par des Grecs au 17e siècle*, I, pp. 159–70. John Matthew Caryophyllus, Ἔλεγχος τῆς ψευδοχριστιανικῆς κατακλήσεως Ζαχαρίου τοῦ Γεργάνου, published in Greek and Latin at Rome in 1631. For Critopoulos see below, pp. 269, 286, 294–5.

CHAPTER 6

THE CHURCH AND THE CHURCHES:
THE CALVINIST PATRIARCH

On 13 November 1572 there was born at Candia in Crete to the
wife of Stephen Lucaris, a prosperous butcher, a son whom his
parents named Constantine.[1] He was a bright, precocious boy;

[1] The chief authority on Cyril Lucaris's career is the *Collectanea de Cyrillo Lucario*,
published in 1707 by Thomas Smith, former English chaplain at Constantinople
(see below, pp. 292–3). This contains a life of Cyril by Smith himself, which is
taken from an appendix called 'The State of the Greek Church under Cyrillus
Lucaris', which he had already published in his *An Account of the Greek Church*
(Latin version, 1678; English version, 1680); a long letter from Cornelius van
Haag, Dutch Ambassador at Constantinople during Cyril's Patriarchate; a
'Fragmentum Vitae Cyrilli' written by Cyril's friend Antoine Léger, Calvinist
chaplain at Constantinople; and a 'Narratio epistolica Turbarum inter Cyrillum
et Jesuitas', for which see below, p. 271, n. 1. Smith only arrived at Constantinople thirty years after Cyril's death. It is unlikely that he obtained much information from the local Greeks, to whom Cyril's theology was by now an
embarrassment. But he had access to his Embassy's papers, and he had read most
of what had been already published about Cyril, in Catholic sources, such as
Allatius and Arnauld (A. Arnauld, *La Perpetuité de la Foi*, pts. III and IV, *Preuves
authentiques de l'Union de l'Eglise d'Orient avec l'Eglise*, published in 1670), and in
hostile Protestant writers such as Grotius (see Smith, *An Account of the Greek
Church*, pp. 276, 280). He also had conversed with Edward Pococke (see below,
p. 292), who had been in Constantinople at the time of Cyril's death; and he
drew largely from a shorter account of Cyril's career given in J. H. Hottinger's
Analecta Historico-Theologica (1652), pp. 552 ff. He notes that Hottinger was a
close friend of Léger, from whom he obtained his information (Smith, *op. cit.*
p. 282). J. Aymon's *Monuments authentiques de la réligion des Grecs et de la fausseté
de plusieurs confessions de foi des Chrétiens*, published in 1708, gives a hotch-potch
of information about Cyril, including some of his letters. Sir Thomas Roe's
letters, written while Ambassador at Constantinople, give further information.
The greater part of Cyril's own surviving letters are given in E. Legrand's
*Bibliographie Hellénique: description raisonnée des ouvrages publiés en Grec par des
Grecs au 17e siècle*, IV. His letters to Roe are unpublished; they are to be found in
State Papers 97, in the Public Record Office. The fullest modern life of Cyril is
G. A. Hadjiantoniou, *Protestant Patriarch*, a work filled with useful information
but passionately prejudiced against both the Latin and the traditional Greek

and his father determined to give him a good education. Venetian policy in Crete was hostile to the Orthodox Church, which it regarded as potentially seditious.[1] In consequence there were few Greek schools there. But Cretan boys were freely allowed to come to Venice. It was therefore to Venice that his father sent Constantine when he was twelve years old, to attend the school attached to the Greek Church there. Its headmaster was Maximus Margunius, a man of independent mind who had already been in trouble with the Orthodox authorities for suspected Latinizing tendencies and was later in difficulties with the Inquisition for being anti-Latin. He had recently been appointed Bishop of Cythera, but many years passed before the Venetian authorities allowed him to reside in his see; and he continued to teach at the school.[2] He was struck by Constantine and gave him special attention. After four years Stephen Lucaris summoned his son back to Crete, perhaps because of financial troubles. The boy spent a year there, attending classes given by a learned monk, Meletius Vlastos, at the monastery of Saint Catherine, in the outskirts of Candia, and writing numerous letters to Margunius. He had difficulty in finding books, other than those which Margunius had left in his old home—the Opuscula of Plutarch, a book of Aristotle's (we do not know which), the Orations of Demosthenes, two volumes of Eusebius's History, two books by Cicero, the Logic of Flaminius and a Latin dictionary.[3] Local tradition adds that owing to the crisis in the family finances his mother took in washing and he himself was apprenticed to a fisherman and had now and then to go on some fishing voyage.

Churches, and not wholly reliable on details or on background information. Cyril's birth is dated at 'about 1558' by Archbishop Laud in a note published in Smith, *Collectanea*, p. 65. But the date 13 November 1572, given by Léger, *ibid.* p. 77, is almost certainly correct.

[1] See D. J. Geanakoplos, *Greek Scholars in Venice*, pp. 45–7; W. Miller, *Essays on the Latin Orient*, pp. 177–80.

[2] For Margunius see above, pp. 214–15.

[3] Legrand, *Bibliographie Hellénique au 17e siècle*, IV, pp. 177–8. For St Catherine's see D. J. Geanakoplos, *Byzantine East and Latin West*, pp. 141–2, 165, 168.

The Calvinist Patriarch

One of these voyages brought him to Alexandria, where he called upon a relative, Meletius Pegas, who was then political secretary to the Patriarch of Alexandria. The tradition is doubtful. More probably he met Meletius when the latter was visiting his family in Crete.[1]

In 1589 Constantine Lucaris was back in Italy and enrolled as a student at the University of Padua, thanks probably to Margunius, who kept a fatherly eye on him, reproving him when he neglected his lectures or when he bought himself an expensive sword to wear. Padua was now the home of Neo-Aristotelianism. To counter the influence of this materialistic philosophy, Margunius used to send Constantine essay-subjects on more spiritual aspects of Greek thought and generally coached him.[2] The boy probably travelled during his vacations. He is said to have visited Germany; and it is possible that he went to Geneva, where there was a small Greek colony founded by a Cretan professor of Italian origin, Franciscus Portus, who had become a Calvinist.[3]

He passed his examinations with honours in 1595 and received his degree of *laureatus*. He had probably already decided to enter the priesthood as that offered the best career for a boy with no taste for commerce or for medicine. His decision was confirmed by an encouraging letter from his cousin Meletius Pegas, who had been elected in 1590 to the Patriarchal throne of Alexandria.[4]

The duties of a Patriarch of Alexandria were not onerous. The vast majority of Egyptian Christians belonged to the Coptic Church; and his flock was composed mainly of immigrant Greek merchants. The Patriarch Meletius therefore spent much of his time at Constantinople, where he had better access to the Sublime

[1] N. C. Papadopoulos, *Historia Gymnasii Patavini*, II, pp. 292–3.
[2] Legrand, *Bibliographie Hellénique au 17e siècle*, IV, pp. 190–5.
[3] For Portus see Legrand, *Bibliographie Hellénique au 17e siècle*, II, pp. vii–xx, III, pp. 93–133; Geanakoplos, *Byzantine East and Latin West*, pp. 158–9. Portus himself had died in 1581. He was succeeded in his Chair at Geneva by his famous pupil, Isaac Casaubon.
[4] Legrand, *Bibliographie Hellénique au 17e siècle*, IV, pp. 214–15.

Porte and where he could help his overworked fellow-Patriarch, particularly in seeing to the Orthodox congregations living beyond the bounds of the Ottoman Empire. In 1595, when Lucaris left Padua, Meletius was living at Constantinople, probably acting as locum tenens of the Patriarchate, where there was a vacancy at the time. It was to Constantinople that Lucaris now went, to be ordained deacon and priest by his cousin. On his ordination, probably at the end of 1595, he followed the usual custom of giving up his baptismal name and taking another, beginning with the same initial letter. Henceforward he was Cyril Lucaris.[1]

The Church authorities at Constantinople were concerned at the time over the fate of the Orthodox in Poland. The Polish kingdom had of recent years been expanding eastward and now controlled Ruthenia and most of the Ukraine, where the population was entirely Orthodox; and there had long been large Orthodox congregations in Galicia and in Lithuania, which had been formally united to Poland in 1569. There were also in Poland large numbers of Lutherans and a few Calvinists. King Stephen Bathory, to whom much of this expansion was due, had been a tolerant Catholic; and, though he encouraged the Jesuits to work among the Orthodox, he allowed Orthodox and Lutheran bishops the right enjoyed by the Catholic bishops to a seat in the Polish Senate. Stephen's sucessor, Sigismund III, elected in 1587, belonged to the Catholic branch of the Swedish Vasa dynasty. His mother, the Lithuanian heiress Catherine Jagellon, had been passionately Catholic; and Sigismund was himself to lose the Swedish throne because of his religion. Sigismund soon took measures against Protestants and Orthodox alike. He ordered that all public offices should be reserved for Catholics; and there were some 20,000 of them in his gift. He deprived non-Catholic bishops of their seats in the Senate. He had been particularly

---

[1] Smith, *Collectanea*, pp. 7, 77. Meletius Pegas was certainly locum tenens of the Patriarchate during the next interregnum from March 1597 to March 1598 (M. Le Quien, *Oriens Christianus*, I, p. 331).

irritated by a progress through the Ukraine made by the Patriarch Jeremias II of Constantinople on his way back from visiting Moscow in 1588, and had ordered the Jesuits to increase their propaganda among all his Orthodox subjects. They won over Michael, Metropolitan of Vilna, and Ignatius, Bishop of Vladimir, with whose help the King was able to summon a Council of the Polish Orthodox bishops to meet at Brest-Litovsk in 1595, to discuss their submission to Rome, along the lines agreed at the Union of Florence. Not many bishops attended the Council, where a slight majority of those present voted to accept Papal supremacy, provided that the Orthodox could keep their liturgy, communion in both kinds for the laity, the marriage of secular clergy and the Julian calendar. When the terms were referred to Rome, Pope Clement VIII accepted them and on 23 December 1595 announced the foundation of the Uniate Orthodox Church of Poland. A second Council was then summoned to meet in October 1596, again at Brest-Litovsk, to endorse the settlement.[1]

When the news reached Constantinople it was decided to send representatives to attend the Council. The Patriarch of Constantinople nominated a certain Nicephorus Cantacuzenus as exarch, or Patriarchal deputy, and Meletius nominated Cyril Lucaris as his exarch. The two young priests set out for Poland, bringing with them three letters on doctrine written by Meletius for the benefit of the faithful.

Orthodox Poles had been horrified by the first Council. Their bishops hastened to Brest to record their protest, and with them a number of eminent laymen, headed by Constantine Basil, Prince of Ostrov and Voyevod of Kiev, a man reputed to be aged more than a hundred, who many years previously had set up the first Slavonic printing-press, to print liturgical books. His opposition

---

[1] For a contemporary account of the Catholic efforts to convert the Orthodox in Poland and the Ukraine see A. Regenvolscius, *Systema Historico-Chronologicum Ecclesiarum Slavonicarum* (1652), pp. 462–80. See also L. Pastor, *History of the Popes from the Close of the Middle Ages*, XXIV, pp. 110 ff.; T. Ware, *The Orthodox Church*, pp. 103–6. See also E. Winter, *Byzanz und Rom im Kampf um die Ukraine*, pp. 56–70.

was formidable, as was shown some years later, during Sigismund's wars against the Turks, when the Ukrainian Cossacks who revered him refused to aid the King. But Sigismund was obdurate. His deputy, Prince Radziwill, refused to allow any dissident bishop into the Church of the Virgin where the Council was held and the Pope's gracious message read out, followed by a *Te Deum*. The dissident bishops were obliged to meet in a private house nearby. It was only there that Pegas's letters on doctrine could be read.[1]

There followed a series of measures against the Orthodox who refused to join the Uniate Church. Bishoprics were given only to Uniates, including the Metropolitan see of Kiev, though the Uniate nominee never ventured to reside there. The endowments of dissident sees were confiscated, and their holders deprived of episcopal privileges: though there was no actual persecution of the lower clergy. Cyril and his companion decided to stay on in Poland. He saw that the Orthodox, priests and laity alike, were at a disadvantage owing to their lack of education. He went to Vilna, where there was an Orthodox school, which he reformed and reorganized, basing himself there for twenty months. Then, at the request of a Galician Orthodox priest, Gabriel Dorotheides, he moved to Lvov, where he founded a school to be run on similar lines. But meanwhile the King's agents watched his actions with suspicion. Early in 1598 he and Nicephorus Cantacuzenus were denounced as Turkish spies. Nicephorus was arrested by Sigismund's police and put summarily to death. Cyril had time to escape to Ostrov, where the Prince gave him shelter until he could be smuggled out of the country. By August 1598 he was in Constantinople; and he spent that Christmas with his family in Crete.[2]

While he was in Vilna Cyril had met various Lutheran divines;

---

[1] Smith, *Collectanea*, pp. 9–10; A. Regenvolscius, *op. cit.* p. 466.

[2] Smith, *Collectanea*, pp. 10–12, 78–9: Legrand, *Bibliographie Hellénique au 17e siècle*, IV, pp. 220–1, 225–9. See also Winter, *op. cit.* pp. 58–60. Cyril's preaching is recorded in the *Codex of the Metochion of the Holy Sepulchre at Constantinople*, no. 408, fols. 44–9.

and they had discussed the possibility of uniting their Churches. The Lutherans suggested some formulae on which inter-communion could be based, which Cyril and his Orthodox friends promised, hesitantly, to accept provided they were endorsed by the Patriarchs of Constantinople and Alexandria. Neither Matthew II of Constantinople nor Meletius was much impressed by the proposals, and would have let the matter drop. But in 1599 Sigismund issued a decree forbidding foreigners to enter or leave his country without his permission, and wrote to Meletius informing him of it and urging him to cease his contumacy and submit to Rome. Meletius wrote a letter in reply, asking leave very politely to be allowed to send to Poland such spiritual guides as the Orthodox might need; and he entrusted it to Cyril, ordering him back to Poland with a note commending him to the King's clemency. At the same time he gave Cyril a letter to deliver to the Lutheran divines in which he suggested consultation on matters of mutual political interest but avoided theological points. When Cyril reached Poland Sigismund received him coldly but allowed him to stay in the country. Cyril did not, however, deliver the letter to the Lutherans, for fear that he and they would be accused of conspiracy.[1]

Cyril spent a year in Poland on this second visit, mainly at the school which he had founded at Lvov. Seventeen years later a Jesuit, Peter Scarga, produced a letter which he said Cyril had written in January 1601 to the Catholic bishop of Lvov, Demetrius Solicowski, in which he referred to the See of Saint Peter with deep reverence and expressed the hope that the Churches would soon be reunited. The letter, which was to be used by the Jesuits to undermine his position with the Orthodox, if genuine, was certainly amended to suit the Jesuits' purpose. Cyril may well have tried to reach some understanding with the Catholic authorities for the sake of his school, and he may have expressed the perfectly Orthodox view that reunion was desirable and that the Bishop of Rome would be treated with the highest honours

---

[1] Smith, *Collectanea*, pp. 11–12.

were he to give up his heresies. But the implication that Cyril was buying personal immunity by becoming a crypto-Catholic is quite out of keeping with his all too obstinate and outspoken character.[1]

In the spring of 1601 Cyril received a letter from Meletius Pegas, who was back in Egypt, offering him the abbacy of an Egyptian monastery and virtually promising him the succession to the Alexandrian Patriarchate.[2] He therefore left Poland and, after a short stay in Moldavia, where the Patriarchate owned large estates, he arrived at Alexandria on 11 September. Two days later Pegas died; and the Alexandrian synod elected Cyril as their Patriarch. The Greek Catholic, Leo Allatius, later published a rumour that Cyril bought the throne with money collected for the Patriarchate in Moldavia, bribing the bishops when they were about to elect a certain Gerasimus Spartaliotes. This is unlikely, as Spartaliotes was henceforward one of Cyril's most devoted followers.[3]

Cyril was an efficient Patriarch of Alexandria. He moved the seat of the Patriarchate from the dying seaport to Cairo, to be at the governmental centre of the province. He reorganized its finances, and he reformed its schools. He settled a quarrel in the Church of Cyprus; and he went to Jerusalem for the enthronement as Patriarch there of his friend Theophanes.[4] But life was lonely in Egypt for a man of his energy and intellect, with only Greek merchants and provincial clerics for company. He had spent little of his life among fellow-Greeks. His studies at Padua and his Protestant contacts in Poland had given him an interest in new trends in Western religious thought.

This interest was enhanced by his friendship with a Dutchman, Cornelius van Haag, whom he probably first met when van Haag

[1] Smith, *Collectanea*, pp. 12–13, 79–80. See below, p. 287.
[2] Legrand, *Bibliographie Hellénique au 17e siècle*, IV, p. 215.
[3] Leo Allatius, *De Ecclesiae Occidentalis atque Orientalis Perpetua Consensione*, III, p. 1072: Smith, *Collectanea*, pp. 13, 80.
[4] Philip of Cyprus, *Chronicon Ecclesiae Graecae* (ed. H. Hilarius), p. 447; Hottinger, *op. cit.* p. 52: Legrand, *Bibliographie Hellénique au 17e siècle*, IV, pp. 230–7.

was travelling in the Levant in 1598. In 1602 van Haag was appointed first ambassador from the States-General to the Sublime Porte. Henceforward Cyril would visit the Dutch Embassy whenever business took him to Constantinople. At his request van Haag procured for him a number of theological works from Holland and put him in touch with the theologian Jan Uytenbogaert, the pupil of Arminius. With him Cyril kept up a correspondence that lasted for many years. His Dutch contacts were strengthened by the visit to the Levant in 1617–19 of a Dutch divine, David Le Leu de Wilhem, with whom also he remained in correspondence.[1] In his letters to his Dutch friends he began to show a growing sympathy with Protestant doctrine. In 1613 he wrote to Uytenbogaert that he believed in only two Sacraments and that they could not confer grace without faith, though faith without the Sacraments was equally valueless. He added that the Greek Church maintained many erroneous practices, though it always admitted the possibility of error.[2] In a series of letters to de Wilhem he stressed the need for the Greeks to replace superstition by 'evangelical simplicity' and to depend on the authority of the Scriptures and the Holy Spirit alone. He told of his distress at what he saw at Jerusalem, where the behaviour of the faithful seemed to him almost pagan. He was glad to find himself in perfect agreement with de Wilhem on all theological matters.[3] A letter written in 1618 to an Italian, Marco Antonio de Dominis, who had given up a Catholic archbishopric to become a Protestant, is even more outspoken. Cyril says that he finds the doctrines of the Reformers more in accord with the Scriptures than those of the Greek or Latin Churches. He begins to discount the authority of the Church Fathers. 'I can no longer endure to hear men say that the comments of human tradition are of equal weight with the Scriptures', he writes. He adds that in his opinion image-worship is disastrous and is even ashamed to confess that he finds

---

[1] Aymon, *op. cit.* pp. 172–5.
[2] The correspondence is given in Aymon, *op. cit.* pp. 130–64.
[3] *Ibid.* pp. 182–95.

the contemplation of a crucifix helpful to his prayers. The invocation of saints is, he adds, an insult to Our Lord.[1]
It is unlikely that Cyril aired these views to the Greeks. They merely knew him to be an efficient and virtuous Patriarch who had a number of foreign friends and was staunch in his opposition to Rome.

It was during these years that the Constantinopolitan Patriarchate was occupied by Neophytus II and Raphael II, both of whom leaned towards union with Rome. When Neophytus licensed an Italian Greek's sermon which openly advocated union, Cyril was asked to preach the counter-blast and to remain in Constantinople to direct anti-Roman activities.[2] He was there when Neophytus died in January 1612. A majority in the Synod elected him to succeed to the Patriarchate. But he could not or would not pay the sum demanded by the Sublime Porte for the confirmation of his election. His opponents on the Synod therefore put up a rival candidate, Timothy, Bishop of Marmora, who promised the Sultan and his ministers a sum larger than was usual; and the Synod was ordered to elect him.[3]

Timothy, a man distinguished only for his wealth, jealously tried to stir up trouble for Cyril in Egypt. Cyril had to retire for a while to Mount Athos, and then visited Wallachia, whose Prince, Michael Bassaraba, had been a fellow-student of his at Padua. He was back in Cairo before 1617, keeping up with his Dutch connections. Thanks to them his reputation was high in Protestant Europe. In about 1618 he received a letter from George Abbot, the somewhat Calvinistic Archbishop of Canterbury, which con-

[1] Legrand, *Bibliographie Hellénique au 17e siècle*, IV, pp. 329–40. De Dominis was a very disreputable character who after doing well out of the Anglican Church, thanks to his flattery of James I, in the end reverted to Catholicism. See the article by G. G. Perry, 'Dominis, Marco Antonio de', in the *Dictionary of National Biography*.
[2] G. Hofmann, *Griechische Patriarchen und Römische Päpste, Orientalia Christiana*, XXV, 76, pp. 43 ff. Cyril was not, however, consistently hostile to Rome. *Ibid.* XV, 52, pp. 44–6, publishes a letter written by Cyril in 1608 in which he addresses Pope Paul V in friendly and even deferential terms, asking for his good will.
[3] Smith, *Collectanea*, pp. 14–15; Philip of Cyprus, *loc. cit.*; Le Quien, *loc. cit.*

tained an invitation to send a few young Greeks to study theology in England at the expense of King James I. In reply Cyril sent a Macedonian youth, Metrophanes Critopoulos, to England. The outcome, as will be related later, was not altogether happy. But henceforward Abbot was among Cyril's correspondents.[1] The Patriarch Timothy tried to harm Cyril's good name by denouncing him as a Lutheran. Cyril answered that, as Timothy knew nothing of Luther nor of his doctrine, he had no idea how far it might resemble his own; he had better keep quiet.[2]

Probably after a reconciliation with Timothy, Cyril visited Constantinople again in the autumn of 1620. While he was there Timothy suddenly died, shortly after attending a dinner-party given by Cyril's friend, the Dutch Ambassador. The Jesuits promptly circulated a rumour that van Haag had poisoned him in order to leave the throne vacant for Cyril. If this were so, the Holy Synod certainly did not object. Cyril was promptly and unanimously elected Patriarch. On this occasion he paid the required sum to the Sublime Porte.[3]

The Greeks might be uninformed about Cyril's theological tendencies; but they were well known to the foreigners at Constantinople. 'As for the Patriarke himself', Archbishop Abbot wrote to the English Ambassador, Sir Thomas Roe, soon after Cyril's election, 'I do not doubt but that in opinion of religion he is, as wee terme him, a pure Calvinist, and so the Jesuites in these parts do brande him.'[4] The Jesuits, with their connections all over Europe, were well aware of his connection with Dutch divines; and they soon began to make sure that the Greeks heard of them.

[1] Legrand, *Bibliographie Hellénique au 17e siècle*, IV, pp. 340–2; Allatius, *op. cit.* III, pp. 1073–4. Abbot's letters are given in P. Colomesius, *Clarorum Virorum Epistolae Singulares*, pp. 557–61.
[2] Legrand, *Bibliographie Hellénique au 17e siècle*, IV, pp. 279–80.
[3] Smith, *Collectanea*, p. 15; Allatius, *op. cit.* III, pp. 1074–5; Philip of Cyprus, *op. cit.* pp. 438–9.
[4] Letter, dated 20 November 1622, in Sir Thomas Roe, *The Negotiations of Sir Thomas Roe in his Embassy to the Ottoman Porte*, p. 102. Sir Thomas had already described Cyril as a 'direct Calvinist' in a letter dated 29 April 1622, written to John Williams, Bishop of Lincoln (*ibid.* p. 36).

Nevertheless the reign began well. When Sir Thomas Roe, a diplomat of distinction who had already been accredited to the court of the Great Moghul, arrived at Constantinople in December 1621, he quickly made friends with the Patriarch and was his mainstay until he returned to England in 1628. The friendship with the Dutch Ambassador continued; and the Jesuits, though they had the full support of the French Ambassador, the Comte de Cési, found it difficult to attack a prelate so powerfully protected; while the Greeks were impressed to see their Patriarch so intimate with distinguished foreigners.

Cyril's troubles began when the Jesuits, playing on the suspicions of conservative members of the Synod, persuaded Gregory, Archbishop of Amasea, to stand as a rival candidate for the Patriarchate. In return Gregory privately promised to submit to Rome. Cyril heard of the intrigue; and Gregory was excommunicated. The Jesuits, undeterred, went to the Grand Vizier, Hussein Pasha, and told him that Cyril had corresponded with the Russian Tsar. This was true. At the previous Vizier's request he had written to Moscow to secure the Tsar's good will for Turkey in a war against Poland. They added, less truthfully, that he had encouraged some Greek islanders to welcome a Florentine invasion. The Vizier was alarmed. Without waiting to hear Cyril's defence, he ordered the Synod to depose Cyril, whom he exiled to Rhodes, and to elect Gregory of Amasea in his place, Gregory having offered 20,000 dollars to the Sublime Porte. But Gregory's reign only lasted for two months. He was a poor man; and the Greek congregations refused to provide the promised money. He appealed to the Jesuits; but subsidies that they expected from Rome had not arrived. To avoid arrest as a defaulter he resigned and fled from Constantinople. In his place the Jesuits persuaded the Porte to demand the election of Anthimus, Metropolitan of Adrianople. He was wealthy and was able to pay 10,000 out of his own resources, and by bribing the Turkish police extracted the remaining 10,000 from the Greeks of the city. It was a triumph for Rome. Pope Urban sent a message to the Comte de Cési to thank him for having displaced 'the son of darkness and athlete of Hell', as he described Cyril. But when he wrote the situation had changed. Sir Thomas Roe had secured Cyril's return from exile. Then Anthimus, a weak and amiable man, had pangs of conscience. He wrote to Cyril to apologize for his usurpation. In spite of pleas from the French Ambassador and the arrival, at last, of the subsidies from Rome, he insisted on resigning. In October 1623, Cyril was back on the Patriarchal throne.[1]

Cyril made it is his first task to improve education. He reformed the Patriarchal Academy, putting in as its head in 1624 his former fellow-student at Padua, Theophilus Corydalleus. The materialistic and scientific curriculum that Corydalleus introduced might seem to many Greek ecclesiastics unsuitable for a Church school, and created for the Patriarch enemies in old-fashioned circles. But it meant that Greek boys were less dependent than heretofore on Jesuit establishments if they wanted an up-to-date education. But Cyril also saw that education cannot be given without good teachers and plentiful books. To obtain the former he took advantage of his Western connections to send promising pupils to finish their studies in Holland, Germany and England. To procure books, he not only had agents to collect

[1] The fullest account of these troubles is given in the tract 'Narratio historica, quas Constantinopoli moverunt Jesuitae adversus Cyrillum Patriarcham & alia notatu dignissima. A viro docto qui fuit αὐτόπτης fideliter conscripta', written in Latin by a certain C. P. and published as an appendix to an anonymous work, *Mysteria Patrum Societatis Jesu*, published with the imaginary imprint 'Lampropoli, apud Robertum Liverum', in 1633. Smith already knew the work when he wrote his account of the Greek Church; he discusses it in his appendix on Cyril (*An Account of the Greek Church*, pp. 251–2), and remarks that it had infuriated Allatius. He reproduced it with minor corrections in his *Collectanea*, pp. 84–109, as 'Narratio epistolica Turbarum inter Cyrillum et Jesuitas'. Aymon, *op. cit.* pp. 201–36, publishes it, with a French translation, as a letter from Chrysosculus the Logothete to David Le Leu de Wilhem. Chrysosculus, who was a Patriarchal official at the time, may well have written it. The same ground is covered by an almost identical account sent as a dispatch, dated 10 February 1627/8, by Roe to London and published in his *Negotiations*, pp. 758–63. Smith's and Léger's own accounts, *Collectanea*, pp. 25–30, 75–80, are based on these sources. For the events of 1623 see also Roe, *op. cit.* pp. 134–5, 146, 213.

for him abroad but he determined to have his own printing-press.[1]

In 1627 this desire was gratified. A young Greek from Cephallonia, called Nicodemus Metaxas, had been visiting his brother, who was a merchant in London, and there had set up a small printing-house for the benefit of the London Greeks. He realized that the press would be more useful in Constantinople. He arrived there in June 1627 with his equipment and a valuable consignment of books. Hearing that he was coming the Patriarch sought the help of Sir Thomas Roe to get the packing-cases through the Turkish customs. Sir Thomas, backed by the Dutch Ambassador, obtained the necessary permit from the Grand Vizier. Cyril wished the press to be installed within the safe precincts of the English Embassy; but Sir Thomas could not agree to that. Instead, it was placed in a small house close by. At once, under Cyril's guidance, Metaxas began to print a number of theological works in Greek, most of them being anti-Roman tracts.

The Catholics were not pleased. Pope Urban VIII, whose Greek press had been set up only a year before, summoned the *Congregatio de Propaganda Fide* to discuss the problem. The *Congregatio* had already tried to take action against Cyril. A Greek Catholic, Canachio Rossi, had been sent to Constantinople to try to lure Cyril over to a friendlier attitude. When that failed Rossi was ordered to organize Jesuit activities to secure his downfall. At its meeting in November 1627 the *Congregatio* decided that the press must at all costs somehow be destroyed. Among the books

---

[1] See above, p. 222. We do not know the names of any pupil that Cyril sent abroad, apart from Critopoulos. Pantogalos and Hierotheos retired to Holland and Conopius to England only after Cyril's death. Zacharias Gerganos, who published a catechism of pronounced Protestant tendencies at Wittenberg in 1622, seems to have been regarded at Rome as one of Cyril's disciples; but he was almost as old as Cyril and had gone to Germany on the express invitation of the Elector of Saxony in 1619 (Legrand, *Bibliographie Hellénique au 17e siècle*, I, p. 159). Cyril probably circulated this catechism in his Patriarchate. In October 1624 de Cési complained to Paris that 'Calvinistic catechisms in manuscript' were being distributed at Constantinople (E. de Hurmuzaki, *Documente Privatore la Istoria Românilor*, IV, 1, p. 225).

printed by Metaxas was a short and ironical tract on the Jews written by Cyril himself. It contained an incidental passage pointing out Muslim dogmas which Christians could not accept. The Jesuits obtained a copy, which the French Ambassador took to the Grand Vizier with the passage underlined; and the Ambassador added that he believed the press to be used for printing false versions of the Sultan's decrees. The Vizier was shocked and was easily persuaded to order the arrest of Metaxas and a search of his office for other evidence of impiety and treason. The Ambassador suggested that it would be appropriate to do so on the afternoon of Epiphany, 6 January 1628, when there was to be a dinner at the English Embassy in the Patriarch's honour. 'This', said the Comte de Cési, 'would add sauce to the dishes.'

On the arranged afternoon the Vizier's Janissaries broke into the building to arrest Metaxas. He was not there; and, when a few minutes later he passed down the street in the company of a secretary at the English Embassy, they could not believe that this elegant gentleman wearing an English suit was the man that they wanted. They vented their disappointment in destroying the press, carrying off fragments of manuscript and type.

The printing-press was put out of action. But otherwise the plot misfired. The Grand Mufti, to whom the Vizier had sent Cyril's tract, pronounced it to be harmless. The Christians were entitled, he said, to state their beliefs, even if they were contrary to Islam. The Vizier had hardly received this ruling when Sir Thomas Roe demanded an interview and stormed at him for insulting a friendly power and reminding him that he himself had given permission for the press to be imported. The Vizier, shaken by the Grand Mufti's verdict and knowing Sir Thomas to be popular with the Sultan, changed his policy. The men who deceived him must be punished. Three Jesuit brothers and Canachio Rossi were cast into prison. When the Comte de Cési came to protest, he was not received by the Vizier but by his deputy, the Grand Kaimakam, who told him that if he could not behave as an Ambassador should he had better leave the country. Some two months later all Jesuits were expelled from the Sultan's dominions. 'They are ready to burst with chagrin at being thrown out', wrote Sir Thomas Roe. 'I hope that hereafter they will trouble as little as possible the poore Greek Church, to whom their practices have cost twelve thousand dollars, to say nothing of this last insurrection against the life and authority of the Patriarch, and against my honour.'[1]

Sir Thomas Roe retired from Constantinople later that year, carrying with him as a token of the Patriarch's regard the great manuscript of the Bible known as the Codex Alexandrinus, which Cyril had brought from Alexandria and sent as a gift to Sir Thomas's sovereign, King Charles I.[2] The Comte de Cési left some three years later. His successor, the Comte de Marcheville, was allowed to reintroduce Jesuits to be his chaplains. But the credit of the French Embassy was low. It was decided at Rome to entrust operations against Cyril in future to the Emperor's Ambassador, Rudolf Schmid-Schwarzenhorn, who arrived early in 1629. His predecessor, Kuefstein, had been a Protestant, but he was a devoted Catholic. Meanwhile the Jesuits' work should be taken over by the Capuchins. The famous Father Joseph, Richelieu's Grey Eminence, was ordered to Constantinople to organize the campaign; but Richelieu forbade him to leave France. Meanwhile the *Congregatio* debated how far bribery and trickery could lawfully be used to destroy so dangerous a heretic.[3]

Cyril Lucaris was to play into their hands. Sir Thomas Roe's departure was a blow to him. He quickly made friends with Sir

---

[1] The story of the printing-press is given in the sources cited above p. 271, n. 1. For a full and valuable discussion of its work see R. J. Roberts, *The Greek Press at Constantinople in 1627 and its Antecedents*, published by the Bibliographical Society in 1967. Roe published the instructions given to Canachio Rossi by Cardinal Bandini in his *Negotiations*, pp. 469–71, with a covering letter to Cyril.

[2] The dispatch of the Codex Sinaiticus, popularly supposed to have been copied by Thecla the Protomartyr, is recorded by Smith, *Collectanea*, pp. 63 ff. See Roberts, *op. cit.* pp. 25–6.

[3] L. Pastor, *History of the Popes from the close of the Middle Ages*, XXIX, pp. 233–7; Hofmann, *Griechische Patriarchen, Orientalia Christiana*, XV, 52, pp. 21 ff. De Cési returned as Ambassador in 1634 and remained there till 1640.

Thomas's successor, Sir Peter Wych. In 1635 he stood as godfather to Sir Peter's son Cyril, a future President of the Royal Society; and he was on good terms with Edward Pococke, chaplain at Aleppo from 1630 to 1638, who used occasionally to visit Constantinople. But his old correspondent Archbishop Abbot had been in disgrace since 1627 and died in 1633. Neither his successor, Archbishop Laud, interested though he was in the Greek Church, nor King Charles I, could sympathize very far with a prelate noted for his Calvinism. Cyril had to depend more and more on his Dutch friends. In the autumn of 1628 a new chaplain arrived at the Dutch Embassy. He was a Savoyard Huguenot by birth, called Antoine Léger, who had been educated at Geneva and was in touch with the leading Calvinists there. He soon was an intimate friend of the Patriarch's, encouraging him in his theological views and eventually persuading him to come into the open about them. The printing-press at Constantinople might be destroyed; but Léger arranged that Genevan presses would print and publish any work that Cyril might wish to submit to them.[1]

The first book that Cyril commissioned was a translation of the New Testament into modern Greek, made by a learned monk, Maximus Callipolites. To many of the Orthodox the idea of tampering with Holy Writ was outrageous, however obscure the text might be to modern readers. To appease them Cyril had the original and modern versions printed in parallel columns, and only added a few uncontroversial notes and references. As Callipolites died soon after delivering the manuscript, Cyril himself read the proofs. The book appeared in 1630. In spite of Cyril's precautions it roused a storm of disapproval from many of his bishops.[2]

[1] Smith, *Collectanea*, pp. 42–3. The correspondence concerning Léger's appointment and arrival in Constantinople is given in Legrand, *op. cit.* IV, pp. 352–82. There is reason to suppose that Cyril tried to arrange through Critopoulos to have books printed in Venice, but Critopoulos's tactless handling of the affair caused it to fail. See below, p. 295.
[2] For Cyril's New Testament see Legrand, *Bibliographie Hellénique au 17e siècle*, I, pp. 104–8.

The bishops were all the more alarmed as it was known by then that the Patriarch himself had written a highly controversial book. Cyril Lucaris's *Confession of Faith* was published in Latin at Geneva in March 1629, with a dedication to van Haag. A manuscript of the Greek text written in Cyril's own hand and dated 1631 is preserved at Geneva. This text was published along with the Latin translation at Geneva later that year and was reissued in 1633. It contained an appendix absent in the first Latin edition. Translations into various European languages followed; indeed an English version, without the appendix, had been published in London, by Nicolas Bourne, in 1629. The full English translation was only published in 1671, in Aberdeen, the translator being William Rait.[1]

The Orthodox Church has never cared for compendia of doctrine. The *De Fide Orthodoxa* of John of Damascus has said all that need be said, though later Councils may have had to elucidate obscure or debated points. But various Patriarchs had from time to time issued brief statements on doctrine, usually for some practical purpose. Gennadius himself had prepared one at the request of Sultan Mehmet the Conqueror; and Jeremias II's answer to the Lutherans was of the same nature. These statements were purely individual.[2] They commanded respect from the prestige of the Patriarchal office and from the personal reputation of the writer. But they could not be binding on the Church unless they were endorsed by a General Council. Their purpose was to serve as guidance, not to enunciate dogmas. Cyril clearly issued his Confession in the hope of strengthening his flock against Romanizing tendencies, of laying the foundation of a reformed and up-to-date Orthodox Church, and of providing a basis for negotiations with other Churches.

Besides the appendix, which contains four supplementary responses, the Confession consists of eighteen articles. The first, on

---

[1] For the various editions and translations of the Confession see Legrand, *op. cit.* I, pp. 237–42, 315–21, 376–80.

[2] For Gennadius's and Jeremias II's statements of doctrine see above, pp. 183, 249–54.

the Trinity, declares that the Holy Spirit proceeds from the Father through the Son. The second declares that the Holy Scriptures are inspired by God and that their authority exceeds the authority of the Church. The third declares that God before the beginning of the world predestined his elect to glory without respect to their works, while others are rejected, the condemnation having as its remote cause the will of God and its immediate cause the justice of God. The fourth declares that God is the creator of everything but not the author of evil; the fifth that God's providence is inscrutable and not to be scrutinized; the sixth that original sin is universal; the seventh that Jesus Christ is God and man, the Redeemer and the judge to come; the eighth that He is sole mediator, high priest and head of the Church. The ninth declares that justification by faith in Christ is necessary for salvation. The tenth says that the Universal Church includes all who have died in the faith as well as the living faithful and repeats that its only head is Christ; the eleventh that only those who are elected to eternal life are true members of the Church, the others are tares amidst the wheat. The twelfth article declares that the Church can stray, mistaking the false for the true, but the light of the Holy Spirit will rescue us through the labours of faithful ministers. The thirteenth maintains that man is justified by faith alone; good works are insufficient for salvation but not to be neglected as they testify to faith. The fourteenth article says that free will in the unregenerate is dead and they cannot do good; the regenerate do good with the assistance of grace. The fifteenth says that only two Sacraments were instituted by Christ and handed down to us as the seals of God's promises to us, but they cannot confer grace unless faith is present. The sixteenth declares baptism to be necessary for the remission of both original and actual sin. In the seventeenth Cyril declares his belief in the real presence of Christ in the Eucharist but only in its administration, only operating when faith is there; there is no material transubstantiation, since the body of Christ is not that which is visible in the Sacrament but that which faith spiritually apprehends. The eighteenth article insists that there are only two conditions after death, heaven and hell; as a man is found at his death so is he judged; and after this life there is neither power nor opportunity to repent. Purgatory is a mere figment. Those justified in this life have no pains to suffer hereafter, but the reprobate pass straight to everlasting punishment.

The supplementary responses say, first, that the Scriptures should be read by every one of the faithful and it is a real injury to a Christian to deprive him of the chance of reading them or of having them read to him; secondly, that the Scriptures are clearly intelligible to all who are regenerate and illumined; thirdly, that the canonical books are those listed at the Council of Laodicea; and, fourthly, that the cult of images is condemned in the Scriptures and is to be detested: but, as painting is a noble art, pictures of Christ and the saints may be made, so long as no form of worship is paid to them.[1]

It should be noted that the Confession contains no doctrine specifically denied by any of the Oecumenical Councils, with the exception of the Response on images, which would be hard to reconcile with the rulings of the Seventh Oecumenical Council. Nevertheless, as anyone could see, it contained statements that scarcely fitted into the Orthodox tradition. However much the Greeks of the time might have welcomed guidance to preserve them from the wiles of Rome, Cyril's declared views could not fail to give many of them a shock.

Many of the articles were unexceptionable. The Orthodox could admit without argument the first, on the procession of the Holy Ghost; the fourth on the Creation; the fifth, on the inscrutability of God's providence; the sixth, on original sin; the seventh and eighth, on Christ as the head of the Church and redeemer; the tenth, on the nature of the Church; the twelfth, that it might err without the help of the Holy Spirit; and the

---

[1] A useful summary of the Latin text of the Confession, together with the supplementary responses, is reproduced in M. Jugie, *Theologia Dogmatica Christianorum Orientalium ab Ecclesia Catholica Dissidentium*, i, pp. 506–7.

sixteenth, on the necessity for baptism. Of the Responses, those concerning the reading of the Scriptures and the list of canonical books were perfectly acceptable. Others of Cyril's views reflected those held by Orthodox theologians in the past and never specifically abandoned. Till the thirteenth century the two Sacraments of baptism and the eucharist had been generally considered as the essential Sacraments, the other five ranking below them.[1] But Orthodox belief had always been that these five were implicitly ordered in the recorded words of Christ, even if their ritual had no spiritual foundation. Indeed, it would be difficult to justify a belief in the apostolic succession of the priesthood if ordination had no sacramental element; and that was a belief held firmly by the Orthodox. We do not know what Cyril thought about it. Again, many of the Orthodox would not be happy to have transubstantiation flatly denied. The Church had never yet defined its belief on the doctrine. Thomas Smith, in his account of the Greek Church written a few decades later, believed that the word μετουσίωσις, which exactly means 'transubstantiation', was first used by Gabriel Severus late in the sixteenth century in his book on the Seven Mysteries. This is not quite accurate. The word had often been used before; but Severus seems to have been the first Greek theologian to take the doctrine for granted. As Smith points out, in the Liturgy of Saint Basil, the bread and wine are said to become 'anti-types' of Christ's body and blood. Jeremias II, in his answer to the Lutherans, follows an older tradition in avoiding the word μετουσίωσις. The words that he uses, μεταβολή and μεταποίησις, and the word μεταστοιχείωσις, often used by earlier theologians, do not necessarily imply a material change in the elements. His statement was, as we have seen, deliberately vague. The Church had hitherto preferred to regard the matter as a mystery on which no precise dogma was necessary or possible. Cyril's absolute denial of transubstantiation was therefore offensive to some of his fellow-Orthodox and embarrassing to others.[2]

---

[1] For the history of the Orthodox doctrine about the Sacraments see Ware, *The Orthodox Church*, pp. 281–3.   [2] See below, pp. 306–7.

Nor was his absolute denial of Purgatory universally acceptable. Some Greek theologians, his cousin Meletius Pegas amongst them, had opposed the doctrine; but the general Orthodox view was that mortal man could not claim to know what plans God may have for the souls of the dead, as God has not chosen to give any revelation on the subject. We cannot say whether Purgatory does or does not exist. Cyril's views on the transcendent authority of the Scriptures could be approved by all the Orthodox; but it was shocking to find no mention made of the Oecumenical Councils or of the Fathers of the Church. They too, though of lesser authority, provided revelations granted by the Holy Spirit. Nor was it proper to omit mention of the unwritten Tradition of which the Church was guardian except to hint that it was fallible.[1]

These omissions, however, caused less disquiet among the faithful than did the positive statements of the Confession. The Response on images distressed almost every Greek. The worship (λατρεία) of images had indeed been forbidden by the Fathers of the Seventh Oecumenical Council. But they had approved of reverence (δουλεία) being given to them; for the image is the antitype of the original and acquires something of its holiness. Cyril seemed to disapprove even of reverence: to him icons were only permissible as a sort of pious decoration. In this he was clearly going against the traditions of the Church. But serious theologians were far more deeply worried by his unqualified advocacy of predestination and of justification by faith.

Neither doctrine had been expressly forbidden by the Church; but neither accorded with accepted tradition. There were two traditional views on predestination. Mark Eugenicus had maintained that God's prescience was absolute but predestination relative; only good actions are predetermined as well as foreknown by God because only they conform to His will. In general the Church preferred the rival, more deterministic doctrine of George Scholarius Gennadius: which is, with slightly different termino-

---

[1] For the Orthodox view on Purgatory see Ware, *The Orthodox Church*, pp. 259-60.

logy, the doctrine of John of Damascus. This holds that prescience precedes predestination. The initiative for good or evil comes from the created will. Predestination is controlled by but does not control God's knowledge and wisdom. This was the view briefly summarized by Jeremias II in his answer to the Lutherans.

Cyril's insistence on justification by faith alone, without works, was equally unacceptable. Here again we may assume that the attitude of the Orthodox of the time was reflected in Jeremias II's pronouncement when the Lutherans raised it: namely that faith needs works and works need faith; either without the other is dead. The Orthodox Church never approved of Pelagianism and it disliked the sort of arithmetic of merit that seemed to be implied by the Roman doctrines of indulgences and Purgatory. It could go further along the road towards justification by faith than could the Catholics; but it could hardly accept the doctrine of justification by faith alone.[1]

So revolutionary were Cyril's doctrines in Orthodox eyes that to this day there have always been Orthodox who refuse to believe that a Patriarch of Constantinople could have written such a Confession. The work has been denounced as a forgery, attributed by some to Antoine Léger, by some to the divines at Geneva who printed it, by some even to the Jesuits, who, they believe, must have put it forward in Cyril's name to ruin his reputation. Why, they argue, did it appear first in Latin? And why was it printed at Geneva? But Cyril himself claimed the authorship in a number of letters and in a stormy interview with the French Ambassador, the Comte de Marcheville, late in 1631.[2] He published the book at Geneva because the press at Constantinople had been wrecked; and a Latin version was needed as he wished to inform the Churches of the West of his views. His letters corroborate the doctrines pronounced in the Confession and even go further.

[1] See above, p. 249.
[2] Letter from van Haag, printed in Smith, *Collectanea*, pp. 71–3. Hadjiantoniou, *op. cit.* pp. 102–8, discusses at length the attitude taken by contemporary and later Greek divines on the question of Cyril's authorship of the Confession.

Writing to Léger and to his Dutch friends he made no secret of his admiration for Calvin and his doctrines.[1]

Cyril did not consider himself revolutionary. He may have known that he was going against accepted tradition; but, so long as the tradition was unwritten, who could say exactly what it was? In a letter to his Polish friends he expressed surprise at being called heterodox. He was an intellectual by temperament, with a logical mind and no sympathy with the apophatic attitude traditionally followed by Orthodox theologians. His education had fortified his natural tastes. A student who had sat under the Neo-Aristotelian professors at Padua was unlikely to be satisfied by a negative theology.[2]

It was some time before many copies of the Confession could arrive in the East. In 1630 the Patriarch Theophanes of Jerusalem wrote to assure the Metropolitan of Kiev that Cyril was not a heretic. He knew Cyril's opinions, he said, and he considered them admirable. Cyril's attitude to icons was perfectly reverent and his definition of predestination was not dissident with the traditions of the Church. But Theophanes could not have yet seen the full text of the Confession.[3]

The Catholics, foreseeing the trouble that the Confession would cause, did their best to make its contents known at Constantinople. Thomas Smith, who derived his information from Edward Pococke, declared that the opposition was artificially whipped up by the Jesuits and Capuchins. The Dutch Ambassador wrote that 'there is scarce one among the Metropolitans, of which a great number are present at Constantinople, who would not venture his estate, life and person in defence of the said Patriarch and his Confession'. Monsieur van Haag was over-optimistic. Within a few months there was a conspiracy against the Patriarch planned by no less than five of his metropolitans, those of Adrianople,

---

[1] Legrand, *Bibliographie Hellénique au 17e siècle*, IV, p. 455. In a letter to Léger Cyril calls himself in quotation marks a 'Calvinist Patriarch', Aymon, *op. cit.* p. 101.

[2] Aymon, *op. cit.* p. 102.

[3] Legrand, *Bibliographie Hellénique au 17e siècle*, III, p. 71.

Larissa, Chalcedon, Cyzicus and Naupactos. It resulted in the elevation to the Patriarchate in October 1633 of Cyril Contari, Metropolitan of Berrhoea (Aleppo). But to secure his election Cyril Contari had promised 50,000 dollars to the Sublime Porte, and he could not raise the money. After a few days he gave up the effort and was exiled to Tenedos. From there he wrote an apology to Cyril Lucaris, who restored him to his see.[1]

Six months later the dissident metropolitans, some of whom by now had read the Confession and were genuinely distressed by it, returned to the attack. But they saw that the only way to displace a Patriarch who had the backing of the Protestant Embassies was to appeal to the Catholic Embassies. This meant that they must put forward a candidate. Athanasius Pattelaras, Metropolitan of Thessalonica, owed his see to Cyril Lucaris, who had preferred him to Cyril Contari; but he felt no gratitude. By offering the Sultan 60,000 dollars and paying it in cash, most of the sum being provided by the French and Imperial Embassies, he secured an order for Cyril's deposition and his own elevation. The Dutch Ambassador then set to work and produced the sum of 70,000 dollars, which restored Cyril to the throne. Athanasius fled to Rome, hoping to be rewarded with a cardinal's hat. But the Papal authorities summed him up as being unreliable and incompetent. They merely gave him his fare back to Thessalonica.[2]

Cyril Contari was a tougher adversary. It was he that the Imperial Ambassador, Schmid-Schwarzenhorn, persuaded the Catholics to support. Schmid-Schwarzenhorn did not personally like him. 'The Patriarch of Berrhoea', as he always called him, was, so he wrote to the Emperor, 'a good and virtuous prelate, good towards the wicked and severe towards the good, generous when it is

---

[1] Smith, *Collectanea*, pp. 56–7; Hottinger, *op. cit.* pp. 558–9; Philip of Cyprus, edition to *Chronicon*, pp. 451–3; Allatius, *op. cit.* III, p. 1077; Hofmann, *Griechische Patriarchen, Orientalia Christiana*, XV, 52, pp. 33 ff.

[2] Smith, *Collectanea*, pp. 57–8; Hottinger, *op. cit.* p. 559; Philip of Cyprus, *loc. cit.*; M. Le Quien, *Oriens Christianus*, I, p. 334. Smith says that Pattelaras's Christian name was Anastasius (*Account of the Greek Church*, p. 284, n. 1), and that Hottinger wrongly calls him Athanasius. But other sources agree with Hottinger.

unnecessary and stingy when he should be generous.' Contari was shrewd enough not to commit himself openly to Rome but to rely on the opposition aroused by Cyril I's theology. This was growing; and it enabled Contari to persuade the Holy Synod to depose Cyril I in March, 1635. After paying the Porte 50,000 dollars, raised with Schmid-Schwarzenhorn's help, Contari became Patriarch for the second time as Cyril II. Some of his supporters suggested that Cyril Lucaris should be quietly murdered; but Schmid-Schwarzenhorn, who did not wish his embassy to be suspected of encouraging murder, had a better idea. The Grand Vizier agreed to banish Cyril I to Rhodes. Schmid-Schwarzenhorn offered to supply a boat for the purpose and arranged that this boat would sail instead to Italy and deposit Cyril at Rome, to be dealt with by the Inquisition. But the hire of the boat involved a sum of 800 dollars, and 500 dollars were needed to bribe the crew. Cyril II, when asked to produce the money, said that they must find a cheaper boat. Meanwhile the Dutch Ambassador heard of the plot. He sent post-haste to warn the Governor of Rhodes, and himself bribed the captain of the boat which Contari finally hired, to put in at Chios. There the Governor of Rhodes was waiting and himself escorted the ex-Patriarch to his island, while the boat was sent back in ignominy to Constantinople.

Cyril Lucaris spent fifteen months in Rhodes. In March 1636 Cyril II held a Council at Constantinople which anathematized Cyril I as a heretic. But the Holy Synod was soon suspicious of Cyril II's connections with Rome. In June 1636 it met to depose him; and he in his turn went to Rhodes, his ship being ordered to bring back Cyril I. Meanwhile Neophytus, Metropolitan of Heraclea, was elected Patriarch. He was a loyal friend of Cyril I and took on the office temporarily in order to arrange for the cancellation of the anathema. By March next year Cyril Lucaris was again Patriarch.[1]

[1] Smith, *Collectanea*, pp. 58-9; Philip of Cyprus, *op. cit.* p. 454; Hottinger, *op. cit.* pp. 559-60; A. Papadopoulos-Kerameus, *Analecta*, IV, pp. 98-9; Le Quien, *loc. cit.*; Legrand, *op. cit.* IV, p. 450. For Schmid-Schwarzenhorn's letters, E. de Hurmuzaki, *Documente Privatore la Istoria Românilor*, IV, 1, pp. 639 ff.

He was, however, no longer so influential. His views were too well known. Many of the Orthodox who supported him against Rome were distressed by them. He could no longer count on the support of the English Embassy. Sir Peter Wych had left Constantinople in 1633 or 1634; and his successor, Sir Sackville Crowe, kept clear of the controversy. Monsieur van Haag was planning his retirement. Antoine Léger had left Constantinople, and his amiable successor, Sartoris, died soon after his arrival.[1] Meanwhile Schmid-Schwarzenhorn redoubled his efforts to destroy him, partly for the Catholic cause, partly to weaken Dutch influence, and partly to show that the Imperial Ambassador was more competent that the French had been. A judicious bribe recalled Cyril Contari from Rhodes. Then in May 1638 Sultan Murad IV declared war on Persia; and the Grand Vizier, Bairam Pasha, preceded him to prepare his way across Anatolia. One of Cyril Contari's chaplains, called Lamerno, hurried to his camp and persuaded him, with the help of a large bribe provided by Schmid-Schwarzenhorn, to accuse Cyril Lucaris before the Sultan of treason. The Vizier chose his time well. The Don Cossacks, instigated by the Persians, had attacked Ottoman territory on the Sea of Azov. When he met the Sultan the Vizier assured him that Cyril Lucaris had plotted this. Murad, who may well have considered Cyril a tiresome cause of trouble, let himself be convinced. A message was sent to the Governor of Constantinople, who on 20 June 1638 arrested Cyril and imprisoned him in a castle on the Bosphorus. Five days later he was told that he was to be deported. He was put on a small boat, and when the boat reached the Sea of Marmora the soldiers on board strangled him and buried his body on the foreshore. Next day, according to their custom, they sold the meagre possessions that he had with him. Someone recognized his pectoral cross; and his fate became known. Angry crowds of Greeks massed outside of Cyril Contari's door, crying: 'Pilate, give us the body.' To prevent a riot the Governor told the soldiers to exhume the body. They did so, but flung it into the sea.

[1] Legrand, *Bibliographie Hellénique au 17e siècle*, IV, pp. 458–9, 461, 498.

There some Greek fishermen found it and recovered it. It was buried in the little monastery of Saint Andrew on an island off the Asiatic coast.[1]

On the Sultan's orders Cyril Contari returned to the Patriarchal throne. In September 1638 he held a Council, attended by the Patriarchs of Alexandria, Cyril's former pupil Critopoulos, and of Jerusalem, his old friend Theophanes, at which Cyril and his theology were again anathematized. But in December of that year Cyril II signed a paper giving his allegiance to Pope Urban VIII. When news of this leaked out, both the Holy Synod and the Sultan were furious. Cyril II was deposed in June 1639, branded in his turn as a heretic and exiled to North Africa, where he died. A moderate cleric, Parthenius I, was elevated in his place. But Parthenius rashly allowed Cyril Lucaris's friend, Theophilus Corydalleus, to preach a sermon at his inauguration; and Corydalleus pronounced a eulogy of Cyril I and his works. This loyalty revived bitterness at a moment when the Orthodox world longed for the controversy to cease. In reply to Corydalleus the Cretan Meletius Syrigos was allowed a few months later to preach a sermon in which Cyril's Calvinistical doctrines were condemned, though Cyril himself was barely mentioned. Syrigos was also encouraged to write a tract repeating the condemnation. It appeared in 1640; but to many of the Orthodox it appeared to go too far in the other direction. Indeed, apart from its rejection of the dual procession of the Holy Ghost, it might have been written by a Roman divine. The quarrels continued. In 1641 the Prince of Moldavia, Basil Lupul, a tough Albanian businessman who was trying to restore order to the Patriarchal finances, wrote beseech-

---

[1] The main account of Cyril's death is given in a letter written by Nathaniel Conopius to Léger, published in Legrand, *Bibliographie Hellénique au 17e siècle*, IV, pp. 514–16. Hottinger (*op. cit.* pp. 564–6) copies it, and Smith (*Collectanea*, pp. 59–62) uses it, adding a few details derived from Edward Pococke, whose account, written for Archbishop Laud, was printed by Pococke in the supplement (p. 33) to his *Historia Dynastiarum*. It gives the date of Cyril's death as January, not June, which, so Pococke assured Smith, was a printer's error. Cyril's death is also described by Allatius, *op. cit.* III, p. 1077, and by Schmid-Schwarzenhorn (de Hurmuzaki, *op. cit.* IV, 1, pp. 639–41).

ing the bishops to cease from their strife. In May 1642 Parthenius held a Council at which Cyril's Confession was examined clause by clause and several of its articles were condemned. To silence Cyril's supporters Parthenius produced the document supplied by the Jesuit Scarga in which Cyril was supposed to have shown sympathy for Rome. Subsequent Councils repeated this condemnation. The most remarkable of seventeenth-century theologians remains branded as having promulgated heresy.[1]

His disciples were scattered. Corydalleus seems to have made an apology for his sermon and was appointed to the bishopric and metropolitan see of Naupactos and Arta; but he was soon deposed and retired into private life. His pupil Nathaniel Conopius retired hurriedly to England. Meletius Pantogalos, whom Cyril had appointed Metropolitan of Ephesus, was deposed by Parthenius I and fled from Constantinople rather than sign a document condemning his friend. He had been closely acquainted with van Haag and with Antoine Léger; so he retired to Holland, to study at the University of Leyden. He was well liked there, especially after he had signed a confession endorsing Cyril's. In 1645 he planned to return to Constantinople, armed with letters of recommendation from the Dutch States-General; but he died on the journey. He had been joined at Leyden by a Cephallonian, Hierotheus, Abbot of Sisia, a friend of Nicodemus Metaxas, who had been appointed to the see of Cephallonia after the destruction of his printing-press. Hierotheus never met Cyril, but seems to have made friends with van Haag during a visit to Constantinople after Cyril's death. In 1643 he went to Venice, vainly trying to raise money to repair his monastery, devastated by an earthquake. From Venice he decided to go on to Holland, where he remained till 1651, apart from a visit to England. In Holland he translated into Greek a number of Calvinist theological works, with which he was in complete agreement. Afterwards he spent some years

---

[1] For Cyril II's and Parthenius I's Councils, see J. D. Mansi, *Sacrorum Conciliorum Collectio*, xxxiv, pp. 1709–20. Cyril II's death is described in a letter by Schmid-Schwarzenhorn in de Hurmuzaki, *op. cit.* iv, 1, p. 689.

in Geneva, and returned to Cephallonia, to his monastery, in 1658, dying some time before 1664. He seems to have suffered from no persecution for his views; but his writings seem not to have circulated at all in the East.[1]

Cyril Lucaris failed. He had involved his Church in a controversy which was to push it into issuing statements of doctrine different from but almost as controversial as his own. His was the only attempt to bring the Orthodox Church into line with the livelier Churches of the West. Lutheran evangelism had little appeal to the Greek temperament; and Anglicanism had nothing important to offer. Lutheran and Anglican overtures met with only a small response. But the hard, logical intellectualism of Calvinism attracted the realistic and cerebral side of the Greek character. Had Cyril achieved his objects the intellectual level of the Orthodox Church might have been immeasurably raised and much of its later obscurantism checked. But the Greek character has its other side, its taste for the Mysteries. The Greek is a mystic as well as an intellectual; and the Orthodox Church derived much of its strength from its old mystical tradition. Its power of survival through worldly disasters lay largely in its acceptance of the transcendental mystery of the divine. This Cyril never understood. To him and his followers the apophatic approach led merely to ignorance and stagnation. He could not appreciate the sustaining force of tradition. The logic of Geneva was no better answer to the problems of the Orthodox than was the disciplined legalism of Rome.

---

[1] For Pantogalos and Hierotheos see the account given in K. Rozemond, *Archimandrite Hierotheos Abbatios*. For Conopius's subsequent career see below, pp. 295–6. Pantogalos's confession was used by Claude in his answer to Arnauld (see below, p. 307). It was poorly printed, with unfavourable comments, by the Catholic priest Richard Simon in his *Histoire critique de la créance et les coutumes des nations du Levant* (pp. 215–16).

THE CHURCH AND THE CHURCHES:
THE ANGLICAN EXPERIMENT

Though the doctrines of Wittenberg or Geneva might be unacceptable to the Orthodox, there was one Church in the West with which they seemed to have much in common. The Church of England rejected Roman supremacy but retained a hierarchy with an apostolic succession. It believed in the charismatic equality of bishops. It followed a ritual that embodied much that was traditional and known to the East. Its attitude to the laity, to whom it allowed communion in both kinds and a share in the councils of the Church, was akin to Eastern tradition, as was its readiness to regard the monarch as the head of the Christian community. It was, moreover, almost as shy of making definitive pronouncements on articles of faith as were the most apophatic theologians, though its motives therein were different.

Neverthless nearly a century passed after the English Reformation before the two Churches made any contact. Few Greeks had ever penetrated to England, other than mercenaries, 'estradiots', as they were called, such as Nicander Nucius of Corfu, men who tended to be disorderly and thievish.[1] Two distinguished refugee scholars from Constantinople, John Argyropoulos and Andronicus Callistus, visited the country in the later fifteenth century but disliked the climate and soon left. William of Waynflete's secretary, Emmanuel of Constantinople, arrived earlier and remained, and helped his employer to draft the statutes for Eton.[2] Few

---

[1] See *The Second Book of Nicander Nucius* (ed. J. H. Cramer), Camden Society, XVII (1841). It gives a lively if inaccurate account of England in the later years of Henry VIII's reign. Nicander took service under a famous estradiot, Thomas of Argos.

[2] For Greek scholars and studies in Renaissance England see R. Weiss, *Humanism in England during the Fifteenth Century*, pp. 143–8.

Englishmen penetrated into Greek lands, apart from pilgrims to Palestine passing through Cyprus. William Wey included in his pilgrims' handbook a few Greek phrases for such travellers, though he recommended them not to stay long in that insalubrious island.[1] John Locke, when on a journey to Jerusalem in 1553, took the trouble to attend a Greek church-service in Cyprus; but he found it unintelligible. He remarked however that Greek monks were obviously chaste and austere, as he never saw one who was fat.[2] Two of the scholars of the English Renaissance went to study Greek from Greeks, William Grocyn, who sat under Demetrius Chalcondylas at Florence, and William Lily, who went to Rhodes and lived with a Greek family there. The leading English Reformers, such as Thomas Cranmer, were conversant with ancient Greek, as was Queen Elizabeth herself. They studied the early Greek Fathers.[3] But of contemporary Greeks they knew little. As late as 1614 Edward Brerewood's huge inquiry into the principal languages and religions of the world is dependent on second-hand sources in its account of the Greek Church, which is muddled and not very accurate, though not hostile.[4] Robert Burton, in his *Anatomy of Melancholy*, published seven years later, accuses the Greeks, on similarly insufficient evidence, of having added so many superstitions to the True Faith that 'they be rather semi-Christians than otherwise'.[5]

---

[1] William Wey, *The Itineraries of William Wey* (Roxburgh Club edition), pp. 102–15 for Greek vocabulary. Of Cyprus he complains (pp. 4–5) that the 'eyre ys so corupte ther abowte'.

[2] John Locke, *Voyage to Jerusalem*, in Hakluyt, *Voyages* (Glasgow edition), v, pp. 84, 96.

[3] See J. H. Lupton, *Life of John Colet*, pp. 46–7, 170–1. Cranmer's interest in the old Greek liturgies led him to introduce a form of the Epiklesis into his first (1549) prayer-book. It should be noticed that Henry Savile says in the commentary of his great edition of Chrysostom's *Opera Omnia* that he was indebted to the collaboration of Greek scholars at Venice such as Margunius and G. Severus. See D. J. Geanakoplos, *Byzantine East and Latin West*, p. 176.

[4] Edward Brerewood, *Enquiries of Languages by Edw. Brerewood, lately Professor of Astronomy at Gresham College*, in *Purchas His Pilgrimes* (Glasgow edition), I, pp. 348–57. Later in the volume (pp. 422–49), Purchas translates Christopher Angelos's *Encheiridion*, for which see below, p. 294.

[5] R. Burton, *The Anatomy of Melancholy* (Everyman Edition), I, p. 70.

Brerewood and Burton should have known better; for by that date fuller information was available. English Philhellenism, however, owes its real origin to the interests of commerce. English trade with the Ottoman dominions was rapidly growing throughout the sixteenth century. In 1579 William Harborne, representing his queen, obtained from Sultan Murad III letters promising special protection for English merchants. This was confirmed in a charter the following year. In 1581 Queen Elizabeth licensed the Turkey Company, which changed its name to the Levant Company in 1590, on the renewal of its charter. In 1583 Harborne returned to Constantinople as a fully accredited ambassador to the Sublime Porte.[1]

The merchants of the Levant Company found themselves dealing almost entirely with Greeks. Greeks grew the currants and made the sweet wines that they bought and provided them with the other commodities that they desired, gems and drugs and spices, carpets and damasks. They found the Greeks to be enterprising and reliable businessmen. Englishmen who began to settle in the Levant to further their trade moved freely in Greek circles; and by the beginning of the seventeenth century there was a small but increasing Greek colony in London. A mutual sympathy grew up. Sir Anthony Sherley, who visited the East in 1599, believed that it would be both right and feasible to rescue the Greeks from their servitude; and his brother, Sir Thomas, who was in Constantinople from 1603 to 1607, had, so he wrote, many discussions 'with wise and wealthy Greeks that do wish for this help with tears'.[2]

The merchants were not particularly interested in the Greek Church. But their increasing numbers and the establishment of a permanent embassy at Constantinople and consulates at Smyrna and Aleppo made it seem desirable to appoint chaplains of the

---

[1] A. C. Wood, *A History of the Levant Company*, pp. 8–26.
[2] Sir Anthony Sherley, *His Relation of his Travels* (1613), pp. 6–7; Sir Thomas Sherley, *Discours of the Turkes* (ed. E. Denison Ross), *Camden Miscellany*, XVI (1936), p. 9.

Church of England at each of these centres. The appointments were made by the Levant Company, with the approval of the ambassador. These chaplains could not fail to be interested in the forms of Christianity that they saw around them; while many of the ambassadors had theological tastes. William Biddulph, the first of these chaplains, was briefly in Constantinople in 1599 and did not care much for the Greeks. He remained only briefly;[1] but from 1611 there was a regular sequence of chaplains, beginning with a Fellow of Trinity College, Cambridge, William Foord, who arrived in company with a new ambassador, Sir Peter Pindar. Of him and of his immediate successors, most of whom came from Oxford, we know little. Indeed the English chaplain from 1627 to 1638, that is to say, during the critical years of Cyril Lucaris's career, was a certain Mr Hunt, of whom nothing is known except his surname. Doubtless he kept in the background because of the direct interest taken in the Patriarchate by his two successive ambassadors, Sir Thomas Roe and Sir Peter Wych. The next chaplain from Trinity College, Cambridge, William Gotobed, who was transferred from Smyrna in 1642, is known only because he helped to bring about the removal of an unpopular ambassador, Sir Sackville Crowe. Far more distinguished was a chaplain who resided at Aleppo from 1630 to 1638, Edward Pococke, who often visited Constantinople and was there, on his way home, when Cyril Lucaris was martyred. He wrote a moving account of the Patriarch's fate for Archbishop Laud. He used his time in Aleppo to perfect his knowledge of Arabic and later became the first and perhaps the greatest of English Orientalists.[2]

Later in the century two distinguished theologians served at Constantinople, Thomas Smith (1668–70) and John Covel (1670–76). Smith, a Fellow of Magdalen, Oxford, wrote on his return

[1] For Biddulph and his chaplaincy see *The Travels of Certaine Englishmen*, compiled by Theophilus Lavender (1609) from letters written by Biddulph.

[2] J. B. Pearson, *A Biographical Sketch of the Chaplains to the Levant Company maintained at Constantinople, Aleppo and Smyrna*, pp. 12–27. Pearson does not mention Biddulph but begins his list with Foord.

a well-informed, frank but fairly sympathetic account of the Greek and Armenian Churches, and published as well a collection of documents on Cyril Lucaris. He later became one of the non-juror clergy.[1] Covel, Fellow and later Master of Christ's, Cambridge, was less attractive. While chaplain he amassed a large fortune in the silk trade. He disliked the Greeks. 'The Greeks are Greeks still', he wrote. 'For falseness and treachery they still deserve Iphigeneia's character of them in Euripides: *Trust them and hang them.*' He too wrote a book later on about the Greek Church, with less sympathy than Smith, though he considered himself to be the chief English authority on the subject and expected to be consulted whenever Greek prelates visited England.[2]

Such works informed England about the Greek Church; and the presence of the chaplains in the Levant informed the Greeks about the English Church. Soon Greek theologians began to want to visit England. The first to come arrived half by accident. Early in the seventeenth century a Peloponnesian youth called Christopher Angelos went to study at the newly founded academy at Athens. He had not been there long before the Turkish governor arbitrarily expelled him as a Spanish spy. He fled to the West, armed with letters of recommendation from two Peloponnesian bishops, and found his way through Venice to Germany, where someone suggested to him that he might go to England, because there, he was told, 'I might find wise men, with whom I might keep my religion, and not lose my learning; they told me, in England you may have both, for the English men love the Grecians and their learning.' He landed at Yarmouth in 1608 and presented his episcopal letters to the Bishop of Norwich, who sent

[1] Thomas Smith, *An Account of the Greek Church* (published in 1680). It had already been published in Latin in 1676. His *Collectanea de Cyrillo Lucario* was published in 1707, though the material had clearly been collected many years previously, and his life of Cyril forms an appendix to the *Account.*

[2] Extracts from Covel's diary, kept when he was chaplain, were published by J. T. Bent (Hakluyt Society, 1st series), LXXXVII (1893). See especially p. 133. Covel's *Some Account of the Present Greek Church* was published in 1722. See below, p. 319.

him to Trinity College, Cambridge. To quote him again, 'The Doctors of Cambridge received me kindly, and frankly: & I spent there almost one whole year, as the testimony of Cambridge can witness. Then I fell sick, that I could scarce breathe: and the Physicians and Doctors counselled me to go to Oxford, because (said they) the air of Oxford is far better than that of Cambridge.' He settled at Oxford, at Balliol, in 1610 and remained there till his death in 1638. He was not a great scholar, but well liked. Anthony à Wood, the Oxford historian, calls him a 'pure Grecian and an honest and harmless man'. He published in English an autobiographical essay called *Christopher Angell, a Grecian who tasted of many Stripes inflicted by the Turkes for the Faith*, and a tract fulsomely praising the English universities, and in Greek and Latin a short *Encheiridion*, a handbook giving a simple and ingenuous account of the organization and ceremonies of the Greek Church.[1]

We do not know whether Archbishop Abbot, himself a Balliol man, was inspired by this amiable Grecian or by one of the Levantine chaplains or by mutual friends in Holland when he wrote in 1617 to Cyril Lucaris and invited him to send four young Greeks to study theology in England. In return Cyril sent a young Macedonian, Metrophanes Critopoulos, whom he had met on Mount Athos in 1613 and whose intelligence had impressed him. Critopoulos arrived in England in about 1621 and was sent to Oxford, to Balliol. He did well at first; but by 1625 Abbot was writing to Sir Thomas Roe to complain of the young man. He was quarrelsome; he ran up debts which the Archbishop had to settle; he was an intriguer, trying to push his way into Royal

---

[1] For Christopher Angelos see E. Legrand, *Bibliographie Hellénique: description raisonnée des ouvrages publiés en Grec par des Grecs au 17e siècle*, III, pp. 208–9; Anthony à Wood, *Athenae Oxonienses* (ed. P. Bliss), II, p. 633; T. Spencer, *Fair Greece, Sad Relic*, pp. 91–3: and his own works, *Christopher Angell, A Grecian...*, published at Oxford in Greek in 1617 and in English in 1618: *An Encomium of the famous Kingdom of Great Britain, and of the two flourishing Sister Universities Cambridge and Oxford*, published in parallel Greek and English versions at Cambridge in 1619: and *Encheiridion*, in Greek and Latin at Cambridge the same year.

circles by making friends with the Archbishop's enemies. Finally, when the time came for him to return to the East, the Archbishop having undertaken to pay his fare, he refused to travel cheaply on a Levant Company boat but insisted on going through Germany, as he had been invited to lecture there. He was clearly a good lecturer and had some success there and in Switzerland; but when staying in Venice he offended the authorities by trying to browbeat a publisher into publishing some very controversial works of his own. He was back in Constantinople in 1631. In 1633 Cyril secured for him the metropolitan see of Memphis in Egypt; and the following year he became Patriarch of Alexandria. But gratitude was not his strongest virtue, as Archbishop Abbot had discovered. He turned against Cyril and was one of the prelates to anathematize him.[1]

Another of Cyril's disciples was more satisfactory. His Protosyncellus, the Cretan Nathaniel Conopius, found it prudent to leave hastily for England. He too studied at Balliol, with such distinction that when he obtained his degree Archbishop Laud had him appointed a minor canon of Christ Church. He was an inconsistent theologian. When visiting Holland he announced his intention of translating Calvin's *Institutes* into Greek, perhaps as a gesture to please his Dutch hosts, or perhaps as a tribute to Cyril's memory. But in 1647 the Puritans expelled him from Oxford because of his Laudian connections, or perhaps for his fondness for singing the Akathistos hymn on all occasions. He seems never to have published anything, but he had another claim to fame. To quote Anthony à Wood: 'While he continued in Balliol College he made the drink for his own use called coffee, and usually drank it every morning, being the first, so the ancients of that house have informed me, that was ever drunk in Oxon.' A fellow-student at Balliol, John Evelyn, remembered him well. 'He was the first I ever saw drink coffee,' he wrote, 'which custom came not into

---

[1] Legrand, *Bibliographie Hellénique au 17e siècle*, v, pp. 192–218, giving also the text of Abbot's and Roe's correspondence about Critopoulos; à Wood, *op. cit.* II, p. 895.

20-2

England till some thirty years after.' Conopius ended his days drinking coffee as Archbishop of Smyrna.[1]

Nicodemus Metaxas, the printer, never went to a university. He had been sent to England by his uncle, the Bishop of Cephallonia, but lived amongst his brother's mercantile circles in London.[2]

These students did not venture to pronounce upon the theology of their Church, about which there was some confusion in English minds. Sir Thomas Roe had written openly to Archbishop Abbot about Cyril Lucaris's Calvinistic views. But Edward Pococke, writing to Archbishop Laud, skimmed over his theology, stressing merely that he was a martyr to Romish intrigue. The ensuing theological debates at Constantinople were not reported in England. The next Greek priest to study at Oxford, Jeremias Germanus, who was there in 1668–9, had no wish to offend his hosts and tactfully agreed with them on questions on theology;[3] nor were definite doctrinal opinions pronounced by a far more distinguished prelate, Joseph Georgirenes, Archbishop of Samos.

Georgirenes journeyed to England in 1676 in order to have a liturgical work for his flock printed there. In fact the work was never printed: Georgirenes was kept too busy on another project. There was by now a considerable Greek colony in London, mainly in the City, but spreading into Soho, where Greek Street perpetuates its memory. Many of these Greeks were rich and well known, such as Charles II's personal doctor, Constantine Rodokanaki, who had recently died after making a fortune out of a patent medicine called Spirit of Salt.[4] These Greeks had a resident priest, Daniel Vulgaris, but no church building. In 1674 Vulgaris, with two other Greeks, appealed to the Privy Council for permission to erect a church in the City, apparently on condition that

---

[1] Legrand, *Bibliographie Hellénique au 17e siècle*, IV, pp. 514–15, V, pp. 294–8; à Wood, *op. cit.* IV, p. 808; John Evelyn, *Diary*, 10 May 1639 (Everyman edition), I, p. 10. For Conopius's activities in Holland see K. Rozemond, *Archimandrite Hierotheos Abbatios*, pp. 32, 57, 61, 63–5. For his report on the murder of Lucaris see above, p. 286, n. 1.   [2] See above, p. 272.

[3] See below, p. 308.

[4] Legrand, *Bibliographie Hellénique au 17e siècle*, II, pp. 148, 188–93.

they became English subjects. Vulgaris was naturalized the following March. But no site had yet been found. Georgirenes made contact with a leading builder-speculator, Nicholas Barbon, who
promised his co-operation, and then approached the Bishop of
London, Henry Compton, who was most sympathetic. But
Compton had his own favourite builder, Richard Firth, who
offered a piece of land in Hog Lane (now Charing Cross Road),
which he sub-leased from a brewer, Joseph Girle, who held it from
the Crown lessee, the Earl of Saint Albans. It was in the parish of
Saint Martin in the Fields; and Compton persuaded the parish to
take over Girle's lease and assign it to the Greeks. But, though
Georgirenes, whose knowledge of English was, as he admitted,
faulty, did not realize it, the parish authorities so worded the
document that they could take back the land when they chose.

The site was officially given to the Greeks in the summer of
1677. Georgirenes had already raised sufficient money for the
work to begin; and Firth had already started on the building.
King Charles II gave £100, and his brother James, Duke of York,
though an acknowledged Catholic, was particularly generous. In
a few months Georgirenes raised £1,500. Though Firth was fined
for using bad bricks, supplied by his former landlord Girle, the
building was ready for use by the end of 1677. Georgirenes then
raised further sums for its decoration and upkeep by publishing
in 1678 a short book on Samos and on other parts of Greece that
he knew, translated into English by 'one that knew the author in
Constantinople'—actually a former Levant Company chaplain,
Henry Denton. The book was dedicated to the Duke of York, in
recognition of his generosity, even though the preface emphasized
the differences between the Roman and Greek Churches. It was
hoped to raise a regular income for the upkeep through a relative
of Georgirenes, one Laurence Georgirenes, who came to England
with a special method for pickling mackerel. The English government was interested and was prepared to give Laurence a patent;
but the scheme came to nothing.

The church was not fully complete till early in 1680. Meanwhile things were going badly. A Greek servant of Georgirenes called Dominico Cratiana absconded with some of the church funds and fled to Bristol. The Archbishop followed to bring a case against him, but, hampered by his bad English, he made a poor impression on the Bristol justices; and Cratiana was acquitted. Cratiana then accused Georgirenes of being a secret Papist and of having boasted that mass would soon be sung in Bristol Cathedral and that, when the Duke of York became king, he would be given an English bishopric. The accusation was well timed, as the excitement engendered by the 'Popish plot' unearthed by Titus Oates had reached a climax owing to the murder of Oates's confidant, Sir Edmund Godfrey. At Georgirenes's request the accusations were examined by the House of Lords, and he was cleared. But suspicions rose again when the informer, Prance, declared that Godfrey's corpse had been moved from a sedan-chair to the back of a horse just outside of the Greek Church. Georgirenes must have regretted his grateful dedication to the Duke of York.

This crisis was barely over before the archbishop had to warn the public against a Greek priest called Ciciliano who was collecting funds nominally for the church but actually for his own lewd purposes. But worse was to follow. Bishop Compton and the Vicar of Saint Martin's, both strong Protestants, objected to some of the usages of the Greek church as being too papistical. They were probably shocked by the presence of icons and the devotions shown to them. Foreseeing some such trouble, the Patriarch had asked the Ambassador at Constantinople, Sir John Finch, that the church in London should be put directly under the Patriarchate, as was the Greek church at Venice. Finch, hearing from Compton of the practices in the church in London, reported in a dispatch dated February 1679, that he considered this undesirable. Compton, whose suspicions had perhaps been first aroused by Cratiana's libels and were being fanned, it seems, by the Vicar of Saint Martin's, felt himself entitled to interfere in the Greek services.

Meanwhile Georgirenes, who was probably aware of the vicar's hostility, decided that the church would be better sited in the City of London, where the majority of the Greeks lived, than in Soho. Bishop Compton gave his approval. But when the Greeks tried to sell the building, on which they had already spent £800, they found that their title to it was legally unsound. The parish was ready at first to appoint assessors jointly with Georgirenes. But, when these assessors valued the building at £626, the vicar produced other assessors who valued it at £168, which he offered to the Greeks for the conveyance of their 'pretended rights'. Georgirenes, who had found a purchaser willing to pay £230 in spite of the legal uncertainty, refused this. The parish then offered £200. When this too was refused, the vicar turned the Greeks out of the building and annexed it, early in 1682. Georgirenes could not obtain any redress. Bishop Compton supported the parish for fear, he said, that the Greeks might sell the building to Dissenters: which was exactly what the parish proceeded to do. In the summer of 1682 the building was leased to French Huguenots, who held the lease until 1822. It then became an English Dissenters' chapel, but reverted to the Church of England in 1849 and was pulled down in 1934.[1]

The Greeks were again without a church until 1717, when Tsar Peter of Russia agreed to provide funds for a new Orthodox church in London. After 1731, when there was regular Russian diplomatic representation in London, it served also as the Russian Embassy chapel; but for several decades the priests were Greek and the Greek liturgy was used. Even after Russian priests and the

---

[1] J. Georgirenes, *A Description of the Present State of Samos, Nicaria, Patmos and Mount Athos* (1678), and 'From the Archbishop of the Isle of Samos in Greece, an account of his building the Grecian Church in So-hoe fields, and the disposal thereof by the masters of the parish St Martins in the fields', a broadsheet bound in *Tracts relating to London, 1598–1760*, in British Museum Library, 816. m. 9. (118). For the full history of the Greek Church in Hog Lane see the admirable account given in the Greater London Council, *Survey of London*, XXXIII (1966), pp. 278–87, 335–6, giving sources, in manuscript and printed, from the Public Record Office, the Journal of the House of Lords, the Westminster Public Library, the Historical Manuscripts Commission, the Bodleian and other collections. I am grateful to the author of the chapter, Mr P. A. Bezodis, for having allowed me to see the chapter before publication.

Slavonic liturgy were introduced the Greek colony made use of it until well into the nineteenth century, when they were able to build another church of their own.[1]

The Archbishop of Samos left the country disappointed and indignant soon afterwards, certainly before 1685. He had already proposed another scheme. In an undated letter, written probably in 1682, he sent a petition to the Archbishop of Canterbury, William Sancroft, to be transmitted to the Bishop of London, to ask that up to twelve Greek theological students should 'be constantly here to be instructed and grounded in the true Doctrine of the Church of England, whereby (with the blessing of God) they may be able Dispensers thereof, and so return into Greece to preach the same, by which means your petitioner conceives the said people may be edified'. He asked the Archbishop to set aside funds for the purpose.[2]

No answer from Sancroft survives. But in 1692 a distinguished Classical scholar, Dr Benjamin Woodroffe, became Principal of Gloucester Hall, Oxford, a bankrupt and empty institution which was to be refounded in 1714 as Worcester College. A few months after his appointment he appeared in person before the Board of the Levant Company in London, on 30 August 1692, to ask the Company to give a free passage on its ships to Greek students visiting England. The Company was not unsympathetic but told Dr Woodroffe to work out a full scheme. It took him some time. His treatise, *A Model of a College to be settled in the University for the Education of some Youths of the Greek Church*, of which the original manuscript is in the Library of Lambeth Palace, bears no date; but it was only on 3 March 1695 that Dr Woodroffe was able to write to the Patriarch of Constantinople, Callinicus II, with a definite invitation to send some boys.

[1] For the history of the Orthodox church founded in 1721 I am indebted to Mr Igor Vinogradoff for a résumé supplied by him in Russian from the records of the Russian church in London.

[2] Letter from Georgirenes to Archbishop Sancroft, in the Bodleian, Tanner MSS. xxxiii, fol. 57, printed in G. Williams, *The Orthodox Church of the East in the Eighteenth Century*, p. lxvi.

According to the *Model* the Greek College was to be in a building attached to Gloucester Hall. When complete it was to house
twenty students coming in yearly batches of four and remaining
there for five years. The Patriarchs of Constantinople and Antioch
were to choose the candidates in consultation with the Levant
Company's representatives at Constantinople, Smyrna and Aleppo.
The Company was to make the final decision; but no directions
were given on how to assess rival candidates from different districts. On their arrival at Oxford the students were to converse in
Ancient Greek for the first two years and then in Latin. They were
first to study Plato and Aristotle and other Classical authors, and
then the early Greek Fathers, particularly those who wrote commentaries on the books of the Bible. As for their dress, 'their habit
is to be the gravest worn in their country'. Yearly reports were to
be sent on each of them to the Bishop of London and to the
Governor of the Levant Company. The financial provisions were
left unfortunately vague.

Dr Woodroffe's letter to the Patriarch, which enclosed a copy
of the *Model*, was written in elegant Classical Greek. In it he spoke
warmly, even fulsomely, of the debt owed by England to Classical
and Christian Greek learning, in the arts, the sciences and theology.
In an attempt to repay the debt 'we have', he wrote, 'established
a common college at Oxford, that famous academy of ours, just
as Athens was once your famous academy'.

The Patriarchate and the Levant Company were ready to
co-operate. The Patriarch was flattered; and the Company seems
to have thought that even if the students failed to become priests
they would be useful as dragoman-interpreters, a class of men
much needed. The first students arrived in October 1698. There
were probably only three of them, as in the following March the
Levant Company voted the sum of forty pounds for the passage of
five Greek youths to set out that summer. Two at least of the
first batch did well. They applied to return home at the end of
1702 and were allowed twenty-five dollars each for their passage
and the transport of their books. At the end of 1703 another three

were allotted a similar sum, together with twenty-seven pounds, which had been advanced to them when they had been arrested at Gravesend for money owing on their original passage from Leghorn. A few days later a fourth student was allowed a free passage home.

But already the Greek College was running into difficulties. The Levant Company was growing less enthusiastic. It was hard to find suitable students; and when they arrived at Oxford they soon ran out of money and began to run up debts which the Company had to pay. Dr Woodroffe, who financed the College largely from his own purse, seems to have supposed that because they were receiving free board and lodging and tuition at Oxford they would need no other money. The building which he had erected for them was shoddy and barely fit for human occupation. It was known locally as 'Dr Woodroffe's Folly'. Many of the students resented its discomforts and were bored by wearing grave habits at Oxford, and made their way to London to enjoy a little gaiety. They wrote discouraging letters home; and Greek parents became unwilling to send their sons to England. The Jesuits, who had viewed the foundation of the College with alarm, made strenuous efforts to pervert the boys. In 1703 Dr Woodroffe reported the case of two of them, brothers called George and John Aptologi, who were offered by mysterious friends in London money for their homeward journey, and, when they accepted and set sail, were kidnapped and taken to Antwerp and thence to Rome, their captors regretting not to have taken the star pupil of the College, a boy called Homer, whom the Levant Company wished to secure as a dragoman. Next, the Jesuits persuaded Louis XIV to establish a Greek College in Paris. The French are always ready to spend money generously on cultural propaganda; and the Paris college was well endowed and comfortable. But, though it accepted non-Catholic students and though the glamour of Paris attracted boys who might otherwise have been ornaments to Oxford, it sought to convert its pupils. The Greek Church authorities could not approve of it. They preferred a competent and well-run seminary founded for Greek students a few years later by the Lutherans at Halle, even though it emphasized philosophy rather than theology. It seems to have been the most successful of these institutions. But in fact most bright Greek boys continued, if they went abroad, to go to Italy, to Venice or to Padua. It was closer to their homes; and financial arrangements were easier.

Dr Woodroffe meanwhile was soon over £1,000 in debt as a result of his venture. His only assets were salt-mines that he owned in Cheshire; but the Treasury refused to release him from the excise-duty due on his salt. Queen Anne's Bounty soon after its institution provided £400; but that was soon used. He spent the next few years continually petitioning the Treasury to stay the proceedings threatened against him for his debts.

On 6 July 1704, the Directors of the Levant Company wrote to Sir Robert Sutton, the Ambassador at Constantinople, to say that they did not intend to send any more students to Oxford. 'Those who have already been there', they said, ' do not give us encouragement enough to make further trial of that kind, having no prospect of advantage, but the experience of a great deal of trouble and charge over them, for which reason we are resolved to have nothing more to do with them.' The Patriarch of Constantinople shared their attitude. On 2 March 1705, the Registrar of the Great Church wrote on behalf of the Patriarch Gabriel III, Callinicus II's successor, to say that: 'The irregular life of certain priests and lay-men of the Eastern Church living in London is a matter of grave concern to the Church. Wherefore the Church forbids any to go and study at Oxford, be they never so willing.' It seems unfair that Oxford should thus be blamed for the shortcomings of London; but it is clear that the students were all drifting to London and behaving very badly there.

We do not know how Dr Woodroffe took the failure of his scheme. He had been too hopeful. An Oxford education, however admirable it might be, was hardly a suitable training for a priest who was to spend his life ministering to a Christian minority in the Ottoman Empire. And it was hardly reasonable to expect that Greek boys coming from oriental homes would readily adapt themselves to a sober academic life at Oxford. None of the students at the Greek College made any mark in later life. Apart from the Jesuits' victims, the name of only one has survived, Francis Prossalenos, who several years later published a friendly little book describing Dr Woodroffe's quirks and foibles.[1]

But Dr Woodroffe had had his moment of glory, especially when in 1701 Neophytus, Metropolitan of Philippopolis and Exarch of All Thrace and Dragovia, came with his suite to England and was given the honorary degree of Doctor of Divinity at a special encaenia at Oxford. The Archdeacon Athanasius, the Archimandrite Neophytus and the Protosyncellus Gregory, who accompanied him, were all given honorary Masterships of Arts, and his doctor, whose name is not known, received a Doctorate of Medicine. Mr Edward Thwaites, who was present, noted that the Metropolitan 'made us a very excellent speech, all in plain proper Hellenistick Greek', and that 'Dr Woodroffe has exerted himself and shown us that he does understand Greek'. The Metropolitan went on to Cambridge, where, at the request of Archbishop Tenison of Canterbury, he was received by Dr Covel, now Master of Christ's. But Cambridge gave no special honour to the distinguished visitor, no doubt owing to the influence of Dr Covel, who was less starry-eyed about Greece than was Dr Woodroffe. Besides, Dr Covel was not going to encourage any move towards inter-communion until he was satisfied about certain doctrines held by the Greek Church. And he was beginning to

---

[1] For Dr Woodroffe's Greek College see Lambeth Palace Library, Codices MSS. Gibsoniani, x, 938, 38 (model of College by Dr Woodroffe), and xiv, 951, 1 (Dr Woodroffe's letter to the Patriarch); *Calendar of Treasury Books*, xix, p. 446, xx, pp. 149, 552, xxii, pp. 194, 423, and *Calendar of Treasury Papers*, iii (1702–7), pp. 42, 207–9, 362, 399–400, 407 (Dr Woodroffe's expenses and debts); W. H. Hart, 'Gleanings from the Records of the Treasury', no. vi; *Notes and Queries* (2nd series), ix, pp. 457–8; G. Williams, *op. cit.* pp. xix–xxii; W. P. Courtney, 'Benjamin Woodroffe', in *Dictionary of National Biography*, lxii: A. C. Wood, *op. cit.* p. 227: J. B. Pearson, *A Biographical Sketch of the Chaplains to the Levant Company maintained at Constantinople, Aleppo and Smyrna*, pp. 43–5.

wonder, also, what exactly some of these visiting prelates were doing.[1]

In September 1689, to complete the Revolution settlement, a Royal Commission was set up to look into the prayer-book. The Rev. Dr George Williams, writing in 1868, claims to have seen at Lambeth a folio prayer-book of the 1683–6 edition, used by the Commissioners, with interleaved blank sheets for their notes. Opposite the words in the Nicene Creed on the Holy Ghost 'Who proceedeth from the Father and the Son' was a note saying: 'It is humbly submitted to the Convocation whether a Note ought not here to be added with relation to the Greek Church, in order to our maintaining Catholic Communion.' The note shows that there were responsible members of the Church of England who were prepared to humour the Greek disapproval of the *filioque* clause in the Creed. They no doubt held the view, rejected by the Greeks, that the addition merely clarified the sense and therefore could be omitted.[2] But there were other doctrines held by the Greeks which, some wondered, might prove a bar to inter-communion.

The Anglicans had sympathized with Cyril Lucaris and had deplored his martyrdom. But they had not inquired too deeply into his doctrine. It was perhaps as well that he was dead and his Calvinistic leanings repudiated before any of them began seriously to study Orthodox theology.

The first Anglican to make a direct inquiry was a priest of French origin, Dr Isaac Basire. He had been one of Charles I's chaplains; and, when the Commonwealth drove him into exile, he wandered round the East as an apostle of Anglicanism, 'planting

---

[1] Williams, *op. cit.* p. xxii.

[2] *Ibid.* p. xviii. The Librarian of Lambeth has had the kindness to inform me that no such copy of the prayer-book exists in the Library at present, nor can he trace any reference to show that such a copy ever existed. I have seen in the Library an undated manuscript entitled 'A Good and Necessary Proposal for the Restitution of Catholick Communion between the Greek Churches and the Church of England' which seems to belong to the same period and which takes the same line (MSS. Gibsoniani, VII, 935).

the Church of England in divers parts of the Levant and Asia', as Evelyn reports. He enjoyed a success among the Greeks. He was twice invited by the Metropolitan of Achaea to preach before an assembly of bishops; and he became a close friend of the Patriarch of Jerusalem, whom he thought to be ready for union. 'It hath been my constant design', he wrote, 'to dispose and incline the Greek Church to a communion with the Church of England, together with a canonical reform of some grosser errors.' When he returned to England he was hailed as an authority on the East. Evelyn heard him preach in Westminster Abbey in 1661 and was much impressed. But in fact Dr Basire never returned to the East. The grosser errors remained unreformed.[1]

What were these grosser errors? Basire was no doubt distressed by the prevalence of icons and, perhaps, of monks. He does not say if he ever discussed the Procession of the Holy Ghost. But he was certainly interested in a question that was troubling many theologians in Western Europe. What was the actual Greek dogma about the Real Presence at the eucharist?

Attention had been drawn to the question in about 1660, in the course of a controversy between the French Huguenots, led by Jean Claude, and the Port-Royal school, led by Antoine Arnauld. They were disputing over the nature of the eucharist; and each party hoped to have the support of Eastern Christian tradition. Anyone acquainted with the general attitude of the Orthodox towards the niceties of dogma would have realized that a

[1] Dr Isaac Basire's 'A Letter, Written by the Reverend Dr Basier [*sic*] Relating His Travels, and Endeavours to propagate the Knowledge of the Doctrine and Discipline, established in the Britannick Church, among the Greeks, Arabians, etc.' is published as part of his *The Ancient Liberty of the Britannick Church* (1661), and, more accessibly, in *The Correspondence of Isaac Basire, D.D.* (ed. N. Darnell, 1831). I quote from the latter, pp. 115–16. See also John Evelyn, *Diary*, 10 November 1661 (Everyman edition), I, p. 363. Williams, *op. cit.* p. xi, quotes a letter from Basire to Antoine Léger, in which he says that he sent a translation in 'Romaic' of the Anglican catechism to the four Eastern Patriarchs. The Patriarch of Alexandria seems not to have replied, but the other three greatly praised it.

categorical answer would not be easy to obtain. Jeremias II's attitude on the subject had been deliberately vague. He had believed in a change in elements, effected by the appeal to the Holy Spirit, but he had been shy of using the word 'transubstantiation'. Cyril Lucaris had flatly denied transubstantiation. But before his time Gabriel Severus had accepted it; and, in the reaction against Lucaris, the Church of Constantinople had recently accepted the Confession of Moghila, who had stated it with confidence. Consequently, when the French disputants referred the question to the French Ambassador to the Sublime Porte, the Marquis de Nointel, His Excellency replied, with some hesitation, that a study of recently published Confessions inclined him to believe that the Greeks accepted the doctrine of transubstantiation; and eventually, in 1671, he obtained a statement from the Patriarch Parthenius IV that that was indeed the official doctrine of the Church.[1]

The Anglicans had hoped to find that the Orthodox would agree with their doctrine of consubstantiation: that is, that though the body and blood of Christ are really present at the Sacrifice, there is no material change in the elements. The Anglican chaplains at Constantinople were asked to make further researches. Thomas Smith, who was there from 1668 to 1670, said that the word 'μετουσίωσις' had only recently been introduced and that the doctrine had only been endorsed as yet by a Council held in 1643 in 'the lesser Russia'. He was probably thinking of the Councils of Kiev (1640) and of Jassy (1642), neither of which were in any sense Oecumenical; though the findings of the Council of Jassy had been confirmed by the Holy Synod under

---

[1] For the debate between Claude and Arnauld see A. Arnauld, *La Perpetuité de la foy*, and Claude's reply, *Réponse au Livre de Mr. Arnauld entitulé La Perpetuité de la foy*; also J. Aymon, *Monuments authentiques de la réligion des Grecs et de la fausseté de plusieurs confessions de foi des Chrétiens*, pp. 38 ff.: Thomas Smith, *An Account of the Greek Church*, pp. 277–9. The Huguenots seem to have derived their information from Meletius Pantogalos, a disciple of Lucaris, who spent several years in Holland and published there a declaration of faith in support of Lucaris's Confession; Claude quotes it as supporting his contentions (*op. cit.* pp. 443–4). See K. Rozemond, *op. cit.* pp. 30–1.

Parthenius II.[1] Covel, who succeeded Smith, noted that Jeremias Germanus when visiting Oxford had assured everyone that 'the Greeks believed no such thing'. But Germanus was wrong; for Covel had himself obtained from the Patriarch, at the request of the Bishops of Chester and Chichester and the future Archbishop Sancroft, a statement called *A Synodical Answer to the Question, What are the Sentiments of the Oriental Church of the Grecian Orthodox: sent to the Lovers of the Greek Church in Britain in the Year of Our Lord 1672.* It was signed on 10 January 1672 by the Patriarch Dionysius IV, four ex-Patriarchs of Constantinople and the Patriarch of Jerusalem and thirty-one other metropolitans, and contained a clear statement of belief in the Real Presence in a full material sense, as well as insisting on the infallibility of the Church, the mediation of saints and seven Sacraments.[2]

Sir Paul Ricaut, secretary at the Constantinopolitan Embassy from 1661 to 1668 and then Consul at Smyrna, was not so positive. In the very perceptive and sympathetic work on the Greek Church that he published in 1676, at the request of Charles II, he agreed with Smith that the word 'μετουσίωσις' was comparatively modern. 'The question about Transubstantiation', he wrote, 'hath not been long controverted in the Greek Church, but, like other abstruse notions, not necessarily to be determined, hath lain quiet and dissentangled [*sic*], wound upon the bottom of its own thread, until Faction, and Malice, and the Schooles, have so ravelled and twisted the twine, that the end will never be found.' This was a fair description of the situation; and Ricaut shrewdly attributes the prevalence of the doctrine in his own time to the influence of 'such as have had their education in Italy'.[3] The pious

---

[1] Smith, *Account of the Greek Church*, pp. 148–53. See above, p. 293.

[2] This statement was extracted from the 'Confession of Dositheus' (see below, pp. 350-3), and is signed by the signatories of the Confession. It is given in full by G. Williams, *op. cit.* pp. 67–76.

[3] Sir Paul Ricaut (or Rycaut), *The Present State of the Greek and Armenian Churches, Anno Christi 1678* (1679). Sir Paul also wrote *The History of the Turkish Empire from 1623 to 1677* and *The Present State of the Ottoman Empire*, the former published to continue the second volume of R. Knolles, *The Turkish History* (6th edition, 1679), and a supplementary volume, *The History of the Turks, 1679–99* (1700).

Sir George Wheler, who travelled widely in Greek lands in the 1670s and published an account of his travels in 1682, believed that the average Greek did not hold with the doctrine. It had its supporters such as Anthimus, the cultured Metropolitan of Athens, whose library Wheler's fellow-traveller, the Frenchman Spon, greatly admired. Anthimus told Wheler that he had been present when the Patriarch Parthenius had signed his declaration for the Marquis de Nointel, and added that he fully endorsed the doctrine. But the Bishop of Salona, whom Wheler met at the Monastery of Holy Luke in Styris, insisted that the Greek view was exactly that which Wheler enunciated; and Wheler found many other Greek clerics who agreed. He himself was of the opinion that the doctrine prevailed only among Greeks living in centres where the Roman Church exercised some influence, in particular in Constantinople itself and in islands under Venetian rule.[1]

All these pundits were right. There was no doubt that at the time the Church authorities at Constantinople, in reaction against Lucaris and under the influence of Italian ideas, did accept the doctrine; but the acceptance was not universal throughout the Church. Wheler was perhaps the nearest to the truth. The average Greek preferred to treat the matter as a mystery; and in the long run that view prevailed. Today the Greek Church fights shy of the word μετουσίωσις. Nineteenth-century catechisms merely declare that the bread and wine become the body and blood of Christ but, in the words of a modern historian of Eastern Christendom, the Orthodox 'are reluctant to define either the character or the exact moment of the change'.[2]

Thus Greek clerics who came to England and denied that their Church believed in transubstantiation were not telling lies to please their hosts. They probably did not believe that the doctrine was obligatory. Germanus's denial might have been too categorical. But Joseph Georgirenes was probably quite honest when he

[1] Sir George Wheler, *A Journey into Greece* (1682), pp. 195, 196, 198.
[2] For the catechisms see below, p. 353.

wrote in the preface to his book on Greece that: 'In the Sacrament of the Eucharist, the Greek Church doth not bear that conformity with the Romish Church, as the great champions for Popery would affix upon them.'[1]

All the same, the Anglicans were left with the nasty suspicion that the Greeks did in fact subscribe to transubstantiation. When the Metropolitan of Philippopolis told Dr Covel at Cambridge in 1701 that the Greeks did not hold the doctrine, Covel frankly did not believe him. Under such circumstances it was difficult for the Anglican hierarchy to pursue discussions on inter-communion.[2]

There were, nevertheless, elements in the Anglican Church which still thought that union with the ancient Church of the East would be both spiritually and politically advantageous. The Non-Juror clergy were never very numerous, but they had vigorous and enterprising leaders. They disliked the path that the Church of England had been taking since the Revolution settlement. Though they abjured the Papacy they did not care for Protestantism. In their own eyes they formed the Old Catholic Church. Thomas Ken, former Bishop of Bath and Wells and last survivor of the Non-Juring bishops of the seventeenth century, who died in 1711, wrote in his will: 'I die in the holy and apostolic faith professed by the whole Church before the division of East and West.' To his followers it was therefore almost a sacred duty to try to achieve union with the Orthodox.[3]

Their opportunity came in 1716. The Patriarchate of Alexandria was in financial difficulties. Cosmas, Archbishop of Sinai, had offered huge bribes to the Governor of Egypt and to the Grand Vizier at Constantinople to secure the Patriarchal throne; and the actual Patriarch, Samuel Capasoulis, had borrowed still larger sums to outbid him. He was now 30,000 dollars in debt. Believing the English to be rich and charitable, he sent to England Arsenius, Metropolitan of the Thebaid, and the senior abbot of the Patriar-

[1] J. Georgirenes, *A Description*, Epistle to the Reader, 9th page (unnumbered).
[2] G. Williams, *op. cit.* pp. lix–lx.
[3] Thomas Ken's will, given in W. Hawkins, *Short Account of Ken's Life*, p. 27.

chate, the Archimandrite Gennadius, a Cypriot by birth. They travelled in style, with four deacons, a reader and a cook, and arrived in England in the summer of 1714, armed with letters to Queen Anne. Though they were embarrassed for a time by a rumour, put about, they said, by the Jesuits, they were well received. They made friends with the antiquary, Humphrey Wanley, who had recently retired from the post of Secretary of the Society for the Promotion of Christian Knowledge; and he and his circle entertained them hospitably. Arsenius wrote joyfully to his friend Chrysanthus, Patriarch of Jerusalem, to report in what favour he and Gennadius were held. He told of parties given in their honour, and he boasted of the wonderful effect that they made on the British public by always wearing their robes when they went about.[1]

In 1715 Arsenius published a touching tract entitled *Lacrymae et Suspiria Ecclesiae Graecae: or the Distressed State of the Greek Church, humbly represented in a Letter to Her late Majesty, Queen Anne*. In response the Bishop of London, John Robinson, sent them a few months later £200 provided from Queen Anne's Bounty and £100 given by King George I, but with the expressed hope that they would then leave the country. He had procured another £100 for them, but held it back until they should announce their departure. They were, however, enjoying themselves too well to take this clear hint that they had outstayed their welcome. Wanley still entertained them, even though Dr Covel wrote to him sternly from Cambridge to warn him that they would be no more reliable theologically than previous Greek visitors and would be certain to say that they did not believe in transubstantiation. Arsenius avoided that trap. Wanley wrote back to Covel to say that the Greek hierarchs modestly declared that: 'they believed as Saints Basil and Chrysostom believed, and they would not meddle in what did not concern them'. Their answer satisfied

---

[1] M. Constantinides, *The Greek Orthodox Church in London*, pp. 9–10. The archives of the Russian church in London (see above, p. 300, n. 1) report that the Jesuits put it about that they were Papal spies.

Wanley, who wrote three days later, on 24 December 1715, to Cambridge to his friend, Dr Tudway, to ask him to tell Dr Covel that the Greeks were coming to visit him there. We do not know how they were received.[1]

Meanwhile they made other friends. Arsenius reported to Chrysanthus of Jerusalem that not only had two Members of Parliament offered to help in the building of a new Greek church in London, but also that many Englishmen were seeking to be received into the Orthodox communion. This surprising remark is to be explained by the fact that the Greeks were beginning to repay the generosity of their hosts by intriguing with the Non-Jurors.

According to Thomas Brett, who had recently been consecrated a Non-Juring bishop, and who later recorded the transactions, it was in July 1716 that the Scottish Non-Juror, Archibald Campbell, happened to meet Arsenius and spoke to him of the possibilities of a closer connection. 'Having', as the historian Skinner records, 'a scheming turn for everything which he thought of the general usefulness for the Church, [Campbell] took occasion in conversation to hint something of this kind.' Arsenius was sympathetic. So Campbell and Jeremy Collier, *primus* of the English Non-Jurors, together with Thomas Brett, Nathaniel Spinkes, James Gadderer and a few others, met to prepare proposals for transmission to the Eastern Patriarchs.[2]

It was probably early in 1717 that a copy of the proposals was given to Arsenius, who dispatched it to Constantinople. It was a lengthy document, translated into elegant Greek by Spinkes, with the help of Mr Thomas Rattray of Craighall. The proposals

[1] G. Williams, *op. cit.* pp. lx–lxi; T. Lathbury, *History of the Non-Jurors*, p. 356.

[2] The history of the Non-Jurors' dealings with the Orthodox was first told by T. Lathbury in 1845 (*op. cit.*, pp. 309–61). He derived his information from Bishop Jolly's manuscript records. It was told more fully by G. Williams, in 1868 (*op. cit.*), which is entirely concerned with the transactions and their background. Some minor corrections to Williams's narrative are given in J. H. Overton, *The Non-Jurors, their Lives, Principles and Writings* (1902), pp. 451 ff. See also J. Skinner, *Ecclesiastical History of Scotland*, II, pp. 634–40.

numbered twelve, but they were supplemented by a list of twelve points on which the Non-Jurors believed themselves to be in complete agreement with the Orthodox and five points on which they disagreed and on which discussion would be necessary.

The twelve proposals were: first, that Jerusalem be recognized as the mother-church of Christendom, and, secondly, that the Church of Jerusalem be given precedence over all others. Thirdly, the canonical rights of the Alexandrian, the Antiochene and the Constantinopolitan Patriarchates should be recognized, and, fourthly, that Constantinople's equality of honour with Rome be accepted. Fifthly and sixthly, the Catholic remnant of the British Churches (as the Non-Jurors called themselves) should recognize that they had received Christianity from Jerusalem and should return to that 'ancient godly discipline'. Seventhly, conformity of worship throughout the Churches should be as near as possible. Eighthly, the British should restore the old English liturgy. Ninthly, the homilies of John Chrysostom and other works by Greek Fathers should be translated into English. Tenthly, the Bishop of Jerusalem should be expressly commemorated in the prayers for the Patriarchs in the Communion service. Eleventhly, the Britannick Churches should be prayed for. Finally, letters should be exchanged to confirm acts of mutual concern.

The twelve points of mutual agreement were stated to be: first, the twelve articles of the Creed are accepted as laid down in the first two Oecumenical Councils. Secondly, the Trinity is consubstantial and the Father the fount and origin from which the Holy Ghost proceeds. Thirdly, the Holy Ghost's procession 'from the Father by the Son' means no more than that. Fourthly, the Holy Ghost has spoken through the Prophets and the Apostles and is the only true author of the Scriptures, and, fifthly, that it assisted the Oecumenical Councils. Sixthly, both parties share the same belief in the number and nature of the charismata of the Spirit. Seventhly and eighthly, Christ is the only founder and only head of the Church. Ninthly, all Christians must be subject to the Church, which can censure and discipline its ministers.

Tenthly, the eucharist is to be given in both kinds to all the faithful. Eleventhly, baptism is necessary, the other holy mysteries being not so generally necessary but to be celebrated by all. Lastly, the doctrine of Purgatory is erroneous.

Disagreement was admitted on five points. The Non-Jurors could not accept that the canons of the Oecumenical Councils commanded the same authority as the Scriptures. Though they considered the Mother of God to be blessed, she could not as a creature be given the glory due to God. Mediation could not be made through the saints, not even through the Mother of God, as that would detract from Christ's mediation. They could accept the Epiklesis as part of the communion service, but insisted that the change in the elements be recognized as taking place 'after a manner which flesh and blood cannot conceive'. They also wished the ninth canon of the Seventh Oecumenical Council to be explained so as to make it clear that no worship was given to pictures.[1]

The Non-Jurors had to wait a long time for an answer. Jeremias III of Constantinople probably received their proposals about the end of 1717. He then had to consult with his fellow-Patriarchs before drafting a reply. The Patriarchal answer is dated 12 April 1718. But three more years elapsed before it reached England. In the meantime Arsenius had at last left England, to try to raise more money in Russia. The date of his departure—we may hope, with the money held back by Bishop Robinson—is unknown. The Russian Tsar had already sent him 500 roubles to England; and in 1717 he was in Holland, to meet Tsar Peter on his return from a state visit to Paris. It was on that occasion that the arrangements were made for the building of a new Greek church in London. Arsenius had probably told the Patriarchs to send their answer to Russia to await him there; and the delay was due to the postponement of his journey. By 1721 he was installed in St Petersburg. In the meantime, no doubt on his suggestion, the Non-Jurors decided to interest the Tsar in their scheme. A letter was sent to him,

[1] G. Williams, *op. cit.* pp. 3–11.

dated 8 October 1717, which referred to His Imperial Majesty's well-known interest in unionist movements and asked for his help. Anyone who really knew Peter the Great might have wondered whether his interest was due to anything but purely political considerations. But he seems to have sent back a benevolent reply.[1]

The Non-Jurors' letter to the Tsar had probably been conveyed by one of Arsenius's deacons, the Pro-Syncellus James, who had joined the Tsar's suite in Holland. In the autumn of 1721 James returned to London with the Patriarchal answer and a covering letter from Arsenius, dated 18 August. The Patriarchal comments were friendly but not very encouraging. On the first five of the Non-Jurors' proposals the Patriarchs inquired why the order of Patriarchal precedence laid down by the Oecumenical Councils needed any alteration. If the British wish to put themselves under Jerusalem, let them do so; but whatever does their reference to 'ancient discipline' mean? Their wish for a close conformity of worship was admirable if obscure; but the Patriarchs could not give their approval of 'the old English Liturgy' as they had never seen it. They naturally commended the proposal to translate works of the Greek Fathers into English. As for the desire for mutual commemoration and consultation, that was admirable 'if so be that the querents will consent to the divine and holy articles of our pure faith'.

The Patriarchs concurred with the points on which the Non-Jurors claimed to be in agreement with the Orthodox. But they remarked, on the procession of the Holy Ghost, that it was unnecessary to add to the Creed and that the prepositions 'ἐκ' and 'διά' (the latter being the preposition used by John of Damascus) were not the same. They commented also that, while Christ was indeed sole head of the Church, for practical and mundane purposes the prince could be regarded as acting head—an idea that did not commend itself to the Non-Jurors. Finally, while not

---

[1] *Ibid.* pp. 12–14: T. Lathbury, *op. cit.* pp. 318–19: archives of the Russian church in London.

admitting the existence of Purgatory, they believed in the validity of prayers for the dead.

On the five points of disagreement the Patriarchs were unyielding. The Oecumenical Councils must be regarded as being fully inspired, they said. They were glad to hear that the British were willing to insert the Epiklesis into the Communion service, but they insisted on the full doctrine of transubstantiation. As for the honour paid to the Mother of God and the saints, they quoted the Psalmist: 'Then were they in great fear where no fear was.' The glory given to the Mother of God is 'hyperdulia', not 'latreia', which is given to God alone. After all, we are told to honour the king, which is, to give him 'dulia'. As for mediation, do we not ask the faithful to pray for us? Even Saint Paul did so. Is it not better, then, to ask the saints to pray for us? Again, the worship of icons is not 'latreia' but relative worship. As Basil says, the honour paid to the image ascends to the proto-type.

The Patriarchs then referred the Non-Jurors to the *Synodical Answer* given by the Patriarch Dionysius IV to Dr Covel. They added a short encyclical statement signed in 1691 by Callinicus II of Constantinople and Dositheus of Jerusalem, explaining that the elements at the eucharist are 'truly the very Body and Blood of Christ under the visible symbols of bread and wine', there having been a material change: which is what is meant by transubstantiation.[1]

The Non-Jurors were disappointed by this answer. The moderates among them, led by Nathaniel Spinkes, refused to continue with the negotiations. But Campbell, Gadderer, Collier and Brett met to compose a reply. In it they modified their original proposals. They would not ask for a change in the precedence of the Patriarchs, merely that the British bishops should be under none of them, except for disciplinary powers to be given to Jerusalem. They accepted the Orthodox rulings about the other proposals. On the points of agreement and disagreement they required some details, not stated, to be adjusted on the procession

---

[1] G. Williams, *op. cit.* pp. 15–83; T. Lathbury, *op. cit.* pp. 319–35.

of the Holy Ghost and felt that there was still some divergence in the interpretation of its role. They agreed, but with qualifications, about the inspiration of the Oecumenical Councils; but they could not accept any form of worship being given to the saints or to icons. They ventured to remind the Patriarchs that there was no such thing as gradual religion. The faith was perfect from the beginning. Therefore the earliest traditions were best. They could accept decisions reached in the first four centuries of Christendom; but why should they be bound by a decision of the late eighth century? They also could not accept transubstantiation; and to support their view they added a number of apposite quotations from John Chrysostom, Cyril of Jerusalem, Epiphanius and Theodoret, as well as from Tertullian and Augustine, showing that the early Fathers did not believe in a substantial change in the elements. It may be remarked that, while their argument that earliest doctrines were best would not have convinced the Orthodox, who believe that the Holy Spirit can at any time add to the revelation of divine truths, the evidence that they cited on the doctrine of the Sacraments held by the Fathers was less easy for the Orthodox to answer.[1]

This document was dated 29 May 1722. It was sent to Arsenius, who was now at Moscow, with a letter, dated 30 May, asking him to transmit copies to the Patriarchs, to the Tsar and to the Russian Synod. Another letter of the same date was sent directly to the Russian Synod, and one dated 31 May to the Imperial Grand Chancellor, Count Golovkin (whom they called Galowskin), asking for their co-operation. The letters were entrusted to James the Pro-Syncellus, who wrote on 9 September to announce his safe arrival in Russia. Arsenius wrote on 9 December to say that the documents had been forwarded and that all was going well in Russia. He also sent some liturgical books, for which the Non-Jurors thanked him on 28 January 1723, adding a tribute to the Archimandrite Gennadius, who had remained in London, apparently as priest at the new Orthodox church. In February

---

[1] G. Williams, *op. cit.* pp. 83–102; T. Lathbury, *op. cit.* pp. 311, 336–41.

Theodosius, Archbishop of Novgorod, representing the Russian Synod, wrote to ask the Non-Jurors to send two of their number to Russia for discussions with the Synod. The Non-Jurors then wrote to Arsenius to ask that his kinsman, Bartholomew Cassano, who was in England, might be allowed to accompany the delegates as interpreter.

Then things began to go badly. It was not easy to find delegates willing and able to go to Russia, especially as the negotiations were being kept secret from the British government. In July 1724 they had to apologize to Arsenius and the Russians for the delay. In the meantime they received from Constantinople a copy of the 'Confession of Dositheus', with a letter signed by each of the Eastern Patriarchs saying that it embodied his beliefs and that he had no further observations to make. The Confession contained a clear statement of the honour to be paid to saints and icons and of transubstantiation. Then came news of the death of Tsar Peter in January 1725. His widow and successor, Catherine I, was not interested in the affair.[1]

The final blow soon followed. Thomas Payne, the Levant Company's chaplain at Constantinople, discovered about the whole correspondence and reported it to Archbishop Wake of Canterbury. The archbishop wrote in September 1725 to Chysanthus of Jerusalem, whom he knew to be a friend of Arsenius; and, after thanking him cordially for a copy of Adam Zoernikoff's work on the Dual Procession, which the Patriarch had sent through the British Embassy to Oxford, he warned him sternly that Arsenius and his friends had been intriguing with a small and schismatic body in Britain which in no way represented the Anglican Church. He added that his 'faithful presbyter Thomas Payne' would inform His Illustrious Reverence about the true position in England.[2]

This letter ended the affair. The Eastern Patriarchs had never been enthusiastic; and the Russians had lost interest. The Catholic Remnant of the British Churches was left in isolation. Indeed, the

[1] G. Williams, *op. cit.* pp. 103–68; T. Lathbury, *op. cit.* pp. 342–57.
[2] G. Williams, *op. cit.* pp. xxxviii–xxxix.

general temper of the Anglican Church in the eighteenth century was not likely to produce any sympathy with Greek Orthodoxy. Dr Covel's book on the Greek Church had appeared in 1722. While not wholly unfriendly, it stressed the ignorance and corruption of the Orthodox clergy, and discouraged the few English clerical philhellenes that remained. Over a century had to pass before there was any revival of oecumenism along such lines.

Looking back from the vantage-point of later centuries, we can see that attempts to bring the Orthodox and Protestant Churches into communion with each other were premature. The only strong common basis was a mutual fear and dislike of Rome. But the Protestants, even the Anglicans, were nervous of anything that might be labelled as superstition. They had not freed themselves from the superstitions of Rome in order to ally themselves with a Church that must have seemed to them equally enslaved to holy pictures and relics and monasteries. Moreover, though they had reacted from Rome, there was still a Scholastic background to their theology. They wanted clear-cut definitions and logical arguments, even when they were dealing with the problem of grace. The Orthodox, with their mysticism, their taste for the apophatic approach and their loyalty to their old traditions, belonged to a different world, a world which the West could not understand. The Protestant overtures offered to the Orthodox an opportunity to revivify their whole attitude to religion. But it was an opportunity that none of the Orthodox really wished to take, with the exception of Cyril Lucaris and his disciples; and, for all Cyril's personal qualities, his efforts ended in failure. The Orthodox were willing to make use of the Protestants but not to join up with them. With the coming of the eighteenth century the West lost interest in the Orthodox faith, except to denounce it as obscurantist and debased. Even the Roman missionary effort was reduced. The Orthodox Greeks were left to turn in again on themselves, or to seek protection from an Orthodox power more traditionally hostile to the West than ever they had been, the Empire of Holy Russia.

CHAPTER 8

CONSTANTINOPLE AND MOSCOW

The proudest achievement of the old Byzantine Church had been the conversion of the Russians. The political calculations of the Russian princes had played their part in producing the happy result; and on the Byzantine side the element of politics had not been lacking. But it was also the product of a genuine missionary spirit; and Byzantine churchmen always retained a special affection towards their Russian godchildren, while to the Russians Byzantium long remained the source of civilization and light.

With the close of the middle ages the relations between Byzantium and Russia began to alter. The Mongol occupation of Russia, which lasted from the mid-thirteenth to the mid-fifteenth century, put a brake on Russian civilization. Russia was cut off from most of Europe, and her own internal development was distorted. The educated laity which had begun to emerge disappeared. The various princely courts which, quarrelsome though they had been, provided vitality and enterprise, were disrupted. When the Mongol tide began to ebb there was just one great prince in Russia, the Grand Prince of Muscovy, a crude autocrat whose court was closer in outlook to that of the Mongol Khan of the Golden Horde than to that of the Emperor at Constantinople. Though trade connections with the Baltic were precariously maintained, it was the Church alone which preserved a tradition of culture throughout the dark ages and which by its connection with Constantinople kept a door open to Europe. But at the same time Byzantium was rapidly declining, whereas by the beginning of the fifteenth century Muscovy had begun to shake off the Mongol yoke. With the shrinking of the Byzantine Oecumene there were already many more Orthodox in Russia than in all the Greek world. Inevitably, the Grand Prince of Muscovy was beginning to wonder whether he, and not the impoverished Basileus at

Constantinople, were not the proper head of the Orthodox
Oecumene, as the stern letter from the Patriarch Antony to the
Grand Prince Vasssily I, written in about 1395, bears witness.[1] The
Russians had meanwhile become more Orthodox than the Greeks
in that they were even more hostile to other forms of Christianity.
The Roman Church meant to them hostile Poles, Hungarians and
Swedes along the western frontiers. They were passionately in-
dignant at the crime of the Fourth Crusade, though it had no
direct effect on them. The West had done nothing to preserve
them from the Mongols; and now they were rescuing themselves
without its help, indeed, in spite of its hostility. In consequence
Russia had no sympathy with those Byzantines who sought aid
from the West and were ready to pay the price of Church union.
Byzantium still kept a direct control over the Russian Church.
Whether by chance or by design, every alternate Metropolitan
of Russia seems to have been appointed by the Emperor at Constantinople; and the others, appointed by the Grand Prince, had
to be confirmed by the Patriarchate.[2] The last of these Constantinopolitan appointments was that of Isidore of Monemvasia, who,
when metropolitan, had been one of the most eager advocates of
the Union of Florence. When he returned to Russia the whole
Russian Church and people repudiated his work, and he was
forced to leave the country. Not only had he let them down, but
it was felt that the Byzantines who had appointed him and had
accepted union at his side had been traitors to Orthodoxy. When
Constantinople fell to the Turks a few years later, all Russia was
sure that this was the divine punishment for the crime.[3]

The fall of Constantinople entirely altered the situation. The
Russians were already feeling self-righteously disillusioned by the
Greeks. Now, as a result of Greek backsliding, there was no
longer a Holy Emperor reigning at Tsarigrad, the Imperial City;
and the Holy Patriarch, though he had reverted to true Orthodoxy, was the slave of infidel masters. One by one the Orthodox
monarchs of the old Byzantine sphere were being eliminated or

[1] See above, p. 71.   [2] See above, p. 76.   [3] See above, pp. 108–110.

reduced to vassalage, till, with the exception of the distant and isolated King of Georgia, the Grand Prince of Muscovy was left the only independent Orthodox sovereign in the world. And, while other Orthodox princes were tottering, his power was steadily increasing. The Mongol Khanate was in decline. The Muscovite prince was uniting the Russians under his rule, till in 1480 Ivan III could declare himself independent of the Golden Horde and sovereign of All the Russias. Henceforward he bore the title of Tsar.[1]

In 1441 Prince Vassily II had written a letter to the Emperor John to seek confirmation from the Byzantine authorities of the Metropolitan Jonah, whom he had appointed to succeed Isidore. In it he boasted of Russia's long tradition of Orthodoxy since the days of 'the great new Constantine, the pious Tsar of the Russian land, Vladimir'. The phrase is ominous; it shows that Vassily was prepared to claim the inheritance of the successors of Constantine. He did not send the letter because he heard a rumour, without foundation, that John had fled to Rome. But a few years later he wrote again, to announce that he had appointed Jonah without waiting for Byzantine confirmation. 'We have done this', he wrote, 'from necessity, not from pride or insolence. Till the end of time we shall abide in the Orthodoxy that was given to us; our Church will always seek the blessing of the Church of Tsarigrad and will be obedient in all things to the ancient piety'; and he goes on to beg 'Thy Holy Majesty' to be well inclined towards the metropolitan. The deference was still there; but the Prince had decided to act on his own.[2]

In a letter written in 1451 the Metropolitan Jonah predicted the

[1] S. M. Soloviev, *History of Russia from the Earliest Times* (in Russian), v, coll. 1483–5; V. Savva, *Muscovite Tsars and Byzantine Emperors* (in Russian), pp. 46–9, 54–5, 272–3; *Journal of the Imperial Russian Historical Society* (in Russian), XLI, no. 19, p. 71. Ivan did not however venture to use the title of Tsar when writing to his former overlord, the Khan of the Golden Horde, till 1493. *Ibid.* no. 48, pp. 180–1.

[2] *Historical Acts, collected and edited by the Archaeographical Commission* (St Petersburg; in Russian), I, no. 39, p. 72, no. 41, p. 82; E. Golubinski, *History of the Russian Church* (2nd edition; in Russian), II, 1, p. 478.

fall of Constantinople, the Second Rome. We are moving towards the notion of Moscow as the Third Rome and the Grand Prince of Muscovy as Holy Emperor.[1]

There was still enough respect for the Byzantine past for the move not to be rapid. Though henceforward the Grand Prince always appointed the Metropolitan of Russia, after a nominal election in the Byzantine manner, and though in 1470 Ivan III declared the Patriarchate as being deprived of any right over the Russian Church, the elected metropolitan still sought confirmation from the Patriarch, whom he recognized as his superior. But the absence of an Orthodox Emperor had to be filled. The Greeks might be obliged to regard the Sultan as heir to the Caesars. The Russians had no such obligation. In 1492 we find the Metropolitan Zosimus writing: 'The Emperor Constantine built a New Rome, Tsarigrad; but the sovereign and autocrat of All the Russias, Ivan Vassilievitch, the new Constantine, has laid the foundation for a new city of Constantine, Moscow.'[2] This new Constantine, Ivan III, had married in 1472 Zoe Palaeologaena, niece of the last Byzantine Emperor. She had been brought up as a Catholic; and her marriage had been arranged by the Pope, with the intention of winning Muscovy over to Rome. But the princess, rechristened Sophia on her marriage, went over wholeheartedly to Orthodoxy. Ivan thus connected himself with the last Imperial dynasty; though, curiously, he and his descendants claimed Imperial descent not from this marriage but from the far-distant marriage of Vladimir, the first Christian prince of Kiev, with the Porphyrogennete Anna, sister of Basil II, a marriage which had in fact been childless.[3] In February 1498 Ivan III had himself crowned by the Metropolitan Simon as 'Tsar, Grand Prince and Autocrat of All the Russias', at the same time co-opting his grandson and heir, Dmitri, as Grand Prince. In the

[1] *Historical Acts*, I, no. 47, p. 94.
[2] See W. K. Medlin, *Moscow and East Rome*, p. 78.
[3] S. J. Pierling, *La Russie et le Saint-Siège*, I, pp. 152 ff.; Medlin, *op. cit.* pp. 76–7; Savva, *op. cit.* p. 27.

coronation ceremony, which was a rough copy of the Byzantine, the metropolitan charged the Tsar 'to care for all souls and for all Orthodox Christendom'. The title of Tsar had now become the official title and brought with it the implication that the Russian monarch was, before God, the head of the Orthodox, that is, of the true Christian world.[1]

The Greeks were not entirely averse to the idea of a powerful monarch whose duty it was to care for the Orthodox. In 1516 the Patriarch Theoleptus I wrote to Vassily III as 'the most high and benevolent Tsar and Great King of all the Orthodox lands of Great Russia', and hinted that a Russo-Byzantine Empire might soon be created.[2] The Russians themselves went further. It was a monk of Pskov, called Philotheus, who in an address to the Tsar, delivered in 1511, made the most complete statement of Russian claims. 'It is', he declared, 'through the supreme, all-powerful and all-supporting right hand of God that emperors reign...and It has raised thee, most Serene and Supreme Sovereign and Grand Prince, Orthodox Christian Tsar and Lord of all, who art the holder of the dominions of the holy thrones of God, of the sacred, universal and apostolic Churches of the most holy Mother of God...instead of Rome and Constantinople... Now there shines through the universe, like the sun in heaven, the Third Rome, of thy sovereign Empire and of the holy synodal apostolic Church, which is in the Orthodox Christian faith... Observe and see to it, most pious Tsar, that all the Christian empires unite with thine own. For two Romes have fallen, but the third stands, and a fourth there will not be; for thy Christian Tsardom will not pass to any other, according to the mighty word of God.'

The pious monk added to his treatise a list of rules according to which the Tsar should govern. The Tsar was to obey Christian principles, of which the Church was guardian; he was to respect

---

[1] *Collection of State Charters and Treaties* (Moscow, 1813–28; in Russian), II, no. 25, pp. 27–9; Medlin, *op. cit.* pp. 78–80.
[2] *Historical Acts*, I, no. 121.

the rights, the privileges and the authority of the Church. His state was to be a theocracy, after the model of Byzantium. But the Byzantines, with their Greek common sense, had been chary of ideology. Their Emperor had been the representative of God before the people; but he was also the representative of the people before God. The ultimate sovereignty of the people had never been forgotten. At the same time centuries of secular education had prevented the Byzantine Church as an organization from dominating Byzantine life. Many members of the laity had considered themselves to be as learned in theology as any ecclesiastic. There had always been, too, an element within the Byzantine Church which had passionately disliked the power and pomp of the hierarchy and its connection with the government. Philotheus and the Russian theorists, however, knew nothing of the democratic traditions that stemmed from ancient Greece and Rome. To them the authority of the Russian monarchy came entirely from above. They added to Byzantine theory an eschatological precision that was far more extreme. Russia was the kingdom mentioned by the Prophet Daniel 'which shall never be destroyed'. It was in Russia that the woman clothed with the sun had sought refuge. The Russian theocracy, with Tsar and Church working in harmony, was instituted by God and above all earthly criticism.[1]

This view did not triumph without a struggle. At the beginning of the sixteenth century there were two distinct parties in the Russian Church. They are usually called the 'Possessors' and the 'Non-Possessors', because the one, to which the Monk Philotheus belonged, believed that the Church in order to fulfil its mission should hold property of its own; while the other believed that it should be free from the ties of property and from the connections with the State which property involved. The Possessors are sometimes called the Josephians, from their first great leader, Joseph Volotski (1440–1515) founder and abbot of the monastery of Volokolamsk, a stern, uncompromising man devoted to the cause

[1] *Historical Acts, Supplements*, I, no. 23; Soloviev, *op. cit.* v, col. 1725; Medlin, *op. cit.* pp. 93–4. See Daniel ii. 44, and Revelation xii. 1, 5, 6.

of making the Church the chief organ in a theocratic State. The Non-Possessors are sometimes called the Zavolghetsi, the men from beyond the Volga; for it was there, where the monarch's power was weaker, that they sought refuge.[1]

The Non-Possessors derived their tradition from Mount Athos, not from the Athos of rich monasteries with wide mainland estates and with splendid churches and refectories and well-stocked libraries, but from the sterner Athos of the ascetes and eremites, of the Hesychasts and Arsenites. Their spiritual ancestor was Gregory of Sinai, who had left the Holy Mountain because it was too sociable, preferring to live a life of greater solitude in the Balkan hills. Gregory's leading pupil had been the Bulgarian Euthymius, an erudite scholar who had become the last Patriarch of Tirnovo, but who had used his authority to enforce poverty and asceticism on the Bulgarian Church. After the Turks occupied Bulgaria many of his disciples migrated to Russia, bringing with them not only a knowledge of Greek mystical and hesychastic literature but also a close connection between the ascetic elements on Mount Athos and the Russian Church. The tradition that they introduced was akin to that of the Arsenites of Byzantium and the old tradition which had always opposed state control. Its first great exponent in Russia was Nil, Abbot of Sor. He was a fierce enemy to any form of state intervention in Church matters. He particularly disliked any attempt to use the arm of the State against heretics. Heresy, he maintained, was the affair of the Church alone; and the Church's weapons should be education and persuasion. For a time he exercised an influence over Ivan III; but he was no match politically for Joseph Volotski, whose ideas were far more attractive to an autocrat. He had fallen into disfavour some time before his death in 1508.[2]

The Non-Possessors were soon to find a greater leader in Maximus, surnamed the Haghiorite, or sometimes simply the Greek,

---

[1] Golubinski, *op. cit.* II, 1, pp. 620 ff.: Medlin, *op. cit.* pp. 80–5, 94–6.
[2] For Gregory of Sinai and Euthymius of Tirnovo see above, pp. 155–7. For Nilus of Sor, Golubinski, *op. cit.* pp. 555–6, 571, 581 ff.

who, as we have seen, was sent by the Patriarch Theoleptus I to Russia in response to Vassily III's request for a skilled librarian. Maximus, whose original name was Michael Trivolis, had been born in Epirus, at Arta, in 1480. During his travels through France and Italy in search of education he had arrived in Florence when it was under the influence of Savonarola, whom he greatly admired and in whose memory he joined the Dominican Order. But he was not happy in Renaissance Italy. After a short time he returned to Greece and settled on Athos, where he occupied himself principally with the libraries of the Mountain. When he came to Russia the Tsar employed him not only to build up libraries for the Russian Church but also to translate Greek religious works into Slavonic, a language which he had actually learnt from the Latin, not the Greek. His literary output, both of translations and original works, was enormous. More than anyone else he was the father of later Russian theology. But politically he was a steadfast Non-Possessor. Vassily III, who at first showed him high favour, became irritated by his refusal to admit the spiritual authority of the Tsar; and in 1525 the Metropolitan Daniel arrested him for heresy on this count. After a series of trials he was condemned and spent twenty years in imprisonment in the monastery of Volokolamsk, his opponents' headquarters. He continued to produce theological works while in detention; and when he emerged, in 1551, five years before his death, his personal prestige was immense. Even the Tsar, Ivan IV, the Terrible, went out of his way to show him honour. But his political influence was gone.[1] The Tsar placed complete reliance in the metropolitan, Macarius of Luzhetski, a prominent Josephian, who was determinedly driving the Non-Possessors underground. In Byzantium the whole tradition of the Church, going back to the days of John Chrysostom, had required it to keep a moral check upon the Emperor, while whole monasteries and even high clerics had kept

[1] For Maximus the Greek see above, p. 213; E. Dénissoff, *Maxime le Grec et l'Occident*, and 'Les Editions de Maxime le Grec', *Revue des études slaves*, XXI (1944), pp. 111–20; G. Papamichael, Μάξιμος ὁ Γραικός; and Golubinski, *op. cit.* pp. 675–712.

up a running fight against state control. This opposition was quelled at times, but it was never silenced for long. Macarius was determined to silence all opposition. He saw that it was in the smaller and poorer monasteries that the Non-Possessors flourished. He therefore forbade monasteries of the smaller type, whether coenobitic or of the older *lavra* type, which seems to have found its way to Russia, to operate. They were either closed or merged into larger units with a tighter organization, itself strictly controlled by the hierarchy; and the hierarchy was to work in close co-operation with the sovereign Prince; which meant that it followed the Prince's orders.[1]

The immediate result of Macarius's policy was seen in 1569, when the Metropolitan Philip, braver than his predecessors, ventured to reprove Ivan the Terrible for his notorious cruelty and oppression. A subservient synod deposed Philip and handed him over for punishment to the Tsar, who put him to death.[2] There were further results which made nonsense of the Possessors' claim that Moscow was the Third Rome. The Third Rome, for the nature of the claim, should have been an empire with an oecumenical outlook. But the policy of subordinating the Church to the lay ruler could not fail to make it a nationalistic policy. It was anyhow difficult for the adherents of the Third Rome theory to retain any allegiance to the Patriarch of the Second Rome, or even to pay much deference to the Pentarchy of Patriarchs—now a Tetrarchy, since Rome had lapsed into heresy. Russian clergy began to resent and despise their Greek brothers and the members of any Church that might seem to challenge their transcendental divine mission. They began to close their frontiers intellectually and temperamentally. Holy Russia became a land apart from the rest of the world.

Nevertheless the prestige of Constantinople could not be forgotten; and, in spite of Macarius's reforms, wandering monks went to and fro to visit Athos and to remind the Russians of the holy Greek tradition. The Patriarch of Constantinople was still Oecumenical Patriarch and senior official in the Orthodox Church.

[1] Medlin, *op. cit.* pp. 99–100.   [2] Soloviev, *op. cit.* VI, col. 171.

Even the most passionate advocate of the Third Rome did not quite know how to degrade him. The Tsar himself not only desired recognition from the Patriarch because of his traditional prestige, but he also realized that he could not become the heir of the Byzantine Caesars and lay head of the Orthodox oecumene without the Patriarch's good will and support. The Patriarch on his side could not afford to alienate what was now the largest, richest and most powerful section of the Orthodox Church; and, though in virtue of the arrangement made with Mehmet the Conqueror the Ottoman Sultan was lay protector of the Church and the Patriarch himself was the administrative and juridical head of the Orthodox within the Ottoman Empire, yet he could not but welcome a great lay potentate who might be able to alleviate by his influence the lot of the captive Orthodox and might some day perhaps be ready to rescue them from bondage. Just as in the middle ages the Orthodox Christians under Arab rule looked to the Byzantine Emperor for protection and the ultimate hope of freedom, so the Orthodox under Turkish rule began to look to the Russian Tsar.

In 1547 Ivan IV was crowned by his metropolitan in a ceremony which was a closer copy of the Byzantine than that of his grandfather half a century earlier. He was anointed with holy oil and underwent a form of semi-ordination, honours which Ivan III had not received.[1] In 1551 the Tsar summoned a synod of the Russian Church to discuss the ritual practices that had grown up in Russia which did not conform with those of the Greek Church. The decrees issued by the Synod, known as the *Stoglav*, or Hundred Chapters, rule that they were all correct. This unilateral decision shocked many of the Orthodox. The monks of Athos protested and the Russian monks there regarded the decisions of the synod as invalid.[2] The Patriarch of Constantinople began to be alarmed

---

[1] Medlin, *op. cit.* pp. 101–4.

[2] E. Duchesne, *Le Stoglav, passim;* Golubinski, *op. cit.* II, 1, pp. 773 ff.; N. Kapterev, *The Character of Russian Relations with the Orthodox East in the 16th and 17th Centuries* (in Russian), pp. 384 ff. It is interesting that the Stoglav makes use of the 'Donation of Constantine'.

by the high-handed actions of the Tsar. In 1561 the Patriarch Joasaph II, to whom Ivan IV had sent a number of handsome gifts, wrote to confirm his title of Tsar but delicately suggested that he should send a legate to perform a new coronation in the Patriarch's name. The Tsar ignored the proposal, which Joasaph did not venture to press.[1] Instead, the Russians put forward with increasing vigour a demand that their metropolitan be raised to the rank of Patriarch.

It was, however, difficult to achieve this ambition if the Russian Church adopted a policy of isolationism. If the elevation was to be recognized by the Orthodox world it could not be done by the Russians alone; it would need the co-operation and approval of the existing Patriarchates. Serious negotiations were only opened in 1587, when Ivan the Terrible had been dead for three years. His heir, Feodor, was a less truculent character, while the Patriarch of Constantinople, Jeremias II, was a subtle and realistic diplomat. A prudent declaration by the Tsar explicitly denied the implication given by the Synod of 1551 that the Russian Church was more Orthodox than that of Constantinople. Instead, his Church sent a deferential request to Constantinople asking that its next metropolitan should be raised by the ancient Patriarchs to Patriarchal rank, adding the hope that he should rank third in the list, after Constantinople and Alexandria, but before Antioch and Jerusalem.

The Patriarchates hesitated. Jeremias first suggested through his agent at Moscow that the Patriarch of Jerusalem should go to Russia to perform the ceremony of elevation, thus delicately indicating that Moscow would have to rank below Jerusalem. Nothing came of the suggestion; but the following autumn Jeremias himself came to Russia on an alms-gathering mission. He was promptly invited to Moscow, and early next year he presided over a ceremony in which the Metropolitan Job was raised to Patriarchal rank. After giving the new Patriarch his

---

[1] The letter is given in *Russian Historical Library* (St Petersburg; in Russian), XXII, 2, coll. 67–75.

personal blessing Jeremias added a general blessing 'for all Patriarchs of Moscow hereafter, appointed with the sanction of the Tsar, according to the election of all the holy Synod of the Russian Church'. That is to say, Constantinople recognized the permanence of the Moscow Patriarchate as well as the right of the Russian bishops to elect him in independence of Constantinople and of the Russian ruler to control the election. In the exchange of instruments that followed the election the Tsar addressed Jeremias as 'Patriarch by the grace of the holy and life-giving Spirit, coming from that most exalted apostolic throne, heir and pastor of the Church of Constantinople, Father of Fathers'. In reply Jeremias addressed the Tsar as 'Orthodox and Christ-loving, God-crowned Tsar, honoured of God and God-adorned...most serene and glorious of sovereign rulers'; and he added: 'Since the first Rome fell through the Apollinarian heresy and the second Rome, which is Constantinople, is held by infidel Turks, so then thy great Russian Tsardom, pious Tsar, which is more pious than previous kingdoms, is the third Rome...and thou alone under heaven art now called Christian Emperor for all Christians in the whole world; and therefore our act to establish the Patriarchate will be accomplished according to God's will, the prayers of the Russian saints, thy own prayer to God, and according to thy counsel.' Jeremias thus makes it clear that he recognizes Russia's claim to be the third Rome politically but not ecclesiastically. The rights and duties of the secular head of the Oecumene have passed from the Emperors of Old Rome and the Emperors of New Rome to the Emperors of Muscovy. But the supreme ecclesiastical authority is still the Pentarchy of Patriarchates, with Constantinople at its head, and Moscow added at the bottom of the list, to make up the pentad, now that Rome had been removed for heresy.[1]

---

[1] The negotiations and ceremonies are given in *Collection of State Charters and Treaties* (ed. A. Malinovsky), II, no. 59, pp. 95–103. See also Kapterev, *Character of Russian Relations with the Orthodox*, pp. 55 ff. An account in verse by Archbishop Arsenios, who was on Jeremias II's staff, is given in C. Sathas, Βιογραφικὸν Σχεδίασμα, pp. 35–81.

Jeremias's solution was ingenious and intelligent. It provided the Orthodox with a powerful lay protector in terms sufficiently flattering for the protector to abandon greater ecclesiastical claims. The Russians did not entirely give up their belief in their own superior holiness; but their relations with the Greeks henceforward improved. The Orthodox under Turkish domination felt now that they were not entirely friendless. Their confidence revived. This friendship did not, it is true, facilitate their relations with their Turkish masters, who naturally looked upon it with suspicion, nor did it in the future help them in their dealings with the Western powers. But it helped to preserve Orthodoxy.

Unfortunately the accord was soon followed by evil days for Russia. The old dynasty of Rurik came to an end with the death of Tsar Feodor in 1598. The troubled reigns of Boris Godunov, of Vassily Shiusky and of the False Dmitri led to a period when it seemed likely that the country would be overrun by the Catholic Poles. During those troubled years it was the Church that held the Russian people together. The Patriarch appeared at first as the deputy head of the State. The Patriarch Job secured the succession of Boris Godunov to the throne in 1598, and the Patriarch Hermogenes (1606–12) attempted even to act as regent during the Polish wars. But on his death the Patriarchate fell into abeyance.[1] In 1613 the Russian boyars met to elect a new Tsar, Michael Feodorovitch Romanov, a young noble of a rich and well-connected but somewhat parvenu family. Michael's father Feodor, after a distinguished lay career, had been obliged to enter the Church, under the name of Philaret, in order to avoid prosecution by Boris Godunov. He had done well there. Basil Shiuski had thought of making him Patriarch in 1606 but had changed his mind; and Philaret had become anti-Patriarch under the aegis of the False Dmitri. But the Poles mistrusted him and put him in prison. The young Tsar was determined to have Philaret as his Patriarch. After a peace-treaty with Poland was signed at Deulino in December 1618, Philaret was released, and arrived in Moscow

---

[1] See Medlin, *op. cit.* pp. 127–9.

the following June. The Patriarch of Jerusalem, Theophanes, happened to be in Russia at the time, begging for alms. He presided over a ceremony in which the Tsar first announced his choice of Philaret as Patriarch and, on Philaret's acceptance, asked Theophanes to consecrate him. A message from the Patriarch of Constantinople was read out, giving his blessing and confirming the right of 'the Russian throne of God's Church' to appoint Patriarchs in the future.[1]

From 1619 till 1633, when Philaret died, Russia enjoyed the spectacle of a father and son as Patriarch and Tsar. As Philaret not only possessed his son's filial respect but also had far the stronger personality, the Church gained enormously in power. Acts were passed in the Patriarch's as well as the Tsar's name; and the Patriarch in fact presided over the government.[2] Philaret's successors, Joasaph and Joseph, were mild and pious men without political ambitions; but the prestige of the Church remained high.[3] This might have led to a renewal of the claim that Moscow should be the Third Rome ecclesiastically, to the detriment of Constantinople. But, owing to the international position, even Philaret found that he needed the whole-hearted good will of his Greek colleagues. The period of troubles had left the Poles in control of the whole Ukraine, including the holy city of Kiev, the cradle of Russian Christianity. The Poles, with Jesuit help, were determined to bring the Churches of the conquered provinces of Ruthenia and the Ukraine into the Roman fold. Where they found local traditions too strong they set up Uniate Churches, which should keep their liturgy and ritual and Slavonic language unchanged, so long as they admitted the complete supremacy of the Roman Pontiff. Moscow needed the help of the other Orthodox Patriarchates to meet the attack. The careers of Meletius Pegas of Alexandria and of Cyril Lucaris illustrated how Greek prelates, from Egypt as well as from Constantinople, occupied themselves with the task of rescuing these threatened Orthodox. The Jesuits were well aware of the position. Their sedulous in-

[1] *Ibid.* pp. 130–4. [2] *Ibid.* pp. 135–8. [3] *Ibid.* p. 139.

trigues in Constantinople were largely aimed at neutralizing these efforts and at driving a wedge between the uncompromising Orthodoxy of Moscow and the more elastic faith of the seventeenth-century Greeks.

The Church of Kiev was saved more by its own efforts than by those of the Greeks. The need of the Greeks to find allies against Roman infiltration, backed as it was by the great Catholic powers, had obliged them to seek the friendship of the Protestants. Cyril Lucaris, when working in Poland, had definitely co-operated with Protestants. But Protestantism was no more attractive to the Ukrainians than was Catholicism. Greek help became slightly suspect.[1]

It had nevertheless been of some value. The Poles had arrested or exiled all the Orthodox prelates who would not submit to Rome. The Patriarch of Jerusalem, Theophanes, passed soon afterwards through the Ukraine on his way to induct Philaret at Moscow. He paused at Kiev, where he secretly ordained seven Orthodox bishops. When the Poles discovered about the ordination they attempted to arrest the bishops. But the Orthodox found an unexpected ally. The Cossacks of the Dnieper and the Don, semi-nomadic freebooters who lived on the frontier-lands between Slav and Turco-Tatar territory and who had never hitherto shown signs of piety, came out fiercely in favour of Orthodoxy and threatened to attack the Poles. The Poles needed the good will of the Cossacks to preserve their south-eastern frontier. The persecution of the Orthodox in the Ukraine ceased. They were allowed to reopen their schools and reorganize their church life.[2]

At this juncture they found a leader. Peter Moghila was the son of a Moldavian prince and had been educated at Paris, but had then taken orders in the Orthodox Church. He came to Kiev in about 1630 and in 1633, at the age of thirty-seven, was elected to its Metropolitan see. During the fourteen years of his episcopate he changed the whole attitude of the Ukrainian Church. Realizing that to combat the Catholics it was necessary to understand

---

[1] See above, pp. 262–6, and below, pp. 339–40.   [2] See above, p. 264.

their theology and practices, he founded schools for the Orthodox clergy and laity where Latin was taught as well as Greek and Slavonic and Western lay and clerical writings and modern science were studied. Under his vigorous guidance the Theological Academy at Kiev became one of the best schools of the time, and was to play an important part in the future; for many of the reformers of Peter the Great's time were educated within its walls. Moghila had tried to persuade Philaret to establish a similar academy at Moscow. Had Philaret lived longer the school might have come into being; but when in 1640 Moghila approached the new Patriarch with definite proposals, they were politely shelved.[1]

Moghila had little use for the Church of Constantinople, distracted as it was in his time by the struggle between Cyril Lucaris and his enemies. He was far better grounded in Latin than in Greek theology; and his training had left him with a sympathy for the doctrinal outlook of the Romans. Cyril's Calvinism was abhorrent to him. As we shall see later, he tried to introduce into Orthodox belief a degree of precision that was somewhat alien to its spirit.[2] But, apart from the theological details of his reforms, he had a great effect on the whole Russian Church. The young Tsar Alexis Mikhailovitch (1645–76), whose reign saw the recovery of Kiev and the Ukraine for Russia, was deeply interested in them. He was devoutly religious but no obscurantist. The most influential man at his court was his confessor, Stephen Vonifatiev, who believed that the Russian Church should not be allowed to stagnate in isolation. The Tsar not only snubbed the efforts of his Patriarch, Joseph, to curb Stephen and the reformers, but sent to Kiev for teachers to translate books of all sorts, historical and scientific as well as theological and liturgical, into Russian. But he found that Moghila's pupils were most of them insufficiently grounded in Greek and too deeply affected by Latin scholasticism. He came to the conclusion that it would be better to emphasize

---

[1] Kapterev, *Character of Russian Relations with the Orthodox*, p. 482.
[2] See below, pp. 340–3.

the Greek background of Orthodoxy and to bring his Church into line with the older Patriarchates.[1]

In this he was influenced by a learned Greek, the Patriarch Paisius of Jerusalem, who visited Moscow in 1649. While in Moscow Paisius was greatly impressed by a priest called Nikon, born Nikita Minin, whom he persuaded the Tsar to make Metropolitan of Novgorod in 1649, and who became Patriarch of Moscow in 1652. In six years, until he was forced to abdicate in 1658, Nikon reformed the whole Russian Church. The details of his reforms, most of them concerned with ritual practices, do not concern us here, except in so far as they brought the Russian Church once more into line with Constantinople. As a result the Tsar became once more accepted as the great lay protector of all the Orthodox; and the Greeks were no longer tempted to flirt with the Protestants or with Rome in their search for friends. Amongst the Russians themselves the reforms roused passionate opposition in many quarters, especially in the monasteries. The Old Believers, as they were called, ably led by the saintly Archpriest Avvakum, held that Holy Russia had no need for foreign-inspired reforms. She was the Third Rome and the sole recipient of divine guidance. By a curious twist of history the spiritual heirs of the Non-Possessors of the sixteenth century, who had been driven underground for their attachment to Greek ways, were these pious monks and holy men who were driven underground for refusing to countenance a revived association with the Greeks. Even the Russians established on Mount Athos amongst Greeks—but Greeks who were themselves suspicious of Constantinople—felt little sympathy for Nikon's progressive activities. But Nikon himself went too far, not in his ritual or administrative reforms, but in an attempt to assert the supreme authority of the Church to an extent more akin to the spirit of the medieval Papacy than that of Byzantium. He forced Tsar Alexis to do penance for Ivan the Terrible's murder of the Metropolitan Philip

[1] Kapterev, *Patriarch Nikon and his Beginnings* (in Russian), pp. 164 ff., and pp. 19–22: W. K. Medlin, *op. cit.* pp. 148–53.

nearly a century before; but, when he began to call himself Great
Ruler (Veliki Gossudar) of Russia, a title that had been given to
Philaret, but only because he was the physical as well as the
spiritual Father of the Tsar, Alexis, grown self-reliant in his
middle age, would not endure it. Nikon fell. But his reforms
lasted.[1]

The Patriarchate of Moscow was never again to enjoy such
power. Alexis's son, Peter the Great, saw in it too great a potential
challenge to his authority. On the death of the Patriarch Adrian in
1700 he refused to appoint a successor, merely nominating an
'Exarch in charge of the Patriarchal see'. A few years later he
formally abolished the Patriarchate; which was not revived till
after the Communist revolution. The abolition of the Patriarchate
had no effect on the relations between Russia and the Greeks.
By strict canonical law the Russian Church should have come
again under the Constantinopolitan Patriarchate; but in fact the
Metropolitan of Moscow was held to be the locum tenens of the
Patriarchal see, in independence of Constantinople. Meanwhile
the Tsar, with his growing power and the title of Emperor that
he had assumed, was regarded more than ever as the Protector of
the Orthodox Churches; while the conquest of Constantinople,
the city of the Patriarchs, became a dominant aim of Tsarist
policy. Russia was henceforward to play a dominant role in the
history of the Greeks.[2]

---

[1] The earliest life of Nikon was written by his disciple I. Shusherin, *Life of the
Holy Patriarch Nikon* (in Russian), published by the Imperial Academy of
Sciences, St Petersburg, in 1817. For his career see also N. Kapterev, *Patriarch
Nikon and his Beginnings*, and *Patriarch Nikon and Tsar Alexis* (both in Russian);
William Palmer's 6-volume *The Patriarch and the Tsar*; and the well-referenced
account in Medlin, *op. cit.* pp. 152–210. For the Old Believers see the auto-
biography of the Archpriest Avvakum, *La Vie de l'Archiprêtre Avvakum, écrit
par lui-même*, translated and edited by P. Pascal. See also F. C. Conybeare,
Russian Dissenters, pp. 79 ff. For a description of the Russian Church in Nikon's
time see Paul of Antioch, *The Travels of Macarius*, selected by W. L. Ridding,
pp. 26–90.

[2] Medlin, *op. cit.* pp. 211–23; R. Wittram, 'Peters des Grossen Verhältnis zur
Religion und den Kirchen', *Historische Zeitschrift*, CLXXIII (1952), pp. 261–96.

CHAPTER 9

THE DEFINITION OF DOCTRINE

Negotiations with the great Protestant Churches of the West and the need to meet the attack of the Church of Rome obliged the Orthodox to give thought to their own doctrines. Their potential friends as well as their enemies continually asked them for precise information about details of their belief. It was embarrassing, at times even humiliating, to have so often to reply that there was no authorized doctrine on these points. There was no doubt that relations with the Anglican Church were seriously damaged by the variety of answers given by responsible Greek ecclesiastics when questioned on transubstantiation. It was not surprising that the questioners, however well disposed they might be, began to suspect the honesty of the Greek episcopate. Confronted by theologians who liked clarity and accuracy, the Orthodox found that their traditional apophatic avoidance of precision was out of date and harmful to themselves. The West did not share their spiritual modesty. It considered their answers dusty; it was hot for certainties.

Among the Greek divines there were now many who had received their higher education in Italian or other Western universities; and this education predisposed them towards the Western attitude. In spite of the traditions of their Church they began to search for a more systematic and philosophical pattern. Their searching took forms that were all the more varied because of the lack of definitions in the past. We find Cyril Lucaris on the one hand and Peter Moghila on the other both sincerely believing that they were interpreting Orthodox doctrine along legitimate lines. There was nothing inherently wrong in this. Indeed, Orthodoxy owed much of its power of endurance to the breadth of its basis. But in a world of religious polemics this breadth might be a weakness. The Orthodox could not defend their doctrines if they did not know what they were. There arose a demand for religious Confessions which should guide them in their relations with others.

Hitherto the only *summa* of theology accepted by the Orthodox had been the *Fountain of Knowledge*, written in the eighth century by John of Damascus.[1] It had been written at a time when Christological problems were the chief concern of theology; it omitted to pronounce on many of the problems that worried the theologians of the seventeenth century. And, even though John was generally held to be the last of the inspired Fathers of the Church and his opinions were deeply respected, they did not constitute essential articles of faith. It was possible for a divine as learned and pious as Mark Eugenicus to suggest a doctrine of predestination that was not quite consonant with the Father's. Others of the Father's rulings could be interpreted in a number of ways. After all, the Church of Rome, too, regarded the *Fountain of Knowledge* as being theologically correct. It did not answer the present need. Later Byzantine scholars had produced short summaries of Orthodox theology, notably the Emperor Manuel II and the Patriarch Gennadius. But both had been writing to explain Christianity to a Muslim public; they had avoided controversial details.[2]

The first attempt to explain Orthodox belief to a non-Orthodox Christian audience, apart from the detailed polemical arguments of anti-Roman theologians, is found in the answers that the Patriarch Jeremias II sent to the Lutherans. Jeremias belonged to the old school with its apophatic traditions, and at the same time he wanted to assure the Lutherans that even though he disagreed with them he wished them well. He was therefore less concerned in making a full statement of his own theology than in pointing out courteously but firmly the points on which he could not accept Lutheran theology.[3]

Cyril Lucaris's Confession, issued some thirty years later, was

[1] John of Damascus, *De Fide Orthodoxa* (Πηγὴ Γνώσεως), in *M.P.G.*, xcIV.
[2] See above, p. 193.   [3] See above, pp. 248–54.

intended to cover the whole range of his belief. But, though Cyril hoped for its acceptance by the Church, it was a personal statement, unlike Jeremias's, which had been issued with the concurrence of the Holy Synod; and its Calvinistic tendencies raised such a storm that an authoritative Confession seemed more than ever necessary.[1]

It was such a Confession that Peter Moghila, Metropolitan of Kiev, hoped to provide, both to check the controversies that Cyril had aroused, and to keep his own Ruthenians and Ukrainians firm in the Faith. But Moghila, though a Moldavian by birth, had been educated in the West. He was strongly opposed to the Roman Church, but his opposition was political rather than theological. He saw the Roman clergy as the instruments of Polish imperialism; he disliked Papal supremacy because of the political activities of the Papacy. It is possible that he would have been quite willing to accept some sort of Uniate status for his Church had he not been convinced that the Papacy would use submission to enforce its integration with some Catholic power. Doctrinally he was far more in sympathy with Rome than with any Protestant Church or even than with the old traditions of Orthodoxy. His whole training inclined him towards a scholastic definition of the Faith.[2]

Peter Moghila composed his *Orthodoxa Confessio Fidei* some time before 1640. He wrote it in Latin, which he knew far better than Greek; indeed, he was an indifferent Greek scholar. As in the case of Cyril Lucaris and his Confession, attempts have been made to show that it was not his own work. But, though he may have consulted with such men as Isaiah Kozlovsky, higoumene of the monastery of St Nicholas at Kiev, he was too self-confident and domineering a man not to have taken full personal responsibility

[1] See above, pp. 276–81.
[2] The best work on Peter Moghila and his Confession is A. Malvy and M. Viller, *La Confession Orthodoxe de Pierre Moghila, Orientalia Christiana, Analecta* x (1927), giving the full text. For his life see *ibid.* pp. ix–xvii. See also E. Legrand, *Bibliographie Hellénique; description raisonnée des ouvrages publiés en Grec par des Grecs au 17e siècle*, IV, pp. 104–60; A. Florovski, *Le Conflit de deux traditions*, pp. 50–6.

for it. In 1640 he summoned a Council to meet at Kiev, in order to decide what liturgical and educational books should be circulated amongst the clergy of his metropolitan see, to counter the works in Polish circulated by the Jesuits. Various books written by his pupils and friends were officially recommended. But the main purpose of the Council was to approve and adopt Moghila's Confession. Moghila did not have the complete success that he desired. There were points in the Confession which troubled many members of the Council. At the end of the discussions it was decided to accept the Confession provisionally, but to send a copy to Constantinople for confirmation by the Patriarch.[1]

The Patriarch at the time was Parthenius I, a man of broad sympathies who was desperately trying to restore peace to the Church after the disputes that had arisen out of Cyril Lucaris's career. He reserved judgment over Moghila's Confession. Instead, he sent back to Kiev a treatise, drawn up by the Holy Synod, dealing only with the Calvinistic errors in Lucaris's Confession. He asked the Council to study and endorse it. But Moghila wanted more definite support. He had recourse to his friend Basil, Prince of Moldavia.[2]

Basil, surnamed Lupul, the Wolf, was the son of an Albanian adventurer and a Moldavian heiress, who had secured the Moldavian throne in 1634 after a series of complicated intrigues and managed to hold it for twenty years. He was a capable administrator and a brilliant financier and soon was the richest man in the Christian East. Judiciously placed gifts kept him on good terms with the Ottoman authorities. Partly from ambition and partly from genuine piety he was ready to show generosity towards the Orthodox Churches. His chief religious adviser was Cyril Lucaris's opponent, Meletius Syrigos, who prejudiced him against Lucaris. So, till Lucaris's death, he would not help the Church of

[1] Malvy and Viller, *op. cit.* pp. xlv–xlvii; Legrand, *Bibliographie Hellénique au 17e siècle*, pp. 104–10.
[2] Malvy and Viller, *op. cit.* pp. lii ff.; J. Pargoire, 'Meletios Syrigos', *Echos d'Orient*, XII (1920), p. 24.

Constantinople, though he gave lavish presents to the Eastern Patriarchates. But since 1638 he had not only paid off all the debts of the Constantinopolitan Patriarchate but had reorganized the management of its finances. He saw himself now as the chief lay patron of Orthodoxy and even dreamed of reviving Byzantium. It was said that at his request the Patriarch Parthenius had prepared a ritual for his Imperial coronation and that his crown had already been made. His pretensions were naturally resented by the Tsar of Russia; but Michael Romanov, after the death of his forceful father, Philaret, Patriarch of Moscow, was too ineffectual to make any successful protest. Michael's resentment was all the more bitter because the Church of Kiev, under Moghila's leadership, looked to the Prince of Moldavia rather than to the Tsar for lay support. This did not improve the relations between Kiev and Moscow.[1]

Basil wished the Church that he patronized to be orderly and united. Urged by Moghila and supported by Syrigos he demanded that a Council should be summoned where a definitive Confession should be authorized. On his insistence a Council was convened to meet at his capital, Jassy, in September 1642. The Church of Constantinople was represented by Meletius Syrigos and by the ex-Metropolitan of Nicaea, the Church of Kiev by Isaiah Kozlovsky and two other prelates. The Church of Moscow sent three delegates, and the Oriental Patriarchs, all of them on Basil's pay-roll, were also represented, though they were careful to maintain that this was only a local Council, without Oecumenical significance. The Prince of Moldavia presided.[2]

Syrigos was an astute politician. Fearing trouble, he insisted that the deliberations of the Council should be held in private. In consequence our only reliable information about its meetings comes, unexpectedly, from a Protestant, a Danish subject of Italian origin called Scogardi, who was Prince Basil's private physician and was in his employer's confidence. According to his

---

[1] For Basil Lupul see N. Jorga, *Byzance après Byzance*, pp. 163–81.
[2] J. D. Mansi, *Sacrorum Conciliorum Collectio*, XXIV, p. 1720.

account, the first item on the agenda was the condemnation of Cyril Lucaris's Confession. The Muscovites at once protested, no doubt more from contrariness than from any love for Lucaris. The Confession, they said, was irrelevant; it was a personal statement with nothing to do with Orthodoxy in general and was probably anyhow a forgery. To avoid an open quarrel Basil supported the Russian request that the item be passed over. Instead, the Council condemned as heretical a short Catechism attributed to Lucaris but in fact written by one of his followers, without making any mention of the late Patriarch himself. The next, and chief, item was a discussion of Moghila's Confession, which Meletius Syrigos had translated from Latin into Greek and which he had undertaken to present to the Council. But Syrigos shrewdly suspected that much of Moghila's doctrine might be a little too Latin for Orthodox tastes. In making the translation he had therefore made certain emendations and omissions in the text. Moghila himself seems to have accepted some of the alterations, while, with his imperfect knowledge of Greek, he may not have noticed others of them.[1] In a Shorter Catechism which he prepared later for the benefit of Russian readers some of the alterations appear but others are omitted.[2]

The Council of Jassy endorsed Moghila's Confession in the form submitted by Syrigos, and concluded its business with recommendations for a few minor administrative reforms. Soon afterwards the Patriarch Parthenius II of Constantinople summoned a special meeting of the Holy Synod, which gave its approval to the decrees passed at Jassy. They were also endorsed by the Patriarchs Joannicius of Alexandria, Macarius of Antioch and Paisius of Jerusalem.[3] All this approval did not, however, raise the Confession into becoming part of the official dogma of the Church. Only an Oecumenical Council could have done so; the Council

---

[1] Scogardi's account is given in E. de Hurmuzaki, *Documente Privatore la Istoria Românilor*, IV, I, p. 668; Malvy and Viller, *op. cit.* pp. xlix–li.

[2] For the catechism see Malvy and Viller, *op. cit.* pp. cxlv–cxxx.

[3] *Ibid.* pp. li–liii, lxii; C. Delikanis, Πατριαρχικὰ Ἔγγραφα, III, pp. 31–2.

of Jassy was not Oecumenical, and the support of the various Patriarchal Synods could not make it so. Thus, though we find the Patriarch Paisius of Constantinople writing in 1654 to Nikon of Moscow recommending the Confession, two years later the Patriarch Parthenius III held a synod at Constantinople which denounced it as being tainted with Roman doctrine. But Parthenius III, who respected Cyril Lucaris's memory sufficiently to give his remains decent reburial and who was anxious to please the Muscovite Church and support it in its disputes with Kiev, was put to death by the Turks in 1657 on the grounds that he was intriguing with the Tsar.[1] There was a reaction in favour of the Confession. In 1662 the Patriarch Nectarius of Jerusalem declared that it 'is absolutely pure in doctrine and contains no novelty taken from another religion';[2] and in 1667 a Greek edition was printed in Syrigos's version at Amsterdam and was circulated round the Orthodox Churches with the full approval of the Constantinopolitan Patriarchate.[3] But its doctrines have never been regarded as essential articles of faith.

As a complete compendium of dogma Moghila's Confession is full of deficiencies. Nevertheless, if we exclude Lucaris's personal Confession, it represents the first attempt since the days of John of Damascus to give precision to the main beliefs of the Church; and it tries to answer questions that had recently arisen during discussions with the Western Churches. On the question of the Procession of the Holy Spirit Moghila's formula runs that: 'the Holy Spirit proceeds from the Father alone, in so far as the Father is the source and principle of divinity'. This is a formula which many Roman divines had been prepared to accept at the Council of Florence and which many today have pronounced to be

[1] Delikanis, *op. cit.* p. 39.

[2] The text of Nectarius's commendation is given in the preface to *The Orthodox Confession of the Catholic and Apostolic Eastern Church, faithfully translated from the Original from the version of Peter Mogila* (ed. J. J. Overbeck), pp. 6–9. Nectarius admits that he has not read the Latin version so cannot pronounce on it.

[3] For the various editions see Malvy and Viller, *op. cit.* pp. lvii–lix.

unobjectionable. It is also the formula which was accepted when the Anglican Church had discussions with the Old Catholic communities and the Orthodox at Bonn in 1875.[1] But to many Orthodox the qualifying clause has always seemed to be unnecessary and undesirable, even though not actually heretical; indeed, it is open to a number of interpretations.

Moghila himself is known to have accepted the Roman doctrine of Purgatory and the immediate entry into Paradise of the souls of the saints. At the Council of Kiev Isaiah Kozlovsky, acting as his spokesman, advocated both doctrines; but, after a long discussion the matter was referred to the decision of the Patriarch of Constantinople, who avoided a direct answer. Syrigos foresaw that the doctrines would arouse bitter controversy at Jassy and when translating the Confession entirely altered the text, so as to deny the existence of Purgatory and any knowledge of the fate of the souls of the saints. When preparing his own Shorter Catechism later, Moghila prudently omitted the whole question.[2] On Predestination and the Foreknowledge of God the Confession follows the doctrine of George Scholarius Gennadius, itself based on that of John of Damascus. This represented the general view of the Orthodox. On the question of Faith and Works the Confession adopted verbally the doctrines enunciated by the Patriarch Jeremias II in his reply to the Lutherans, but added categorically: 'They sin who hope to be saved by Faith alone, without good works.'[3]

On Transubstantiation both Moghila and Syrigos in his translation accepted a doctrine similar to the Latin, interpreting it in a definitely material sense.[4] But the Greek doctrine of the Epiklesis, the belief that the change in the bread and wine was only completed by the invocation to the Holy Spirit, was rejected by Moghila, who took the Latin view that it was completed when the words of Christ were repeated. This aroused fierce argument at the Council of Kiev; and the matter was included with those to

[1] Malvy and Viller, *op. cit.* pp. 127–8 and notes.
[2] *Ibid.* pp. 144–52, xlvi–xlvii, cxvii.
[3] *Ibid.* pp. 19–21, 107–8.   [4] *Ibid.* pp. 34, 60–1.

be referred to the Patriarch. In his translation of the Confession Syrigos altered the text to include the doctrine of the Epiklesis. Had it been rejected it is doubtful whether the Confession would have been endorsed. But Moghila, when he discovered the alteration, was not pleased. He held to his view, which he restated in his Shorter Catechism.[1]

Certain phrases in the Confession which Syrigos allowed to remain indicate that Moghila did not accept Palamas's doctrine of the Energies; but it was nowhere categorically denied and did not come up for discussion.[2]

Various minor points on which the Confession's formulae were perhaps a little more precise than the Greeks would have preferred, were accepted without opposition. There had been some discussion at the Council of Kiev over the origin of the human soul; but this was because some of the Ruthenian divines had traducianist notions. Moghila's formula, that the soul was created by God and immediately infused into the body as soon as the body was formed by generation, was accepted by the Council of Jassy.[3]

To a student of Orthodoxy Peter Moghila's Confession has a curiously alien ring. It was clearly inspired by a Latin-trained mind. The explanation of the Creed and the Seven Sacraments, the listing and arrangement of the Three Theological Virtues and the Seven Deadly Sins, as well as much of the actual phrasing, show how deeply Moghila was steeped in scholastic theology. Some Orthodox theologians have believed that the Confession is little more than an adaptation of the Catechism published a few decades earlier by the Latin saint, Peter Canisius. Meletius Syrigos had done his best to render it into a more acceptable form; and at the time it seemed to answer a need. It was difficult for the Orthodox to reject it, after the approval given to it by so many Patriarchs and synods. Even the Russians, in spite of their coolness towards Moghila, signified their acceptance. The Patriarch Joachim of Moscow ordered in 1685 its translation into Slavonic, a transla-

[1] Malvy and Viller, *op. cit.* pp. l, lxxxviii. See Scogardi's account, above, p. 343, n. 1.   [2] Malvy and Viller, *op. cit.* pp. 71–2.   [3] *Ibid.* pp. 12–13.

tion that was eventually published in 1696, by order of Tsar Peter and his mother, the Tsaritsa Elizabeth; and the Patriarch Adrian pronounced it to be divinely inspired. Peter the Great himself, with his liking for Western modes of thought, ranked it with the works of the old Church Fathers.[1] But there was always a current of reserve about it in the East. In the tradition of the Orthodox Church Moghila's Confession ranks as a personal expression of faith which is perfectly Orthodox but which carries no obligatory authority.[2]

By 1691 criticism of the Confession was growing again. The Patriarchs Callinicus of Constantinople and Dositheus of Jerusalem tried to check the critics by pronouncing it to be orthodox and irreprehensible;[3] while Dositheus showed his approval still further by writing a long preface to an edition published in Greek in 1699 at Snagov by the hieromonk Anthimus of Iberia.[4] But it seemed clear that a wider exposition of the Faith was needed and that Dositheus was the right man to prepare it. He was a Peloponnesian, born near Corinth in 1641 into a family that claimed descent from the Notaras family of Constantinople. The Patriarch Paisius of Jerusalem, himself also a Peloponnesian, had been a friend of his parents and offered to arrange for his education at Constantinople, where his chief teacher was the philosopher John Caryophyllus. Caryophyllus, who was a close friend of Cyril Lucaris and shared many of his unorthodox views, was a brilliant teacher who, in spite of his personal taste for Neo-Aristotelianism, inspired many of the best Greek theological brains of his time. In Constantinople Dositheus learnt Latin and Italian as well as Turkish and Arabic. Paisius took him into his service. When he was nineteen he accompanied Paisius as his secretary on a voyage to the Caucasian countries, and was with him when he died at Castelorizzo in 1660. Paisius's successor on the Patriarchal throne

---

[1] *Ibid.* p. lxvii. See Mansi, *op. cit.* xxxvii, pp. 27–8.
[2] E.g. S. Bulgakov, *The Orthodox Church* (trans. E. S. Cram), p. 47.
[3] Mansi, *op. cit.* xxxvii, pp. 465–6.
[4] Legrand, *Bibliographie Hellénique au 17e siècle*, iii, pp. 68–9, iv, pp. 151–2.

of Jerusalem, Nectarius, appointed him soon afterwards to be his representative in Moldavia, a post of responsibility, as the Patriarchate was endowed with large estates there. In 1668 he was raised to the metropolitan see of Caesarea in Palestine. Next year, when Nectarius abdicated, he became at the age of twenty-seven Patriarch of Jerusalem. He reigned there for thirty-nine years, until his death in 1707. During these years his learning, his energy and his high probity made him the most influential and revered figure in the Christian East.[1]

Dositheus was deeply worried about the state of the Orthodox Church. It had, as he indicated in his preface to Moghila's Confession, four outward dangers to face. First there was Lutheranism and, secondly, Calvinism, both of them attractive because they shared with Orthodoxy the enmity of Rome, and both of them with many worthy adherents, but both of them frankly heretical. Thirdly there was the reform of the calendar, carried out by Pope Gregory XIII in 1583. Dositheus disliked this reform, not only because it altered in the name of science a traditional and hallowed system, but also, and perhaps still more, because it had been imposed unilaterally by the Papacy; and one by one the countries of the world were beginning to accept it. Fourthly, and worst of all, there was the Jesuit Order. Dositheus was frankly terrified of the Jesuits. When he had been working in Moldavia he had learnt about their operations in neighbouring countries and had been told horrifying tales of their behaviour, many of which he noted down, such as the story of the Ruthenian princess whom they had converted and then persuaded to exhume the rotting corpse of her father so as to have him baptized in the Latin rite. He was

---

[1] There is a vast literature about Dositheus. His nephew and successor, Chrysanthos Notaras, inserted a short and eulogistic biography at the beginning of his *History of the Patriarchs of Jerusalem*, which Chrysanthos edited after his death. For summaries of his career see T. H. Papadopoullos, *Studies and Documents relating to the History of the Greek Church and People under Turkish Domination, Bibliotheca Graeca Aevi Posterioris*, I, pp. 154–6; M. Jugie, *Theologia Dogmatica Christianorum Orientalium ab Ecclesia Catholica Dissidentium*, I, pp. 516–17. See also A. P. Palmieri, *Dositeo, Patriarca Greco di Gerusalemme*, passim, a full biography from a Latin point of view.

particularly alarmed by the successs of their propaganda which hinted that the Orthodox hierarchy was tinged by Protestant heresies. He even suspected them of having altered if not entirely rewritten Cyril Lucaris's famous Confession to prove their point.[1] It was to prove that his Church was clear of such Protestant tendencies that he gave his support to Moghila's Confession. But the Jesuits' example showed him what was the greatest internal need of his Church. The Jesuits were successful because of their excellent educational system. It was in their education that the Orthodox were most deficient. Dositheus encouraged the creation and reform of schools and academies. In 1680 he erected at the expense of his Patriarchate a printing-press at Jassy in Moldavia, where he had funds at his disposal and where it would be free from the difficulties which the Turkish authorities would have created at Jerusalem or Constantinople. Hitherto, since the destruction of the short-lived press that Lucaris had instituted at Constantinople, the Orthodox had been obliged to have their books printed abroad, mostly at Venice, Geneva or Amsterdam, or in the Ukraine, where the standard of printing was low. The Jerusalem Press at Jassy now became the most important printing house in the Orthodox world.[2]

He himself wrote many of the Press's publications. His literary activity was unending. He prepared editions of a number of the Fathers of the Church as well as of works by more recent theologians, such as his predecessor Nectarius. Indeed, he rescued many works from being entirely lost. Of his own works three treatises, strongly attacking the Church of Rome, were published in his lifetime, the *Tomos Katallagis*, the *Tomos Agapis* and the *Tomos Charas*, the last appearing two years before his death. These were

[1] E. Legrand, *Bibliographie Hellénique au 17e siècle*, III, pp. 68–9 (Dositheus's 'four dangers'). Dr J. Covel, *Some Account of the Present Greek Church*, p. liv, says that he had received letters from Dositheus in which the Pope is called 'Savage Beast, wild Bear, the Abomination of Desolation...', and the Franciscans 'wild Beasts, most unmerciful Murderers, Devils'. For Dositheus's doubts over Lucaris's authorship of his Confession see his Ἱστορία, p. 1170.

[2] Papadopoullos, *op. cit.* pp. 155–6: T. Ware, *Eustratios Argenti*, pp. 31–2.

short but clearly expressed homilies, largely compiled from earlier theological works. His greatest work did not appear until 1715, eight years after his death, edited and produced by his nephew and successor, Chrysanthos Notaras. It is called a *History of the Patriarchs of Jerusalem* but is in fact a history of the whole Eastern Church, its councils, its schisms and its leading figures, with comparatively little about Jerusalem itself. It contains numerous digressions on theology and history. Dositheus made full use of his wide reading, not only in the Church Fathers and the Byzantine and neo-Byzantine historians but also in the Arabic chroniclers and in Western writers such as Gregory of Tours. It is a frankly polemical work, missing no opportunity for underlining the errors of the Latins. Dositheus dates the beginning of the schism with the West, with some reason, back to the days of the early Church. His standards of scholarship were not perhaps those of today; and a number of his statements can be proved to be inaccurate in the light of modern research. But he was the equal of any scholar of his time. If his interpretation of events was never very objective, he was no less objective than were, in their different ways, writers such as Voltaire or even Gibbon. He deserves to rank as a great historian.[1]

Dositheus believed that the Church was in need of a wider statement of doctrine than that provided by Moghila's Confession. In 1672, early in his Patriarchate, he asked his brother of Constantinople, Dionysius IV, surnamed 'The Muslim', because he had a number of Muslim relatives, to send him an encyclical letter which he could present to the Synod of Jerusalem as a statement of the true faith. Dionysius therefore composed a statement with the help of three of his predecessors, Parthenius IV, Clement and Methodius III, who countersigned it; and he dispatched it to Jerusalem to be read out to the synod which Dositheus had convened. The Synod of Jerusalem endorsed it. Dositheus then edited it for publication. A few years later it appeared as one of the first

[1] The History was published at Bucharest in 1715. For its contents see Jorga, *Byzance après Byzance*, pp. 196–8.

The Definition of Doctrine

productions of the Jerusalem Press at Jassy. It became generally known as the 'Confession of Dositheus'.[1] The 'Confession of Dositheus' lacks the neat scholastic arrangement of Moghila's Confession. It treats each essential doctrine one by one but not in any logical order; and the treatment is discursive. There is a tendency to qualify dogmatic definitions wherever possible, in the old tradition which holds that our knowledge about theology must necessarily be incomplete apart from what has been already divinely revealed. Nevertheless the Confession did attempt to give clear answers on the main dogmas that had recently been in dispute. In opposition to the Latins it declared categorically that the Holy Spirit descended from the Father alone, without the qualifying phrase inserted in Moghila's Confession. It disallowed the doctrine of Purgatory. It insisted on the use of leavened bread in the Sacrament and stated that the Epiklesis was necessary to complete the change in the elements. It maintained that only the Orthodox calendar of fasts and feasts was correct. It explicitly denied the claim of the Roman see to have any superior position in the Church. Unlike Moghila's Confession, which implicitly denied Palamism, its phraseology on the Vision of God was Palamite. But it was equally outspoken in denying aspects of Protestant theology. It came out firmly in favour of transubstantiation, using the word μετουσίωσις, and declaring that the bread and wine of the Sacrament became truly and fully the body and blood of Christ. It approved the intercession of saints and the plenary remission of sins by a ceremony of extreme unction. The number of Sacraments was definitely stated to be seven. It laid down that reverence should be paid to holy images, along the lines fixed by the Second Council of Nicaea. Indeed, it went further than the Council of Nicaea in permitting icons of the Father and the Holy Spirit, whereas the

[1] The full Greek text of the 'Confession of Dositheus' is given in J. N. Karmiris, Τὰ Δογματικὰ Συμβολικὰ Μνημεῖα τῆς Ὀρθοδόξου καθολικῆς Ἐκκλησίας, ii, pp. 746–73. See also J. N. W. B. Robertson, *The Acts and Decrees of the Synod of Jerusalem, sometimes called the Council of Bethlehem*, which contains an English translation of the Confession (pp. 110–62).

Byzantines had held that only the Incarnate Divinity could be depicted. It denied Predestination in the Calvinist sense, insisting on the freedom of the human will and following the doctrine laid down by John of Damascus and Gennadius. It opposed the doctrine of Justification by Faith alone. Salvation, it declares, is achieved 'by faith and charity, that is, by faith and works'.

The Synod of Jerusalem was not an Oecumenical Council; and neither Dionysius nor Dositheus would have claimed that the Confession was absolutely correct in all details, but merely that it represented what, with their human limitations, they believed to be correct. Taken in its entirety it represented the general view of the Orthodox of the time, and, apart from its precise definition of transubstantiation, it is still generally valid today. When the Non-Juror Anglican divines needed an authoritative statement on Orthodox doctrine, it was a copy of the 'Confession of Dositheus' which the Patriarch Jeremias III sent to England, politely suggesting that Anglicans should subscribe to it before any discussions about union could be profitably held.[1] But even with all its qualifying clauses the Confession was a little too precise for many of the Orthodox. The formula on transubstantiation was soon to cause trouble.

In 1680, at the request of the Patriarch Joachim of Moscow, Dositheus sent to Russia two of his most learned followers, the Cephallonian brothers Joannicius and Sophronius Likhoudes. The Church of Kiev was making strenuous efforts to impose its Latinized doctrine of the Eucharist on the whole Russian Church. One of Peter Moghila's pupils, the Ukrainian monk Symeon Polotsky, had settled in Moscow and by his charming and courtly manners had made himself a favourite in the Tsar's household. Tsar Alexis entrusted him with the education of his children, including his young son Peter; though, as the future Peter the Great was only aged eight when Symeon died, Symeon's direct

---

[1] See H. T. F. Duckworth, *Greek Manuals of Church Doctrine*, summarizing four nineteenth-century Greek catechisms.

influence on him cannot have been great. Symeon knew no Greek but was fluent in Latin and Polish; and his knowledge of Western scientific discoveries and methods greatly impressed the Muscovites. He had nothing but contempt for the Russian clergy; and, relying on the Tsar's friendship, he attempted to secure an official ruling that the Russian Church accepted the full doctrine of transubstantiation and rejected the doctrine of the Epiklesis. The Patriarch Joachim and his clergy were alarmed; they therefore sent to Dositheus for help.

The worst of the crisis was over by the time that the Likhoudes brothers arrived at Moscow, as Symeon had just died. His friend and disciple, Sylvester Medvedev, who carried on his cause, was less erudite and less able. He was no match for the Likhoudes brothers, who themselves had received an excellent Western education at Padua and Venice, and knew Latin and Italian and all the up-to-date trends in philosophy and science. The Tsar began to withdraw his favour from Medvedev and to realize how strongly public opinion disliked the Ukrainian doctrines. At a Council held in Moscow in 1690, just before the Patriarch Joachim's death, Symeon Polotsky's teachings were repudiated. The dogma of the Epiklesis was established; and a deliberately imprecise phrase about transubstantiation was approved. Various theological textbooks published at Kiev were withdrawn. In their place new textbooks were compiled by the Likhoudes brothers. They re-edited Moghila's Confession, so that the edition which appeared in 1696 contained a number of modifications on the Persons of the Trinity and on the doctrine of the Sacrament. In spite of their Western education the Likhoudes brothers belonged to the old apophatic tradition. They seem even to have found the 'Confession of Dositheus' a little too cataphatic for their tastes. They represent a movement back from the search for precision that characterized the seventeenth century into the older traditional lines. In the nineteenth century, when fresh catechisms were prepared, in Russia as well as in Greece, the phraseology on the Sacrament, on free will and justification by faith, were deliberately vague, stressing the mystery of God.[1]

The eighteenth century was not in any part of the world a great age of theologians. In Russia the secular control of the Church instituted by Peter the Great, and based on Lutheran rather than on Byzantine models, discouraged theological enterprise. The Imperial court began to associate itself more and more with lay Western culture. Of the three remarkable women who dominated the destinies of Russia during the century two, Catherine I and Catherine II, were born Protestants, and their conversion to Orthodoxy was political rather than spiritual, while the third, Elizabeth Petrovna, was superstitious rather than pious and had no taste for theological niceties. Catherine II deliberately filled the high positions in the Church with free-thinkers and tended to regard the monasteries as being inimical to the State. Russian holy men, such as Tikhon, Bishop of Voronezh, whom Dostoievsky was greatly to admire, or the mystic monk Paisy Velichkovsky, received no support or approval from the government.[2]

Amongst the Greeks, owing to the influence of the Phanariot nobility, lay learning became the fashion, at the expense of religious learning. One of the few men to combine the two learnings was Nicodemus of the Holy Mountain, whose *Pidalion*, published in 1800 at Leipzig, is still the chief authority on the duties and range of Greek canon law, but who was also a mystic in the old tradition, though the mystical exercises that he recommended owed more to Loyola and the Western mystics than to the Hesychasts. But he stood alone as a spiritual figure.[3] There was no longer any interest in debates with divines of other faiths.

---

[1] For the Likhoudes brothers see M. Smertsovsky, *The Brothers Likhudy* (in Russian), giving a full account of their career and writings. See also Jugie, *op. cit.* I, pp. 517–18.

[2] For the later Russian mystics see E. Behr-Sigel, *Prière et sainteté dans l'Eglise russe.*

[3] See Ware, *Eustratios Argenti*, pp. 101–2, 170–2, also M. Viller, 'Nicodème l'Agiorite et ses emprunts à la littérature spirituelle occidentale', *Revue d'Ascétique et de Mystique*, V (1924), pp. 174–7.

The Orthodox had a protector of their own faith in Russia, though Russia was not always so helpful or quite as disinterested as they had hoped. The one constant danger was still the propaganda of the Roman Church. The Jesuits had lost some of their influence; many potentates were turning against them in the West. But they were still active in the East, as were the Dominican and Franciscan Orders; and the Catholic powers, in particular France, however much they might disapprove of them at home, were ready to make use of them for political purposes within the Ottoman Empire.

The dispute over the custodianship of the Holy Places in Palestine continued without ceasing. The Franciscans claimed to be special guardians of the sites; and the Catholic powers would back their claims. The Sultan, though for administrative convenience he preferred to leave them under Orthodox control, was often ready for diplomatic reasons to promise concessions to the Franciscans. He also had his Coptic, Jacobite and Arabian subjects to consider. In the later seventeenth century the influence of the eminent Phanariots at the Sublime Porte secured for the Greeks the most favoured position at the Holy Places. But the Latin rivalry could not be eliminated. Later it was to be one of the causes of the Crimean War.[1] At the same time Latin propaganda never ceased at Constantinople, even invading the Patriarchal court. The Patriarch Athanasius V, a distinguished musicologist who reigned from 1709 to 1711, was strongly suspected of Romanizing tendencies; and similar suspicions were harboured against one or two of his successors. Finally the rivalry between the Churches gave rise to the one great theological controversy within Orthodoxy during the eighteenth century.

There had always been discussion on the proper procedure for receiving into the Church converts from the Roman or other Churches. The problem often arose because of the number of Greeks born in Venetian territory, such as the Ionian islands, who, either because they came to settle within the Ottoman Empire or

---

[1] See above, p. 236.

because they married Orthodox spouses, wished to return to the Church of their forefathers. The Council of 1484, the first council to be held at Constantinople after the fall of the city, had dealt with that very question. It had ordained a ritual in which the convert abjured his doctrinal errors and was reconfirmed; but he did not have to be rebaptized. But as time went on doubts arose whether this was sufficient; was a heretic baptism valid? These doubts were not purely occasioned by dislike for the Latins, though that motive was certainly not absent, but from a genuine suspicion that the Latin ritual of baptism was not canonically correct. The Orthodox, following the practice of the early Christians, baptized by immersion. The Church allowed that in an emergency any baptized Christian, whatever his sect, could perform a valid baptism, so long as the Holy Trinity was invoked; but the ritual should include immersion in so far as it was physically possible. The Latins baptized by aspersion. Many of the Orthodox considered this to be uncanonical. They demanded that the convert be re-baptized, not because he had already been baptized by a heretic but because, in their opinion, he had not really been baptized at all. Ecclesiastical opinion among the Orthodox, particularly in monkish circles, had for some time been moving in this direction. Baptismal practices were not mentioned in the seventeenth-century Confessions; but by the beginning of the eighteenth century there was a definite move to insist upon re-baptism. It is probable that the Russians, always more Orthodox than the Orthodox, were the protagonists. In 1718 Peter the Great wrote to ask the Patriarch Jeremias III of Constantinople whether he should rebaptize converts and was told that it was unnecessary. But in saying so Jeremias did not speak for the whole of his Church. He had on his side the Phanariot aristocrats and intellectuals, who prided themselves on their Western culture and their freedom from bigotry, and most of the upper hierarchy, men many of whom owed their posts to Phanariot influence and many of whom came from the Ionian Islands, where the Orthodox lived on good terms with the Catholics and conversion was frequent. Such men saw no need for changing the existing practice. There was nothing in the Canon Law, as derived from the Scriptures and the Oecumenical Councils, which insisted on immersion as the only valid form of baptism or in any way demanded the rebaptism of anyone baptized in the name of the Trinity. On the other side were ranged most of the monasteries, which always saw themselves as the guardians of Tradition, the Orthodox in Russia and the Orthodox in Syria and Palestine, where feeling against the Catholics ran high and where few converts were ever made, and the lower clergy in general, nearly all of them influenced by the monasteries.

In the middle of the eighteenth century this second party found leaders in two remarkable men. One of them, Eustratios Argenti, was a layman from Chios, born in about 1690 and educated in philosophy and medicine in Western Europe. He became one of the best-known physicians in the Near East; but he was also a passionate theologian. His reading convinced him that in fact immersion was the only canonical form of baptism. It was, he thought, worldly and wrong to countenance other forms. He received no sympathy from the intellectual circles in which he moved; but he convinced one eminent divine, Cyril, Metropolitan of Nicaea. Cyril was a Constantinopolitan of humble birth but of good education who had risen in the hierarchy on his merits. He was considered to be very able by his fellow-metropolitans but was not popular amongst them. However the Patriarch Paisius II was still more unpopular. Paisius, who had already been deposed once, was aware that the synod was intriguing against him and was said to have made all his metropolitans swear on oath that if he were deposed again none of them would replace him. Cyril swore with the rest, but, only a few days after Paisius's deposition in September 1748, he was appointed to the Patriarchal throne. The story that Cyril broke his oath was only circulated some years later by his enemies; and they offered no explanation for his easy succession to the throne. As Patriarch, Cyril had three objects in view, to improve monastic education, to reform the finances of his office, and to establish the need for the rebaptism of converts. His first object, which culminated in an attempt to found an academy on Mount Athos, ended in failure. His stringent financial measures had some success. He laid heavy taxes on the metropolitanates and richer bishoprics and relieved the burden on the poorer congregations. This increased his popularity with the Greek populace in Constantinople, which already sympathized with his known views on rebaptism; but it infuriated the metropolitans. Before he could implement his religious policy they secured his deposition, in May 1751, and reinstated Paisius. Paisius seems to have borne no rancour against Cyril and was himself mildly in favour of the need for rebaptism; but he was in no position to enforce his views or to prevent a number of metropolitans from openly denouncing them. There was at the time in Constantinople a monk called Auxentius, who was considered by the populace to possess thaumaturgical powers and who was certainly an effective demagogue. Though Cyril denied, probably truthfully, any connection with him, he roused feeling against Paisius and the metropolitans and instigated such riots in favour of Cyril that in September 1752 the Turkish authorities felt it necessary to insist on Paisius's deposition and Cyril's reinstatement. After such a demonstration of his popularity Cyril could defy the metropolitans. In 1755 he issued an encyclical, written in colloquial Greek, probably by himself, in which he advocated rebaptism in the case of converts from the Roman and Armenian Churches. He followed this a month later by an official order, known as the Oros, in whose drafting Argenti had a hand, which insisted on canonical grounds that rebaptism should be applied in the case of every convert. The Patriarchs of Alexandria and Jerusalem countersigned the order. The Patriarch of Antioch would have done so, had he not been on an alms-seeking visit to Russia and had his throne not been snatched in his absence by a usurper.

The Oros was met with an angry outcry from the metropolitans; but, somewhat to their embarrassment, they found that they had become the allies of the envoys of the Catholic powers, who at once protested to the Porte against this insult to the Catholic Faith. It was ambassadorial pressure rather than that of the Synod which led to Cyril's deposition in January 1757. But when his successor Callinicus IV, formerly Metropolitan of Braila in Roumania, attempted to annul the Oros six months later, there were such riots that the Turks demanded his abdication. The next Patriarch, Serapheim II, was too prudent to repeat the attempt. So, though for some time to come Cyril's memory was subjected to bitter abuse, rebaptism for converts is to this day the official rule in the Orthodox Church. Whether, as some of Cyril's opponents have claimed, it was a piece of reactionary obscurantism, or, as others have claimed, an act of religious chauvinism, or whether, as is more likely, it was a result of a sincere conviction, Cyril's Oros is still regretted by many of the Orthodox and has proved a bar to any possible reunion of the Churches. It was the last theological enterprise of the Orthodox Church until we come to the controversies of the nineteenth century. In the meantime the Church had been caught up in the political strivings of the Greek people.[1]

[1] The baptism controversy has been admirably covered by Ware, *Eustratios Argenti*, pp. 65–107. For Cyril V's career the basic authority is the chronicle of Sergios Macraios, part I (in Sathas, Μεσαιωνικὴ Βιβλιοθήκη, III, pp. 203–37). See also Papadopoullos, *op. cit.* pp. 159–264.

24-2

THE PHANARIOTS

It was fortunate for the Church in its struggle to maintain its standards against oppression and increasing debt that there were classes amongst the Greeks to whom Ottoman rule had brought prosperity. The spread of one great Empire over the Near East had broken down national trade-barriers. In spite of local octrois and the rapacity of individual governors commerce flourished throughout the Empire; and more and more merchants from the West came to Turkish ports to buy the silks and carpets, the olives and dried fruits, the herbs and spices and tobacco which the Empire produced. The Turks themselves had no taste for trade, and they had ejected the Italians who in the old days had dominated Levantine commerce. They left trading activities to their subject races, to Jews, Armenians, Syrians and Greeks; and the Greeks, largely because they were the best sailors, were the dominant group. There was always great poverty amongst them. The majority of Greek peasants, whether in Europe or in Asia, barely scraped a living from the barren soil. But where nature had been kinder, as on Mount Pelion with its gushing streams, flourishing communities arose, with small industrialists banded together in associations or corporations. The silks of Pelion were famous by the end of the seventeenth century, and the growers enjoyed special privileges from the Sultan. At Ambelakia in Thessaly and Naoussa in Western Macedonia there was a flourishing cotton-making industry.[1] About the same time the fur-trade of the Empire was centred round the Macedonian town of Castoria, whose citizens bought furs in the distant north and made

---

[1] See A. Hadjimichali, 'Aspects de l'organisation économique des Grecs dans l'Empire Ottoman', *Le Cinq-centième anniversaire de la prise de Constantinople*, *L'Hellénisme contemporain* (fascicule hors série; 1953), pp. 264–8; N. G. Svoronos, *Commerce de Salonique au XVIIIe siècle*, p. 250. D. Sicilianos, Ἡ Μακρινίτζα καὶ τὸ Πήλιον, pp. 92–4.

them up into pelisses and caps in their own workshops.[1] In the tobacco lands of Macedonia, though the big money went to the Turkish landlords, the peasants who worked the fields were not downtrodden.[2] Not only was local shipping round Constantinople and the flourishing fishing industry largely manned by Greeks or by Christian Lazes, who being Orthodox ranked as Greeks, but the carrying-trade in the Eastern Mediterranean was in the hands of Greek shipowners living in the Aegean islands, in Hydra or in Syra.[3] Greek merchants carried Malmsey wine to the markets of Germany or Poland or collected cottons and spices in the further East for re-export.[4] But it was in the larger seaport cities, in Smyrna or in Thessalonica or, above all, in Constantinople itself, that great fortunes could be made. Koranic law as well as their natural distaste kept the Turks from taking an interest in banking. Soon it was the Jews and, still more, the Greeks who became the bankers and financiers of the Empire.

In the East money-making has never, as it was in the feudally minded West, been considered to be incompatible with aristocracy. A moneyed nobility began to emerge among the Greeks, closely

[1] For the fur-trade see Hadjimichali, *art. cit.* pp. 272–5; C. Mertsios, *Monuments de l'histoire de la Macédonie*, pp. 209 ff.

[2] Reports by the French Consuls Arasy, de Jonville and Beaujour, in M. Lascaris, *Salonique à la fin du XVIIIe siècle*; Svoronos, *op. cit.* pp. 261–4.

[3] For maritime trade within the Ottoman Empire in the seventeenth century see R. Mantran, *Istanbul dans la seconde moitié du XVIIe siècle*, pp. 425 ff., esp. pp. 487–92. For the part played by Greeks see Eremiya Çelebi Kömürcüyan, *Istanbul Tarihi: XVII asîrda Istanbul* (trans. into Turkish by H. D. Andreasyan), p. 47 (the account of a contemporary Armenian traveller), and Mantran, *op. cit.* pp. 55–7. There is no good general survey of the trade of the Aegean islands in the eighteenth century, when the islanders took over most of the Levantine trade. According to L. S. Bartholdy (*Voyage en Grèce fait dans les années 1803–1804*, II, p. 63) the islands of Hydra, Spetsai, Psara and Chios owned from 300 to 400 ships. For Hydra the best monograph is still G. D. Kriezis, Ἱστορία τῆς Νήσου Ὕδρας πρὸ τῆς Ἐπαναστάσεως τοῦ 1821. See also, for the islands' privileges, J. Z. Stephanopoli, *Les Iles de l'Egée: leurs privilèges, passim*.

[4] See N. Jorga, *Byzance après Byzance*, pp. 234–5: also T. Stoianović, 'The conquering Balkan Orthodox Merchant', *Journal of Economic History*, XX, pp. 234–313. There were chapels for the use of Greek merchants at Leipzig, Breslau and Posen: M. Gedeon, Πατριαρχικοὶ πίνακες, pp. 638, 641, 669.

knit by common aims and interests and by intermarriage, but open to newcomers. These rich families were ambitious. Authority among the Greeks was in the hands of the Patriarch. It therefore became their object to control the Patriarchate. Calling themselves the 'Archontes' of the Greek nation, they built their houses in the Phanar quarter of Constantinople, to be close to the Patriarchal buildings. They obtained for their sons positions in the Patriarchal court; and one by one the high offices of the Great Church passed into lay hands. Their members did not enter the Church itself. That was considered to be beneath their dignity. The bishops and the Patriarch himself continued to be drawn mainly from bright boys of humbler classes who had risen through intelligence and merit. But by the end of the seventeenth century the Phanariot families, as they were usually called, dominated the central organization of the Church. They could not control it completely. Occasionally, as in the case of the Patriarch Cyril V, they would be overridden by public opinion. But the Patriarchate could not do without them; for they were in a position both to pay its debts and to intrigue in its favour at the Sublime Porte.[1]

It was a matter of pride amongst the Phanariots to claim for their families a high Byzantine ancestry or at least a descent from one of the eighteen noble provincial families which Mehmet II had transported to Constantinople, or even from some great Italian house. The claims were hard to prove in a society where a whole household usually took its master's surname, but they were impressively put forward; and newcomers into the group hastened to ally themselves by marriage to these illustrious names.[2] The

---

[1] For the 'archontes', see Jorga, *Byzance après Byzance*, pp. 90–1, 113–25.

[2] For these claims see *Le Livre d'Or de la noblesse phanariote par un Phariote* (ed. E. R. Rhangabé), *passim*. The Cantacuzeni, probably correctly, and the Argyropouli, the Aristarchi and the Rhangabe, less convincingly, claimed Byzantine Imperial descent. The Mouroussi and the Ypsilanti claimed to be families transported by Mehmet II from Trebizond and to be related to the Grand Comneni. The Mano came from Sicily via Genoa; the Mavroyeni claimed descent from the Venetian Morosini; the Scarlati came from Florence. The Mavrocordato were to claim descent from Othello in the male line and Fabius Maximus Cunctator in the female. See below, p. 367.

Phanariots thus impregnated themselves with memories of Byzantium. While they sought to increase their riches and through their riches to obtain influence at first the Patriarch's and then the Sultan's courts, they dreamed that the influence might ultimately be used to recreate the Empire of Byzantium.

It had taken roughly a century for the Greek laity to recover from the shock of the conquest. Then we come to the first Greek millionaire of the Ottoman era, Michael Cantacuzenus, Shaitan-oglu, 'the devil's son', as the Turks called him. Though he was put to death and his vast possessions confiscated, other members of the family kept their wealth and ranked high in Phanariot circles.[1] His slightly younger contemporary, John Caradja, a man of humbler origin, made vast sums as caterer to the Ottoman army, a rewarding post to which his son-in-law Scarlatos, surnamed Beglitsi, succeeded. Scarlatos became even richer than Shaitanoglu but was more prudent. He too died a violent death, murdered by a janissary in 1630; but his heirs succeeded to all his possessions.[2]

These sixteenth-century millionaires built up their fortunes as merchants; but they learnt that wealth could best be won and maintained by co-operation with the Ottoman government. By the beginning of the next century rich merchants began to send their sons, together with young scholars and theologians, to study at the universities of Italy, mainly at Padua, though some went to Rome or to Geneva or to Paris. There the boys tended to concentrate on medical studies. There were very few Turkish doctors; and the best way of winning the confidence of an eminent Turk was to cure him of some disease, probably the indigestion which his inordinate love of sweetmeats, combined often with a surreptitious indulgence in alcohol, invariably brought on. Greek doctors enjoyed a high reputation. As we have seen, King Charles II of England's favourite physician was a Greek, Dr Rodocanaki.[3]

The system soon proved its value. In about 1650 there arrived

[1] See above, pp. 197–8.
[2] For Scarlatos Beglitsi see Gerlach, *op. cit.* pp. 270, 296; Jorga, *Byzance après Byzance*, pp. 119, 123.   [3] See above, p. 296.

back in Constantinople from the West a young Chiot doctor called Panayoti Nicoussios Mamonas, nicknamed the 'Green Horse', because of a saying that you could as easily find a green horse as a wise man in Chios. He had been educated by Jesuit fathers in Chios; but they had not converted him, and he had gone on to study philosophy under Meletius Syrigus at Constantinople and from there to the medical school at Padua. On his return he attracted the attention of the great Albanian-born vizier, Ahmet Köprülü, who employed him first as his family doctor but then, noting his general ability and his remarkable gifts as a linguist, found him still more useful in drafting foreign dispatches and interviewing foreign envoys. In 1669 Köprülü created for him the post of Grand Dragoman of the Sublime Porte, that is to say, interpreter-in-chief and acting permanent head of the Foreign Ministry. In that capacity Panayoti was allowed to grow a beard, a privilege hitherto denied to Christian laymen in Turkey, to ride in public with four attendants, and to wear, together with his servants, bonnets trimmed with fur.[1] At the same time the post of Dragoman of the Fleet was created, reserved for Phanariots. In spite of its name, the office really gave its holder authority over the Greek laity, to the detriment of the Patriarch's power.[2]

So well did Panayoti serve the vizier that the system was continued after his death four years later, when Köprülü appointed to the office of Grand Dragoman a rich young Greek called Alexander Mavrocordato, who belonged to the innermost circle of the Phanariot aristocracy. With his appointment there opened a new chapter in the history of Phanariot power and aspirations.[3]

In their desire to consolidate their position both economically and politically the Phanariots looked for land in which they could invest their wealth and which could be a base for the rebuilding of Byzantium. Fortunes could easily be made in Constantinople

[1] K. Daponte, Χρονογράφος, in Sathas, Μεσαιωνικὴ Βιβλιοθήκη, III, pp. 6, 10, 12, 15. Anastasius Gordius says that he was a pupil of Meletius Syrigus (Βίος Εὐγενίου Αἰτωλοῦ, in Sathas, *op. cit.* III, p. 483). See also J. von Hammer-Purgstall, *Geschichte des Osmanischen Reiches*, VI, pp. 11, 27.
[2] See Papadopoullos, *op. cit.* pp. 48–9.   [3] See below, pp. 368–9.

but as easily lost or could be suddenly confiscated; and it was difficult for a Christian to acquire lands within the Ottoman Empire, and the lands might at any time be expropriated. There were, however, beyond the Danube territories which admitted the Sultan's suzerainty but which were self-governing. The Principalities of Wallachia and Moldavia, which we now collectively call Roumania, were inhabited by an indigenous race speaking a Latin language with Illyrian forms and Slavonic intrusions, with a Church that was Slavonic-speaking and had earlier been under the Serbian Church but now depended upon Constantinople. From the fourteenth to the seventeenth century the reigning princes of both Principalities, who succeeded each other with startling rapidity, had been connected by birth, often illegitimate, or by marriage to the family of Bassaraba, which gave its name to Bessarabia. Wallachia had accepted Turkish overlordship in the fourteenth century; but in the late fifteenth century Prince Stephen the Great of Moldavia had conquered Wallachia and had been the main bulwark of Christendom against the Turks. His successors had not been able to maintain the struggle. They submitted voluntarily to the Sultan and were permitted to reign on autonomously as his vassals. The two provinces were divided again, under princes of the dynasty who were nominally elected by the boyars, the heads of the local noble families, and whose elections were subject to the Sultan's confirmation. Vassals though they were, the Princes of Wallachia and Moldavia were the only lay Christian rulers left within the sphere of the old Byzantine world. They saw themselves as being in some way the heirs of the Byzantine Caesars. Some of the more ambitious even took the title of *Basileus*; and all of them modelled their courts on the lines of the old Imperial court.[1]

Their ambitions disposed them favourably towards the Greeks. They liked to receive special notice from the Patriarchate; and they realized that it was advisable to have friends in Constantinople who could intrigue for them at the Sultan's court, the more

---

[1] Jorga, *Byzance après Byzance*, pp. 126–54.

so as the Sultan increasingly nominated the princes for election. On their side the Phanariots saw that here was territory in which they could entrench themselves. More and more Greeks began to flock across the Danube and to marry into the Moldavian and Wallachian nobility. The Princess Chiajna of Wallachia, Stephen the Great's granddaughter, was famed for the number of handsome Greek gentlemen that she collected at her court. One of her daughters married the Patriarch's nephew, the other a Cantacuzenus, the brother of Shaitan-oglu. Her brother, Prince Iancu of Moldavia, married a Greek widow and gave his stepsons high posts in his administration. Michael the Brave, Prince of Wallachia at the end of the sixteenth century, was the son of a Greek woman and employed Greek poets to sing his praises.[1]

The Cantacuzeni were the first great Phanariot family to interest itself in the Principalities. Shaitan-oglu's youngest son, like his uncle, married a Wallachian princess; and, of his eldest son's children, the daughter became Princess of Moldavia and the youngest son married Stanca Bassaraba, heiress of the senior branch of the princely line.[2] The Greek Cantacuzeni thus became the leading family in the Trans-Danubian nobility. Their cousins, the Rosetti, soon joined them, with the Chrysosculei and lesser families such as the Caradja and the Pavlaki.[3] Their example was followed by Orthodox Albanian families who had settled in Constantinople and had married Greek wives. At their head was George Ghika, the head of a family connected with the Köprülüs and wisely on good terms with his Muslim cousins.[4]

Scarlatos Beglitzi followed the same policy. He had no sons, and of his four daughters it was the youngest, Roxandra, to whom he left the bulk of his fortune. He determined that she should make a match suitable to her wealth and her lineage; for Scarlatos

---

[1] Jorga, *Byzance après Byzance*, pp. 135–6, 148–9. For Chiajna's excessive love for Greek gentlemen, see poem by George the Aetolian in N. Banescu, *Un Poème grec vulgaire*; and poem by Stavrinos the Vestiary, 'Ανδραγαθίες τοῦ εὐσεβεστάτον καὶ ἀνδρειοτάτον Μιχαὴλ βοεβόδα, in E. Legrand, *Recueil des poèms historiques*.
[2] For the Cantacuzene family, see above, p. 197. [3] Daponte, Χρονογράφος, p. 17.
[4] Daponte, 'Ιστορικὸς Κατάλογος, in Sathas, *op. cit.* III, pp. 172–5.

claimed to belong to a noble Florentine family that had come to Greece with the Acciaiuoli. In 1623, when Roxandra was aged fourteen, she was married to the only son of Rudolph Bassaraba, Prince of Moldavia, a boy of seventeen who himself had just been elected to the Moldavian throne. But the young Prince Alexander died in 1630, having for one year been Prince also of Wallachia. Scarlatos was murdered that same year; and Roxandra was left a childless widow aged twenty-one. She was not beautiful; and an attack of smallpox left her marked and blind in one eye. But she had been superbly educated; Italian as well as Greek writers paid tribute to her culture; and she was immensely wealthy. She refused to marry the next Prince of Wallachia, her late husband's cousin, Matthew Bassaraba (though unkind rumour said that it was he who rejected the marriage, on hearing of her pock-marks). Instead, she fixed her choice on a young merchant from Chios, named Nicholas Mavrocordato. His father claimed descent from a Greek general in Venetian service, Mavros, whose name was distorted in drama to Othello, the Moor of Venice, whose heiress had married into the Genoese-Chiot family of the Cordati. His mother was also a Genoese Chiot by origin, belonging to the Genoese branch of the Roman family of the Massimi, descended from Fabius Maximus Cunctator. Despite his boasted lineage it was his marriage to Roxandra that made the fortune of the Mavrocordato family; and his descendants for several generations gratefully added the surname of Scarlatos to their own.[1]

Alexander, the younger but only surviving son of the marriage,

[1] Daponte, Χρονογράφος, pp. 15–16, and Ἱστορικὸς Κατάλογος, pp. 166–7. Demetrius Cantemir, *The History of the Growth and Decay of the Othman Empire* (trans. N. Tindal), pp. 356–8, tells of Roxandra's pockmarks and of Matthew of Wallachia's refusal to marry her; but his evidence is suspect, as he hated the Mavrocordato family and was writing some seventy years later. Daponte speaks highly of her erudition, as does the scholar James Manos of Argos (in his preface to her son Alexander Mavrocordato's Ἱστορία τῶν Ἰουδαίων). See A. Stourdza, *L'Europe Orientale et le rôle historique des Maurocordato*, pp. 32–4, 408–9, which cites all the relevant sources but is careless over dates and names. For a romanticized account of Roxandra, written by a descendant and based on the family papers, see Princesse Bibesco, *La Nymphe Europe*, I, pp. 63–71.

was born in 1642. His father died ten years later; and his mother, who seems to have had Catholic sympathies, sent him when he was fifteen to Rome, to the Jesuit College of Saint Athanasius. Three years later he went on to the University of Padua, where he studied philosophy and medicine. Riotous behaviour caused him to be sent down from Padua; and it was at Bologna that he obtained his doctoral degree, with a thesis on the circulation of the blood. He returned to Constantinople soon afterwards, and in 1666, when he was twenty-four, he was appointed Grand Orator of the Great Church and Director of the Patriarchal Academy. There, influenced by the ex-Director, John Caryophyllus, he lectured on Neo-Aristotelian philosophy as well as on ancient Greek philology; but he continued to practise medicine; and it was as a physician that he attracted the notice of Ahmet Köprülü, who was looking for a replacement for Panayoti, recently elevated to be Grand Dragoman. He was an excellent doctor. The Sultan and many of the foreign ambassadors were his patients. But, as in the case of Panayoti, the vizier decided to make fuller use of his abilities. On Panayoti's death Alexander Mavrocordato was appointed Grand Dragoman, at the age of thirty-one. Three years previously he had married a Phanariot lady, Charis Chrysoscoleo, whose mother Cassandra was a Moldavian princess.

Alexander was Grand Dragoman for twenty-five years, with a brief interval early in 1684, when he was cast into prison as one of the scapegoats for the Turkish failure before Vienna. His mother, who joined him in prison, died soon after their release, in August 1684. Alexander was soon reinstated. In 1688 he led an Ottoman embassy to Vienna. In 1698 a still higher post was created for him. He became Exaporite, Minister of the Secrets, Private Secretary to the Sultan, with the title of Prince and Illustrious Highness. In 1698 he was chief Turkish delegate at the peace conference of Carlowitz, where the Habsburg Emperor gave him the title of Prince of the Holy Roman Empire. He died in 1709, honoured and immensely rich. His career had opened up new vistas for Greeks of ambition.

Though none of the later Phanariots quite measured up to Alexander Mavrocordato's stature, he set the pattern for them. He was remarkably intelligent and highly educated, and always eager to maintain intellectual contacts with the West. The Jesuits believed him to be a secret Catholic; but his actions scarcely confirmed their belief. He took an active part in the affairs of the Orthodox Church, fighting for its rights. As Grand Dragoman he secured a relaxation of the rules restricting the building of new churches, and he arranged for the transference of many of the Holy Places at Jerusalem from Latin to Greek ownership, in co-operation with the great Patriarch Dositheus of Jerusalem. But he was far from fanatical. He gave strict orders to the Greeks at Jerusalem that they were to welcome and aid Christians of all sects who visited the shrines under their care; and he seems to have believed that it might be possible to reunite the Churches of Christendom on a new philosophical basis, resting on the foundation of the unity of the old Graeco-Roman world. His attitude revealed his Jesuit training. He was a philosopher and an intellectual, eager to be an up-to-date European, with little sympathy with the old apophatic traditions of Orthodoxy. He did much in practice for his Church; but the school of thought that he represented was to add to its problems.[1]

The Phanariots had meanwhile consolidated their hold upon the Principalities. The local Church helped in the hellenization of the country. It continued to use a Slavonic liturgy until the end of the seventeenth century, when the Roumanian language was introduced, though the Slavonic script was not replaced by a Latin script till well into the nineteenth century. But, whatever the language of the liturgy, the upper clergy were Greek or Greek-

---

[1] There is no satisfactory life of the great Exaporite. He is frequently mentioned in the Constantinopolitan sources of the time, in particular Daponte and Cantemir, and in all contemporary works dealing with the Levant, and with the diplomacy of the period. See Jorga, *Byzance après Byzance*, pp. 203–7; Stourdza, *op. cit.* pp. 35 ff.; E. Legrand, *Généalogie des Maurocordatos de Constantinople*, pp. 10 ff. See also the romanticized account in Princesse Bibesco, *op. cit.* pp. 72–114. For his educational reforms see above, pp. 222–3.

educated; and Greek schools and seminaries were founded in both Principalities. This did not represent a crude exploitation of the natives. Rather, it was the voluntary work of the native Church in order to secure the support of Greek learning and Phanariot money and influence and to strengthen itself against Latin missionaries operating from the Habsburg dominions and from Poland. The Greek academies at Bucharest and Jassy were established not for racial purposes but in the general interest of Orthodoxy.[1]

The Bassaraba dynasty had become thoroughly hellenized before its extinction, at about the end of the first quarter of the seventeenth century. When it was gone the princely thrones were left open to adventurers who could combine local connections with influence at the Phanar and the Sultan's court. There were two main factions, on the one hand families such as the Cantacuzeni and the Rosettis who had acquired by purchase or by marriage large estates in the Principalities and made their homes there, and on the other families such as the Ghikas and the Mavrocordatos, who wished to control the Principalities from the Phanar and used their Roumanian estates chiefly as sources of income. Of the outstanding princes who succeeded to the Bassarabas the first was an Albanian with a Moldavian mother, Basil, surnamed the Wolf, who reigned in Moldavia from 1634 to 1654. He was, as we have seen, the friend of Peter Moghila and a great figure in Orthodox politics. After paying the debts of the Patriarchate and the yearly taxes due from the communities on Mount Athos he won such prestige that he was employed to arbitrate in ecclesiastical quarrels, such as that between the Patriarch of Alexandria and the autonomous monastery of Saint Catherine on Mount Sinai. The Constantinopolitan ex-Patriarch Athanasius Pattellaras called him the New Achilles and the heir of all the Emperors; and he secretly planned his Imperial coronation. But when he plotted to annex Wallachia to his throne the Sublime Porte was alarmed, and he was deposed.[2]

[1] For the Church in the Principalities see N. Jorga, *Istoria la Biserica Românilor, passim.* [2] Jorga, *Byzance après Byzance*, pp. 163–79. See above, pp. 341–3.

Four years later Gregory Ghika intrigued himself on to the Moldavian throne and next year secured the Walachian throne also. He had no Roumanian blood in his veins; and his success was due to his influence at Constantinople, in particular with his Köprülü cousins.[1] For the next half-century the thrones passed with bewildering rapidity alternately between the Ghikas and their connections and the Cantacuzeni and theirs. The three eminent princes of the time belonged to the latter faction. Sherban Cantacuzenus, the son of a Bassaraba heiress, became Prince of Wallachia in 1679. He was a local patriot who did much to encourage local industry and art; and it was he who established the liturgy in Roumanian. Though outwardly loyal to the Sultan he dreamed of independence and intrigued with the Habsburg and Russian Emperors, the former giving him the title of Prince of the Holy Roman Empire. But he moved faster than was prudent. When he died suddenly in 1689 rumour said that he had been poisoned by his more cautious brother and nephew.[2] His brother barely survived him; and his nephew, Constantine Brancovan, whose mother, Helena Cantacuzena, had thus inherited all the Bassaraba and Cantacuzenus estates, succeeded to the Wallachian throne. He ruled prosperously for twenty-five years. Like his uncle he did much for his country and its culture and was himself in close touch with the intellectual life of the Phanar and of Italy. But he too worked secretly with foreign powers and dreamed of becoming the Christian Emperor of the East. Eventually his personal enemies warned the Sultan of his ambitions; and one day in 1714 the Prince and his sons were haled off to Constantinople to be beheaded.[3]

His contemporary and rival, Demetrius Cantemir, had a shorter princely career, though he escaped execution. Demetrius Cantemir was a remarkable man. His father's family was Tatar in origin,

[1] Daponte, Χρονογράφος, pp. 9–17.
[2] *Ibid.* pp. 7–41; Cantemir, *op. cit.* pp. 370–1.
[3] For the career of Constantine Brancovan see Stourdza, *op. cit.* pp. 47 ff., giving references to original Roumanian sources. Cantemir, *op. cit.* pp. 371–2, gives a gossipy and prejudiced account of his life and family.

but his mother was Greek, and he himself married into the Cantacuzenus family. He spoke eleven languages. He wrote a standard history of the Ottoman Empire, which is still useful, a history of Moldavia, a Greek translation of the Koran, a dialogue on Dualist philosophy and a treatise on Oriental music; and he composed popular songs which can still sometimes be heard in the streets of Istanbul. He was a trained lawyer and for many years acted as legal adviser to the Patriarchate. It was his intervention that saved for the Christians the church of Saint Mary of the Mongols. He secured the throne of Moldavia in 1710 and at once began negotiations with Peter the Great of Russia, encouraging him to invade the province. But the invasion was a fiasco. There was no popular support. Peter was surrounded near the river Pruth and only escaped captivity owing to the venality of the Ottoman vizier. Cantemir had to flee to Russia, where he ended his days.[1]

Such careers frightened the Sultan and played into the hands of the Phanariots who wished to govern the Principalities from Constantinople. The Phanar disliked any sort of Roumanian separatism. It wished to keep the Ottoman Empire intact until the whole could be transferred to the Greeks of Constantinople. Its influence at the Sublime Porte secured the establishment of a new policy. Henceforward Phanariots from Constantinople should govern the Principalities. This had been the aim of the great Exaporite. Shortly before his death he had obtained the Moldavian throne for his eldest son, Nicholas, whose wife, Cassandra Canta-cuzena, had Bassaraba blood. Nicholas had been displaced soon afterwards by Cantemir; but in 1716 he was appointed to the Wallachian throne and proved his loyalty to the Sultan by spending two years in captivity in an Austrian prison. The Porte was im-pressed. It decided to entrust the thrones to the Mavrocordato clan and their kinsmen the Ghikas and the Rakovitzas.[2]

---

[1] For Demetrius Cantemir's life and writings see Cantemir, *op. cit.* pp. 455–60. The *History* naturally gives a rather biased account of his career.

[2] Jorga, *Byzance après Byzance*, pp. 224–5. See also A. C. Hypsilantis, Τὰ μετὰ τὴν Ἅλωσιν (*1453–1789*), pp. 320 ff.

From 1711 to 1758 in Moldavia and from 1716 to 1769 in Wallachia members of these three families followed each other as princes, in rapid succession. After 1731 the farce of election by the local boyars was dropped. Henceforward the Sultan frankly appointed the Prince himself, in return for payments in cash to himself and to his ministers. Henceforward, therefore, as with the Patriarchate, it was in the Sultan's interest to make as many changes as possible, to depose a Prince, then oblige him to buy back his throne, or to transfer him from one Principality to the other, or to threaten the Prince of Wallachia with transference to the poorer throne of Moldavia unless he paid an indemnity. It was usual for the Prince to have previously held the office of Grand Dragoman, as the Sultan then had some idea of his capabilities and he would probably have made enough money to afford the position. The titles of the princely family were regulated, descendants in the male line being allowed to use the title of Prince. The court and the administration were reorganized in imitation of the Patriarchal court; but it included a Turkish Resident whose duty it was to see to the welfare of the Muslims in the Principality, and also to spy upon the Prince. The most important of the Prince's officials was the Kapikehaya, his agent at Constantinople, upon whose loyalty, influence and tact his tenure of office depended. The Prince was appointed at Constantinople and consecrated there by the Patriarch. He had to arrive at his new capital within thirty days, or else pay a fine of some sixteen gold pounds to the Aga of the Janissaries for every day over the thirty till he arrived. Tactful princes were never over-punctual. On his arrival he was ceremonially blessed by the local metropolitan. Grounds for his deposition could easily be found. He would be accused of intrigues with foreign powers or of witholding revenue or of maltreating his subjects. A *firman* would then be sent from the Sultan to the metropolitan to announce the deposition. The metropolitan communicated it to the assembly of boyars and was himself responsible to see that the Prince did not abscond. As soon as possible the Prince would be sent under guard to Constantinople and was usually banished for a while to a specified place of exile; but very often after a few months he bought back the throne. Local government was in the hands of the boyars, with Phanariot officials regularly inspecting them and giving them advice. Any Greek who had married into a boyar's family and possessed land ranked as a boyar.[1]

Phanariot rule in the Principalities compared well with that of most Pashas in other parts of the Empire and with the rule of the last native princes. The corruption was not excessive by eighteenth-century standards. Justice was fairly honestly administered, without excessive delays. But the Princes were hampered by their uncertainty of tenure. For example, Constantine Mavrocordato, the Exaporite's grandson, was a conscientious and enlightened ruler who issued a reformed constitution for each Principality, making the incidence of taxation fairer and its collection less wasteful; and he improved the lot of the serfs, whom he planned entirely to liberate. But, though between 1730 and 1769 he reigned for six periods in Wallachia and four in Moldavia, the longest of these periods lasted for only six months. Such frequent coming and going made good government and a consistent policy almost impossible.[2] In particular the uncertainty encouraged the Princes to extract all the money that they could from their subjects. The Principalities were naturally rich and the princely income large; but Moldavia had to pay a yearly tribute of some 7,000 gold pounds to the Sultan, and Walachia a yearly tribute of some 14,000 gold pounds. By 1750 the Moldavian throne cost the successful candidate roughly 30,000 gold pounds, and the Wallachian roughly 45,000. Transference from one throne to the other

---

[1] The best account of Phanariot rule in the Principalities is given by William Wilkinson (*An Account of the Principalities of Wallachia and Moldavia*, published in 1820), who was for several years previously British Consul at Bucharest, a post which in the mid-seventeenth century had been held by the historian Daponte. See also the very hostile account in M. P. Zallonis, *Essai sur les Fanariotes*, and J. L. Carra, *Histoire de la Moldavie et de la Valachie* (1781).

[2] Wilkinson, *op. cit.* pp. 95–8; A. D. Xenopol, *Histoire des Roumains*, II, pp. 207–12. For Constantine Mavrocordato see Hypsilantis, *op. cit.* pp. 340–9; Jorga, *Byzance après Byzance*, pp. 231–2. See the list of Princes given in Stourdza, *op. cit.* pp. 89–90.

cost about 20,000 gold pounds. In a good year Moldavia might produce up to 180,000 gold pounds in taxes and Wallachia up to 300,000. But the Prince had not only to recover his outlay and pay the annual tribute. He had to maintain his court and administration; he had constantly to bribe Turkish officials, and he was expected to give generous financial support to the Patriarchate. In consequence he taxed his people to the utmost. If he remitted one tax, he invented another. The Roumanians began to sigh nostalgically for the less efficient but less exacting rule of their native princes. Eighteenth-century travellers all commented on the oppressive taxation and the harm that it was doing to the Principalities' prosperity. Yet every Prince ended his reign a poorer man.[1] By the middle of the eighteenth century the Mavrocordato family, rich though it had been, could no longer afford to provide princes; and the Rakovitsas were ruined. Different Phanariot clans, the Ypsilanti, the Mouroussi and the Callimachi, took their place. In 1774, to ensure more continuity, the Sultan agreed to restrict the princedom to members of these three families and the Ghikas. In 1802 each Prince was promised a reign of at least seven years.[2]

In view of the financial burden why did anyone ever wish to be Prince? Partly the desire came from a love of pomp and of titles and a taste for power, even though the power was limited. A British visitor in 1817 remarked on 'the extraordinary phenomenon of a pure despotism exercised by a Greek prince who is himself at the same time an *abject slave*'.[3] But chiefly it was in pursuit of the Imperial idea, the rebirth of Byzantium. Under

---

[1] Wilkinson, *op. cit.* pp. 60–71.

[2] See R. W. Seton-Watson, *A History of the Roumanians*, pp. 126–43. In the early nineteenth century Dr Robert Walsh says that eight Phanariot families were allowed the title of Prince, the Mavrocordato, Mouroussi, the Ypsilanti, the Callimachi, Soutzo, Caradja, Hantcherli and Mavroyeni families (*Residence at Constantinople during the Greek and Turkish Revolutions*, II, pp. 402–3). He omits the Cantacuzeni, Ghika and Rakovitsa families, who also had princely ancestors.

[3] W. MacMichael, *Journey from Moscow to Constantinople*, p. 107. He describes the pomp and luxury of the Phanariot courts, *ibid.* pp. 92 ff. Comte de Hauterive made a similar comment on a prince's glory thirty years earlier (*Voyage en Moldavie*), p. 368.

Phanariot princes a neo-Byzantine culture could find a home in the Principalities. A Greek-born nobility could root itself in lands there; Greek academies could educate citizens for the new Byzantium. There, far better than in the shadowy palaces round the Phanar, with Turkish police at the door, Byzantine ambition could be kept alive. In Roumania, in Rum beyond the Danube, the revival of New Rome could be planned.

But the plans needed the co-operation of the Church. The Patriarch had become the pensioner of the Phanariots, but he was still the head of the Orthodox community. The Patriarchate gained much from the connection. If from 1695 to 1795 there were only thirty-one Patriarchal reigns, in contrast with the sixty-one between the years 1595 and 1695, this was due to Phanariot influence at the Sublime Porte. Though the sum to be paid to the Sultan for the confirmation of a Patriarchal election was still high, the Phanariots saw to it that it was not now increased and they paid the greater part of it. They used their power and their wealth to ease the burden on the Great Church. But the Great Church had to repay them for their help. The reforms of 1741 and 1755, by reducing the power of the synod and therefore of the lay officials that dominated it, freed the Church to some extent from their influence over appointments. But they imposed their ideas upon it; they forced it to become an instrument of their policy.[1]

Many of the Phanariots' ideas were excellent. They had a high regard for education. There had been several scholars and distinguished authors amongst them; and many of the princes, especially those of the Mavrocordato family, were men of wide culture, able to converse on equal terms with the most sophisticated visitors from the West. Under their influence the Patriarchal Academy at Constantinople had been revitalized. The academies founded at Bucharest and Jassy by the hellenized princes of the seventeenth century were encouraged and enlarged. Greek scholars

[1] For the reforms see T. H. Papadopoullos, *Studies and Documents relating to the History of the Greek Church and People under Turkish Domination, Bibliotheca Graeca Aevi Posterioris*, I, pp. 48–57. See above, p. 176.

flocked to them, preferring to teach there rather than in the restricted atmosphere of Constantinople. The Bucharest Academy was modernized at the close of the seventeenth century by the learned Sevastus Kymenites; and his work was carried on by other scholars, George Hypomenas, George Theodorou of Trebizond, Demetrius Pamperis Procopius, James Manos of Argos, and others. Sevastus's contemporary, the Cretan Jeremias Kakavala, similarly modernized the Academy at Jassy. The Phanariot example was copied by wealthy patrons throughout Greek lands, who founded academies at Smyrna, in Chios, at Janina, at Zagora on Pelion and at Dimitsana in the Peloponnese, and elsewhere. These schools were devoted to the necessary task of improving Greek lay education; and their founders and patrons were most of them men who had themselves been educated in the West. Their model was more the University of Padua than anything in the old Byzantine tradition. The Greek Fathers of the Church might still be studied; but the emphasis was, rather, on Classical philology and ancient and modern philosophy and science. The professors were loyal members of the Orthodox Church, conscientiously opposed to Latins and Protestants alike; but they were themselves affected by the occidental fashions of the time, the tendency towards rationalism and the dread of anything that might be labelled as superstition. They wanted to show that they and their pupils were as enlightened as anyone in the West.[1]

It was good for the Church to have to meet an intellectual challenge; but the challenge was too abrupt. The strength of the Byzantine Church had been the presence of a highly educated laity that was deeply interested in religion. Now the laity began to despise the traditions of the Church; and the traditional elements in the Church began to mistrust and dislike modern education, retreating to defend themselves into a thickening obscurantism. The cleavage between the intellectuals and the traditionalists, which had begun when Neo-Aristotelianism was introduced into the curriculum of the Patriarchal Academy, grew wider. Under

[1] See above, pp. 220–3, and Jorga, *Byzance après Byzance*, pp. 231–40.

Phanariot influence many of the higher ecclesiastics followed the modernist trend. In the old days Orthodoxy had preferred to concentrate on eternal things and modestly to refuse to clothe faith in the trappings of modish philosophy. The Phanariots in their desire to impress the West had no use for such old-fashioned notions. Instead, seeing the high prestige of ancient Greek learning, they wished to show that they were, by culture as well as by blood, the heirs of ancient Greece. Their sons, lively laymen educated in the new style, were now filling the administrative posts at the Patriarchal court. As a result the Patriarchate began to lose touch with the great body of the faithful, to whom faith meant more than philosophy and the Christian saints more than the sophists of pagan times.

Above all, the Phanariots needed the support of the Church in the pursuit of their ultimate political aim. It was no mean aim. The *Megáli Idéa*, the Great Idea of the Greeks, can be traced back to days before the Turkish conquest. It was the idea of the Imperial destiny of the Greek people. Michael VIII Palaeologus expressed it in the speech that he made when he heard that his troops had recaptured Constantinople from the Latins; though he called the Greeks the *Romaioi*. In later Palaeologan times the word Hellene reappeared, but with the conscious intention of connecting Byzantine imperialism with the culture and traditions of ancient Greece.[1] With the spread of the Renaissance a respect for the old Greek civilization had become general. It was natural that the Greeks, in the midst of their political disasters, should wish to benefit from it. They might be slaves now to the Turks, but they were of the great race that had civilized Europe. It must be their destiny to rise again. The Phanariots tried to combine the nationalistic force of Hellenism in a passionate if illogical alliance with the oecumenical traditions of Byzantium and the Orthodox Church. They worked for a restored Byzantium, a New Rome that should be Greek, a new centre of Greek civilization that

---

[1] See J. Voyatzidis, 'La Grande Idée', *Le Cinq-centième anniversaire de la prise de Constantinople, L' Hellénisme contemporain* (fascicule hors série), pp. 279–85.

should embrace the Orthodox world. The spirit behind the Great Idea was a mixture of neo-Byzantinism and an acute sense of race. But, with the trend of the modern world the nationalism began to dominate the oecumenicity. George Scholarius Gennadius had, perhaps unconsciously, foreseen the danger when he anwered a question about his nationality by saying that he would not call himself a Hellene though he was a Hellene by race, nor a Byzantine though he had been born at Byzantium, but, rather, a Christian, that is, an Orthodox. For, if the Orthodox Church was to retain its spiritual force, it must remain oecumenical. It must not become a purely Greek Church.

The price paid by the Orthodox Church for its subjection to its Phanariot benefactors was heavy. First, it meant that the Church was run more and more in the interests of the Greek people and not of Orthodoxy as a whole. The arrangement made between the Conquering Sultan and the Patriarch Gennadius had put all the Orthodox within the Ottoman Empire under the authority of the Patriarchate, which was inevitably controlled by Greeks. But the earlier Patriarchs after the conquest had been aware of their oecumenical duties. The autonomous Patriarchates of Serbia and Bulgaria had been suppressed when the two kingdoms were annexed by the Turks; but the two Churches had continued to enjoy a certain amount of autonomy under the Metropolitans of Peć and of Tirnovo or Ochrid. They retained their Slavonic liturgy and their native clergy and bishops. This did not suit the Phanariots. It was easy to deal with the Churches of Wallachia and Moldavia because of the infiltration of Greeks into the Principalities, where anyhow the medieval dominance of the Serbian Church had been resented. The Phanariot Princes had not interfered with the vernacular liturgy and had, indeed, encouraged the Roumanian language at the expense of the Slavonic. The upper clergy was Graecized; so they felt secure. The Bulgarians and the Serbs were more intransigent. They had no intention of becoming Graecized. They protested to some effect against the appointment of Greek metropolitans. For a while the Serbian Patriarchate of

Peć, was reconstituted, from 1557 to 1755. The Phanariots demanded tighter control. In 1766 the autonomous Metropolitanate of Peć was suppressed and in 1767 the Metropolitanate of Ochrid. The Serbian and Bulgarian Churches were each put under an exarch appointed by the Patriarch. This was the work of the Patriarch Samuel Hantcherli, a member of an upstart Phanariot family, whose brother Constantine was for a while Prince of Wallachia until his financial extortions alarmed not only the taxpayers but also his ministers, and he was deposed and executed by the Sultan's orders. The exarchs did their best to impose Greek bishops on the Balkan Churches, to the growing anger of both Serbs and Bulgarians. The Serbs recovered their religious autonomy early in the nineteenth century when they won political autonomy from the Turks. The Bulgarian Church had to wait till 1870 before it could throw off the Greek yoke. The policy defeated its own ends. It caused so much resentment that when the time came neither the Serbs nor the Bulgarians would cooperate in any Greek-directed move towards independence; and even the Roumanians held back. None of them had any wish to substitute Greek for Turkish political rule, having experienced Greek religious rule.[1]

Only the Church of Montenegro, the tiny mountain-land into which the Turks never managed to penetrate, kept its religious freedom, under a dynasty of episcopal governors whose title descended from uncle to nephew. The Prince-Bishop Peter I Petrovitch Niegoch was recognized as an independent ruler by Sultan Selim III in 1799; and thenceforward even the Phanar admitted Montenegro's complete religious autonomy.[2] The Rus-

---

[1] For the Bulgarian Church see I. Snegarov, *History of the Archbishopric-Patriarchate of Ohrid* (in Bulgarian), *passim*. For the Serbian Church see L. Madrovics, *Le Peuple serbe et son église sous la domination turque*, *passim*. Both S. Macraios, Ὑπομνήματα Ἐκκλησιαστικῆς Ἱστορίας, in Sathas, *op. cit.* pp. 250–2, and Hypsilantis, *op. cit.* p. 410, declare that the authorities of both sees asked for their autonomy to be abolished. This was no doubt because the higher clergy, who were Greek, needed support against growing Balkan nationalism.

[2] For the Montenegran Church see Madrovics, *op. cit.*

sian Church was in a different position. Even the most imperially minded of the Constantinopolitan Patriarchs could not hope to control it, administered as it was by the Tsars practically as a department of State. Peter the Great's abolition of the Moscow Patriarchate was not displeasing to Constantinople, as it restored, nominally at least, the overriding ecclesiastical authority to the Oecumenical Patriarch. But the Patriarchs knew better than to try to interfere uninvited into Russian Church affairs.[1] Nor could they hope to govern the autonomous Church of Georgia, though its metropolitan acknowledged the Patriarch as his superior and officially had his appointment confirmed from Constantinople.[2]

Since the Ottoman conquest of Syria and Egypt the Greeks had dominated the older Patriarchates of the East. The Patriarch of Constantinople officially exercised no authority over his fellow-Patriarchs, but from his position at the capital of the Empire he tended to act as their agent before the Sultan and could largely control them, all the more easily because their hierarchies were almost entirely Greek. This was reasonable enough in the case of the Alexandrian Patriarchate, whose congregation was mainly composed of Greek traders and industrialists settled in Egypt, the native Christians belonging almost all of them to the separated Monophysite Church of the Copts. In 1651 the whole Orthodox congregation in Cairo was estimated at only 600; and Roman propaganda in the Patriarchate was very active there in the eighteenth century. But the Greeks remained faithful to Orthodoxy, largely owing to the intervention of Eustratios Argenti.[3] In the Patriarchates of Antioch and Jerusalem the majority of the

---

[1] See above, pp. 335-7.   [2] See above, pp. 75-6.

[3] For the Church of Alexandria see K. A. Uspenski, *The Patriarchate of Alexandria* (in Russian), I, pp. 340 ff.; C. A. Papadopoulos, Ἱστορία τῆς Ἐκκλησίας Ἀλεξανδρείας, *passim*: and Ware, *op. cit.* pp. 50-9. One Patriarch, Samuel Capasoulis, made a secret submission to Rome (Hofmann, *Griechische Patriarchen und Römische Päpste, Orientalia Christiana*, XIII, no. 47, *passim*, and XXXVI, no. 97, pp. 41-60). Eustratios Argenti also tried to set the finances of the Patriarchate on a better footing (Ware, *Eustratios Argenti*, pp. 52-3). Hypsilantis says that in 1744 the Patriarch's income was insufficient to pay the interest on his debts (*op cit.* p. 352).

Orthodox belonged to local races, now Arabic-speaking and using in their village churches an Arabic liturgy. They tended to resent the superimposed Greek hierarchy. Though they enjoyed a slightly superior position in comparison with the other religious minorities owing to Phanariot influence at the Sublime Porte, they were listless in their loyalty, and many slipped over to Rome or to other sects. The Patriarch of Antioch, now seated at Damascus, was closer in touch with the Arabs than his brother of Jerusalem. His upper clergy contained a larger proportion of indigenous members. But he was the poorest and the least influential of the Patriarchs and would never venture to oppose his brother of Constantinople, especially after a schism beginning in 1724 when pro-Roman bishops in Damascus elected a pro-Roman Patriarch, Serapheim (Cyril VI), and the remaining members of the synod fled to Constantinople and there elected a Greek, Sylvester. It was over forty years before the Orthodox party prevailed. Sylvester himself paid due attention to his Arabic congregation; but his successors tended to spend most of their time at Constantinople.[1] The Patriarch of Jerusalem, though the lowest in rank, was the least indigent of the Patriarchs. He enjoyed special prestige as bishop of the holiest of cities and the custodian of the chief shrines of Christendom. Since the sixteenth century the Princes of Wallachia and Moldavia had showered gifts on the Patriarchate and endowed it with large estates in the Principalities; and the Russian Tsars had been almost as generous. The Patriarch of Jerusalem could afford to finance schools not only in Palestine but also in other parts of the Orthodox world. He ran his own printing-press, safely located away from Muslim interference in the Moldavian capital of Jassy. But its organization was entirely Greek. If any Orthodox Palestinian wished for advancement he had to learn Greek and entirely identify himself with Greek interests; and the Patriarch himself spent much of his time at Constantinople or in the Principalities. The Greeks were not prepared to let

[1] For the Church of Antioch see C. A. Papadopoulos, Ἱστορία τῆς Ἐκκλησίας Ἀντιοχείας, *passim*: Ware, *op. cit.* pp. 36–41.

this luscious plum fall into other hands.[1] Yet it is doubtful whether in the long run the Greek nationalism that was being increasingly infused into the whole Orthodox organization was beneficial to Orthodoxy. It was not in the old Byzantine tradition. Though within the Empire itself a knowledge of Greek was necessary for any official position, there had been no distinction of race; and the Byzantines had encouraged vernacular liturgies and had been cautious in trying to impose a Greek hierarchy upon other peoples. But the Great Idea encouraged the Greeks to think of themselves as a Chosen People; and chosen peoples are seldom popular, nor do they fit well into the Christian life.

This attempt to turn the Orthodox Church into an exclusively Greek Church was one of the outcomes of Phanariot policy. It led also to a decline in spiritual values, by stressing Greek culture as against Orthodox traditions and seeking to turn the Church into a vehicle of nationalist feeling, genuine and democratic up to a point, but little concerned with the spiritual life. At the same time it placed the Patriarchate on the horns of a moral dilemma. It involved the Church in politics, and subversive politics. Was it not the duty of the Church to render unto Caesar the things which were Caesar's? Could a Patriarch justifiably jettison the agreement reached between the Sultan and his great predecessor Gennadius? Could he abjure the oath that he had sworn to the Sultan when his election was confirmed? On a more practical level, had he the right to indulge in plots which if they failed would undoubtedly subject his flock to ghastly reprisals? The more thoughtful hierarchs could not lightly support revolutionary nationalism. Yet if they failed to join in the movement from a sense of honour or

[1] For the properties of the Jerusalem Patriarchate in the Principalities see Jorga, *Byzance après Byzance*, pp. 132, 159–60, 188, 193. The Patriarch Chrysanthos Notaras, Dositheus's nephew and successor, spent most of his time in Moldavia and Wallachia (*ibid.* p. 227). James Dallaway, in his *Constantinople, Ancient and Modern* (published in 1797), p. 380, says that the Patriarchs of Antioch and Jerusalem have to live at Constantinople because their poverty obliges them to depend upon the bounty of the Patriarch of Constantinople. This is not quite accurate with regard to the Patriarch of Jerusalem, who liked to live in Constantinople in order to keep in touch with his properties in the Principalities.

from prudence or from spiritually minded detachment, they would be branded as traitors to Hellenism. The Church would lose its hold over the livelier and more progressive elements of its congregation. The rebirth of Greece was to involve a gallows erected at the gate of the Patriarchate and a Patriarch's corpse swinging thereon.

CHAPTER II

THE CHURCH AND THE GREEK PEOPLE

The Phanariots with their political and intellectual ambitions
threatened to damage what had hitherto been the greatest asset of
the Orthodox Church. If there was no Reformation in Eastern
Christendom, nor even any heretical movement as powerful as
that of the Cathars in the medieval West, it was because the Church
had never lost touch with the people. The rule that chose the
village priest from among the villagers, so that he differed from
them only in having received the education and training needed
to perform the Mysteries, meant that there was never a serious
cleavage between him and his congregation. He could never be
an absentee. He could not aspire to a higher place in the hierarchy;
he had no reason to go off to intrigue for preferment at the bishop's
palace. He was humble and content with his lot. If he felt the need
for spiritual guidance he could seek it at some nearby monastery.
The congregation respected him because he was empowered to
conduct the services of the Church. But his material lot was so
little better than that of his parishioners that none of them could
resent him. The parish was a united whole, deriving its strength
from the communal reading of the Gospels and celebration of the
eucharist; and, after the Turkish conquest, the sense of unity was
enhanced by awareness of the infidel oppressor. These Christian
villages, by the very simplicity of their Christianity, could maintain their integrity against the local Turkish landowner or aga or
the envoys of the Sultan from distant Istanbul.

There was always a danger in this simplicity that the religious
ceremonies of the village would become mere magical practices,
mixed up with superstitions inherited from old pagan days. If
village religion was to mean more than magic, if it was to keep a
real spiritual force, it must be supervised. The village might be
fortunate enough to have in the neighbourhood a monastery that

was a centre of active spiritual life. But even the monasteries needed supervision if their standards were to be maintained. The local bishop must be in touch with the parishes and monasteries of the diocese; and he himself must be worthy. The metropolitan must supervise the bishop; and his worthiness depended upon the summit of the Church hierarchy, the Patriarchal court. The local parish or monastery might be so self-sufficient that it could survive even if connection with the higher authorities was interrupted; but unless the higher authorities took a constant interest in its welfare it would stagnate.[1]

This interest lessened as time went by. It had never been part of the village priest's duties to be a scholar; but morally he was expected to give an example to the parish. While foreign travellers in the seventeenth century lament the ignorance of the priests and monks, by the end of the eighteenth century visitors to Greek lands were reporting instance after instance of greed and extortion of which not only priests and monks but even bishops were guilty. William Turner, for instance, tells of the Archbishop of Cos refusing, in his presence, to send a priest to a dying woman because she could not pay the sum that he demanded. To many of the Greeks themselves it began to appear that the whole ecclesiastical organization was rotten to the core.[2]

In the sixteenth century, as in Byzantine times, the Patriarchal Court had been filled by earnest clerics, most of whom came from the provinces and had started their careers in some provincial monastery. As they mounted up the hierarchy they might learn the value of intrigue and of bribery, but they were essentially men of religion, and most of them remembered their provincial origins. But the Turkish conquest had obliged the Patriarchate to take on secular duties. Its high officials had to be administrators. Worldly laymen were more useful for the work than spiritually minded ecclesiastics. From the seventeenth century onwards, under the

---

[1] For the organization of the parish, which has remained unaltered to the present day, see P. Hammond, *The Waters of Marah*, pp. 28 ff.

[2] W. Turner, *Journal of a Tour in the Levant*, III, pp. 509–10.

influence of the Phanariots, this laicization was increased. The rich merchants of Constantinople, on whose benefactions the Patriarch depended for his financial security, coveted posts at his Court for their relatives and began to use the offices for their political ends. These new ministers had nearly all been born and brought up in Constantinople. They regarded the provinces as being uninteresting and barbarous. Their attention was concentrated on Constantinople itself or on the rich lands of the Principalities, where many of them now owned estates. Their education made them unsympathetic with the older traditions of the Church. By the eighteenth century it was a matter of pride for them to be versed in Western philosophy and the rationalism fashionable at the time. The improvement in educational facilities provided by the schools and academies that they patronized meant a corresponding decline in religious education. Few of the hierarchs at the Patriarchal court ventured to brave Phanariot contempt by protesting against the fashions. But amongst the pious in the provinces there was a reaction against this new-fangled learning, which led to a suspicion of all learning, and to a defiant obscurantism. If studying books led to such godless rationalism, then surely it was better not to study books at all.[1]

It was in the monasteries that the decline in learning was most clearly apparent and most harmful; for the religious standards of a district depended mainly on its monasteries, which provided the spiritual advisers and confessors on whom the country-folk, the priests among them, depended. Even in Byzantine times many of the provincial monasteries had been humble and unpretentious and their monks simple men without much book-learning. But a monastery was required to have a library, even though it might contain little more than a few liturgical books and lives of saints. By the end of the sixteenth century libraries in the smaller monasteries began to be neglected, chiefly from lack of funds. By the end of the eighteenth century, with indifference and even hostility added to the poverty, these small libraries had virtually disap-

---

[1] See above, pp. 220–2.

peared. In such that remained the books were undusted and unread, if they had not been lost or sold. With few exceptions the average monk had forgotten how to read. Eighteenth-century travellers remarked that often when a monk seemed to be reading out the Gospels he was merely repeating what he had learnt by heart. The monks went through their liturgical rites devoutly enough but mechanically. Otherwise they tilled their fields and orchards or felled their timber like co-operative farmers. Their establishments could hardly give a spiritual direction to the neighbourhood.[1]

The greater monasteries preserved their cultural life for longer. The establishments in the Constantinopolitan suburbs were still centres for study.[2] The great Pontic monasteries of Sumela,

[1] J. Pitton de Tournefort, *Relation d'un voyage du Levant, fait par ordre du roi*, I, p. 98, says that the Greek clergy cannot really read the service-books and do not understand what they are repeating, and, p. 114, that they are no longer capable of preaching sermons. Even the sympathetic Ricaut had complained that English mechanics were 'more learned and knowing than the Doctors and Clergy of Greece' (*The Present State of the Greek and Armenian Churches, Anno Christi 1678*, preface, p. 28). J. Spon, *Voyages d'Italie, de Dalmatie, de Grèce, et du Levant*, II, pp. 200–2, had been impressed by the library of the Archbishop of Athens, Anthimos III, in 1674. But Athens was exceptional in its cultural traditions. English travellers of the early nineteenth century, such as W. M. Leake, *Travels in Northern Greece*, published in 1838 but based on travels made in the early years of the century, H. Holland, *Travels in the Ionian Islands, Albania, Thessaly, Macedonia, etc., during the years 1812 and 1813*, and Dr Hunt, *Mount Athos: An Account of the Monastic Institutions and Libraries*, published in 1818 in R. Walpole, *Memoirs relating to European and Asiatic Turkey* (2nd edition), all continually accuse Greek monks of utter ignorance and worthlessness, as do later R. Curzon, *Visits to Monasteries in the Levant* (1848), and Edward Lear, who refers to the monks of Athos as 'these muttering, miserable, mutton-hating, man-avoiding, Misogynic, morose and merriment-marring, monotoning, many-mule-making, mocking, mournful, minced fish and marmalade-masticating Monx' (letter to C. Fortescue (1856), quoted in A. Davidson, *Life of Edward Lear* (Penguin edition), p. 98). But it must be remembered that most of these travellers equated learning with Classical learning and would have been annoyed had the monks been sufficiently sophisticated to prevent their purloining of Classical manuscripts. On the other hand Dean Waddington in his book on *The Present Condition of the Greek or Oriental Church*, based on his travels to Greece in 1823–4, wrote with some respect of the monasteries (pp. 79–94), though he was shocked by the ignorance of the parish priests (p. 108).

[2] Libraries of monasteries in the outskirts of Constantinople now transferred to the Phanar contain a number of Classical works copied after the conquest,

Vazelon and Piristira maintained and added to their libraries, which were still well tended in the nineteenth century.[1] The Meteora monasteries in Thessaly, which had suffered terribly at the time of the Turkish conquest, were restored in the late sixteenth century by a Wallachian prince, who provided them with collections of books.[2] In the seventeenth century many other monasteries were rebuilt or founded by rich patrons and were attached to a rich institution, such as the Jerusalem Patriarchate or a monastery of princely foundation in the Principalities, which would be responsible for maintaining its standards.[3] But by the eighteenth century the foundation of monasteries was no longer fashionable.

The decline was particularly noticeable on Mount Athos. The disgruntled Catholic traveller, Pierre Belon, who disliked the Greeks, declared that in the sixteenth century it was impossible to find more than three or four literate monks in any of the monasteries there.[4] This is hard to believe when we remember that the Athonite monasteries co-operated in 1578 to buy Michael Cantacuzenus's splendid library. In 1602 Margunios bequeathed nine cases of books to the monastery of Iviron on Athos; and in 1684 the Patriarch Dionysius IV bequeathed his many books to the same monastery. Catalogues show that throughout the seventeenth century the other greater Athonite houses were also adding to their libraries.[5] Even in the eighteenth century Patriarchs such as

especially the Kamariotissa, which had MSS of Demosthenes, Homer, Theocritus and Lucian, copied in the sixteenth century and later. See the draft catalogue in the Phanar library. The catalogue of the monastery of Agia Triada on Halki has a note remarking that many of the best MSS were taken away by Sir Thomas Roe in 1628 and are now at Oxford. See above, p. 279.

1 See F. and E. Cumont, *Voyage d'exploration archéologique dans le Pont et la Petite Arménie*, pp. 371–2.

2 See D. M. Nicol, *Meteora, the Rock Monasteries of Thessaly*, pp. 169–70; N. Jorga, *Byzance après Byzance*, pp. 130, 142–3.

3 Jorga, *Byzance après Byzance*, pp. 142, 158–60.

4 P. Belon, *Les Observations de plusieurs singularitez et choses memorables trouvées en Grèce, Asie, Indie, Arabie et autres pays estranges* (1583 edition), p. 83.

5 For Michael Cantacuzenus's books, see above, p. 197; for a full account of Margunius's bequests see D. J. Geanakoplos, *Byzantine East and Latin West*, pp. 181–90; for Dionysius IV see Gedeon, Πατριαρχικοὶ Πίνακες, p. 593. His will is dated 1678.

Jeremias III or Serapheim II, men used to educated surroundings, were happy to retire there.[1] But Cyril V's brave attempt to found an Athonite academy showed by its failure that the monks refused to accept the intellectualism of the Phanar.[2] There was a growing lack of sympathy between the monasteries even on Athos and the Greeks of Constantinople. With the monastic atmosphere growing hostile to culture, Athos lost its appeal to men of education. The monasteries received cruder and less worthy recruits. By the end of the eighteenth century the rate of literacy on the Holy Mountain had seriously declined; and by the early nineteenth century the monks had sunk into the state of boorish ignorance so brilliantly and maliciously described by travellers such as Robert Curzon.[3]

These travellers were not guiltless of exaggeration. They remarked on the exploitation by the clergy, but seldom mentioned that there were also kindly and saintly priests. They noticed how narrow were the interests of the monks and how neglected were most of their libraries. But there were still houses on Athos, such as the Grand Lavra, where the treasures of the past were still tended with care, as they were, too, in monasteries such as Sumela or Saint John on Patmos. Moreover, this distressing anti-Western anti-intellectualism was in its way an expression of integrity. The Republic of the Holy Mountain was trying to avoid the infection of worldly pride and ambition which seemed to be pervading Greek society. It was trying to keep alive the true Orthodox tradition of concentration on the eternal verities unharmed by man-made philosophies and scientific theories. The monks had been made to listen to Vulgaris's lectures on German philosophy in the days of the Athonite academy; and they had been shocked. Yet this was what they were now offered when they sought for spiritual guidance from Constantinople. Their resentment was deplorable and uncreative; but it represented a positive striving to preserve the essence of the Faith.

[1] Gedeon, *op. cit.* pp. 631–2, 650.   [2] See above, p. 220.
[3] Curzon, *op. cit.* pp. 279–311, 357–449.

Yet even on Athos nationalism reared its head. The Greek monasteries began to show hostility to the Serbian and Bulgarian houses and soon, also, to the Roumanian and the Russian; and the hostility was to grow in the nineteenth century.[1]

Nationalism on Mount Athos was self-contained, an expression of rivalry between Christian peoples. Outside of the Mountain it was directed against the infidel oppressor. The Greek in the provinces could not understand the subtle politics of the Patriarchate. He could not appreciate the delicacy that the Patriarch and his advisers had to show in their dealings with the Sublime Porte. He looked to his village priest or to the local abbot or the bishop to protect him against the Turkish governmental authorities, and he gave his support to anyone who would champion him against the government. In the great days of the Ottoman Empire, when the administration had been efficient and on the whole just, Greek nationalism could be kept underground. But by the eighteenth century the administrative machinery was beginning to run down. Provincial Turkish governors began to revolt against the Sultan and could usually count on the support of the local Greeks. A growing number of outlaws took to the mountains. In Slav districts they were known by the Turkish name of *haidouks*; in Greece they were called the Klephts. They lived by banditry, directed mainly against the Turkish landowners; but they were quite ready to rob Christian merchants or travellers of any nationality. They could count on the support of the local Christian villagers, to whom they were latter-day Robin Hoods; they could almost always find refuge from the Turkish police in some local monastery.[2]

At the same time a spirit of revolt was growing in more educated Greek circles. There was a closer contact between Ottoman Europe and the rest of the continent. The Ionian Islands had

[1] See F. W. Hasluck, *Athos and its Monasteries*, pp. 55–60.
[2] For the Klephts see A. Phrantzis, Ἐπιτομὴ τῆς Ἱστορίας τῆς ἀναγεννηθείσης Ἑλλάδος, I, pp. 40 ff. See also Papadopoullos, *Studies and Documents relating to the History of the Greek Church and People under Turkish Domination, Bibliotheca Graeca Aevi Posterioris,* I, pp. 147–9.

remained under Venetian rule; and, after the close of the last war between Venice and the Turks early in the eighteenth century, it was easy to go to and fro between the islands and the mainland. The French conquest of Venice at the end of the century brought French revolutionary ideas within the reach of the Greeks. The spreading interest in Greek antiquities brought travellers of all nationalities to Greece; and the French Revolutionary wars, which made travel in Italy difficult for the British, resulted in numbers of them making their way to Athens. Meanwhile the Greeks in the Principalities were in constant touch with Austria and Russia. On the whole the Greeks were no more illiterate than any other European people of the time. In the villages only the priest, the schoolmaster and one or two farmers could read; but in the towns, small as well as large, literacy was general. Visitors to modern Greece always remark upon the inordinate passion of the Greeks for reading newspapers. In the late eighteenth century hand-bills and tracts took their place. It was an age all over Europe of secret societies; in particular it saw the spread of Freemasonry. Freemasonry appealed to the Greeks of the time. Though there does not seem to have been any Lodge within the Ottoman Empire, a number of Phanariots and of other Greeks became Masons in the course of journeys to the West; and in 1811 a lodge was founded at Corfu. The ideas of eighteenth-century Freemasonry were hostile to the old-established Churches. There were even a few Greek ecclesiastics among the Masons; but the effect of the movement was to weaken the influence of the Orthodox Church.[1]

The prophet of the new dispensation amongst the Greeks was a remarkable man called Adamantios Korais. He was born at Smyrna in 1748 and went as a young man to Paris, which he made his headquarters for the rest of his life. There he made contact with the French *Encyclopédistes* and their successors. From them he learnt a dislike for clericalism and for tradition. From reading

[1] For Freemasonry in Greece see N. Botzaris, *Visions balkaniques dans la préparation de la révolution grecque*, pp. 71–81; E. G. Protopsaltis, Ἡ Φιλικὴ Ἑταιρεία, pp. 19–20.

Gibbon he came to believe that Christianity had ushered in a dark age for European civilization. His friend Karl Schlegel taught him to identify nationality with language. 'Language is the nation,' he wrote; 'for when one says *la langue de France* one means the French nation.' The Greeks of his time were therefore of the same race as the ancient Greeks. But to make the identification closer he sought to reform the language so that it would be nearer to the Classical forms. He was, in fact, primarily responsible for the *katharevousa*, that artificial language which has had even to this day a disastrous effect in inhibiting the development of modern Greek literature. For the Byzantine past of Greece and for the Orthodox Church he had no use at all. His writings were eagerly read by the young intellectuals at the Phanar and by men of education all over Greece.[1] Almost more influential was the poet Rhigas, who was born, probably in 1757, at Velestino in Thessaly and whose real name was probably Antonios Kyriazis. Rhigas's stirring songs continually reminded the Greeks of their glorious past and urged them to rise against the Turks; and he himself developed schemes for liberating the whole of Turkey-in-Europe, working out a constitution which should safeguard the interests of the Balkan Slavs and Vlachs and Albanians, and founding a secret society for the furtherance of his aims. Unfortunately he and some fellow-conspirators were arrested by the Austrian police at Trieste in 1798 and handed over to the Turks, who put him to death.[2]

The Church authorities were well aware of these schemes, which enjoyed the sympathy of many of the younger Phanariots; and they were aware that the liveliest minds among the Greeks were thus turning away from religion, and that many even of the clergy were highly critical of the hierarchy. There appeared in Vienna in 1791 a book in Greek entitled *The New Geography*. It had been written by two Greek monks, Demetrius Philippides and George

---

[1] The basic work on Korais is D. Thereianos, *Adamantios Koraës* (3 vols.). See P. Sherrard, *The Greek East and the Latin West*, pp. 179–86.

[2] See A. Daskalakis, *Les Œuvres de Rhigas Velestinlis, passim;* S. Lampros, Ἀποκάλυψις περὶ τοῦ μαρτυρίου τοῦ 'Ρήγα; K. Amantos, Ἀνέκδοτα ἔγγραφα περὶ 'Ρήγα Βελεστινλῆ.

Constantas, who had smuggled the manuscript out of the Ottoman Empire. It contained a violent diatribe against the Church, accusing the upper ranks of venality and servility to the Turks and the lower ranks of obscurantist ignorance.[1] An equally bitter work, published anonymously in Italy in 1806, called *The Hellenic Nomarchy or a Word about Freedom*, repeated the charges against the whole ecclesiastical organization.

Such attacks convinced many members of the Patriarchal court that maybe Turkish rule was more conducive to a true religious life than was this new spirit of revolt. In 1798 there was published at Constantinople a work called *The Paternal Exhortation*, the author's name being given as Anthimus, Patriarch of Jerusalem. Anthimus was a sick man at the time and not expected to survive; but when he surprised his doctors by making a recovery he indignantly repudiated the authorship. The true identity of the author is unknown, but there is reason to believe that he was the Patriarch Gregory V, then entering on his first spell at the Patriarchate. Gregory, or whoever the author was, clearly knew that the book would arouse angry criticism and hoped that the critics would be checked by the saintly reputation of the moribund Anthimus. *The Paternal Exhortation* opens by thanking God for the establishment of the Ottoman Empire, at a time when Byzantium had begun to slip into heresy. The victory of the Turks and the tolerance that they showed to their Christian subjects were the means for preserving Orthodoxy. Good Christians should therefore be content to remain under Turkish rule. Even the Ottoman restriction on the building of churches, which the author realized might be hard to explain as beneficial, is excused by the remark that Christians should not indulge in the vainglorious pastime of erecting fine buildings; for the true Church is not made by hands, and there will be splendour enough in Heaven. After denouncing the illusory attractions of political freedom, 'an

---

[1] D. Philippides and G. Constantas, Γεωγραφία Νεωτερική, 2 vols., *passim* (for extracts see Papadopoullos, *op. cit.* pp. 136–7). Ἑλληνικὴ Νομαρχία ἤτοι Λόγος περὶ Ἐλευθερίας (ed. Tomadakis), *passim*.

enticement of the Devil and a murderous poison destined to push the people into disorder and destruction', the author ends with a poem bidding the faithful to pay respect to the Sultan, whom God had set in authority over them.[1]

Tactless though it was, the *Paternal Exhortation* was not theologically unsound. It was not the business of the Church to indulge in subversive nationalistic activities. Christ Himself had distinguished between the things which are Caesar's and the things which are God's. Paul had ordered Christians to obey the king, even though the king was the pagan Roman Emperor. The early Church had only defied authority when its freedom of worship was forbidden or its members were required to follow practices that were against a Christian conscience. The Turks had made no such demands. Good churchmen should surely be good citizens, not revolutionary plotters. From the practical point of view also the *Exhortation* was not unjustified. The Turkish Empire might be in decadence; but it had succeeded so far in crushing every revolt against its authority. The Cyprus rebellion of 1764 had fizzled out. The Morean revolt which Catherine II of Russia had encouraged in 1770 had ended in disaster and the rebels sternly punished. The treason of the Wallachian and Moldavian Princes in 1806 was to be ruthlessly crushed. The revolt of the Serbs which broke out under Karageorge in 1805 was to drag on for many years before it achieved success. Another unsuccessful rising could bring interminable misery to the Christians. It was, perhaps, unnecessary for the author of the *Paternal Exhortation* to show so much deference to the Sultan; but his views were not unreasonable for a devout prelate who believed that the Church should be kept free

[1] The full title of the pamphlet is Διδασκαλία Πατρική. Συντεθεῖσα παρὰ τοῦ Μακαριωτάτου Πατριάρχου τῆς ἁγίας πόλεως Ἱερουσαλὴμ κίρ Ἀνθίμου εἰς ὠφέλειαν τῶν ὀρθοδόξων Χριστιανῶν νῦν πρῶτον τυπωθεῖσα δι' ἰδίας δαπάνης τοῦ Παναγίου Τάφου, printed in Constantinople in 1798. See also D. Zakythinos, Ἡ Τουρκοκρατία, p. 82, for a version of the text. S. Macraios, Ὑπόμνημα Ἐκκλησιαστικῆς Ἱστορίας, in Sathas, Μεσαιωνικὴ Βιβλιοθήκη, p. 394, accuses Gregory, whom he did not like, of having taken advantage of Anthimus's moribund state to issue the pamphlet in his name.

from politics and who from the terms of his own appointment had solemnly sworn to guarantee the loyalty of his flock to the Sultan's government, and who for humanity's sake wished it not to run the risk of self-destruction.

Nevertheless it was a document which found little sympathy with its Greek readers. Korais hastened to reply in a tract called the *Fraternal Exhortation*, in which he declared that the *Paternal Exhortation* in no way represented the feeling of the Greek people but was the ridiculous raving of a hierarch 'who is either a fool or has been transformed from a shepherd into a wolf'.[1] It also embarrassed the Phanariots. The older amongst them were aware of the dangers of a premature revolt. Constantine Ypsilanti, who was to be many times Prince of Moldavia and who had known Rhigas since their young days together, pursued an aim like that of Rhigas, a reformed Balkan Empire, but it was to include the Turks and to be inaugurated under the Sultan's suzerainty. Later, so he hoped, the Greeks would take over the government from Turkish hands. His opinion carried weight amongst the older Phanariots, though many of them felt that he was moving a little too fast for safety. Time, they thought, was on their side. The Ottoman Empire would soon collapse from its own weakness. The reforms which Sultan Selim III bravely attempted to introduce to bring it up to date were over-hastily conceived and unwisely executed. Though the power of the Janissaries was destroyed, instead there was chaos in the army; and a number of local pashas, led by Ali Pasha at Janina and Osman Pasvanoglu at Vidin, were in open revolt. Selim himself was deposed in 1807 and murdered the following year. Soon, the older Phanariots hoped, there would be such disorder in the central administration that even the Turks would be content to let the Greeks take over the government. This was a policy which the Patriarchate could

---

[1] A. Korais, Ἀδελφικὴ Διδασκαλία πρὸς τοὺς εὑρισκομένους κατὰ πᾶσαν τὴν Ὀθωμανικὴν ἐπικράτειαν Γραικούς, εἰς ἀντίρρησιν κατὰ τῆς Ψευδωνύμου ἐν ὀνόματι τοῦ μακαριωτάτου πατριάρχου Ἱεροσολύμων ἐκδοθείσης ἐν Κωνσταντινουπόλει πατρικῆς Διδασκαλίας.

bless; for it avoided sedition. But it did not satisfy the younger Phanariots. They were impatient. The time would soon be ripe. They pinned their faith on the Russian sovereign, the enlightened Tsar Alexander I.[1]

But, in spite of the enthusiasm of its younger members, the Phanar was not popular amongst the Greeks as a whole. To men like Korais it seemed to be moving still in the corrupt and shameful atmosphere of Byzantium. Its wealth roused jealousy, which its arrogance did not allay. The financial exactions of the Phanariots in the Principalities had been noticed with disapproval by every Western traveller; but their severest critics were the Greeks themselves. There is a book, an *Essai sur les Fanariotes*, written in about 1810 in French by a Greek called Mark Zallonis, but not actually published till 1824, at Marseilles, which is almost hysterical in its denunciation but tells some bitter truths about the effect of Phanariot domination.[2]

Zallonis tended to confuse the Phanariots with the Patriarchate. Pious Greeks were right to condemn the effects of the Phanariot

---

[1] Botzaris, *op. cit.* pp. 83–100. Dallaway, who knew Constantine Ypsilanti, thought him wise and estimable (*op. cit.* p. 103). The historian, A. C. Hypsilantis, Τὰ μετὰ τὴν Ἅλωσιν (*1457–1789*), writing in 1789, believed that the Greeks had forfeited their chances of liberty owing to their evil ways and only the Russians could save them (*op. cit.* p. 534).

[2] An English translation of the *Essai* is published in C. Swan, *Voyage up the Mediterranean* (1826). There is also a Greek translation by someone who gives his name as 'N. Ηδαιεφαβ' (*sic*, obviously a code of some description) entitled Σύγγραμμα τῶν ἀπὸ τὴν Κωνσταντινούπολιν πριγκίπων τῆς Βγαχομολδαβίας, τῶν λεγομένων Φαναριωτῶν, παρὰ τοῦ Μάρκου Φιλίππου Ζαλλωνη... (Paris, 1831). It is likely that the translator was Korais. Zallonis often makes false accusations, as when he accuses the Phanariots for the Orthodox Church's hostility to Rome (pp. 138 ff. of French edition). The English traveller Thornton is almost as scathing about Phanariot rule (T. Thornton, *The Present State of Turkey*, II, pp. 297–380, published in 1809); but Thornton disliked all Greeks. W. Wilkinson, *An Account of the Principalities of Wallachia and Moldavia*, *passim*, is fairer-minded and gives the Phanariots credit for their efforts to improve education. Dr Adam Neale, passing through Moldavia in 1805, thought well of the government of Alexander Mouroussi, but regarded him as an exception (*Travels through some parts of Germany, Poland, Moldavia and Turkey*, p. 164).

control of the Church. It undoubtedly suited the Phanariots that the Church should be in debt and therefore dependent upon their aid. To some extent, therefore, they encouraged and perpetuated its corruption. But they did not control it absolutely, for they themselves were divided. Their older and more conservative members agreed with the Patriarch in wishing to discountenance open rebellion. A test came early in the nineteenth century when Sultan Selim made a serious effort to suppress brigandage. The Klephts in Greece, thanks to the spirit of revolt and to the hymns of Rhigas, had become popular heroes. It was a patriotic duty for a Greek to give them shelter against the police; and the village priest and the monks of the country monasteries were eager to help them. But they were a menace to orderly rule; and when the Sultan demanded of the Patriarch that he should issue a stern decree threatening with excommunication any priest or monk who would not aid the authorities in their suppression, the Patriarch could not well refuse. The decree was published in the Peloponnese; and, though most of the higher clergy sullenly obeyed it, the villages and the poorer monasteries were outraged; and even at the Phanar there was open disapproval. It became clear that when the moment for revolt arrived the Patriarch would not be at its head.[1]

In spite of the Patriarch the plots continued. At the end of the eighteenth century there were several secret societies in existence, with names such as the *Athena*, which hoped to liberate Greece with French help and which counted Korais among its members, or the *Phoenix*, which pinned its hopes on Russia.[2] In 1814 three Greek merchants at Odessa in Russia, Nicholas Skouphas, Emmanuel Xanthos and Athanasius Tsakalof, the first a member of the *Phoenix* and the latter two freemasons, founded a society which they called the *Hetaireia ton Philikon*, the Society of Friends.

[1] A. Phrantzis, *op. cit.*, *loc. cit.* Phrantzis, a Peloponnesian writing about events that took place within his lifetime, and himself a member of the Hetaireia, is a reliable source. When Leake visited the Great Meteoron in 1810, the abbot and two of his monks were away in prison at Jannina for having sheltered some Klephts, a little unwillingly, from Ali Pasha's police (Leake, *op. cit.* IV, p. 542).
[2] Botzaris, *op. cit.* pp. 71–81; Protopsaltis, *op. cit.* pp. 15–18.

Thanks chiefly to the energy of Skouphas, who unfortunately died in 1817, it soon superseded all the previous societies and became the rallying point of rebellion. Skouphas was determined to include in the society patriots of every description; and soon it had amongst its members Phanariots such as Prince Constantine Ypsilanti and his hot-headed sons, Alexander and Nicholas, all now living in exile in Russia, and members of the Mavrocordato and Caradja families, or high ecclesiastics such as Ignatius, Metropolitan of Arta and later of Wallachia, and Germanus, Metropolitan of Patras, intellectuals such as Anthimus Ghazis, and brigand leaders such as the *armatolos* George Olympios and Kolokotronis. It was organized partly on masonic lines and partly on what the founders believed to have been the early Christian organization. It had four grades. The lowest was that of Blood-brothers, which was confined to illiterates. Next were the Recommended, who swore an oath to obey their superiors but were not permitted to know more than the general patriotic aims of the society and were kept in ignorance of the names of their superiors and were supposed not even to know of the existence of the Blood-brothers. Above them were the Priests, who could initiate Blood-brothers and Recommendeds and who, after solemn oaths, were allowed to know the detailed aims of the society. Above them again were the Pastors, who supervised the Priests and saw that they only initiated suitable candidates; a suitable Recommended could become a Pastor without passing through the grade of Priest. From the Pastors were chosen the supreme authorities of the society, the *Arche*. The names of the members of the *Arche* were unknown except to each other, and their meetings were held in absolute secrecy. This was thought necessary not only for security against external powers but also for the prestige of the society. Had the names of its directors been known, there might have been opposition to several of them, particularly among such a faction-loving people as the Greeks; whereas the mystery surrounding the *Arche* enabled hints to be dropped that it included such mighty figures as the Tsar himself. All grades had to swear unconditional obedience to the *Arche*, which itself operated through twelve Apostles, whose business it was to win recruits and to organize branches in different provinces and countries. They were appointed just before the death of Skouphas; and their names are known. It was first decided to fix the headquarters of the society on Mount Pelion, but later, after the initiation of the Maniot chieftain, Peter Mavromichalis, it was moved to the Mani, in the south-east of the Peloponnese, a district into which the Turks had never ventured to penetrate.[1]

There were however two distinguished Greeks who refused to join the Society. One was the ex-Patriarch Gregory V. He had been deposed for the second time in 1808, and was living on Mount Athos, where the Apostle John Pharmakis visited him. Gregory pointed out that it was impossible for him to swear an oath of unconditional obedience to the unknown leaders of a secret society and that anyhow he was bound by oath to respect the authority of the Sultan. The reigning Patriarch, Cyril VI, was not approached. Still more disappointing was the refusal of the Tsar's foreign minister, John Capodistrias, to countenance the Hetaireia.[2]

John Antony, Count Capodistrias, had been born in Corfu in 1776, and as a young man had worked for the Ionian government there, before going to Russia at the time of the second French occupation of the Ionian Islands in 1807. He was given a post in the Russian diplomatic service and was attached to the Russian Embassy at Vienna in 1811, and next year was one of the Russian delegates at the treaty negotiations at Bucharest. His remarkable abilities impressed Tsar Alexander, who in 1815 nominated him Secretary of State and Assistant Foreign Minister. In his youth

[1] Botzaris, *op. cit.* pp. 83–100; E. G. Protopsalti, Ἡ Φιλικὴ Ἑταιρεία, pp. 21 ff. A good contemporary account of the Society is given by Dean Waddington in his *Visit to Greece, 1823–4*, pp. xvi–xxx. Protopsalti, *op. cit.* pp. 245–55, reproduces the constitution and oaths of the Society.

[2] J. Philemon, Δοκίμιον Ἱστορικὸν περὶ τῆς Ἑλληνικῆς Ἐπαναστάσεως, I, pp. 157–8: Botzaris, *op. cit.* pp. 95–6: T. Kandiloros, Ἱστορία τοῦ Ἐθνομάρτυρα Γρηγορίου τοῦ Ε', pp. 123–34.

Capodistrias had made contact with many of the Greek revolutionary thinkers, and he was well known to be a Greek patriot. In the past many Greeks had looked to France to deliver them from the Turks; but after Napoleon's collapse the whole Greek world turned to Russia, and Capodistrias's accession to power gave them confidence. The Russian sovereign was the great patron of Orthodoxy. The Greeks forgot how little they had gained from Catherine the Great, the imperialistic German free-thinker, who had incited them to revolt in 1770 and then had abandoned them. But at the Treaty of Kučuk Kainarci in 1774 Russia had acquired the right to intervene in Turkish internal affairs in the interest of the Orthodox. Catherine's son, the madman Paul, was clearly unwilling to help the Greek cause; but when Alexander I succeeded his murdered father in 1801 hopes rose. Alexander was known to have liberal views and mystical Orthodox sympathies. Belief in his aid had encouraged the Princes of Moldavia and Wallachia to plot against the Sultan in 1806; and, when they were deposed by the Sultan, the Tsar cited his rights under the Treaty of Kučuk Kainarci and declared war on Turkey. The only outcome of the war had been the annexation by Russia of the Moldavian province of Bessarabia. But the Greeks were not discouraged. Now, with a Greek as the Tsar's Secretary of State, the time had surely come for the War of Liberation. The plotters refused to realize that Capodistrias was the Tsar's servant and a practical man of the world; and they did not know that the Tsar himself was becoming more reactionary and less willing to countenance rebellion against established authority.[1]

The planners of Greek independence could not count on the open support of the Patriarchate. They should have realized that they also could not count on the support of Russia. And the nationalist ecclesiastical policy of the Church during the last century deprived them of the friendship of the other peoples of the Balkans. The leaders of the Hetaireia were aware of this. They made

---

1 There is as yet no good life of Capodistrias. For his early career and his relation to the Society, see Botzaris, *op. cit.* pp. 75, 77, 86–7, 97–100.

earnest attempts to enrol Serbian, Bulgarian and Roumanian members. When Karageorge revolted against the Turks in Serbia Greek armatoles and klephts came to join him. Even the Phanariot princes had offered support; but they were rebuffed. 'The Greek Princes of the Phanar', Karageorge wrote, 'can never make common cause with people who do not wish to be treated like animals.' Karageorge's revolt was put down by the Turks in 1813. Two years later the Serbs revolted again, under Miloš Obrenovitć, a far subtler diplomat, who secured Austrian support and eventually induced the Sultan to accept him as a reliable vassal-prince. Miloš had no contact with the Greeks. The Hetaireia therefore pinned its faith on Karageorge, who was persuaded to become a member in 1817. As Karageorge was greatly admired by the Bulgarians it was hoped that numbers of them would now join the movement. Karageorge was then sent back to Serbia. But the Serbs, who were satisfied with Miloš's achievements, offered him no support; and Miloš regarded him as a rival to be eliminated. He was assassinated in June 1817. With his death any hope of interesting the Serbs in the coming Greek rebellion faded out; and there was no one capable of rallying the Bulgars to the cause. Karageorge alone could have given the Hetaireia the air of not being exclusively Greek.[1]

The Hetaireia had higher hopes of the Roumanians. There a peasant leader, Tudor Vladimirescu, who had led a band to help the Serbs, was defying the Turkish police in the Carpathian mountains and had gathered together a considerable company. He was in close touch with two leading hetairists, George Olympius and Phokianos Savvas, and he himself joined the society, promising to co-ordinate his movements with the Greeks'. But he was an unreliable ally; for he was bitterly opposed to the Phanariot princes, who, he considered, had brought ruin to his country.[2]

[1] Botzaris, *op. cit.* pp. 133–42.
[2] See N. Jorga, *Izvoarele contemporane asupra mişcării lui Tudor Vladimirescu*, introduction, *passim*: Botzaris, *op. cit.* pp. 143 ff.

By the end of 1820 everything seemed to be ready. Ali Pasha of Janina was in open revolt against the Sultan; and had promised help to the Greeks; and, though Osman Pasvanoglu was dead, his pashalik of Vidin was in disorder, tying up Turkish troops south of the Danube. The *Arche* of the *Hetaereia* had a few months previously elected a Captain-General, choosing a young Phanariot Alexander Ypsilanti, son of the ex-Prince Constantine of Moldavia. It is interesting to note that the plotters considered that only a Phanariot had sufficient experience and prestige for the post. Alexander Ypsilanti was born in 1792 and spent his youth in Russia. He had won a reputation for gallantry and military skill when serving in the Russian army and had lost an arm at the battle of Kulm, fighting against the French. He was known to be an intimate friend of the Tsar and the Tsaritsa and of Capodistrias. He made it his first task to improve the efficiency of the Society and summoned the one and only plenary meeting of the *Arche*, which was held at Ismail in southern Russia in October 1820. The original plan had been to start the revolt in the Peloponnese, where there would be a secure base in the Mani and where the sympathy of the inhabitants was assured. Alexander now changed his mind. It would be better to start the main campaign in Moldavia. By the Treaty of Bucharest the Turks had undertaken not to send troops into the Principalities without Russian consent. Vladimirescu would distract what Turkish militia was there already; and a successful army sweeping through Wallachia and across the Danube was the only thing that might induce the Bulgarians and the Serbians to join in. Meanwhile a subsidiary rising in the Peloponnese, which Alexander's brother Demetrius was sent to organize, would further embarrass the Turks.[1]

The invasion of Moldavia was timed to begin on 24 November (O.S.) 1820. Alexander had already gathered together a small army of Greeks and Christian Albanians on the Russian side of the frontier. Almost at the last moment Capodistrias counselled delay. The Austrian secret police had discovered the plans and had sent

[1] Protopsaltis, *op. cit.* pp. 70–84, with documents.

to warn the Sultan; and the Tsar was nervous of international reactions. But, in January 1821, Vladimirescu, encouraged by George Olympius, against the advice of Phokianos Savvas, began to attack Turkish police posts and was scornful of Ypsilanti's hesitation. About the same time the Prince of Wallachia, Alexander Soutzo, died, poisoned it was rumoured by the Hetaireia, of which he was known to disapprove. Demetrius Ypsilanti reported from the Peloponnese that everyone there was impatient of further delays. Alexander Ypsilanti decided that the time had come to act. He sought an audience of the Tsar before leaving St Petersburg, but it was refused. The Tsaritsa, however, sent him her blessing; and he was assured that the Tsar would personally protect his wife. On 22 February (O.S.) Alexander and his little band crossed over the river Pruth into Moldavia.

In his desire to prevent a leakage of news Alexander had not warned his fellow-plotters. When news of his advance reached the Peloponnese, his brother Demetrius hesitated, fearing that it might be a false rumour. But the people would not wait. They found a leader in Germanus, Metropolitan of Patras, who, in defiance of the Patriarchate and of Orthodox tradition, raised the standard of revolt at the monastery of Agia Lavra, near Kalavryta, on 25 March. The Mani had already risen. The islands of Spetsai and Psara and a little later Hydra rose in early April. By the end of April all central and southern Greece was up in arms.

But it was now too late for Alexander Ypsilanti. He had marched unopposed on Bucharest. But there was no news of any rising among the Bulgarians or the Serbs; and when he reached Bucharest he found that Tudor Vladimirescu and his troops were there before him; and they refused to let him into the city. 'I am not prepared to shed Roumanian blood for Greeks,' said Vladimirescu. There were skirmishes between the two forces. Then came news that the Tsar had repudiated the whole rebellion at the Congress of Laibach, and with his permission a huge Turkish army was approaching the Danube, ready to invade the Principalities. Ypsilanti retired north-east, towards the Russian frontier.

Vladimirescu, after lingering for a few days in Bucharest trying to make terms with the Turkish commander, moved back on 15 May into the Carpathians. But he had lost control over his own followers. They allowed George Olympius to take him prisoner and to put him to death, on the evening of 26 May, for his treason to the cause. Phokianos Savvas and a garrison of Albanians held Bucharest for a week, then also retired into the mountains. The Turks entered Bucharest before the end of May, then moved in pursuit of Ypsilanti. On 7 June (O.S.) they routed his army at a battle at Dragasani. His best troops perished. He himself fled over the Austrian frontier into Bukovina, where by Metternich's orders he was arrested. He spent the remainder of his life in an Austrian prison. The remnant of his army was rallied by George Cantacuzenus, who led them back towards the Russian frontier. But the frontier was closed to them. The Turks caught up with them at Sculeni on the Pruth and massacred them there, on 17 June, in sight of Russian territory. Savvas surrendered to the Turks in August and was put to death by them. George Olympius held out till September in the monastery of Secu. When all hope was lost he fired his powder stores and blew up the monastery with himself and all his garrison within it.[1]

The Sultan had already taken vengeance at Constantinople. The news that Alexander Ypsilanti had invaded Moldavia reached the city in early March. The Patriarch and his advisers were taken by surprise. Gregory V, who had been restored to the Patriarchal throne in December 1818, hastened to summon the synod. But, with the Turkish police all around them there was nothing that they could do but pray and keep silence. One or two bishops slipped quietly out of the city to join the rebels, together with a

---

[1] The best contemporary account of the revolt, as seen from Constantinople, is given in R. Walsh, *Residence at Constantinople during the Greek and Turkish Revolutions*, I, pp. 299–333. Events in the Principalities are given by two contemporary Roumanian writers, Ivan Darzeanu, *Cronica Revolutiei din 1821*, and Mihai Cioranu, *Revolutia lui Tudor Vladimirescu*, both published in Jorga, *Byzance après Byzance*. There is a vast literature dealing with the rising in Greece itself.

few of the Phanariot nobility. Had Gregory been able to bring himself to denounce the revolt he might have saved his life. As it was, Turkish police entered the Patriarchate and kept him a prisoner there till 22 April, when he was hanged at the gate of his palace. Two metropolitans and twelve bishops followed him to the gallows. Then it was the turn of the laymen. First the Grand Dragoman, Mouroussi, and his brother, then all the leading Phanariots. By the summer of 1821 the great houses in the Phanar were empty. A new Patriarch had been appointed, a harmless nonentity called Eugenius II. There was a new Grand Dragoman, unrelated to any of the Phanariot clans; and he was executed on the merest suspicion of treason a few months later; and the post was abolished. The powers of the Patriarchate were severely curtailed. The contract made between the Conquering Sultan and Gennadius had been broken by the Patriarchate. The Turks were no longer prepared to trust the Orthodox.[1]

With the holocaust at the Patriarchate the old dispensation was ended. The Orthodox Church had to reorganize itself to face up to a nationalistic world.

[1] The actions of the Holy Synod and the Patriarch and Gregory's death are graphically described by Walsh, *op. cit.* I, pp. 311 ff. He actually witnessed the Patriarch's hanging. See also Kandiloros, *op. cit.* pp. 214 ff.

CHAPTER 12

EPILOGUE

The Patriarchate of Constantinople never recovered from the events of 1821. The Patriarch still remained at the head of the Orthodox *milet*; but his administration was supervised more closely and his powers were steadily curtailed. He could still appear in 1908, at the opening of the Parliament which Sultan Abdul Hamit was forced to summon, together with his fellow-hierarchs, as a high official of the Ottoman Empire. But the triumphant Young Turks had no use for the *milet* system and planned its abolishment. The victory of the Allies in 1918 raised hopes in Patriarchal circles. But they hoped not that the previous power should be restored to the Patriarchate, but rather that Constantinople should be given to the Greeks, in consummation of the Great Idea. It was a vain hope, ruined by the genius of Kemal Ataturk. The Greek defeat in Asia Minor meant that the Turks would recover Constantinople; and Ataturk's conception of government had no place for the *milets*. Henceforward the Patriarch's authority was purely ecclesiastical. He became merely the chief bishop of a dwindling religious community in a secular state, whose rulers mistrusted and disliked him for his faith and for his race. His flock, restricted now within Turkey to Istanbul—the name Constantinople was forbidden— and its suburbs, could look to him for moral guidance and spiritual comfort. But that was all that he could give them. His condition in no way improved in the following decades.

Throughout the nineteenth century, after the close of the Greek War of Independence, the Greeks within the Ottoman Empire had been in an equivocal position. Right up to the end of the Balkan War in 1913 they were far more numerous than their fellow-Greeks living within the boundaries of the Kingdom of Greece, and on an average more wealthy. Some of them still took service under the Sultan. Turkish government finances were still

Epilogue

largely administered by Greeks. There were Greeks in the Turkish diplomatic service, such as Musurus Pasha, for many years Ottoman Ambassador to the Court of St James. Such men served their master loyally; but they were always conscious of the free Greek state, whose interests often ran counter to his. Under the easygoing rule of Sultans Abdul Medjit and Abdul Aziz, in the middle of the century, no great difficulties arose. But the Islamic reaction under Abdul Hamit led to renewed suspicion of the Greeks, which was enhanced by the Cretan question and the war, disastrous for Greece, of 1897. The Young Turks who dethroned Abdul Hamit shared his dislike of the Christians, which the Balkan War seemed to justify. Participation by Greeks in Turkish administrative affairs declined and eventually was ended.

For the Orthodox Patriarch of Constantinople the position throughout the century was particularly difficult. He was a Greek but he was not a citizen of Greece. By the oath that he took on his appointment he undertook to be loyal to the Sultan, even though the Sultan might be at war with the Kingdom of Greece. His flock, envious of the freedom of the Greeks of the Kingdom, longed to be united with them; but he could not lawfully encourage their longing. The dilemma that faced Gregory V in the spring of 1821 was shared, though in a less acute form, by all his successors. He no longer had any authority over the Greeks of Greece. Hardly had the Kingdom been established before its Church insisted on complete autonomy under the Archbishop of Athens. It was to Athens, to the King of Greece, that the Greeks in Turkey now looked for the fulfilment of their aspirations. Had the Christian Empire been restored at Constantinople the Patriarch would indeed have lost much of his administrative powers; but he would have lost them gladly; for the Emperor would have been at hand for him to advise and admonish, and he would have enjoyed the protection of a Christian government. But as it was, he was left to administer, in a worsening atmosphere and with decreasing authority, a community whose sentimental allegiance was given increasingly to a monarch who lived far away, with whom he could not publicly associate himself, and whose kingdom was too small and poor to rescue him in times of peril. In the past the Russian Tsar had been cast by many of the Greeks in the role of saviour. That had had its advantages; for, though the Tsar continually let his Greek clients down, he was at least a powerful figure whom the Turks regarded with awe. Moreover he did not interfere with the Greeks' allegiance to their Patriarch. Whatever Russian ambitions might be, the Greeks had no intention of ending as Russian subjects. As it was, the emergence of an independent Greece lessened Russian sympathy. Greek politicians ingeniously played off Britain and France against Russia, and against each other; and Russia found it more profitable to give her patronage to Bulgaria: which was not to the liking of the Greeks.

We may regret that the Patriarchate was not inspired to alter its role. It was, after all, the Oecumenical Patriarchate. Was it not its duty to emerge as leader of the Orthodox Oecumene? The Greeks were not alone in achieving independence in the nineteenth century. The Serbs, the Roumanians, and, later, the Bulgarians all threw off the Ottoman yoke. All of them were alive with nationalistic ardour. Could not the Patriarchate have become a rallying force for the Orthodox world, and so have checked the centrifugal tendencies of Balkan nationalism?

The opportunity was lost. The Patriarchate remained Greek rather than oecumenical. We cannot blame the Patriarchs. They were Greeks, reared in the Hellenic tradition of which the Orthodox Church was guardian and from which it derived much of its strength. Moreover in the atmosphere of the nineteenth century internationalism was regarded as an instrument of tyranny and reaction. But the Patriarchate erred too far in the other direction. Its fierce and fruitless attempt to keep the Bulgarian Church in subjection to Greek hierarchs, in the 1860s, did it no good and only increased bitterness. On Mount Athos, whose communities owed much to the lavish, if not disinterested, generosity of the Russian Tsars, the feuds between the Greek and Slav monasteries were far from edifying. This record of nationalism was to endanger the very existence of the Patriarchate in the dark days that followed 1922.

Now, owing to the very fact of these disasters, the Patriarchate can be oecumenical once more. In the country of his residence the Patriarch's congregation is small; for the Greeks have almost all, willingly or unwillingly, left Turkey for Greece, where they are under the ecclesiastical rule of the Archbishop of Athens. The Patriarch of Alexandria is responsible for the Orthodox in Africa, and the Patriarchs of Antioch and Jerusalem for those in Asia. But the large and widespread Orthodox congregations in Western Europe, in Australia and in the Americas depend canonically on the Patriarch of Constantinople; and this gives him now the authority to be the real spokesman for Orthodoxy and, if God wills, to play a leading part in bringing closer friendship between the great branches of the Church of Christ.

Nevertheless the importance of the Greek tradition in the survival of Orthodoxy during the Ottoman period must not be forgotten. Throughout all its vicissitudes the Church was determined to keep its flock conscious of the Greek heritage. The monks might be suspicious of pagan learning and of attempts to revive the study of philosophy; but everyone who called himself a Greek, whatever his actual racial origins might be, was proud to think that he was of the same nation as Homer and Plato and Aristotle, as well as of the Fathers of the Eastern Church. This faith in the Greek genius kept hope alive; and without hope few institutions can survive. The Greeks might be languishing by the waters of Babylon; but they still had their songs to sing. It was Orthodoxy that preserved Hellenism through the dark centuries; but without the moral force of Hellenism Orthodoxy itself might have withered.

Hellenism provided hope for this earth. But the true strength of the Orthodox lay in their conviction that so long as they remained loyal to the teaching of Christ they would find beyond this vale of tears real and eternal happiness. More than any other branch of the Christian Church the Orthodox have been mindful of the injunction to render unto Caesar the things which are Caesar's. This has enabled them to submit—too easily, critics have thought—to the secular authority of infidel or godless governments; but it has also enabled them to keep apart the things which are God's and to cling to them with integrity. It might have been more heroic to protest and to face martyrdom; but, if all the members of a Church are martyred, there will be no Church left on earth. As it was, there were martyrs during these centuries, who suffered in defence of their religious integrity. But it was not for men of religion to plunge into worldly politics. The Patriarch was, indeed, forced to assume a political role by becoming ethnarch of the Orthodox *milet*. But it was his duty, both as a religious leader and as an official of the Ottoman Empire, to discourage political activity in his flock; and this gave him a difficult role to play at the time of the movement towards Greek independence. The Patriarchate was blamed for not being in the forefront of the movement. But it was not in the Orthodox tradition that prelates should be warrior politicians. The great Fathers of the Church, such as Basil, would have been horrified by the gallant Peloponnesian bishops who raised the standard of revolt in 1821; nor would they have approved of the politically minded Cypriot ethnarchs of our own day.

The business of the Patriarch was to see that his Church endured. Liberty of worship was more important to him than secular liberty. On the ecclesiastical front he could play politics, to preserve his Church from being absorbed by the great and ambitious Church of Rome, and to seek allies from amongst the vigorous new Protestant Churches, and to ensure the loyalty of the daughter-Church in Russia. Yet even on that front the Orthodox remained on the defensive, seeking not to attack but to maintain what they believed to be their traditions and their rights. They were ready to listen to the overtures of the Protestants, but, except in the eccentric case of Cyril Lucaris and his school, they regarded the Protestants as bringing possible aid against Roman aggression, and also as sources of material assistance. The integrity of the true faith was not to be touched: though in fact the negotiations led to a desire to give to the articles of faith a precision alien to the old apophatic outlook. It was a temporary desire. In the main the Orthodox saw the truths of their faith as eternal. They were not going to alter them for any earthly advantage.

The history of the Orthodox Patriarchate during the long captivity of the Great Church is lacking in heroic bravado. Its leaders were men who found it wise to avoid publicity and outward splendour and grand gestures. If they often indulged in intrigue and often in corruption, such is the inevitable fate of second-class citizens under a government in which intrigue and corruption flourish. The grand achievement of the Patriarchate was that in spite of humiliation and poverty and disdain the Church endured and endures as a great spiritual force. The Candlestick had been darkened and obscured, as the Englishman Peter Heylyn, who disliked the Greeks, noted in the early seventeenth century, but God had not taken it away. The light still burns, and burns brighter. The Gates of Hell have not prevailed.

BIBLIOGRAPHY

BOOK I

1 COLLECTIONS OF SOURCES

Barker, E. *Social and Political Thought in Byzantium from Justinian I to the last Palaeologus.* Oxford, 1957.

Brightman, F. E. *Liturgies Eastern and Western,* I. *Eastern Liturgies.* Oxford, 1896.

Corpus Scriptorum Historiae Byzantinae. Bonn, 1828–97. Cited as C.S.H.B.

Dölger, F. *Regesten der Kaiserurkunden des oströmischen Reiches,* 5 pts. Munich–Berlin, 1924–65.

Gelzer, H. *Texte der Notitiae Episcopatum.* Leipzig, 1901.

Mansi, J. D. *Sacrorum Conciliorum nova et amplissima Collectio,* 31 vols. Florence–Venice, 1759–98.

Meyer, P. *Die Haupturkunden für die Geschichte der Athos-Kloster.* Leipzig, 1894.

Migne, J. P. *Patrologia Cursus Completus. Series Graeco-Latina,* 161 vols. in 166. Paris, 1857–66. Cited as *M.P.G.*

Migne, J. P. *Patrologia Cursus Completus. Series Latina,* 221 vols. Paris, 1844–55. Cited as *M.P.L.*

Miklosich, F. and Müller, J. *Acta et Diplomata Graeca Medii Aevi Sacra et Profana,* 6 vols. Vienna, 1860–90.

Pitra, J. B. *Analecta Sacra et Classica Spicilegio Solesmensi Parata,* 8 vols. Paris, 1876–88.

Zachariae von Lingenthal, K. E. *Collectio Librorum Juris Graeco-Romani Ineditorum.* Leipzig, 1852.

Zachariae von Lingenthal, K. E. *Jus Graeco-Romanum,* 7 vols. Leipzig, 1856–84.

2 ORIGINAL SOURCES

Acta Maximi, in *M.P.G.* vol. XC.

Agapetus, Pope. *Epistolae,* in *M.P.L.* vol. LXVI.

Anagnostes, Johannes. *De Excidio Thessalonicae* (ed. I. Bekker), in C.S.H.B. Bonn, 1838.

Athanasius. *De Sententia Dionysii,* in *M.P.G.* vol. XXV.

Balsamon, Theodore. *Opera,* in *M.P.G.* vol. CXXXVIII.

Basil of Caesarea. *De Spiritu Sancto* and *Epistolae,* in *M.P.G.* vol. XXXII.

Benjamin of Tudela. *Itinerary* (trans. M. N. Adler). Oxford, 1907.

Blemmydas, Nicephorus. *Curriculum Vitae et Carmina* (ed. A. Heisenberg). Leipzig, 1896.

Bibliography

Cantacuzenus, John, Emperor. *Historiarum Libri IV* (ed. L. Schopen), 3 vols. in C.S.H.B. Bonn, 1828–32.

Cecaumenus. *Strategicon* (ed. B. Vassilievsky and V. Jernstedt). St Petersburg, 1896.

Chomatianus, Demetrius. *Responsiones*, in *M.P.G.* vol. cxix.

Cinnamus, Johannes. *Historia* (ed. A. Meineke), in C.S.H.B. Bonn, 1836.

Codinus (Pseudo-Codinus). *De Officialibus Palatii Constantinopolitani et de Officiis Magnae Ecclesiae Liber*, in *M.P.G.* vol. clvi.

Constantine Porphyrogenitus, Emperor. *De Ceremoniis Aulae Byzantinae* (ed. J. J. Reiske), 2 vols. in C.S.H.B. Bonn, 1829–40.

Dion Cassius. *Historia Romana* (ed. U. P. Boissevain). Berlin, 1895–1901.

Ducas, *Historia Turco-Byzantina* (ed. V. Grecu). Bucarest, 1958.

Ecloga Leonis et Constantini, in K. E. Zachariae von Lingenthal, *Collectio Librorum Juris Graeco-Romanorum*.

Epanagoge Aucta, in K. E. Zachariae von Lingenthal, *Jus Graeco-Romanum*, vol. iv.

Eusebius of Caesarea. *Vita Constantini*, in *M.P.G.* vol. xx.

Gennadius, George Scholarius. *Contre les Juifs*, in *Œuvres Complètes*, 8 vols. Paris, 1928–36.

Gregoras, Nicephorus. *Historia* (ed. L. Schopen and I. Bekker), 2 vols. in C.S.H.B. Bonn, 1829–55.

Gregory Nazianzene. *Orationes*, in *M.P.G.* vol. xxxv; *In Pentecosten* and *Supremum Vale*, in *M.P.G.* vol. xxxvi; *Poemata*, in *M.P.G.* vol. xxxvii.

Gregory of Nyssa. *Vita Moysis*, in *M.P.G.* vol. xliv; *De Instituto Christiano*, in *M.P.G.* vol. xlvi.

Irenaeus. *Contra Haereses*, in *M.P.G.* vol. vii.

Isaac of Nineveh. *Homilies* (Greek version, ed. N. Theotoki). Leipzig, 1790.

John Chrysostom. *In Matthaeum*, in *M.P.G.* vol. lvii.

John of Damascus. *De Fide Orthodoxa* (Πηγὴ Γνώσεως), and *Orationes*, in *M.P.G.* vol. xciv.

Justinian I, Emperor. *Novellae* (ed. K. E. Zachariae von Lingenthal), 2 pts. Leipzig, 1881–4.

Leo Diaconus, *Historia* (ed. C. B. Hase), in C.S.H.B. Bonn, 1828.

Mauropus, Johannes. *Poemata*, in *M.P.G.* vol. cxx.

Maximus the Confessor. *Disputatio contra Pyrrhum*, in *M.P.G.* vol. xci.

Méthode de la Sainte Attention (ed. J. Hausherr), *Orientalia Christiana Periodica*, vol. ix, 2. Rome, 1927.

Nicephorus the Hesychast. *De Sobrietate*, in *M.P.G.* vol. cxlvii.

Nicetas Choniates. *Chronicon* (ed. I. Bekker), in C.S.H.B. Bonn, 1835.

Nicetas Stethatus. *Vie de Symeon le Nouveau Théologien* (ed. with French trans. I. Hausherr and G. Horn), in *Orientalia Christiana*, xii. Rome, 1928.

Bibliography

Pachymer, Georgius. *De Michaele et Andronico Palaeologis* (ed. I. Bekker), 2 vols, C.S.H.B. Bonn, 1835.

Palamas, Gregorius. *Défense des Saints Hesychastes* (ed. and trans. J. Meyendorff), 2 vols. Louvain, 1959.

Palamas, Gregorius. *Opera*, in *M.P.G.* vol. CL.

Philokalia, compiled by Macarius of Corinth and Nicodemus of the Holy Mountain, trans. into Russian by Feodor, Bishop of Vladimir-Suzdal, 5 vols. Moscow, 1883–9. Shorter Greek version, Ἡ Φιλοκαλία τῶν Ἱερῶν Νηπτικῶν, pub. Venice, 1782.

Philopatris (ed. C. B. Hase), in C.S.H.B. Bonn, 1828.

Philotheus, Patriarch of Constantinople. *Encomium Gregorae Palamae*, in *M.P.G.* vol. CLI.

Phrantzes (Sphrantzes), Georgius. *Chronicon* (ed. I. Bekker), in C.S.H.B. Bonn, 1838.

Plethon, Georgius Gemistus. *Traité des Lois* (ed. C. Alexandre with trans. by A. Pellisier). Paris, 1858.

Symeon the New Theologian. *Divinorum Amorum Liber*, in *M.P.G.* vol. CXX.

Symeon, Archbishop of Thessalonica. *De Sacris Ordinationibus, M.P.G.* vol. CLV.

Syropoulos, Silvester. Memoirs: S. Sgouropoulos (*sic*), *Vera Historia Unionis non Verae inter Graecos et Latinos* (ed. and trans. R. Creyghton). The Hague, 1660.

Taxeis: Graecorum Episcoporum Notitiae and *De Ordinis Thronorum Metropolitanorum*, in *M.P.G.* vol. CVII.

Terre Hodierne Grecorum et Dominia Secularia et Spiritualia Eorum (ed. S. Lambros), *Neon Hellenomnemon*, vol. VII. Athens, 1910.

Theodore Studites. *Opera*, in *M.P.G.* vol. XCIX.

Theophylact, Archbishop of Bulgaria. *Enarratio in Ioannis Evangelium*, in *M.P.G.* vol. CXXXIII; *De Iis in quibus Latini Accusantur*, in *M.P.G.* vol. CXXVI.

Vita Sancti Lucae Junioris, in *M.P.G.* vol. CXI.

Zigabenus, Euthymius. *Panoplia*, in *M.P.G.* vol. CXXX.

3 MODERN WORKS

Allen, W. E. D. *A History of the Georgian People*. London, 1932.

Amantos, K. Ἱστορία τοῦ Βυζαντινοῦ Κράτους, 2 vols. Athens, 1939–47.

Anastos, M. V. 'Pletho's Calendar and Liturgy', in *Dumbarton Oaks Papers*, IV. Cambridge (Mass.), 1948.

Bakalopoulos, A. E. Ἱστορία τοῦ νέου Ἑλληνισμοῦ. Thessalonica, 1961–7.

Bardy, A. Chapters 5 to 10 in Fliche and Martin, *Histoire de l'Eglise*, IV, pt. I and 1–2, *ibid.* pt. II.

Bibliography

Baynes, N. H. *Byzantine Studies and other Essays*. London, 1955.

Beck, H.-G. 'Humanismus und Palamismus', XII Congrès International des Etudes Byzantines, *Rapports*, III. Ochrid, 1961.

Beck, H.-G. *Kirche und theologische Literatur im Byzantinischen Reich*. Munich, 1959.

Brandon, S. *The Fall of Jerusalem*. London, 1951.

Bréhier, L. *Le Monde Byzantin*, 3 vols. Paris, 1947–50.

Bréhier, L. and Battifol, P. *Les Survivances du culte impérial romain*. Paris, 1920.

Buckler, A. *Anna Comnena*. Oxford, 1929.

Bulgakov, S. *The Orthodox Church*. London, 1935.

Bury, J. B. *A History of the Later Roman Empire*, 2 vols. London, 1923.

Bury, J. B. *Selected Essays* (ed. H. Temperley). Cambridge, 1930.

Cambridge Medieval History, vol. I. Cambridge, 1913.

Cambridge Medieval History, vol. IV, 1 (new edition). Cambridge, 1966.

Candal, M. 'Fuentes palamiticas: dialogo de Jorge Facrasi sobre el contradictorio de Palamas con Niceforo Gregoras', *Orientalia Christiana Periodica*, XVI. Rome, 1950.

Charanis, P. 'The strife among the Palaeologi and the Ottoman Turks 1370–1402', *Byzantion*, XVI, 1. Boston, 1942/3.

Chrysanthos, Mgr. Ἡ Ἐκκλησία τῆς Τραπεζοῦντος. Athens, 1933.

Delehaye, H. *Les Saints Stylites*. Brussels, 1923.

Dictionnaire de théologie catholique (ed. A. Vacant, E. Mangeot, and others), 15 vols. in 18. Paris, 1907–53.

Dinić, M. Chapter XII, 'The Balkans, 1018–1499', in *Cambridge Medieval History*, IV, 1 (new edition).

Dölger, F. *Byzanz und die Europäische Staatenwelt*. Ettal, 1953.

Dvornik, F. *Byzantium and the Roman Primacy*. New York, 1966.

Dvornik, F. *Early Christian and Byzantine Political Philosophy*, 2 vols. Washington, 1966.

Dvornik, F. *The Idea of Apostolicity in Byzantium and the Legend of the Apostle Andrew*. Cambridge, Mass., 1958.

Dvornik, F. *The Photian Schism*. Cambridge, 1948.

Dvornik, F. 'Emperors, Popes and General Councils', *Dumbarton Oaks Papers*, VI. Cambridge, Mass., 1951.

Evdokimov, P. *L'Orthodoxie*. Neuchâtel, 1965.

Fliche, A. and Martin, V. (eds.). *Histoire de l'Eglise*. Paris, 1934– (in progress).

Fuchs, F. *Die Höheren Schulen von Konstantinopel im Mittelalter*. Leipzig, 1926.

Gardner, A. *The Lascarids of Nicaea*. London, 1912.

Gardner, A. *Theodore of Studium, his Life and Times*. London, 1905.

Bibliography

Gardner, A. Chapter 'Religious Disunion in the Fifth Century', in *Cambridge Medieval History*, I.

Gavin, F. *Some Aspects of Contemporary Greek Orthodox Thought*. London, 1936.

Geanakoplos, D. J. *Byzantine East and Latin West*. Oxford, 1966.

Geanakoplos, D. J. *Emperor Michael Palaeologus and the West*. Cambridge, Mass., 1952.

Geanakoplos, D. J. *Greek Scholars in Venice. Studies in the Dissemination of Greek Learning from Byzantium to Western Europe*. Cambridge, Mass., 1962.

Gibbon, E. *The Decline and Fall of the Roman Empire* (ed. J. B. Bury), 7 vols. London, 1896–1900.

Gill, J. *The Council of Florence*. Cambridge, 1959.

Gilson, E. *The Philosophy of Saint Thomas Aquinas* (trans. E. Bullough). Cambridge, 1935.

Golubinsky, E. E. *History of the Russian Church* (in Russian), 2 vols. in 4. Moscow, 1900–11.

Guilland, R. *Essai sur Nicéphore Gregoras*. Paris, 1926.

Hackett, J. *A History of the Orthodox Church of Cyprus*. London, 1901.

Halećki, O. *Un Empereur de Byzance à Rome*. Warsaw, 1930.

Hasluck, F. W. *Athos and its Monasteries*. London, 1924.

Hausherr, I. *La Méthode d'oraison hésychaste, Orientalia Christiana*, IX. Rome, 1927.

Hausherr, I. 'La Traité de l'Oraison d'Evagre le Pontique', *Revue d'ascétique et de mystique*, XV. Paris, 1934.

Hefele, C. J. *Histoire des Conciles* (trans. H. Leclercq), 8 vols. in 16. Paris, 1907–21. Cited as Hefele–Leclercq.

Hill, G. *A History of Cyprus*, 3 vols. Cambridge, 1940–8.

Hussey, J. M. *Church and Learning in the Byzantine Empire, 867–1025*. London, 1937.

Huxley, A. *Grey Eminence* (1st edition). London, 1941.

Ikonnikov, V. *Cultural Importance of Byzantium in Russian History* (in Russian). Kiev, 1869.

Janin, R. *La Géographie ecclésiastique de l'Empire byzantin*, I, iii, *Les Eglises et les monastères*. Paris, 1953.

Janin, R. 'Géorgie', in *Dictionnaire de théologie catholique*, VI.

Jenkins, R. *Byzantium: the Imperial Centuries*. London, 1966.

Jerphanion, G. de. *Les Eglises Rupestres de Cappadoce*, 2 vols. and albums. Paris, 1925–42.

Jirecek, C. J. *Geschichte der Bulgaren*. Prague, 1871.

Jirecek, C. J. *Geschichte der Serben*, 2 vols. Gotha, 1911–18.

Jorga, N. *Histoire de la vie byzantine*, 3 vols. Bucharest, 1934.

Jorga, N. *Histoire des Roumains*, 5 vols. Bucharest, 1937.

Bibliography

Jorga, N. *Istoria Bisericii Românesti*, 2 vols. Valenia, 1908-9.

Jugie, M. *Theologia Dogmatica Christianorum Orientalium ab Ecclesia Catholica Dissidentium*, 5 vols. Paris, 1926-35.

Jugie, M. 'Palamas', in *Dictionnaire de théologie catholique*, XI.

Jugie, M. 'Symeon de Thessalonique', in *Dictionnaire de théologie catholique*, XIV, 2.

Knecht, A. *System des Justinianischen Kirchenvermögensrechtes*. Stuttgart, 1905.

Koukoules, P. Βυзαντινῶν Βίος καὶ Πολιτισμός, 8 vols. Athens, 1947-57.

Krumbacher, K. *Geschichte der Byzantinischen Litteratur* (2nd edition). Munich, 1897.

Langford-James, R. L. *A Dictionary of the Eastern Orthodox Church*. London, 1923.

Laurent, V. 'La direction spirituelle des grandes dames de Byzance', *Revue des études byzantines*, VIII. Paris, 1950.

Laurent, V. 'Les droits de l'empereur en matière ecclésiastique', *Revue des études byzantines*, XIII. Paris, 1954-5.

Leib, B. *Rome, Kiev et Byzance à la fin du XIme siècle*. Paris, 1924.

Lossky, V. *The Mystical Theology of the Eastern Church* (trans. anon.). London, 1957.

Lot-Borodin, M. *Un Maître de la spiritualité byzantine au XIVme siècle: Nicolas Cabasilas*. Paris, 1958.

Masai, F. *Plethon et le Platonisme de Mistra*. Paris, 1956.

Medlin, W. K. *Moscow and East Rome*. Geneva, 1952.

Mercati, G. *Notizie di Procoro e Demetrio Cidone, Manuele Caleca e Teodoro Meliteniota*. Rome (Vatican), 1931.

Meyendorff, J. *L'Eglise Orthodoxe*. Paris, 1960.

Meyendorff, J. *Saint Grégoire Palamas et la mystique orthodoxe*. Paris, 1959.

Meyendorff, J. *A Study of Gregory Palamas* (trans. G. Lawrence). London, 1964.

Miller, W. *Essays on the Latin Orient*. Cambridge, 1921.

Miller, W. *The Latins in the Levant*. London, 1908.

Miller, W. *Trebizond, the Last Greek Empire*. London, 1926.

Mohler, L. *Kardinal Bessarion als Theologe, Humanist und Staatsmann*, 3 vols. Paderborn, 1923-42.

Neale, J. M. *History of the Holy Eastern Church, Patriarchate of Alexandria* and *Patriarchate of Antioch*. London, 1847 and 1873.

Nicol, D. M. *The Despotate of Epiros*. Oxford, 1957.

Nicol, D. M. *Meteora, the Rock Monasteries of Thessaly*. London, 1963.

Nicol, D. M. Chapter VII, 'The Fourth Crusade and the Greek and Latin Empires, 1204-61', in *Cambridge Medieval History*, IV, 1 (new edition).

Norden, W. *Das Papsttum und Byzanz*. Berlin, 1903.

Obolensky, D. 'Byzantium, Kiev and Moscow: a study in ecclesiastical relations', *Dumbarton Oaks Papers*, XI. Cambridge, Mass., 1957.

Bibliography

Ostrogorsky, G. *History of the Byzantine State* (trans. J. M. Hussey). Oxford, 1956.

Ostrogorsky, G. Chapter VIII, 'The Palaeologi', in *Cambridge Medieval History*, IV, 1 (new edition).

Palmieri, A. 'Filioque', in *Dictionnaire de théologie catholique*, V.

Peeters, P. 'Histoires monastiques géorgiennes', *Analecta Bollandiana*, XXXVI–XXXVII. Brussels, 1917–18.

Peeters, P. 'Les débuts de Christianisme en Géorgie', *Analecta Bollandiana*, L. Brussels, 1932.

Petit, L. 'Arsène Antonius et les Arsénites', in *Dictionnaire de théologie catholique*, I, ii.

Pierling, S. J. *La Russie et le Saint-Siège*, 3 vols. Paris, 1896–1901.

Runciman, S. *The Eastern Schism*. Oxford, 1955.

Runciman, S. *The Fall of Constantinople*. Cambridge, 1965.

Runciman, S. 'Byzantine and Hellene in the fourteenth century', Τόμος Κωνσταντίνου 'Αρμενοπούλου. Thessalonica, 1951.

Runciman, S. 'The Byzantine "Protectorate" in the Holy Land', *Byzantion*, XVIII. Brussels, 1948.

Salaville, S. 'Une Lettre et un discours inédits de Théolepte de Philadelphie, *Revue des études byzantines*, V. Paris, 1947.

Schaeder, H. *Moskau das Dritte Rom*. Hamburg, 1929.

Schiwietz, S. *Das Morgenlandische Monchtum*. Mainz, 1904.

Setton, K. M. 'The Byzantine background to the Italian Renaissance', *Proceedings of the American Philosophical Society*, C, 1. Philadelphia, 1956.

Ševčenko, I. 'Nicolas Cabasilas's "Anti-Zealot" Discourse: A Reinterpretation', *Dumbarton Oaks Papers*, XI. Cambridge, Mass., 1957.

Sherrard, P. *The Greek East and the Latin West*. London, 1959.

Tafrali, O. *Thessalonique au quatorzième siècle*. Paris, 1913.

Tatakis, B. *La Philosophie Byzantine*. Paris, 1949.

Toumanov, C. Chapter XIV, 'Armenia and Georgia', in *Cambridge Medieval History*, IV, 1 (new edition).

Tournebize, F. *Histoire politique et religieuse de l'Arménie*. Paris, 1910.

Underwood, P. A. *The Kariye Djami*, 3 vols. New York, 1966.

Viller, M. 'La question de l'union des églises entre grecs et latins depuis le Concile de Lyon jusqu'à celui de Florence', *Revue d'histoire ecclésiastique*, XVI, XVIII. Paris, 1921, 1922.

Waechter, A., *Der Verfall des Griechentums in Kleinasien im XIVten Jahrhundert*. Leipzig, 1903.

Ware, T. *The Orthodox Church*. London, 1963.

Weigand, T. *Der Latmos*, Berlin, 1913.

Wittek, P. *The Rise of the Ottoman Empire*. London, 1938.

Xenopol, A. D. *Histoire des Roumains de la Dacie Trajane*, 2 vols. Paris, 1896.

419

Bibliography

Zakythinos, D. A. *Le Despotat Grec de Morée*, 2 vols. Paris, 1932–53.

Zernov, N. *Eastern Christendom*. London, 1961.

Ziegler, A. 'Isidore de Kiev, apôtre de l'Union Florentine', *Irenikon*, XIII. Chevetogne, 1936.

Zoras, G. Περὶ τὴν Ἅλωσιν τῆς Κωνσταντινουπόλεως. Athens, 1959.

BOOK II

1 COLLECTIONS OF SOURCES

Acta et Scripta Theologorum Wirtembergensium et Patriarchae Constantinopolitani, D. Hieremiae. Wittenberg, 1584. Also reproduced in Gedeon of Cyprus, Κριτὴς τῆς 'Αληθείας, 2 vols. Leipzig, 1759.

Aymon, J. *Monuments authentiques de la religion des Grecs et de la fausseté de plusieurs confessions de foi des Chrétiens*. The Hague, 1708.

Beldiceanu, N. *Les Actes des premiers Sultans*. Paris–The Hague, 1960.

Bent, J. T. *Early Voyages and Travel in the Levant*, Hakluyt Society, series I LXXXVII, London, 1893.

Calendar of Treasury Books, vols. XVIII–XXII. London, 1936–50.

Calendar of Treasury Papers (ed. J. Redington), 6 vols. London, 1868–89.

Carayon, A. *Relations inédits des missions de la Société de Jesus à Constantinople*. Paris, 1864.

Collection of State Charters and Treaties (in Russian; ed. A. Malinovsky), 4 vols. Moscow, 1813–28.

Colomesius, P. *Clarorum Virorum Epistolae Singulares*. Hamburg, 1687.

Corpus Reformatorum, I–XII, *Melancthonis Epistolae, Praefationes Consilia, etc.* (ed. C. G. Bretschneider). Halle, 1834– .

Corpus Scriptorum Historiae Byzantinorum (C.S.H.B.). Bonn, 1828–97.

De Hurmuzaki, E. *Documente Privatore la Istoria Românilor*, 13 vols. in 22. Bucarest, 1876–1909. (Vol. XII ed. N. Jorga, vol. XIII ed. A. Papadopoulos-Kerameus.)

Delikanis, C. Τὰ ἐν τοῖς Κώδιξι τοῦ Πατριαρχικοῦ 'Αρχειοφυλακείου σωζόμενα ἐπίσημα ἐκκλησιαστικὰ ἔγγραφα τὸ ἀφορῶντα εἰς τὰς Σχέσεις Οἰκουμενικοῦ Πατριαρχείου πρὸς τὰς 'Εκκλησίας 'Αλεξανδρείας, 'Αντιοχείας, 'Ιεροσολύμων καὶ Κύπρου (Πατριαρχικὰ Ἔγγραφα), 3 vols. Constantinople, 1904.

Gedeon, M. Πατριαρχικοὶ Πίνακες. Constantinople, 1890.

Gedeon, M. Χρονικὰ τοῦ Πατριαρχικοῦ Οἴκου καὶ Ναοῦ. Constantinople, 1894.

Heyd, U. *Ottoman Documents on Palestine, 1552–1615*. Oxford, 1960.

Historical Acts, collected and edited by the Archaeographical Commission (in Russian), 5 vols. St Petersburg, 1841–2.

Hottinger, J. H. *Analecta Historico-Theologica*. Zurich, 1652.

Bibliography

Jorga, N. *Izvoarele Contemporane asupra mişcârii lui Tudor Vladimirescu.* Bucarest, 1921.

Jorga, N. *Nouveaux Matériaux pour servir à l'Histoire de Jacques Basilikos l'Héraclide.* Bucharest, 1900.

Journal of the Imperial Russian Historical Society (in Russian), v. St Petersburg, 1884.

Karmiris, J. N. Τὰ Δογματικὰ καὶ Συμβολικὰ Μνημεῖα τῆς Ὀρθοδόξου Καθολικῆς Ἐκκλησίας, 2 vols. (vol. i, 2nd edition, Athens, 1960; vol. ii, Athens, 1953).

Legrand, E. *Bibliographie Hellénique: description raisonnée des ouvrages publiés en Grec par des Grecs aux 15e et 16e siècles,* 4 vols. Paris, 1885–1906.

Legrand, E. *Bibliographie Hellénique: description raisonnée des ouvrages publiés en Grec par des Grecs au 17e siècle,* 5 vols. Paris, 1894–1903.

Legrand, E. *Deux Vies de Jacques Basilicos, comte palatin et prince de Moldavie.* Paris, 1889.

Legrand, E. *Recueil des poèmes historiques en grec vulgaire.* Paris, 1877.

Mansi, J. D. *Sacrorum Conciliorum nova et amplissima Collectio,* 31 vols. Florence–Venice, 1759–98.

Miklosich, F. and Müller, J. *Acta et Diplomata Graeci Medii Aevi Sacra et Profana,* 6 vols. Vienna, 1860–90.

Robertson, J. N. W. B. *The Acts and Decrees of the Synod of Jerusalem, sometimes called the Council of Bethlehem.* London, 1899.

Russian Historical Library (in Russian; 2nd edition). St Petersburg, 1908.

Sathas, C. N. Μεσαιωνικὴ Βιβλιοθήκη, 7 vols. Venice, 1872–94.

Smith, T. *Collectanea de Cyrillo Lucario.* London, 1707.

Sokolowski, S. *Censura Orientalis Ecclesiae—De principiis nostri seculi haereticorum dogmatibus—Hieremiae Constantinopolitani Patriarchae, judicii & mutuae communionis caussa, ab Orthodoxae doctrinae adversariis, non ita pridem oblatis. Ab eodem Patriarcha Constantinopolitano ad Germanos Graece conscripta—a Stanislao Socolovio conversa.* Cracow, 1582.

Tappe, E. D. *Documents concerning Rumanian History, collected from British Archives.* The Hague, 1964.

Le Stoglav (ed. E. Duchesne). Paris. 1920.

Zepos, J. and Zepos, P. *Jus Graeco-Romanum,* 8 vols. Athens, 1931.

2 ORIGINAL SOURCES AND WORKS WRITTEN BEFORE 1830

A Wood, A. *Athenae Oxonienses* (ed. P. Bliss), 4 vols. London, 1813–20.

Abbot, G., Archbishop of Canterbury. Letters, in Colomesius, *Selectae Clarorum Virorum Epistolae,* and in E. Legrand, *Bibliographie Hellénique du 17e siècle,* v.

Agallianos, Theodore. Ἀνέκδοτοι Λόγοι (ed. Patrineli), see below (p. 431), Patrineli.

Bibliography

Allatius, L. *De Ecclesiae Occidentalis atque Orientalis Perpetua Consensione*, III. Cologne, 1648.

Allatius, L. *De Libris et Rebus Ecclesiae Graecorum*. Paris, 1646.

Angelos, C. *Christopher Angell, a Grecian who tasted of many Stripes inflicted by the Turkes for the Faith*. Oxford, 1618 (Greek version. Oxford, 1617).

Angelos, C. *Encheiridion*. Cambridge, 1619.

Angelos, C. *An Encomium of the famous Kingdom of Great Britain and of the two flourishing Sister Universities Cambridge and Oxford*. Cambridge, 1619.

'Anthimos, Patriarch of Jerusalem' (false attribution). Πατρικὴ Διδασκαλία. Constantinople, 1798. New edition in Zakythinos, Ἅλωσις (see below, p. 434).

Anthony the Exarch. Letter to Melanchthon, in E. Legrand, *Bibliographie Hellénique des XVe et XVIe siècles*, I.

Arasy, J. V. *Description des pays du départment du Consulat de Salonique*, in Lascaris, *Salonique à la fin du XVIIIe siècle* (see below, p. 430).

Arnauld, A. *La Perpétuité de la Foy*, 3 vols. Paris, 1669–73.

Arsenios, Archbishop. Καθίδρυσις Ρωσσικοῦ Πατριαρχείου, in Sathas, Βιογραφικὸν Σχεδίασμα περὶ τοῦ Πατριάρχου Ἱερεμίου Β' (see below, p. 432).

Avvakum, Archpriest. *La Vie de l'Archiprêtre Avvakum, écrit par lui-même* (trans. and ed. P. Pascal). Paris, 1938.

Bartholdy, L. S. *Voyage en Grèce, fait dans les années 1803–1804*, 2 vols. Paris, 1807.

Basire, I. *The Ancient Liberty of the Britannick Church*. London, 1661.

Basire, I. *The Correspondence of Isaac Basire, D.D.* (ed. N. Darnell). London, 1831.

Baudier, M. *Histoire générale du serrail et de la cour du Grand Seigneur*. Paris, 1623.

Beaujour, F. *Mémoire sur le Commerce de Salonique*, in Lascaris, *Salonique à la fin du XVIIIe siècle* (see below, p. 430).

Belon, P. *Les Observations de plusieurs singularitez e choses memorables trouvées en Grèce, Asie, Indie, Arabie et autres pays estranges*. Paris, 1853.

Bembo, Cardinal P. Oration, in J. Morelli, 'Intorno ad un orazione greca inedita del Cardinale Pietro Bembo alla Signoria de Venezia', *Memorie del Regale Istituto del Regno Lombardo–Veneto*, II, pp. 251–62. Milan, 1821.

Bernardo, Lorenzo. *Viaggio a Constantinopli di ser Lorenzo Bernardo, Miscellanea pubblicata dalla Deputazione Veneta di Storia Patria*, serie 4, vol. IV. Venice, 1886.

Brerewood, E. *Enquiries of Languages by Edw. Brerewood, lately Professor of Astronomy at Gresham College*, in *Purchas His Pilgrims*, I. Glasgow, 1905.

Burton, R. *The Anatomy of Melancholy* (Everyman edition). London, 1896.

Busbecq, O. G. *Legationis Turcicae Epistolae IV*. Hanover, 1605.

Camerarius, J. Letter, in *Corpus Reformationis*, IX. pp. 169 ff.

Cantemir, Demetrius. *The History of the Growth and Decay of the Othman Empire* (trans. N. Tindal). London, 1734.

422

Bibliography

Caryophyllus, J. M. Ἔλεγχος τῆς Ψευδοχριστιανικῆς κατηχήσεως Ζαχαρίου τοῦ Γεργάνου (Greek and Latin). Rome, 1631.

Carra, J. L. Histoire de la Moldavie et de la Valachie. Neuchâtel, 1781.

Celebi, Evliya. Seyahalname (ed. N. Asim). Istanbul, 1898.

Chrysanthos Notaras, Patriarch of Jerusalem. (See Dositheus.)

Chrysosculus, Logothete. Letter to de Wilhem, in Aymon, Monuments authentiques.

Cioranu, M. Revoluţia lui Tudor Vladimirescu, in Jorga, Izvoarele Contemporane.

Claude, J. Réponse au livre de Mr. Arnaud entitulé La Perpétuité de la Foy. Quevilly/ Rouen, 1671.

'Confession of Dositheus', in Karmiris, Τὰ Δογματικὰ καὶ Συμβολικὰ Μνημεῖα, ΙΙ. English translation in Robertson, The Acts and Decrees of the Synod of Jerusalem.

Conopius, N. Letter to Léger, in Hottinger, Analecta, and in Legrand, Bibliographie Hellénique du 17e siècle, IV.

Covel, J. Extracts from diaries, in Bent, Early Voyages and Travels in the Levant (see above, p. 420).

Covel, J. Some Account of the Present Greek Church. Cambridge, 1722.

Critobulus (Kritovoulos). History of Mehmed the Conqueror (trans. C. T. Riggs). Princeton, 1954.

Critopoulos, Metrophanes. Confessio Fidei. Helmstadt, 1651.

Crusius, M. Germanograecia. Basle, 1585.

Crusius, M. Turco-Graeciae, libri octo. Basle, 1584.

Cuperus, G. Tractatus historico-chronologicus de Patriarchis Constantinopolitanis. Venice, 1751.

Cyril (Lucaris), Patriarch of Constantinople. Confessio Christianae Fidei. Geneva, 1629. Greek version, Ὁμολογία τῆς Χριστιανικῆς Πίστεως, ibid. 1633.

Cyril (Lucaris), Patriarch of Constantinople. Letters, in Aymon, Monuments Authentiques, in Colomesius, Clarorum Virorum Epistolae, in Hottinger, Analecta, and in E. Legrand, Bibliographie Hellénique du 17e siècle, IV.

Dallaway, J. Constantinople, Ancient and Modern. London, 1797.

Daponte, K. Χρονογράφος and Ἱστορικὸς Κατάλογος, in Sathas, Μεσαιωνικὴ Βιβλιοθήκη, ΙΙΙ.

Darzeanu, I. Cronica Revoluţiei din 1821, in Jorga, Izvoarele Contemporane.

De Hauterive, Comte. Journal inédit de voyage (ed. Académie Roumaine). Bucarest, 1902.

De Jonville, T. Le commerce annuel avec la Chrétienté au milieu du XVIIIe siècle, in Lascaris, Salonique à la fin du XVIIIe siècle. See below (p. 430).

De la Croix, —. Etat present des nations et églises grecque, arménienne et maronite en Turquie. Paris, 1715.

De Nicolay, N. Les Navigations, peregrinations et voyages. Antwerp, 1576.

Bibliography

De Pauw, C. *Philosophical Dissertations on the Greeks* (trans. into English), 2 vols. London, 1793.

De Villalon, C. *Viaje de Turquia, 1557*, in M. Serrano y Sanz, *Autobiografías y Memorias*. Madrid, 1905.

Des Hayes, L. *Voyages*, in A. L. de Laborde, *Documents sur Athènes*. Paris, 1854.

Dorotheus of Monemvasia. Σύνοψις Ἱστοριῶν. Venice, 1818.

Dositheus, Patriarch of Jerusalem. Ἐγχειρίδιον ἐλέγχον τὴν Καλβινικὴν Φρενοβλάβειαν. Bucarest, 1690.

Dositheus, Patriarch of Jerusalem. Ἱστορία περὶ τῶν ἐν Ἱεροσολύμοις πατριαρχευσάντων. Bucarest, 1715. (With biographical sketch by Chrysanthos Notaras, Patriarch of Jerusalem.)

Drummond, A. *Travels*. London, 1754.

Du Fresne Canaye. *Voyage du Levant, 1573* (ed. M. H. Hauser). Paris, 1897.

Ekthesis Chronica (ed. S. Lambros). London, 1902.

Ἑλληνικὴ Νομαρχία, ἤτοι Λόγος περὶ Ἐλευθερίας. 'Italy', 1806; ed. N. Tomadakis. Athens, 1948.

Evelyn, J. *Diary* (Everyman edition), 3 vols. London, 1906.

Filelfo, F. *Cent-dix Lettres grecques de François Philelphe* (ed. E. Legrand). Paris, 1902.

Forgach, F. *Vita Jacobi Despotae, alias Heraclidae Basilici dicti*, in Legrand, *Deux Vies de Jacques Basilicus*.

Gennadius (George Scholarius), Patriarch of Constantinople. *Confessio Fidei* and *Dialogus*, in *Œuvres complètes*, III (ed. L. Petit, X. A. Sidérides and M. Jugie). Paris.

George the Aetolian. Poem, in N. Banescu, *Un Poème grec vulgaire*.

Georgirenes, J., Archbishop of Samos. *A Description of the Present State of Samos, Nicaria, Patmos and Mount Athos*. London, 1678.

Georgirenes, J., Archbishop of Samos. 'From the Archbishop of the Isle of Samos in Greece, an account of his building the Grecian Church in So-hoe fields, and the disposal thereof by the masters of the parish St Martins in the fields', in *Tracts relating to London* (British Museum Library, 816.m.9. (118)).

Gerganus, Zacharias. *Catechismus Christianus*. Wittenberg, 1622.

Gerlach, S. *Stephan Gerlachs des Aelteren Tagebuch*. Frankfort-am-Main, 1674.

Gordius, A. Βίος Εὐγενίου Αἰτωλοῦ, in Sathas, Μεσαιωνικὴ Βιβλιοθήκη, III.

Graziani, A.-M. *De Joanne Heraclide Despota*, in E. Legrand, *Deux Vies de Jacques Basilicus; Histoire de Jacques Heraclide*, in Jorga, *Nouveaux Matériaux pour servir a l'histoire de Jacques Basilikos Heraclide*. (See above, p. 421.)

Grelot, G. J. *A Late Voyage to Constantinople* (trans. J. Philips). London, 1683.

Gyllius, P. *De Constantinopoleos Topographia*. Leyden, 1632.

Hawkins, W. *Short Account of Ken's Life*. London, 1713.

Helladius, A. *Status praesens Ecclesiae Graecae*. No place, 1714.

Bibliography

Hierax. Χρονικὸν περὶ τῆς τῶν Τούρκων βασιλείας, in Sathas, Μεσαιωνικὴ Βιβλιοθήκη, I.

Hill, A. *A Full and Just Account of the Present State of the Ottoman Empire in all its Branches*. London, 1709.

Historia Patriarchica Constantinopoleos (ed. B. G. Niebuhr), in C.S.H.B. Bonn, 1849. Also in Crusius, *Turco-Graecia*.

Historia Politica Constantinopoleos (ed. B. G. Niebuhr), in C.S.H.B. Bonn, 1849. Also in Crusius, *Turco-Graecia*.

Holland, H. *Travels in the Ionian Isles, Albania, Thessaly, Macedonia, etc. during the years 1812 and 1813*, 2 vols. 1814.

Hunt, Dr. *Mount Athos: An Account of the Monastic Institutions and Libraries*, in R. Walpole, *Memoirs relating to European and Asiatic Turkey* (2nd edition). London, 1818.

Hypsilantis, A. C. Τὰ μετὰ τὴν Ἅλωσιν *(1453–1789)* (ed. A. Germanos). Constantinople, 1870.

Jeremias II, Patriarch of Constantinople. Letters and Confession, in *Acta et Scripta Theologorum Wirtemburgensium et Patriarchae Constantinopolitani D. Hieremiae*.

Knolles, R. *The Turkish History from the Original of that Nation to the Growth of the Ottoman Empire*, 6th edition, 2 vols. London, 1687. (See below, P. Ricaut.)

Kömürcüyan, Eremiya Celebi. *Istanbul Tarihi: XVII asîrda Istanbul* (trans. into Turkish by H. D. Andreasyan). Istanbul, 1952.

Korais, A. Ἀδελφικὴ Διδασκαλία πρὸς τοὺς εὑρισκομένους κατὰ πᾶσαν τὴν Ὀθωμανικὴν Ἐπικράτειαν Γραικούς. Rome (actually Paris), 1798.

Korais, A. *Mémoire sur l'état actuel de la civilisation dans la Grèce*. No place or date (?Paris, 1803).

Lavender, T. *The Travels of Certaine Englishmen*. London, 1609.

Leake, W. M. *Travels in Northern Greece*. London, 1838.

Léger, A. 'Fragmentum vitae Cyrilli Lucaris', in Smith, *Collectanea de Cyrillo Lucario*.

Léger, A. Letters, in E. Legrand, *Bibliographie Hellénique au 17e siècle*, IV.

Locke, J. *Voyage to Jerusalem*, in Hakluyt, *Voyages* (Glasgow edition, v). 1903.

Le Quien, M. *Oriens Christianus*, 3 vols. Paris, 1840.

Luther, M. *Vom Kriege wider die Türcken*. Wittenberg(?), 1529.

Luther, M. *Von den Consiliis und Kirchen* (Weimar edition). 1914.

Luther, M. and von Eck, J. Disputatio. *Der authentische Texte der Leipziger Disputation (1519). Aus bisher unbenutzen Quellen* (ed. O. Seitz). Berlin, 1903.

MacMichael, W. *Journey from Moscow to Constantinople, 1817–18*. London, 1819.

Macraios, S. Ὑπομνήματα Ἐκκλησιαστικῆς Ἱστορίας, in Sathas, Μεσαιωνικὴ Βιβλιοθήκη, III.

Bibliography

Manos, James, of Argos. Λόγος Πανηγυρικός, preface to A. Mavrocordato, Ἱστορία τῶν Ἰουδαίων. Bucarest, 1716.

Margunius, Maximus. Letters, in Legrand, *Bibliographie Hellénique du 17e siècle*, IV.

Mavrocordato, A. Ἀλεξάνδρου Μαυροκορδάτου τοῦ Ἐξαποῤῥήτου Ἐπιστολαί ρ′ (ed. Livada). Trieste, 1879.

Mavrommatis, Neophytos. Κατάλογος τῶν μετὰ τὴν ἅλωσιν Κωνσταντινουπόλεως Πατριαρχευσάντων (ed. J. Sakellios, Εὐαγγελικὸς Κήρυξ, VIII). 1862. Athens,

Meletios, Metropolitan of Athens. Ἐκκλησιαστικὴ Ἱστορία (ed. G. Vendotis), 3 vols. Vienna, 1783–95 (with 4th volume by Vendotis).

Moghila, Peter, Archbishop of Kiev. *Confessio*, text in A. Malvy and M. Viller, *La Confession orthodoxe de Pierre Moghila* (see below, p. 431). Greek text published Amsterdam, 1667. English version: *The Orthodox Confession of the Catholic and Apostolic Eastern Church, faithfully translated from the Original from the version of Peter Mogila* (ed. J. J. Overbeck). London, 1898.

Morelli, J. 'Intorno ad un orazione greca inedita del Cardinale Pietro Bembo alla Signoria di Venezia', *Memorie del Regale Istituto del Regno Lombardo–Veneto*. Milan, 1821.

Narratio epistolica Turbarum inter Cyrillum et Jesuitas', in Hottinga, *Analecta*, and Smith, *Collectanea*; identical in Chrysosculus, Letter (see above).

Neale, A., *Travels through some parts of Germany, Poland, Moldavia and Turkey*. London, 1818.

Nucius, Nicander. *The Second Book of Nicander Nucius* (ed. J. H. Cramer), Camden Society, XVII. London, 1841.

Orthodox Confession, The. (See Moghila.)

Pantagalos, Meletius. *Confession*, partly printed in Simon *Histoire Critique* (see below).

Papadopoli, N. C. *Historia Gymnasii Patavini*, 2 vols. Venice, 1762.

Paul, Deacon of Antioch. *The Travels of Macarius* (selected by Lady Laura Ridding). Oxford, 1936.

Philip of Cyprus, Protonotary. *Chronicum Ecclesiae Graecae* (trans. N. Blancardus, re-ed. H. Hilarius). Leipzig, 1687.

Philippides, D. and Konstantas, G., Γεωγραφία Νεωτερική, 2 vols. Vienna, 1791.

Phrantzes (Sphrantzes), G. Χρονικόν (ed. H. Becker), in C.S.H.B. Bonn, 1838.

Pitton de Tournefort, J. *Relation d'un voyage du Levant, fait par ordre du roi*, 2 vols. Paris, 1717.

Pius II, Pope. *Lettera a Maometto II* (ed. G. Toffanin). Naples, 1953. (Collectio Universalis 8.)

Pococke, E. Supplement to his edition of Abulfaraj, *Historia Dynastiarum*. London, 1663.

Pococke, R. *A Description of the East*, 2 vols. London, 1743–5.

Bibliography

Raybaud, M. *Mémoires sur la Grèce*, 2 vols. Paris, 1824. (With *Introduction Historique*, by A. Rabbé.)

Regenvolscius, A. *Systema Historico-Chronologicum Ecclesiarum Slavonicarum*, Utrecht, 1652.

Ricaut, P. *The Present State of the Greek and Armenian Churches, Anno Christi, 1678.* London, 1680.

Ricaut, P. (name spelt Rycaut on title-page). *The Present State of the Ottoman Empire.* London, 1670.

Ricaut, P. (Rycaut). In vol. II, pt. II, of Knolles, *The Turkish History* (6th edition), 1687; and vol. III (*The History of the Turks, beginning with the year 1687*). London, 1700.

Roe, T. *The Negotiations of Sir Thomas Roe in his Embassy to the Ottoman Porte.* London, 1740.

Roe, T. Letters, in E. Legrand, *Bibliographie Hellénique au 17e siècle*, v.

Schweigger, S. *Ein newe Reyesbeschreibung auss Teutschland nach Constantinopel und Jerusalem.* Nuremberg, 1608.

Schmid-Schwarzenhorn, R. Letters, in E. de Hurmuzaki, *Documente Privatore la Istoria Românilor*, IV, I.

Scogardi, —. Letter, in de Hurmuzaki, *Documente Privatore la Istoria Românilor*, IV, I.

Severus, Gabriel. Πόσαι εἰσὶν αἱ γενικαὶ καὶ πρῶται διαφοραὶ καὶ ποῖαι ἃς ἔχει ἡ ʾΑνατολικὴ ʾΕκκλησία τῇ ʿΡωμαϊκῇ. Constantinople, 1627.

Sherley, A. *His Relation of his Travels.* London, 1613.

Sherley, T. *Discours of the Turkes* (ed. E. Denison Ross), *Camden Miscellany*, XVI. London, 1936.

Shusherin, I. *Life of the Most Holy Patriarch Nikon* (in Russian). St Petersburg, 1811.

Simon, R. *Histoire critique de la créance et les coutumes des nations du Levant.* Frankfort-am-Main, 1684.

Skinner, J. *An Ecclesiastical History of Scotland*, 2 vols. London, 1788.

Smith, T. *An Account of the Greek Church.* Oxford, 1680. (Latin version, *De Graecae Ecclesiae hodierno statu epistola.* London, 1676.)

Smith, T. *Collectanea de Cyrillo Lucario* (see above, p. 21).

Smith, T. *Epistolae Quattuor de Moribus et Institutis Turcarum.* Oxford, 1674.

Sommer, J. *Vita Jacobi Despotae*, in Legrand, *Deux Vies de Jacques Basilicus*.

Spon, J. *Voyage d'Italie, de Dalmatie, de Grèce, et du Levant*, 3 vols. Lyon, 1678.

Stavrinos, the Vestiary, Ανδραγαθίες τοῦ εὐσεβεοτάτου καὶ ανδρειοτατου Μιχαὴλ βοεβόδα in E. Legrand, *Recueil des poèmes historiques* (see above, p. 421).

Le Stoglav (ed. E. Duchesne). Paris, 1920.

'Synodical Answer to Question: What are the Sentiments of the Oriental Church of the Grecian Orthodox—sent to lovers of a Greek Church in Britain in 1672', text in G. Williams, *The Orthodox Church of the East.*

Thornton, T. *The Present State of Turkey.* London, 1807.

Bibliography

Turner, W. *Journal of a Tour in the Levant*, 3 vols. London, 1820.

Van Haag (de Haga), C. Letter, in Smith, *Collectanea*.

Von Harff, A. *The Pilgrimage of Arnold von Harff, Knight* (trans. and ed. M. Letts), Hakluyt Society, series II, XCIV. London, 1946.

Waddington, G. *The Present Condition of the Greek or Oriental Church*. London, 1829.

Waddington, G. *Visit to Greece, 1823–4*. London, 1825.

Walsh, R. *Residence at Constantinople during the Greek and Turkish Revolutions*, 2 vols. London, 1836.

Wey, W. *The Itineraries of William Wey*, Roxburghe Club. London, 1857.

Wheler, G. *A Journey into Greece*. London, 1682.

Wilkinson, W. *An Account of the Principalities of Wallachia and Moldavia*. London, 1820.

Wortley Montagu, Lady M. *Complete Letters* (ed. R. Halsband), 3 vols. Oxford, 1965–7.

Zallonis, M. P. *Essai sur les Fanariotes*. Marseille, 1824.

3 MODERN WORKS, WRITTEN SINCE 1830

Adeney, W. F. *The Greek and Eastern Churches*. Edinburgh, 1908.

Alderson, A. D. *The Structure of the Ottoman Dynasty*. Oxford, 1956.

Amantos, C. Οἱ προνομιακοὶ ὁρισμοὶ τοῦ Μουσουλμανιτισμοῦ ὑπὲρ τῶν Χριστιανῶν, in 'Ελληνικά, IX. Athens, 1936.

Amantos, C. I. 'Ανέκδοτα ἔγγραφα περὶ Ρήγα Βελεστινλῆ. Athens, 1930.

Argenti, P. *Chios Vincta*. Cambridge, 1941.

Argenti, P. *The Occupation of Chios by the Genoese*, 3 vols. Cambridge, 1958.

Arnold, T. W. *The Caliphate*. Oxford, 1924.

Babinger, F. *Mehmed der Eroberer und seine Zeit*. Munich, 1953.

Behr-Sigel, E. *Prière et sainteté dans l'église russe*. Paris, 1950.

Benz, E. *Die Ostkirche im Licht der Protestantischen Geschichtsschreibung*. Freiburg, 1952.

Benz, E. *Wittenberg und Byzanz*. Marburg, 1949.

Bibesco, Princesse. *La Nymphe Europe*. Paris, 1960.

Botzaris, N. *Visions balkaniques dans la préparation de la révolution grecque*. Geneva–Paris, 1962.

Bulgakov, S. *The Orthodox Church* (trans. E. S. Cram). London, 1935.

Camelli, G. *Demetrio Calcocondilo*. Florence, 1954.

Chrysostomos-Papadopoulos, Archbishop of Athens. 'Η 'Εκκλησία τῆς Κύπρου ἐπὶ Τουρκοκρατίας (1571–1878). Athens, 1929.

Constantinides, M. *The Greek Orthodox Church in London*. Oxford, 1933.

Conybeare, F. C. *Russian Dissenters*, Harvard Theological Studies, X. Cambridge (Mass.), 1921.

Bibliography

Courtney, W. P. 'Benjamin Woodroffe', in *Dictionary of National Biography*, LXII.

Cumont, F. and Cumont, E. *Voyage d'exploration archéologique dans le Pont et la Petite Arménie*. Brussels, 1906.

Curzon, R. *Visits to Monasteries in the Levant*. London, 1849.

Daskalakis, A. *Les Œuvres de Rhigas Velestinlis*. Paris, 1937.

Davidson, A. *Life of Edward Lear* (Penguin edition). London, 1950.

Demetracopoulos, A. C. 'Ορθόδοξος 'Ελλάς. Leipzig, 1872.

De Meester, P. *Le Collège pontifical grec de Rome*. Rome, 1910.

Dénissoff, E. *Maxime le Grec et l'Occident*. Louvain, 1942.

Dénissoff, E. 'Les Editions de Maxime le Grec', in *Revue des études slaves*, XXI. Paris, 1944.

Dictionary of National Biography, 63 vols. London, 1885–1900.

Dictionnaire de théologie catholique (ed. A. Vacant, E. Mangeot, and others), 15 vols. in 18. Paris, 1907–53.

Duckworth, H. T. F. *Greek Manuals of Church Doctrine*. London, 1901.

Easterling, P. E. 'Hand-list of the Additional Greek Manuscripts in the University Library, Cambridge', in *Scriptorium*, XVI, 2. London, 1962.

Eleutheriades, N. P. Τὰ Προνόμια τοῦ Οἰκουμενικοῦ Πατριαρχείου. Smyrna, 1909.

Encyclopaedia of Islam (ed. Houtsma, Arnold and Basset), 4 vols. Leyden–London, 1913–34.

Encyclopaedia of Islam (new edition, ed. Lewis, Pellat and Schacht). Leyden–London, 1955, in progress.

Fedalto, G. 'Ancora su Massimo Margounios', *Bolletino dell'Istituto di Storia Veneziano*, V–VI. Venice, 1964.

Florovski, A. *Le Conflit des deux traditions*. Prague, 1937.

Geanakoplos, D. J. *Byzantine East and Latin West*. Oxford, 1966.

Geanakoplos, D. J. *Greek Scholars in Venice. Studies in the Dissemination of Greek Learning from Byzantium to Western Europe*. Cambridge (Mass.), 1962.

Gelzer, H. *Der Patriarchat von Achrida*. Leipzig, 1902.

Golubinski, E. *History of the Russian Church* (in Russian; 2nd edition), 4 vols. in 2. Moscow, 1901–11.

Hadjiantoniou, G. A. *Protestant Patriarch*. Richmond (Va.), 1961.

Hadjimichali, A. 'Aspects de l'organisation économique des Grecs dans l'Empire Ottoman', *Le Cinq-centième anniversaire de la prise de Constantinople, L'Hellénisme contemporain* (fascicule hors série). Athens, 1953.

Hadrovics, L. *Le Peuple serbe et son église sur la domination turque*. Paris, 1947.

Hammond, P. *The Waters of Marah*. London, 1956.

Hart, W. H. 'Gleanings from the Records of the Treasury, no. VI', in *Notes and Queries* (2nd series), IX. London, 1860.

Bibliography

Hasluck, F. W. *Athos and its Monasteries.* London, 1924.

Hasluck, F. W. *Christianity and Islam under the Sultans,* 2 vols. Oxford, 1929.

Hauteriue, Compte de. *Journal inédit de voyage en Moldavie,* Roumanian Academy. Bucarest, 1902.

Hofmann, G. *Athos e Roma, Orientalia Christiana,* v, 19. Rome, 1925.

Hofmann, G. *Griechische Patriarchen und Römische Päpste, Orientalia Christiana,* XIII, 47; XV, 52; XIX, 63; XX, 64; XXV, 76; XXX, 84; XXXVI, 97. Rome, 1928–34.

Hofmann, G. *Il Vicariato Apostolico di Constantinopoli, 1453–1830, Orientalia Christiana Analecta,* CIII. Rome, 1935.

Hofmann, G. *Patmos und Rom, Orientalia Christiana,* XI, 41. Rome, 1928.

Hofmann, G. *Patriarchen von Konstantinopel, Orientalia Christiana,* XXXII, 89. Rome, 1933.

Hofmann, G. *Rom und der Athos, Orientalia Christiana Analecta.* Rome, 1954.

Hofmann, G. *Rom und der Athosklöster, Orientalia Christiana,* VIII, 28. Rome, 1926.

Inalcik, H. 'Mehmed the Conqueror (1453–1481) and his time', in *Speculum,* XXXV. Cambridge (Mass.), 1960.

Janin, R. *Constantinople byzantine. La Géographie ecclésiastique de l'Empire byzantin,* pt. I, iii, *Les Eglises et les monastères.* Paris, 1953.

Jorga, N. *Byzance après Byzance.* Bucarest, 1935.

Jorga, N. *Despre Cantacuzini.* Bucarest, 1902.

Jorga, N., *Geschichte des Osmanischen Reiches,* 5 vols. Gotha, 1908–13.

Jorga, N. *Istoria la Biserica Românilor,* 2 vols. Valenia, 1908–9.

Jorga, N. *Istoria Invatamintului Romanesc.* Bucarest, 1928.

Jugie, M. *Theologia Dogmatica Christianorum Orientalium ab Ecclesia Catholica Dissidentium,* 5 vols. Paris, 1926–35.

Kandiloros, T. Ἱστορία τοῦ Ἐθνομάρτυρος Γρηγορίου τοῦ Ε΄. Athens, 1909.

Kapterev, N. *The Character of Russian Relations with the Orthodox East in the 16th and 17th Centuries* (in Russian). Moscow, 1885.

Kapterev, N. *Patriarch Nikon and his Beginnings* (in Russian). Moscow, 1913.

Kapterev, N. *Patriarch Nikon and Tsar Alexis* (in Russian), 2 vols. Moscow, 1909–12.

Karmiris, J. N. Ὀρθοδοξία καί Προτεσταντισμός. Athens, 1923.

Karolidis, P. Ἱστορία τῆς Ἑλλάδος ἀπὸ τῆς ὑπὸ τῶν Ὀθωμανῶν ἁλώσεως τῆς Κωνσταντινουπόλεως μέχρι τῆς βασιλείας Γεωργίου τοῦ Α΄. Athens, 1925.

Kidd, B. J. *The Churches of Eastern Christendom.* London, 1927.

Kramers, J. H. 'Selim I' in *Encyclopaedia of Islam* (1st edition), IV.

Kriezis, G. D. Ἱστορία τῆς Νήσου Ὕδρας πρὸ τῆς Ἐπαναστάσεως τοῦ 1821. Patras, 1860.

Lascaris, M. *Salonique à la fin du XVIIIe siècle.* Athens, 1939.

Lathbury, T. *History of the Non-Jurors.* London, 1845.

Bibliography

Laurent, V. 'Les Chrétiens sous les Sultans', in *Echos d'Orient*, XXVIII. Constantinople, 1929.

Legrand, E. *Cent-dix Lettres grecques de Fr. Philelphe*. Paris, 1892.

Legrand, E. *Généalogie des Maurocordatos de Constantinople*. Paris, 1900.

Livre d'Or de la noblesse phanariote par un Phanariote, Le (ed. E. R. Rhangabé). Athens, 1892.

Lupton, J. H. *Life of John Colet*. London, 1887.

Lybyer, A. H. *The Government of the Ottoman Empire in the time of Suleiman the Magnificent*. Cambridge (Mass.), 1913.

Malvy, A. and Viller, M. *La Confession orthodoxe de Pierre Moghila, Orientalia Christiana*, x, 39. Rome, 1927.

Mantran, R. *Istanbul dans la seconde moitié du XVIIe siècle*. Paris, 1962.

Medlin, W. K. *Moscow and East Rome*. Geneva, 1952.

Mertsios, C. *Monuments de l'histoire de la Macédonie*. Thessalonica, 1947.

Miller, W. *Essays on the Latin Orient*. Cambridge, 1921.

Molmenti, P. G. *Venice* (trans. H. Brown), pt. II, *The Golden Age*. London, 1907.

Moschovakis, N. Τὸ ἐν Ἑλλάδι δημόσιον δίκαιον ἐπὶ Τουρκοκρατίας. Athens, 1882.

Nicol, D. M. *Meteora, the Rock Monasteries of Thessaly*. London, 1963.

Otetea, A. 'L'Hetairie d'il y a cent cinquante ans', in *Balkan Studies*, VI, 2. Thessalonica, 1965.

Overton, J. H. *The Non-Jurors, their Lives, Principles and Writings*. London, 1902.

Palmer, W. *The Patriarch and the Tsar*, 6 vols. London, 1871–6.

Palmieri, A. P. *Dositeo, Patriarca Greco di Gerusalemme*. Florence, 1909.

Papadopoullos, T. H. *Studies and Documents relating to the History of the Greek Church and People under Turkish Domination, Bibliotheca Graeca Aevi Posterioris*, I. Brussels, 1952.

Papadopoulos, C. A. Ἱστορία τῆς Ἐκκλησίας Ἀλεξανδρείας 62–1934. Alexandria, 1935.

Papadopoulos, C. A. Ἱστορία τῆς Ἐκκλησίας Ἀντιοχείας. Alexandria, 1951.

Papadopoulos, C. G. *Les Privilèges du Patriarcat oecuménique dans l'Empire ottoman*. Paris, 1924.

Papamichael, G. 'Les Editions de Maxime le Grec', *Revue des études slaves*, XXI. Paris, 1944.

Papamichael, G. Μάξιμος ὁ Γραικός. Athens, 1951.

Pargoire, J. 'Meletios Syrigos', *Echos d'Orient*, XII. Constantinople, 1920.

Pastor, L. *History of the Popes from the close of the Middle Ages* (English trans.), 16 vols. London, 1891–1928.

Patrineli, C. G. Ὁ Θεόδωρος Ἀγαλλιανὸς καὶ οἱ Ἀνέκδοτοι Λόγοι του. Athens, 1966.

Bibliography

Paulova, M. 'L'Empire byzantin et les Tchèques avant la chute de Constantinople', *Byzantinoslavica*, XIV. Prague, 1953.

Pearson, J. B. *A Biographical Sketch of the Chaplains to the Levant Company maintained at Constantinople, Aleppo and Smyrna*. Cambridge, 1883.

Perry, C. G. 'Dominis, Marco Antonio de', in *Dictionary of National Biography*, XV.

Perry, W. J. 'Bāyazīd II', in *Encyclopaedia of Islam* (new edition), I.

Petit, L. 'Jérémie II Tranos', in *Dictionnaire de théologie catholique*, VIII, I.

Petrakakos, D. Κοινοβουλευτική Ἱστορία τῆς Ἑλλάδος, 2 vols. Athens, 1925.

Phrantzis, A. Ἐπιτομὴ τῆς Ἱστορίας τῆς ἀναγεννηθείσης Ἑλλάδος, 3 vols. Athens, 1841.

Philemon, J. Δοκίμιον Ἱστορικὸν περὶ τῆς Ἑλληνικῆς Ἐπαναστάσεως, 2 vols. Athens, 1834.

Pierling, S. J. *La Russie et le Saint-Siège*, 3 vols. Paris, 1896–1901.

Popescu, N. *Patriarhii Ţarigradului prin ţerile româneşti in veacul al XVI-lea*. Bucharest, 1914.

Pregor, T. 'Das Kronik von 1570', in *Byzantinische Zeitschrift*, XI. Munich, 1902.

Protopsaltis, E. G. Ἡ Φιλικὴ Ἑταιρεία. Athens, 1964.

Xenopol, A. D. *Historia des Roumains*, 2 vols. Paris, 1896

Roberts, R. J. *The Greek Press at Constantinople in 1627 and its Antecedents*, The Bibliographical Society. London, 1967.

Roth, C. *The House of Nasi: the Dukes of Naxos*. Philadelphia, 1949.

Rozemond, K. *Archimandrite Hierotheos Abbatios*. Leiden, 1966.

Runciman, S. *The Fall of Constantinople*. Cambridge, 1965.

Sathas, C. Βιογραφικὸν Σχεδίασμα περὶ Πατριάρχου Ἱερεμίου Β΄ (*1572–1594*). Athens, 1870.

Savva, V. *Muscovite Tsars and Byzantine Emperors* (in Russian). Kharkov, 1901.

Seton-Watson, R. W. *A History of the Roumanians*. Cambridge, 1934.

Sherrard, P. *The Greek East and the Latin West*. London, 1959.

Sicilianos, D. Ἡ Μακρινίτζα καὶ τὸ Πήλιον. Athens, 1939.

Sicilianos, D. *Old and New Athens* (trans. R. Liddell). London, 1960.

Smertsovsky, M. *The Brothers Likhudy* (in Russian). St Petersburg, 1899.

Snegarov, I. *History of the Archbishopric-Patriarchate of Ohrid, 1394–1767* (in Bulgarian). Sofia, 1936.

Soloviev, S. M. *History of Russia from the Earliest Times* (in Russian; 2nd edition), 6 bks. St Petersburg, 1894–5.

Spencer, T. *Fair Greece, Sad Relic*. London, 1954.

Stamatiades, E. Βιογραφίαι τῶν Ἑλλήνων Μεγάλων Διερμηνέων τοῦ Ὀθωμανικοῦ κράτους. Athens, 1865.

Stephanides, B. Συμβολαὶ εἰς τὴν Ἐκκλησιαστικὴν Ἱστορίαν καὶ τὸ Ἐκκλησιαστικὸν Δίκαιον. Constantinople, 1921.

Bibliography

Stephanopoli, J. Z. *Les Iles de l'Egée: leurs privilèges*. Athens, 1912.

Stephanopoli, J. Z. 'L'Ecole, facteur du réveil national', in *Le Cinq-centième anniversaire de la prise de Constantinople, L'Hellénisme contemporain* (fascicule hors série). Athens, 1953.

Stoianović, T. 'The Conquering Balkan Orthodox Merchant', in *Journal of Economic History*, XX. London, 1960.

Stourdza, A. A. C. *L'Europe orientale et le rôle historique des Maurocordato*. Paris, 1913.

Survey of London (ed. Greater London Council), XXXIII. London, 1966.

Svoronos, N. G. *Commerce de Salonique au XVIIIe siècle*. Paris, 1956.

Tafrali, O. *Topographie de Thessalonique*. Paris, 1913.

Thereianos, D. *Adamantios Koraës*, 3 vols. Trieste, 1889–90.

Tomadakis, N. B. 'Ετούρκευσεν ὁ Γεώργιος 'Αμιρούτзης; in 'Επετηρὶς 'Εταιρείας Βυзαντινῶν Σπουδῶν, VIII. Athens, 1948.

Tsourkas, C. 'Autour des origines de l'Académie Grecque de Bucarest', in *Balkan Studies*, VI, 2. Thessalonica, 1965.

Ulgen, A. S. *Constantinople during the era of Mohammed the Conqueror*. Ankara, 1939.

Uspensky, K. A. *The Patriarchate of Alexandria* (in Russian), I. St Petersburg, 1898.

Üzüncarşîlî, I. H. *Osmanlî Tarihi*, 3 vols. Ankara, 1947–51.

Vailhé, S. 'Constantinople (Eglise de)', in *Dictionnaire de théologie catholique*, III, 2.

Van Millingen, A. *Byzantine Churches in Constantinople*. London, 1910.

Van Millingen, A. *Byzantine Constantinople: the Walls of the City*. London, 1899.

Vaughan, D. *Europe and the Turks, 1350–1700*. Liverpool, 1954.

Viller, M., 'Nicodème l'Agiorite et ses emprunts à la littérature spirituelle occidentale', in *Revue d'ascétique et de mystique*, V. Paris, 1924.

Vlachos, N., 'La Relation des Grecs asservis avec l'Etat Musulman Souverain', in *Le Cinq-centième anniversaire de la prise de Constantinople, L'Hellénisme contemporain* (fascicule hors série). Athens, 1953.

Von Hammer-Purgstall, J. *Geschichte des Osmanischen Reiches*, 10 vols. Pest, 1827–35.

Voyatzidis, J. 'La Grande Idée', in *Le Cinq-centième anniversaire de la prise de Constantinople, L'Hellénisme contemporain* (fascicule hors série). Athens, 1953.

Ware, T. *Eustratios Argenti*. Oxford, 1964.

Ware, T. *The Orthodox Church*. London, 1963.

Weiss, R. *Humanism in England during the Fifteenth Century*. Oxford, 1941.

Williams, G. *The Orthodox Church of the East in the Eighteenth Century*. London, 1868.

Bibliography

Winter, E. *Byzanz und Rom im Kampf um die Ukraine*. Leipzig, 1942.

Wittram, R. 'Peters des Grossen Verhältnis zur Religion und den Kirchen', in *Historische Zeitschrift*, CLXXIII. Munich, 1952.

Wood, A. C. *A History of the Levant Company*. London, 1935.

Zakythinos, D. ʻΗ Ἅλωσις τῆς Κωνσταντινουπόλεως καὶ ἡ Τουρκοκρατία. Athens, 1954.

INDEX

NOTE. Names that constantly recur in the text are not included

Abaga, Mongol Khan, 47
Abbot, George, Archbishop of Canterbury, 268–9, 275, 294–5, 296
Abdul Aziz, Ottoman Sultan, 408
Abdul Hamit II, Ottoman Sultan, 407–8
Abdul Medjit, Ottoman Sultan, 408
Aberdeen, 276
Abraham, Metropolitan of Ochrid, 233
Acciaiuoli family, 367
Achaea, Metropolitan of, 306
Achatius, heretic, 239
Acropolita, George, 98
Adrian, Patriarch of Moscow, 337, 347
Adrianople, 14, 121, 169, 180; Metropolitans of, see Anthimus, Parthenius
Adriatic Sea, 24, 66
Aegean Sea and archipelago, 44, 120, 165, 231
Africa, African Church, 8, 286
Agallianos, Theodore, 185 n., 193 n.
Agapetus I, Pope, 59
Agia Lavra, monastery near Kalavryta, 404
Agia Triada, monastery on Halki, 389 n.
Akyndinus, Metropolitan of Thessalonica, 140–4, 150, 153
Albania, Albanians, 286, 341, 370, 393, 403, 405
Aldus, see Manutius
Aleppo (Berrhoea), 275, 283, 291, 292, 301; Metropolitan of, see Cyril
Alexander I, Tsar of Russia, 396, 400–1, 403–5
Alexander Lapucheanu, Prince of Moldavia, 243–5
Alexandria, 9, 11, 261, 266, 274; Church and Patriarchate of, 10, 20–1, 78, 81, 165, 176–8, 234–5, 261–6, 310, 313, 358, 370, 381; Patriarchs of, see Athanasius, Cyril,

Matthew, Meletius, Metrophanes, Philotheus, Samuel
Alexandrinus, Codex, 274
Alexis I, Mikhailovitch, Tsar of Russia, 335–7, 352–3
Ali Pasha of Janina, 396, 402
Allatius, Leo, 215, 234, 259 n., 266, 271 n.
Alps, 89
Amadeus VI, Count of Savoy, 102
Amalfi, 24
Amasea, see of, 270
Ambelakia, 360
America, 410
Amiroutzes, George, 104, 183, 193, 195
Amsterdam, 344, 349
Anabaptist sect, 55, 251
Anatolia, 12, 136, 285
Anchialus, 197, 213
Ancyra, see of, 33, 34, 65, 194
Andreae, Jacob, of Tübingen, 247, 255
Andrew, Saint, apostle, 20
Andrew, Saint, monastery near Constantinople, 286
Andronicus II, Palaeologus, Emperor, 14, 31, 35, 48–9, 70, 98, 115, 117, 138
Andronicus III, Palaeologus, Emperor, 14, 31–2, 143
Angeli, family, 13, 65
Angelus, Christopher, 217, 293–4
Anglican Church, see England, Church of
Anna of Savoy, Empress, 143–5
Anna, Porphyrogennete, Grand Princess of Russia, 323
Anne, Queen of England, 311
Anthimus II, Patriarch of Constantinople, formerly Metropolitan of Adrianople, 270–1
Anthimus, Patriarch of Jerusalem, 394, 395 n.

435

Index

Anthimus III, Metropolitan of Athens, 309, 388 n.

Anthimus of Iberia, hieromonk, 347

Antioch, Church and Patriarchate of, 9–11, 20–1, 68, 78, 81, 104, 165, 176–7, 228, 234, 301, 313, 358, 381–3, 410; Patriarchs of, *see* Athanasius, Cyril, Euthymius, Ignatius, Macarius, Sylvester

Antony IV, Patriarch of Constantinople, 57, 71–2, 76, 120–1, 321

Antony the Eparch, 229, 240–1, 257

Antwerp, 302

Apocaucus, Alexius, 143, 145

Apollinarian heresy, 331

Apollonia, 65

Apollonius of Tyana, 16

Apostolis, Arsenius (Aristobulus), Bishop of Monemvasia, 199, 229, 240

Apostolis, Michael, 208, 211, 229

Aptologi, George and John, 302

Aquinas, Thomas, 5, 100, 110, 118, 138, 139, 152–3. *See* Thomism

Arabia, 186; Arab conquests, 23

Arabs, Orthodox, 182, 355, 382

Archipelago, Duchy of the, 166, 226

Areopagite, *see* Dionysius

Argenti, Eustratios, 235, 357–8, 381

Argos, 180

Argyri, Argyropouli, family, 196, 362 n.

Argyropoulus, John, 120, 289

Argyrus, Isaac, monk, 154

Arian heresy, 10, 56, 91–2

Aristarchi, family, 362 n.

Aristophanes, 241

Aristotle, Aristotelianism, 113, 117, 122, 127, 139, 212, 260, 301, 410. *See* Neo-Aristotelianism

Arles, Council of (314), 56

Armatoles, 179

Armenians, 191–2, 196, 236, 358, 360

Arminius, 267

Arnauld, Antoine, 259 n., 306, 307 n.

Arsenites, 66–9

Arsenius, Autorianus, Patriarch of Constantinople, 65–9

Arsenius, Metropolitan of the Thebaid, 310–15, 317–18

Arsenius, archbishop, 331 n.

Arta, 213, 217, 327; Metropolitans of, *see* Corydalleus, Damascenus, Ignatius

Asen dynasty, 13

Asia Minor, 165, 407

Ataturk, Kemal, 407

Athanasius I, Patriarch of Constantinople, 28, 48, 138

Athanasius III, Pattelaras, Patriarch of Constantinople, formerly Metropolitan of Thessalonica, 232, 283, 370

Athanasius V, Patriarch of Constantinople, 233, 355

Athanasius I, Saint, Patriarch of Alexandria, 98, 107

Athanasius II, Patriarch of Constantinople, 68, 99

Athanasius III, Patriarch of Antioch, 234

Athanasius, Metropolitan of Ochrid, 233

Athanasius, Saint, of Mount Athos, 44

Athanasius, archdeacon, 304

Athanasius, Saint, College at Rome, 215, 217, 223, 231, 232, 258, 368

Athens, 14, 47, 192, 215, 216–18, 222, 231, 293, 301, 392, 408; Our Lady of, church, *see* Parthenon; Metropolitans of, *see* Anthimus, Theophanes

Athos, Mount (the Holy Mountain), 25, 140, 142, 150, 157, 185, 215, 268, 294, 326, 370, 400; monastic organization, 44–9; mystical life, 136–8, 156; cultural life, 210, 213, 220, 224, 389–90; influence at Patriarchate, 196–8; relations with Rome, 232–3; Russian monasteries, 336, 391, 409

Augsburg, Confession of, 246–54

Augustine, Saint, Bishop of Hippo, 6, 57–8, 97, 129, 317

Australia, 410

436

Index

437

Index

Index

441

Index

Ferdinand I Hapsburg, Emperor, 244

Ferrara, 219 n.; Council of (1438), 104, 122

Filelfo, Francesco, 183

Finch, Sir John, ambassador, 298

Firth, Richard, builder, 297

Flaminius, logician, 260

Flanginis, Thomas, 212 n.

Florence, Florentines, 124, 213, 270, 290, 362 n.; Council of (1439), 15, 51, 72–3, 85, 93 n., 104–10, 122, 124, 226–7, 235, 237, 239, 263, 321, 344

Foord, William, chaplain, 292

Forbach, Heinrich, bishop, 242

France, French, 203, 233, 234, 240, 241, 270, 274, 302, 306, 327, 355, 392, 393, 400–1, 409

Franciscan Order, 214, 231, 355

Francisco of Toledo, Don, 160

Francus, Matthew Irenaeus, 241

Frederick II, King of Denmark, 243

Freemasonry, 392

Gabriel II, Patriarch of Constantinople, 201

Gabriel III, Patriarch of Constantinople, 303

Gadderer, James, Non-Juror, 312, 316

Galata, 144. See Pera

Galesia, see Joseph

Galicia, 262

Gemistus, see Plethon

Geneva, 261, 275–6, 281, 288, 349, 363

Gennadius I, George Scholarius, Patriarch of Constantinople, at Council of Florence, 104–5, 107; leader of anti-Unionist party, 110, 160; theological opinions, 125–7, 276, 280–1, 339, 345, 352; becomes Patriarch, 168–70; arranges settlement with Sultan, 182–5, 186, 383; later life, 193–4; 115, 116, 121, 155, 226, 379

Gennadius, archimandrite, 311, 317

Genoa, Genoese, 13, 84, 100, 144, 159, 160, 165, 218, 219 n., 226–7, 362 n., 367

George I, King of England, 311

George Brankovic, Prince of Serbia, 184

George of Cyprus, see Gregory

George of Trebizond, 104, 124, 211

George Saint, Patriarchal church in Constantinople, 190–1

George, Saint, of the Cypresses, church in Constantinople, 191

George, Saint, church at Thessalonica, 192

Georgia, Georgians, 24, 44, 75–6, 105, 108 n., 195–6, 248, 322, 381. See Caucasian states, Iberia

Georgirenes, Joseph, Metropolitan of Samos, 296–9, 309–10

Georgirenes, Laurence, 297

Gerace, 142

Gerganos, Zacharias, 258

Gerlach, Stephen, chaplain, 188 n., 197 n., 210 n., 247–8, 255

Germanus II, Patriarch of Constantinople, 66

Germanus III, Patriarch of Constantinople, 68, 98

Germanus, Patriarch of Jerusalem, 199

Germanus, Metropolitan of Patras, 399, 404

Germanus, Jeremias, priest, 296, 308, 309

Germany, Germans, 91, 220, 249, 254, 259, 271, 293, 295, 361, 401

Ghazis, Anthimus, 399

Ghika family, 366, 370, 372, 375

Ghika, George, 366

Ghika, Gregory, Prince of Moldavia and Wallachia, 371

Gibbon, Edward, 88, 350, 393

Girle, Joseph, brewer, 297

Giustiniani Longo, Giovanni, 160

Gloucester Hall, Oxford, 300–1

Godfrey, Sir Edmund, 298

Godunov, see Boris

Golden Horde, Mongol state, 320, 322

Golden Horn, harbour of Constantinople, 100, 181

442

Index

Index

445

Index

Kulm, battle of, 403
Kymenites, Sevastus, 223, 377
Kyriazis, Antony, 393

Lacedaemon, Metropolitan of, *see* Chrysanthus
Laibach, Congress of (1821), 404
Lambeth Palace, in London, 300, 305
Lamerno, chaplain, 285
Laodicea, Council of (380?), 278
La Porrée, Gilbert de, 153
Lapuceanu, *see* Alexander
Larissa, Metropolitans of, *see* Gregory, Leontius
Lascaris family, 196. *See* Theodore
Lascaris, James, 211
Latmos, Mount, 44, 45
Laud, William, Archbishop of Canterbury, 260 n., 275, 286 n., 292, 295, 296
Lazes, 361
Leake, W. M., 398 n.
Lear, Edward, 388 n.
Léger, Antoine, chaplain, 259 n., 275, 281, 282, 285, 286 n., 287, 306 n.
Leghorn, 302
Leipzig, 241, 354
Le Leu de Wilhem, David, 267, 271 n.
Leo I, Emperor, 58
Leo III, Emperor, 59, 61
Leo V, Emperor, 60
Leo VI, Emperor, 16, 60, 63, 67
Leo III, Pope, 91
Leonard of Chios, Archbishop of Mitylene, 110–11
Leontius, Metropolitan of Larissa, 178
Lepenthrenus, Athanasius, 119–20
Lesina, 215
Lestarchus, Hermodorus, 218, 219 n., 242
Lettonia, 243
Levant Company, 290–2, 294–5, 300–3, 318
Leyden University, 287
Lighthouse, Our Lady of, church in Constantinople, 188

Likhoudes brothers, Joannicius and Sophronius, 352–3
Lily, William, 290
Lithuania, 262
Locke, John, philosopher, 290
Locke, John, traveller, 219 n.
Lollards, 53
Lombardy, 104
London, 15, 271 n., 272, 276, 296–300, 302, 303, 312, 314–15, 317; Bishops of, *see* Compton, Robinson
Louis XIV, King of France, 302
Loyola, Ignatius, 354
Lucaris, *see* Cyril
Lucaris, Stephen, 259–60
Luke the Stylite, 45–6
Luke, Holy, monastery in Styris, 46, 309
Luther, Martin, 238–9, 243, 269
Lutherans, 200, 238–58, 262, 264–5, 269, 276, 279, 281, 288, 303, 339, 345, 348, 354
Lvov, 264–5; Bishop of, *see* Solicowsky
Lyons, Council of (1274), and Union of, 69–70, 97–9, 101

Macarius III, Patriarch of Antioch, 234, 343
Macarius of Corinth, 158 n.
Macarius of Luzhetski, Metropolitan of Russia, 327
Macarius, 'Pseudo-Macarius', 132–3
Macedonia, Macedonians, 36, 47, 72, 140, 217, 269, 294, 360–1
MacMichael, W., 375 n.
Macraios, historian, 395 n.
Magdalen College, Oxford, 292
Magnaura Palace, in Constantinople, 27
Mahmud Pasha, 183–4, 193
Malatesta, Sigismondo, 124. *See* Cleope
Malaxus, Manuel, 210
Malaxus, Nicholas, 210 n.
Malea, Cape, 98
Malmsey wine, 361
Mammas, *see* Gregory

Index

Mamonas, *see* Nicoussios

Manasses, *see* Maximus

Mani, the, district in the Peloponnese, 400, 403, 404

Manichaean heretics, 146, 239

Mano family, 362 n.

Manos, James, of Argos, 367 n., 377

Mansfeld, Count Wolrad of, 242–3

Manuel I, Comnenus, Emperor, 64

Manuel II, Palaeologus, Emperor, 15, 49, 72, 76, 102–3, 115–16, 118, 121–2, 127, 339

Manuel of Corinth, 209

Manutius, Aldus, printer, 211

Mara Branković, wife of Sultan Murad II, 184–5, 194–5

Marchetti, *see* James

Marcheville, Comte de, ambassador, 274, 281

Marcian, Emperor, 58

Margunius, Maximus, Bishop of Cythera, 214–15, 216 n., 230–1, 257 n., 260–1, 290 n., 389 n.

Maria Palaeologaena, Khatun of the Mongols, 47

Mark, Saint, evangelist, 20

Mark I, Xylocaraves, Patriarch of Constantinople, 193–4

Mark Eugenicus, Metropolitan of Ephesus, 72, 104–10, 116, 125–6, 134–5, 235, 280, 339

Mark, archbishop, 178 n.

Mark, monk, 99

Marmora, Sea of, 159, 180, 181; Bishopric of, 268

Marseilles, 397

Martin V, Pope, 103

Martin's-in-the-Fields, Saint, church in London, 297–9

Mary of the Mongols, Saint, church in Constantinople, 191, 372

Massimi family, 367

Matthew II, Patriarch of Constantinople, 201, 265

Matthew Psaltis, Patriarch of Alexandria, 235, 358

Mavrocordato family, 362 n., 370, 375, 376, 399

Mavrocordato, Alexander, the Exaporite, 204 n., 218 n., 222–3, 236, 364, 367–9

Mavrocordato, Constantine, Prince of Moldavia and Wallachia, 374

Mavrocordato, Nicholas, of Chios, 367

Mavrocordato, Nicholas, Prince of Moldavia, 372

Mavromichalis, Peter, 400

Mavropus, John, Bishop of Euchaita, 115

Mavros, *see* Othello

Mavroyeni family, 362 n., 375 n.

Maximus III Manasses (Manuel Christonymus), Patriarch of Constantinople, 194–5

Maximus IV, Patriarch of Constantinople, 196 n., 198, 212

Maximus the Confessor, Saint, 11, 61, 87 n., 134, 152

Maximus the Haghiorite, the Greek (Michael Trivolis), 213–14, 235, 326–7

Maykov, *see* Nil

Medici, Cosimo de', 124

Medvedev, Sylvester, 353

Megaspilaeon, monastery in the Peloponnese, 48

Mehmet II, the Conqueror, Ottoman Sultan, 16, 159, 161, 186–9, 191, 192 n., 194–5, 197, 276, 329, 362; treatment of Greek subjects, 166–70, 180–4

Melanchthon, Philip, reformer, 239–43, 245

Meletius Pegas, Patriarch of Alexandria, 190, 214, 235, 261–6, 280, 333

Meletius, Metropolitan of Rhodes, 233

Melos, George Antony, 218

Memphis, see of, 295

Messalian heretics (Euchites), 132, 141, 153

Metaphrastes, *see* Symeon

Index

Index

Index

Index

Index

Index